THE NEUROPSYCHOLOGY of FACE PERCEPTION and FACIAL EXPRESSION

NEUROPSYCHOLOGY AND NEUROLINGUISTICS

a series of books edited by **Harry A. Whitaker**

BRUYER:
  *The Neuropsychology of Face Perception and
  Facial Expression*

KELLER/GOPNIK:
  Motor and Sensory Processes in Language

NESPOULOUS/PERRON/LECOURS:
  The Biological Foundations of Gestures

VAID:
  *Language Processing in Bilinguals: Psycholinguistic
  and Neuropsychological Perspectives*

THE NEUROPSYCHOLOGY of FACE PERCEPTION and FACIAL EXPRESSION

edited by
Raymond Bruyer
University of Louvain

LAWRENCE ERLBAUM ASSOCIATES, PUBLISHERS
1986   Hillsdale, New Jersey   London

Lawrence Erlbaum Associates, Inc., Publishers
365 Broadway
Hillsdale, New Jersey 07642

Library of Congress Cataloging-in-Publication Data
Main entry under title:

The Neuropsychology of face perception and facial
   expression.

   Includes bibliographies and index.
   1. Neuropsychology.   2. Face perception.   3. Facial
expression.   I. Bruyer, Raymond.   [DNLM: 1. Face—
physiology.   2. Facial Expression.   3. Neuropsychology.
WE 705 N494]
QP360.N495 1986   612'.82   85-27420
ISBN 0-89859-602-5

Printed in the United States of America
10 9 8 7 6 5 4 3 2 1

List of Contributors

Raymond Bruyer • *University of Louvain*
Ruth Campbell • *University of Oxford*
Isabelle Clerc • *University of Rouen*
Antonio R. Damasio • *University of Iowa Hospitals and Clinics*
Hanna Damasio • *University of Iowa Hospitals and Clinics*
Jules B. Davidoff • *University College of Swansea*
Haydn D. Ellis • *University of Aberdeen*
Pierre Feyereisen • *University of Louvain*
Robert G. Ley • *Simon Fraser University*
Luigi Pizzamiglio • *University of Rome*
Phyllis Ross-Kossak • *New York University Medical Center*
Justine Sergent • *McGill University*
Esther Strauss • *University of Victoria*
Guy Tiberghien • *University of Grenoble*
Gerald Turkewitz • *Hunter College of the City of New York*
Andrew W. Young • *University of Lancaster*
Pierluigi Zoccolotti • *University of Rome*

Contents

Preface

Obviously, the face is an important stimulus both ecologically and psychosocially. An illustration of this importance can be found in the "face-ism" phenomenon: the head involves only 15–20% of the total body, but people (especially men) are generally depicted by means of an impressive overstatement of their face (see, e.g., Archer, Iritani, Kimes, & Barrios, 1983). The face, as a psychological stimulus, supports two main functions: It is the main source of information for discrimination and identification of people, and it constitutes the structural ground of many nonverbal messages, including information about the emotional state of the person (for a similar view, see Ellis, 1983). Due to the importance of the face, a great number of studies in experimental psychology have been conducted dating back to the very outset of the scientific study of behavior and cognitive events. An overview of the field can be found in the book edited by Davies, Ellis, and Shepherd (1981).

This tradition in experimental psychology, together with early observations concerning defects of face recognition after brain damage and with the increasing development of neuropsychology, has generated, in the last 2 decades, a great number of neuropsychological investigations concerning the visual processing of faces and, more recently, the mechanisms of facial expression and the perception of facial expressions. Classically, and in function of their own viewpoint concerning the relationships between cognitive events and cerebral mechanisms, authors consider that natural (pathological) or experimental dissociations evidenced in neuropsychology can contribute to a better understanding of cerebral mechanisms and of functional differences between cerebral regions (in this "neuroscientific" view, cognitive dissociations represent one way among others of studying the brain) or to a better explanation of cognitive mechanisms permitting hypotheses about postulated processes to be tested (in this "cognitivist" view, cerebral properties are one way among others of studying cognition). Both points of view are represented in this book.

The neuropsychology of face processing has developed, logically and chronologically, in three successive periods, the commencement of each period being associated not with the end but with the renewal of the preceding one. This kind of evolution in neuropsychology, however, is not unique for the study of the processing of faces. The first period was characterized by reports of isolated cases suffering from a defect in the recognition of familiar faces. This approach dates back for more than a century and reached a high point in the publication of Bodamer (1947), who proposed the term *prosopagnosia* for this pathological condition. It continues in the light of the findings of the other two approaches. The second series of studies grew out of the first. Since 1966 (De Renzi & Spinnler, 1966), neuropsychologists have given groups of brain-damaged subjects to various tests of faces discrimination and recognition, the subjects being selected only on the basis of lesion localization, thus not specifically as prosopagnosic. New, unfamiliar faces were generally employed. The aim of such studies, as was usual in the 60s, was to search for deficiencies (dissociations) in the mechanisms of face processing and to establish correlations with anatomical localizations and especially lesion lateralization. According to the usual evolution in the field, the third period, starting in 1971 (Geffen, Bradshaw, & Wallace, 1971; Rizzolatti, Umiltà, & Berlucchi, 1971), was characterized by the participation of normal subjects in experiments using lateralized tachistoscopic presentations of the material. It was assumed that the performance would differ in function of the stimulated hemifield, due to the specific mode of processing of the contralateral hemisphere (given the crossed organization of the visual neuronal pathways).

In spite of the amount of empirical data so far collected, and recent books devoted to the right cerebral hemisphere (Perecman, 1983; Young, 1983), no book has yet been published concerning the neuropsychology of face perception and facial expression (at least in English: see Bruyer, 1983). To our knowledge, there are only reviews of empirical data and/or critical and theoretical papers, generally limited to particular aspects of the field (Benton, 1980; Blanc-Garin, 1984; Damasio, Damasio, & Van Hoesen, 1982; Davidoff, 1982; Ellis, 1975, 1983; Hay & Young, 1982; Hécaen, 1981; Jeeves, 1984; Meadows, 1974; Rinn, 1984; Sergent & Bindra, 1981; see also the special issue of *Human Neurobiology*, 1984, *3*). The present book is an attempt to fill this lacune. It could be that this absence is due at least partially to a lack of firm theoretical foundation for the neuropsychological approach to the mechanisms of face processing and to methodological difficulties. There are, indeed, controversies concerning the inferential process toward cerebral asymmetries from observed lateral differences as well as very weak explanatory power: The "theories" are mainly descriptive systems, not models permitting operationalization and predictions. Note again that this kind of limitation in neuropsychology is not specific to the field surveyed in the present book. On the other hand, some important gains have been made during the last decade and it may be that an earlier publication would have been premature. Indeed, up to about 1974 it was well established that the processing of faces was a right-brain competence whereas more recent empirical data have revealed that this asymmetry had to be qualified carefully by characteristics of the input, of the subjects, and of the cognitive requirements of the task. As noted by Ellis (1983), "If research on cerebral asymmetry in processing faces had stopped in the early-to-mid 1970s, we would probably all happily accept that the right hemisphere is better adapted for processing complex patterns, such as faces. (. . .) However, research did not stop" (p. 38).

Therefore, the present book has been designed not to build a coherent and powerful neuropsychological "theory" of face processing. Neuropsychology is still a young scientific field, and the first real theory remains to be elaborated, the main effort being devoted to the production of empirical data. The contributors thus try to present the reader with a complete overview of the published data, together with hypotheses and methodological critical comments, about variables that have been shown to be important. I would like to thank these contributors for their collaboration as well as Harry Whitaker and the editorial board of Lawrence Erlbaum Associates for their fruitful support in this venture.

For the Introduction, Ellis has taken on a hazardous task: He lists the main theoretical problems in face processing from a cognitive point of view. Then, a series of chapters is devoted to reviews concerning neuropsychological data related to face perception, offered by pathological observations (Part I) and studies of lateral differences in normal subjects (Part II). The chapters by Damasio and Damasio (anatomy), and Tiberghien and Clerc (mechanisms), on prosopagnosia, and Bruyer, on the processing of faces after brain damage, are followed by contributions concerning the analysis of lateral differences in normal subjects: methodological considerations (Sergent), familiarity effects (Ross-Kossak and Turkewitz), the question of specificity (Davidoff), and the effects of subjects characteristics (Young—age; Zoccolotti and Pizzamiglio—sex and cognitive style). The third part of the book deals with the non-verbal messages conveyed by the face: Feyereisen reviews data issued from brain-injured subjects and Campbell (expressions) and Ley with Strauss (perception of expressions) survey the data produced by normal subjects.

Raymond Bruyer

REFERENCES

Archer, D., Iritani, B., Kimes, D. D., & Barrios, M. (1983). Face-ism: five studies of sex differences in facial prominence. *Journal of Personality and Social Psychology, 45*, 725–735.

Benton, A. L. (1980). The neuropsychology of facial recognition. *American Psychologist, 35*, 176–186.

Blanc-Garin, J. (1984). Perception des visages et reconnaissance de la physionomie, dans l'agnosie des visages. *L'année Psychologique, 84,* 573–598.

Bodamer, J. (1947). Die Prosop-Agnosie. *Archives fur Psychiatrie und Zeitschrift fur Neurologie, 179,* 6–53.

Bruyer, R. (1983). *Le visage et l'expression faciale: approche neuropsychologique.* Bruxelles: Mardaga.

Damasio, A. R., Damasio, H., & Van Hoesen, G. W. (1982). Prosopagnosia: anatomic basis and behavioral mechanisms. *Neurology, 32,* 331–341.

Davidoff, J. (1982). Studies with non-verbal stimuli: In J. G. Beaumont (Ed.), *Divided visual field studies of cerebral organisation* (pp. 29–55). London: Academic Press.

Davies, G., Ellis, H., & Shepherd, J. (Eds.). (1981). *Perceiving and remembering faces.* London: Academic Press.

De Renzi, E., & Spinnler, H. (1966). Facial recognition in brain-damaged patients. An experimental approach. *Neurology, 16,* 145–162.

Ellis, H. D. (1975). Recognizing faces. *British Journal of Psychology, 66,* 409–426.

Ellis, H. D. (1983). The role of the right hemisphere in face perception: In A. W. Young (Ed.), *Functions of the right hemisphere* (pp. 33–64). London: Academic Press.

Geffen, G., Bradshaw, J. L., & Wallace, G. (1971). Interhemispheric effects on reaction time to verbal and nonverbal visual stimuli. *Journal of Experimental Psychology, 87,* 415–422.

Hay, D. C., & Young, A. W. (1982). The human face: In A. W. Ellis (Ed.), *Normality and pathology in cognitive functions* (pp. 173–202). New York: Academic Press.

Hécaen, H. (1981). The neuropsychology of face recognition: In G. Davies, H. Ellis, & J. Shepherd (Eds.), *Perceiving and remembering faces* (pp. 39–54). London: Academic Press.

Jeeves, M. A. (1984). The historical roots and recurring issues on neurobiological studies of face perception. *Human Neurobiology, 3,* 191–196.

Meadows, J. C. (1974). The anatomical basis of prosopagnosia. *Journal of Neurology, Neurosurgery, and Psychiatry, 37,* 489–501.

Perecman, E. (Ed.). (1983). *Cognitive processing in the right hemisphere.* New York: Academic Press.

Rinn, W. E. (1984). The neuropsychology of facial expression: a review of the neurological and psychological mechanisms for producing facial expressions. *Psychological Bulletin, 95,* 52–77.

Rizzolatti, G., Umiltà, C., & Berlucchi, G. (1971). Opposite superiorities of the right and left cerebral hemispheres in discriminative reaction time to physiognomical and alphabetical material. *Brain, 94,* 431–442.

Sergent, J., & Bindra, D. (1981). Differential hemispheric processing of faces: methodological considerations and reinterpretation. *Psychological Bulletin, 89,* 541–554.

Young, A. W. (Ed.). (1983). *Functions of the right cerebral hemisphere.* London: Academic Press.

Foreword:
From Patchwork to
Melting Pot

PATCHWORK

For psychologists, this book may seem incomplete. Indeed, some important topics related to face processing are not considered here. Three partially inter-related areas of research come to mind in particular: animal studies, psycho-pathology, and self-recognition. Actually, psychopathology and animal studies are only marginally relevant to human neuropsychology, and very few data are available concerning recognition of one's own face and animal studies. These data are briefly reviewed in the first part of this Foreword. First, we examine the visual processing of one's own face (neuropsychological data, animals, psy-chopathology), and then we discuss the other studies concerning the visual processing of faces (animals and psychopathology).

Visual Recognition of One's Own Face

The visual recognition of one's own face (see the readings collected by Mounoud & Vinter, 1981) is mainly studied in developmental psychology. It is generally claimed (but see the critical review of Anderson, 1984a) that the true recognition of oneself follows a period during which the stimulus seen in the mirror is considered to be another person (for empirical data and reviews see Amsterdam, 1972; Boulanger-Balleyguier, 1964, 1967; Brunet & Lézine, 1949; Wallon, 1959; Zazzo, 1948, 1975, 1977a, 1977b). The study of Beardsworth and Buckner (1981), nevertheless, shows that the recognition of oneself by adults is easier kinesthetically than visually. Moreover (but see the critical comments of Ander-son, 1984b), in an evolutionist perspective, it seems that animals are unable to reach this stage of true self-recognition, with chimpanzees being a major exception (for data and reviews, see Anderson, 1983; Boulanger-Balleyguier, 1968; Gallup, 1968, 1970, 1977; Gallup, McClure, Hill, & Bundy, 1971; Hall, 1962; MacLean, 1964; Premack, 1975; Zazzo, 1979). Some data also are available in the field of non-neuropsychological behavioral disturbances (psychiatry). First, we note that some psychiatric hallucinatory syndromes are characterized by the continuous vision of oneself in the visual field (*héautoscopie*) or, conversely, by an absence of image when looking in a mirror (Zazzo, 1948). Second, social behavior without self-recognition has been described when early demented patients (in a psychiatric sense) were presented with a mirror (Abély, 1930; Delmas, 1929). Third, and against a common intuitive notion, Neuman and Hill (1978) have shown that autistic children were able to recognize themselves in a videotape mirror image. Fourth and finally, social behavior without self-recognition has been described for mentally retarded children (Shentoub, Soulairac, & Rustin, 1954; Soulairac, Shentoub, & Rustin, 1954) and Vinter, Mounoud, and Husain (1983) have shown by means of a distorting mirror that mentally retarded adults had a distorded self-image.

Some data are more related to neuropsychological problematics. It has been shown that the level of deficiency of self-recognition in a mirror can be an index of severity of cognitive impairment in senile demented patients (Ajuriaguerra, Strejilevitch, & Tissot, 1963; Postel, 1968). A deficiency in self-recognition also has been noted in Korsakoff patients (Michel, 1978). Prosopagnosics are frequently reported as having difficulties in recognizing themselves in mirror images (examples: Bauer, 1984; Bodamer, 1947, Cases 1 & 2; Bruyer et al., 1983; Charcot, 1883; Cogan, 1979, Cases 11 & 12; Cohn, Neumann, & Wood, 1977, Case 1; Damasio, Yamada, Damasio, Corbett, & McKee, 1980, Case 2; Michel, 1978; Nardelli et al., 1982, Case 2, Schachter, 1976; Shuttleworth, Syring, & Allen, 1982, Cases 1 & 2) or judging their mirror images as modified, strange, or unusual (examples: Bodamer, 1947, Cases 1 & 2; Bruyer et al., 1983; Hécaen, Ajuriaguerra, Magis, & Angelergues, 1952; Lhermitte, Chain, Escourolle, Ducarne, & Pillon, 1972; Whiteley & Warrington, 1977, Case 2). Schachter (1976) has even described a case of prosopagnosia limited to the mirror image (actually, paroxystical). Finally, it seems that split-brain patients are able to recognize their own faces, whatever the stimulated hemisphere or better with the right one (Preilowski, 1975, 1979; Sperry, Zaidel, & Zaidel, 1979).

The representation of one's own face is based mainly on the mirror image; therefore, in the natural face-to-face perception of peers, the perceived face is "reversed" (the right part of the face is seen in the left side of the visual field and vice versa), but not the face perceived in a mirror (the right half-face remains in the right part of the field). Consequently, dissociations can be searched (a) between self-perception and perception of other faces, as well as (b) between self-perception in a mirror and self-perception on a video TV screen (or on photographs). This second kind of dissociation is illustrated by some demented patients with an adequate self-recognition in the mirror and no self-recognition on a video screen (Michel, 1978). As concerns the first type of dissociation, there are cases of prosopagnosic patients able to recognize themselves in photographs or in a mirror, or for which no mention is made by authors concerning self-recognition (we incautiously suppose it was preserved); we also note the study of Mita, Dermer, and Knight (1977), which showed that people prefer the mirrored to the normal photograph of themselves, and the normal to the mirrored photograph of familiars. In a similar line, lateral differences observed by Seinen and Vanderwerff (1969), and Strauss and Kaplan (1980), about the emotional expression of hemifaces issued from the face of the perceiver have to be replicated and confronted with data concerning faces of other people (see Part III of this book): the subjects of the first paper judged their right hemiface as more "positive" and their left hemiface as more "negative"; those of the second study judged the left hemiface to be more similar to their own mental image of themselves when happiness was expressed, the right one more similar for sadness, and the left hemiface more expressive than the right for sadness. Finally, Dimond and Harries (1984) examined the use of the hand to touch one's own face in monkeys, apes (gorillas, chimpanzees, and orangutans), and humans: the authors noted increasing touching behavior from monkeys to humans and a quasi-similar increase in the use of the left-hand (and cross-cultural differences in humans; Hatta & Dimond, 1984); the authors suggest that these data reflect the evolution of right hemisphere dominance for the management of emotional and non-verbal behavior.

Face Perception

Regarding face perception, two kinds of information should be mentioned. First, psychopathology offers some observations concerning the processing of faces. Because autism generally is considered a defect of interpersonal interactions, autistic children have been given tests of face recognition (e.g., Langdell, 1978). There are also rare psychiatric syndromes (cf. Enoch, Trethowan, & Barker, 1967) characterized by "illusions of doubles": the patient is convinced that the person seen is in fact someone else (Capgras' syndrome), that the same individual is seen when two different persons are seen (Frégoli's syndrome), or that various persons are intermetamorphosed (for these conditions, see Christodoulou, 1976, 1977). It is being increasingly suggested that such syndromes could result from a neurological pathology involving the cerebral hemispheres (Alexander, Stuss, & Benson, 1979; Christodoulou, 1976, 1977; Hayman & Abrams, 1977; Luauté, Bidault, & Thionville, 1978; McCallum, 1973; Merrin & Silberfarb, 1976; Morrison & Tarter, 1984; Waghray, 1978; Weston & Whitlock, 1971). Finally, Levin and Benton (1977) have shown that the test of Benton and Van Allen (1968; see Bruyer, this volume) can be used to discriminate psychiatric disorders from brain disease (see also Tzavaras, Luauté, & Bidault, 1986).

Second, some preliminary animal observations shortly may become relevant to neuropsychology. Rosenfeld and Van Hoesen (1979) showed that monkeys are able to discriminate among faces of other monkeys, even if various transformations are made. Overman and Doty (1982) have given monkeys and humans tests of similarity between composite symmetrical chimeras (see Part III of this volume) and the normal face, both groups being presented with both monkeys and human faces. Human subjects displayed the classical asymmetric choice, largely preferring the composite stimulus issuing from the right hemiface; given the face-to-face situation, the right portion of a perceived face falls in the left part of the visual field. The authors present these results as a bias in favor of the left hemifield (however, there apparently was no control condition in which the normal face would be mirrored). Moreover, this asymmetric choice of human perceivers was only observed with human stimuli. Monkeys reacted behaviorally to faces as specific stimuli like the human subjects (comparison conditions with inverted faces, and with naturalistic stimuli of common objects), but, unlike humans, they did not make asymmetrical choices.

Hamilton and his coworkers have developed a program for research on face and facial expression discrimination in split-brain monkeys. In an early, short research report, the authors (Hamilton, Preilowski, Tieman, & Gray, 1972) suggested that the left hemisphere was dominant for such a task in the single split-brain monkey being studied at that moment. Hamilton, Tieman, and Farrell (1974) have examined cerebral asymmetries of split-brain monkeys for the discrimination of pairs of various kinds of stimuli, including faces of monkeys. As a group, the seven monkeys produced a left hemisphere advantage for line orientation and, to a lesser extent, direction of movement, but no asymmetries emerged for control patterns, mirror images, or faces. Nevertheless, on an individual level, two subjects were significantly left dominant and one right dominant for the discrimination of faces. With a larger sample of 20 subjects (Hamilton, 1977), no significant group asymmetry emerged but, again, there were individual differences in both the strength and the direction of asymmetries, but there were related to neither indices of hand preference nor sex. Recently, Hamilton and Vermeire (1983) taught 18 split-brain monkeys to discriminate in pairs of monkey faces; 7 of the subjects were then given tests of generalization to new photographs of the learned faces. During the learning of discrimination, in spite of important individual differences, again no asymmetry emerged as regards the group, and the dominance index was not related to hand preference, but it was to age. Nevertheless, as a group, females evidenced a significant left-hemisphere superiority. No brain asymmetry was apparent as concerns the generalization.

Perrett, Rolls, and Caan (1982), using electrophysiological techniques, observed that 10% of the neurones in the fundus of the superior temporal sulcus responded specifically to faces (human or monkey faces, familiar and new). Some of these cells appeared to be sensitive to modifications of orientation, and it seemed that sub-categories of neurones are specialized for particular facial features. Note that a majority of the cells has been found in the left hemisphere, but this observation must be considered with caution because the sampling was biased toward the left hemisphere (see also Léonard, Rolls, Wilson, & Baylis, 1985; Perrett et al., 1984; Perrett et al., 1986; Rolls, 1984).

MELTING POT

A large part of the data surveyed previously could appear to be relatively remote from neuropsychology; moreover, we can not discuss them in detail here. Nevertheless, these observations concern anatomical and/or cognitive dissociations and it could be that any future neuropsychological theory of face processing will have to integrate these data or at least take them into account. We now examine neuropsychological topics for which no chapter has been planned in this book.

Split-Brain Preparation

Because there are not much data available concerning split-brain preparation, a special chapter devoted to this area has not been planned. First, tests of face recognition using a lateralized mode of presentation (see Part II of this book) have indicated that commissurotomized subjects had behavioral reactions to various kinds of facial stimuli displayed in the left hemifield comparable to those to stimuli of the right hemifield (Preilowski, 1979; Sperry et al., 1979). Second, split-brain subjects have been submitted to composite, centrally displayed stimuli made by apposing the left half of a stimulus to the right half of another ("chimeras": see Part III of this book). Levy, Trevarthen, and Sperry (1972), using facial and non-facial materials, have shown that both hemispheres can independently and simultaneously process such stimuli if the particular kind of task response of each hemisphere is taken into account. This is one of the first studies suggesting that the functional differences between the hemispheres must be conceived in terms of verbal versus visuospatial mode of processing instead of verbal versus visuospatial kind of stimuli (for parallel observations collected in acallosal subjects, see Jeeves, 1979; also Dunne, 1977; MacKay, 1976; both cited by Milner & Jeeves, 1979). Finally, the split-brain subjects studied by Gazzaniga and Smylie (1983) have produced a right-hemisphere superiority for a match-to-sample task of face recognition.

Neuropsychological Paradigms

There are two areas of research in which neuropsychological paradigms have been used to study topics not specifically related to the neuropsychology. First, Phippard (1977) showed both the "classic" left-field advantage for faces in normal subjects, and no lateral differences in deaf subjects using a "total" mode of communication (combination of sign language, finger-spelled English, speech reading). Nevertheless, two qualifications are needed: a sample of deaf subjects using an oral mode of communication exclusively also was included in this research but, unfortunately, not given the test on faces; further, the asymmetry has been observed with a group of normals older than the deaf subjects, but not with normals of approximately matching ages. Other studies have been devoted to the understanding of reading deficiencies. The reading deficiencies seem to be related to anomalies concerning the right-field advantage for the processing of words but not to the left-field superiority for faces in children 7–9-years-old (Marcel & Rajan, 1975) or in subjects 10–14-years-old (Pirozzolo & Rayner, 1979).

Second, neuropsychological paradigms employing faces or facial expressions as stimuli have been used to explore the encoding of visually complex stimuli. Korsakoff patients and right-brain-damaged subjects have defective recognition of unfamiliar faces (see Bruyer, this volume), but it could be that these two kinds of impairment result from different pathological mechanisms. Indeed, Biber, Butters, Rosen, Gerstman, and Mattis (1981) have shown that these two populations did not differ in the standard condition and that the performance of Korsakoff's but not of right-lesioned subjects markedly improved when the patients were invited to encode the to-be-memorized faces in a deeper manner (by judging the likeability of faces). As regards face recognition in normal subjects, Proudfoot (1982) showed contrasted patterns of lateral differences depending on whether the subjects were asked to examine the to-be-memorized faces on the basis of physical features or of "information" concerning habits of the perceived persons. Similarly, contrasting asymmetries were obtained by Galper and Costa (1980) depending on whether the subjects were invited to memorize the faces by means of particular facial features or of the general pattern of the face. As regards the processing of facial expressions by normal subjects, McKeever and Dixon (1981) noted a right-hemisphere advantage when the female subjects were invited to form an emotionally imaged mental representation about the perceived stimulus. In a similar line, different patterns of lateral differences have been observed for the processing of facial expressions depending on whether the subjects were required to encode simuli in a "verbal" (labels) or an "emotional" (empathy) manner, both in a between- (Safer, 1981) and in a within-subjects design (Safer, 1984; for faces, see Thompson & Mueller, 1984).

Direction of Gaze

If we consider that the direction of gaze contributes to facial expression or to facial action (see Campbell, this volume), some data have to be mentioned here. The assumption is that the direction of lateral eye movements reflects the activation of the contralateral hemisphere (Bakan, 1969). Thus, a verbal task induces right-directed deviations, and spatial problem-solving procedures induce left-directed gaze (see, for example, Kinsbourne, 1972; Swinnen, 1984). Similarly, emotionally loaded situations will produce a left-deviation (Schwartz, Davidson, & Maer, 1975; Tucker, Roth, Arneson, & Buckingham, 1977) or a deviation depending on the positive or negative valence of the situation (Ahern & Schwartz, 1979; Natale & Gur, 1980), and a laterally deviated gaze differentially affects the evocation of personal events (Natale & Gur, 1980). Nevertheless, we note that empirical data (Berg & Harris, 1980) and theoretical considerations (Ehrlichman & Weinberger, 1978) do not support this inferential link between direction of gaze and hemispheric activation.

The Question of Hand Dominance

This volume includes two chapters devoted to the subject characteristics (see chapters by Young; Zoccolotti & Pizzamiglio), but none has been assigned to the question of the hand dominance, or handedness, or "laterality." Actually, very few data specifically concerning face processing are available (see following), and what are available are inconclusive. Furthermore, this complex area of research concerns neuropsychology as a whole and not specifically the mechanisms of face perception (see Bryden, 1982; Hécaen, 1984). Let us briefly survey the main data available (except as regards the production of facial action, which is reviewed by Campbell, this volume, and the perception of facial emotion, which is reviewed by Ley & Strauss, this volume).

It is usually claimed (see Damasio & Damasio, this volume) that prosopagnosia is never associated with aphasia and results from a bilateral lesion or, perhaps, from unilateral right-sided damage. Tzavaras, Mérienne, and Masure (1973) have described a patient suffering from both prosopagnosia and language impairment after a surgical lesion in the left temporal lobe. This patient was familial left-handed. Concerning studies devoted to face processing by groups of brain-damaged subjects (Bruyer, this volume), Tzavaras, Hécaen, and LeBras (1971) have been unable to reproduce, with left-handed subjects (familial or not), the specific impairment for face processing resulting from a right-lesion in right-handed subjects (Tzavaras, Hécaen, & LeBras, 1970).

Some additional information has issued from studies of neurologically intact subjects. With non-laterally displayed stimuli, Gilbert (1973) noted that weakly left-handed subjects performed more poorly on a face recognition test than strongly lateralized (left- or right-handed) subjects. This observation was taken to indicate that moderate handedness reflects a weak functional brain asymmetry; nevertheless, the visual hemifield asymmetry (favoring the left-field) remained independent of handedness (Gilbert, 1977). However, Buffery (1974) has observed that the left-field advantage for discrimination of faces was higher for right- than for left-handers; similarly, in a task of face recognition, Piazza (1980) found a left-field advantage only for right-handers without familial sinistrality (no asymmetry emerged for left-handed subjects, or subjects with a history of familial sinistrality whatever their own handedness). On the other hand, it appeared that a test of face recognition interfered in a verbal task of estimation of durations in a manner similar to a test of word recognition, whatever the handedness of the subjects (Hicks & Brundige, 1974). Finally, some authors consider that a kind of facial asymmetry actually results from a perceiver bias favoring the left visual field when seeing faces (see Ley & Strauss, chapter 12; Campbell, chapter 11, this book). Gilbert and Bakan (1973) support such a view, at least when right-handed perceivers are considered: no lateral bias was noted in left-handers. A similar pattern of results has been collected by Lawson (1978) with additional complex qualifications in function of the arm position for writing, and sex.

Studies of EEG Activities

Finally, we mention studies in which EEG activities or cerebral evoked potentials are recorded in subjects processing faces (Butler, Glass, & Heffner, 1981; Dumas & Morgan, 1975; Glass, Butler, & Carter, 1984; Ornstein, Johnstone, Herron, & Swencionis, 1980; Rapaczynski & Ehrlichman, 1979; Small, 1983; Sobotka, Pizlo, & Budohoska, 1984): As a rule, the right hemisphere was predominantly involved, but see Bruyer (submitted) for a critical review.

So, the time has come to get to the heart of the matter!

R. Bruyer

REFERENCES

Abély, P. (1930). Le signe du miroir dans les psychoses et plus précisément dans la démence précoce. *Annales Médico-Psychologiques, 1*, 28–36.

Ahern, G. L., & Schwartz, G. E. (1979). Differential lateralization for positive versus negative emotion. *Neuropsychologia, 17*, 693–698.

Ajuriaguerra, J., Strejilevitch, M., & Tissot, R. (1963). A propos de quelques conduites devant le miroir de sujets atteints de syndromes démentiels du grand âge. *Neuropsychologia, 1*, 59–73.

Alexander, M. P., Stuss, D. T., & Benson, D. F. (1979). Capgras syndrome: A reduplicative phenomenon. *Neurology, 29*, 334–339.

Amsterdam, B. (1972). Mirror self-image reactions before age two. *Developmental Psychobiology, 5*, 297–305.

Anderson, J. R. (1983). Responses to mirror image stimulation and assessment of self-recognition in mirror- and peer-reared stumptail macaques. *Quarterly Journal of Experimental Psychology, 35B*, 201–212.

Anderson, J. R. (1984a). The development of self-recognition: A review. *Developmental Psychobiology, 17*, 35–49.

Anderson, J. R. (1984b). Monkeys with mirror: some questions for primate psychology. *International Journal of Primatology*, *5*, 81–97.

Bakan, P. (1969). Hypnotizability, laterality of eye-movements and functional brain asymmetry. *Perceptual and Motor Skills*, *28*, 927–932.

Bauer, R. M. (1984). Autonomic recognition of names and faces in prosopagnosia: A neuropsychological application of the guilty knowledge test. *Neuropsychologia*, *22*, 457–469.

Beardsworth, T., & Buckner, T. (1981). The ability to recognize oneself from a video-reading of one's movements without seeing one's body. *Bulletin of the Psychonomic Society*, *18*, 19–22.

Benton, A. L., & Van Allen, M. W. (1968). Impairment in facial recognition in patients with cerebral disease. *Cortex*, *4*, 344–358.

Berg, M. R., & Harris, L. J. (1980). The effect of experimenter location and subject anxiety on cerebral activation as measured by lateral eye movements. *Neuropsychologia*, *18*, 89–93.

Biber, C., Butters, N., Rosen, J., Gerstman, L., & Mattis, S. (1981). Encoding strategies and recognition of faces by alcoholic Korsakoff and other brain-damaged patients. *Journal of Clinical Neuropsychology*, *3*, 315–330.

Bodamer, J. (1947). Die Prosop-Agnosie. *Archives fur Psychiatrie und Zeitschrift fur Neurologie*, *179*, 6–53.

Boulanger-Balleyguier, G. (1964). Premières réactions devant le miroir. *Enfance*, 51–67.

Boulanger-Balleyguier, G. (1967). Les étapes de la reconnaissance de soi devant le miroir. *Enfance*, 91–116.

Boulanger-Balleyguier, G. (1968). Comparaison entre l'évolution des réactions du chat et de l'enfant devant le miroir. *Journal de Psychologie Normale et Pathologique*, 73–84.

Brunet, O., & Lézine, I. (1949). Psychologie de la première enfance: une contribution du groupe des jeunes parents. *Enfance*, 355–363.

Bruyer, R. (submitted). *Brain asymmetries in face processing: A critical review of electrophysiological studies from a psychological point-of-view*. Manuscript submitted for publication.

Bruyer, R., Laterre, C., Seron, X., Feyereisen, P., Strypstein, E., Pierrard, E., & Rectem, D. (1983). A case of prosopagnosia with some preserved covert remembrance of familiar faces. *Brain and Cognition*, *2*, 257–284.

Bryden, M. P. (1982). *Laterality: Functional asymmetry in the intact brain*. New York: Academic Press.

Buffery, A. W. H. (1974). Asymmetrical lateralisation of cerebral functions and the effects of unilateral brain surgery in epileptic patients. In S. Dimond & J. G. Beaumont (Eds.), *Hemisphere function in the human brain* (pp. 204–234). London: Elek Science.

Butler, S. R., Glass, A., & Heffner, R. (1981). Asymmetries of the contingent negative variation (CNV) and its after positive wave (APW) related to differential hemispheric involvement in verbal and non-verbal tasks. *Biological Psychology*, *13*, 157–171.

Charcot, J. M. (1883). Un cas de suppression brusque et isolée de la vision mentale des signes et des objets (formes et couleurs). *Progrès Médical*, *11*, p. 568 (more detailed in: *Leçons sur les maladies du système nerveux*. Paris: Delahaye & Lacrosnie, 1887, vol. III, pp. 176–189).

Christodoulou, G. N. (1976). Delusional hyper-identification of the Frégoli type. *Acta Psychiatrica Scandinavica*, *54*, 305–314.

Christodoulou, G. N. (1977). The syndrome of Capgras. *British Journal of Psychiatry*, *130*, 556–564.

Cogan, D. G. (1979). Visuospatial dysgnosia. *American Journal of Ophtalmology*, *88*, 361–368.

Cohn, R., Neumann, M. A., & Wood, D. H. (1977). Prosopagnosia: A clinicopathological study. *Annals of Neurology*, *1*, 177–182.

Damasio, A., Yamada, T., Damasio, H., Corbett, J., & McKee, J. (1980). Central achromatopsia: behavioral, anatomic, and physiologic aspects. *Neurology*, *30*, 1064–1071.

Delmas, A. (1929). Le signe du miroir dans la démence précoce. *Annales Médico-Psychologiques*, *1*, 227–233.

Dimond, S., & Harries, R. (1984). Face touching in monkeys, apes and man: Evolutionary origins and cerebral asymmetry. *Neuropsychologia, 22*, 227–233.

Dumas, R., & Morgan, A. (1975). EEG asymmetry as a function of occupation, task, and task difficulty. *Neuropsychologia, 13*, 219–228.

Ehrlichman, H., & Weinberger, A. (1978). Lateral eye movements and hemispheric asymmetry: A critical review. *Psychological Bulletin, 85*, 1080–1101.

Enoch, M. D., Trethowan, W. H., & Barker, J. C. (1967). *Some uncommon psychiatric syndromes.* Bristol: Wright.

Gallup, G. G. (1968). Mirror-image stimulation. *Psychological Bulletin, 70*, 782–793.

Gallup, G. G. (1970). Chimpanzees: Self-recognition. *Science, 167*, 86–87.

Gallup, G. G. (1977). Self-recognition in primates. *American Psychologist, 32*, 329–338.

Gallup, G. G., McClure, M. K., Hill, S. D., & Bundy, R. A. (1971). Capacity for self-recognition in differentially reared chimpanzees. *Psychological Records, 21*, 69–74.

Galper, R. E., & Costa, L. (1980). Hemispheric superiority for recognizing faces depends upon how they are learned. *Cortex, 16*, 21–38.

Gazzaniga, M. S., & Smylie, C. S. (1983). Facial recognition and brain asymmetries: clues to underlying mechanisms. *Annals of Neurology, 13*, 536–540.

Gilbert, C. (1973). Strength of left-handedness and facial recognition ability. *Cortex, 9*, 145–151.

Gilbert, C. (1977). Non-verbal perceptual abilities in relation to left handedness and cerebral lateralization. *Neuropsychologia, 15*, 779–791.

Gilbert, C., & Bakan, P. (1973). Visual asymmetry in perception of faces. *Neuropsychologia, 11*, 355–362.

Glass, A., Butler, S. R., & Carter, J. C. (1984). Hemispheric asymmetry of EEG alpha activation: Effects of gender and familial handedness. *Biological Psychology, 19*, 169–187.

Hall, K. R. L. (1962). Behaviour of monkeys towards mirror-images. *Nature, 196*, 1258–1261.

Hamilton, C. R. (1977). Investigations of perceptual and mnemonic lateralization in monkeys. In S. Harnad, R. W. Doty, L. Goldstein, J. Jaynes, & G. Krauthammer (Eds.), *Lateralization in the nervous system* (pp. 45–62). New York: Academic Press.

Hamilton, C. R., Preilowski, B., Tieman, S. B., & Gray, G. E. (1972). Cerebral dominance for facial discrimination in monkeys. *Caltech Biology Annual Report*, p. 96.

Hamilton, C. R., & Vermeire, B. A. (1983). Discrimination of monkeys faces by split-brain monkeys. *Behavioral Brain Research, 9*, 263–275.

Hamilton, C. R., Tieman, S. B., & Farrell, W. J. (1974). Cerebral dominance in monkeys. *Neuropsychologia, 12*, 193–197.

Hatta, T., & Dimond, S. J. (1984). Differences in face touching by japanese and british people. *Neuropsychologia, 22*, 531–534.

Hayman, M. A., & Abrams, R. (1977). Capgras' syndrome and cerebral dysfunction. *British Journal of Psychiatry, 130*, 68–71.

Hécaen, H. (1984). *Les gauchers: Étude neuropsychologique.* Paris: Presses Universitaires de France.

Hécaen, H., Ajuriaguerra, J., Magis, C., & Angelergues, R. (1952). Le problème de l'agnosie des physionomies. *L'encéphale, 41*, 322–355.

Hicks, R. E., & Brundige, R. M. (1974). Judgments of temporal duration while processing verbal and physiognomic stimuli. *Acta Psychologica, 38*, 447–454.

Jeeves, M. A. (1979). Some limits to interhemispheric integration in cases of callosal agenesis and partial commissurotomy. In I. Steele Russel, M. W. Van Hof, & G. Berlucchi (Eds.), *Structure and function of cerebral commissures* (pp. 449–474). London: MacMillan.

Kinsbourne, M. (1972). Eye and head turning indicates cerebral lateralization. *Science, 176*, 539–541.

Langdell, T. (1978). Recognition of faces: an approach to the study of autism. *Journal of Child Psychology and Psychiatry, 19*, 255–268.

Lawson, N. C. (1978). Inverted writing in right- and left-handers in relation to lateralization of face recognition. *Cortex, 14*, 207–211.

Léonard, C. M., Rolls, E. T., Wilson, F. A. W., & Baylis, G. C. (1985). Neurons in the amygdala of the monkey with responses selective for faces. *Behavioral Brain Research, 15*, 159–176.

Levin, H. S., & Benton, A. L. (1977). Facial recognition in "pseudoneurological" patients. *Journal of Nervous and Mental Disease, 164*, 135–138.

Levy, J., Trevarthen, C., & Sperry, R. W. (1972). Perception of bilateral chimeric figures following hemisphere deconnexion. *Brain, 95*, 61–78.

Lhermitte, F., Chain, F., Escourolle, R., Ducarne, B., & Pillon, B. (1972). Etude anatomo-clinique d'un cas de prosopagnosie. *Revue Neurologique, 126*, 329–346.

Luauté, J. P., Bidault, E., & Thionville, M. (1978). Syndrome de Capgras et organicité cérébrale. A propos d'une malade étudiée par un test de reconnaissance de visages et par la scanographie. *Annales Médico-Psychologiques, 136*, 803–815.

MacLean, P. D. (1964). Mirror display in the squirrel monkey, *Saimiri Sciureus. Science, 146*, 950–952.

Marcel, T., & Rajan, P. (1975). Lateral specialization for recognition of words and faces in good and poor readers. *Neuropsychologia, 13*, 489–497.

McCallum, W. A. G. (1973). Capgras symptoms with an organic basis. *British Journal of Psychiatry, 123*, 639–642.

McKeever, W. F., & Dixon, M. S. (1981). Right-hemisphere superiority for discriminating memorized from nonmemorized faces: Affective imagery, sex, and perceived emotionality effects. *Brain and Language, 12*, 246–260.

Merrin, E. L., & Silberfarb, P. M. (1976). The Capgras phenomenon. *Archives of General Psychiatry, 33*, 965–968.

Michel, F. (1978). Self-recognition on a TV screen. In P. A. Buser, & A. Rougeul-Buser (Eds.), *Cerebral correlates of conscious experience* (pp. 299–309). Amsterdam: North-Holland.

Milner, A. D., & Jeeves, M. A. (1979). A review of behavioral studies of agenesis of the corpus callosum. In I. Steele Russel, M. Van Hof, & G. Berlucchi (Eds.), *Structure and function of cerebral commissures* (pp. 428–448). London: MacMillan.

Mita, T. H., Dermer, M., & Knight, J. (1977). Reversed facial images and the mere-exposure hypothesis. *Journal of Personality and Social Psychology, 35*, 597–601.

Morrison, R. L., & Tarter, R. E. (1984). Neuropsychological findings relating to Capgras syndrome. *Biological Psychiatry, 19*, 1119–1128.

Mounoud, P., & Vinter, A. (Eds.). (1981). *La reconnaissance de son image chez l'enfant et l'animal.* Neuchatel: Delachaux et Niestlé.

Nardelli, E., Buonanno, F., Coccia, G., Fiaschi, A., Terzian, H., & Rizzuto, N. (1982). Prosopagnosia: Report of four cases. *European Neurology, 21*, 289–297.

Natale, M., & Gur, R. (1980). Differential hemispheric lateralization of positive and negative emotions in normals. *Communication*, Meeting of the International Neuropsychological Society, Chianciano (Italy).

Neuman, C. J., & Hill, S. D. (1978). Self-recognition and stimulus preference in autistic children. *Developmental Psychobiology, 11*, 571–578.

Ornstein, R., Johnstone, J., Herron, J., & Swencionis, C. (1980). Differential right hemisphere engagement in visuospatial tasks. *Neuropsychologia, 18*, 49–64.

Overman, W. H., & Doty, R. W. (1982). Hemispheric specialization displayed by man but not macaques for analysis of faces. *Neuropsychologia, 20*, 113–128.

Perrett, D. I., Rolls, E. T., & Caan, W. (1982). Visual neurones responsive to faces in the monkey temporal cortex. *Experimental Brain Research, 47*, 329–342.

Perrett, D. I., Smith, P. A. J., Potter, D. D., Mistlin, A. J., Head, A. S., Milner, A. D., & Jeeves, M. A. (1984). Neurones responsive to faces in the temporal cortex: Studies of functional organization, sensitivity to identity and relation to perception. *Human Neurobiology, 3*, 197–208.

Perrett, D. I., Mistlin, A. J., Potter, D. D., Smith, P. A. J., Head, A. S., Chitty, A. J., Broenniman, R., Milner, A. D., Jeeves, M. A. J. (1986). Functional organization of visual neurones processing face identity. In H. D. Ellis, M. A. Jeeves, F. Newcombe, & A. W. Young (Eds.), *Aspects of face processing*. Dordrecht: Martinus Nijhoff.

Phippard, D. (1977). Hemifield differences in visual perception in deaf and hearing subjects. *Neuropsychologia, 15*, 555–561.

Piazza, D. M. (1980). The influence of sex and handedness in the hemispheric specialization of verbal and nonverbal tasks. *Neuropsychologia, 18*, 163–176.

Pirozzolo, F. J., & Rayner, K. (1979). Cerebral organization and reading disability. *Neuropsychologia, 17*, 485–491.

Postel, J. (1968). Les troubles de la reconnaissance spéculaire de soi au cours des démences tardives. *L'évolution Psychiatrique, 33*, 605–648.

Preilowski, B. (1975). Facial self-recognition after separate right and left hemisphere stimulation in two patients with complete cerebral commissurotomy. *Experimental Brain Research, 23 (suppl.)*, p. 165.

Preilowski, B. (1979). Consciousness after complete surgical section of the forebrain commissures in man. In I. Steele Russel, M. W. Van Hof, and G. Berlucchi (Eds.), *Structure and function of cerebral commissures* (pp. 411–420). London: MacMillan.

Premack, D. (1975). Putting a face together. Chimpanzees and children reconstruct and transform disassembled figures. *Science, 188*, 228–236.

Proudfoot, R. E. (1982). Hemispheric asymmetry for face recognition: Some effects of visual masking, hemiretinal stimulation and learning task. *Neuropsychologia, 20*, 129–144.

Rapaczynski, W., & Ehrlichman, H. (1979). EEG asymmetries in recognition of faces: comparison with a tachistoscopic technique. *Biological Psychology, 9*, 163–170.

Rolls, E. T. (1984). Neurons in the cortex of the temporal lobe and in the amygdala of the monkey with responses selective for faces. *Human Neurobiology, 3*, –

Rosenfeld, S. A., & Van Hoesen, G. W. (1979). Face recognition in the rhesus monkey. *Neuropsychologia, 17*, 503–509.

Safer, M. A. (1981). Sex and hemisphere differences in access to codes for processing emotional expressions and faces. *Journal of Experimental Psychology: General, 110*, 86–100.

Safer, M. A. (1984). Individual differences in the metacontrol of lateralization for recognizing facial expressions of emotion. *Cortex, 20*, 19–25.

Schachter, M. (1976). Auto-prosopagnosie paroxystique et épilepsie. Corrélation physio-pathologique ou rencontre fortuite? *Archives Suisses de Neurologie, Neurochirurgie et Psychiatrie, 119*, 167–176.

Schwartz, G. E., Davidson, R. J., & Maer, F. (1975). Right hemisphere lateralization for emotion in the human brain: interactions with cognition. *Science, 190*, 286–288.

Seinen, M., & Vanderwerff, J. J. (1969). De Waarneming van asymmetrie in het gelaat. *Nederlands Tijdschrift voor Psychologie, 24*, 551–558.

Shentoub, S. A., Soulairac, A., & Rustin, E. (1954). Comportement de l'enfant arriéré devant le miroir. *Enfance, 7*, 333–340.

Shuttleworth, E. C., Syring, V., & Allen, N. (1982). Further observations on the nature of prosopagnosia. *Brain and Cognition, 1*, 307–322.

Small, M. (1983). Asymmetrical evoked potentials in response to face stimuli. *Cortex, 19*, 441–450.

Sobotka, S., Pizlo, A., & Budohoska, W. (1984). Hemispheric differences in evoked potentials to pictures of faces in the left and right visual fields. *Electroencephalography and Clinical Neurophysiology, 58*, 441–453.

Soulairac, A., Shentoub, S. A., & Rustin, E. (1954). Analyse des réactions de l'enfant arriéré devant le miroir. *Annales Médico-Psychologiques, 1,* 694–700.

Sperry, R. W., Zaidel, E., & Zaidel, D. (1979). Self recognition and social awareness in the deconnected minor hemisphere. *Neuropsychologia, 17,* 153–166.

Strauss, E., & Kaplan, E. (1980). Lateralized asymmetries in self-perception. *Cortex, 16,* 289–293.

Swinnen, S. (1984). Some evidence for the hemispheric asymmetry model of lateral eye movements. *Perceptual and Motor Skills, 58,* 79–88.

Thompson, W. B., & Mueller, J. H. (1984). Face memory and hemispheric preference: Emotionality and extraversion. *Brain and Cognition, 3,* 239–248.

Tucker, D. M., Roth, R. S., Arneson, B. A., & Buckingham, V. (1977). Right hemisphere activation during stress. *Neuropsychologia, 15,* 697–700.

Tzavaras, A., Hécaen, H., & LeBras, H. (1970). Le problème de la spécificité du déficit de la reconnaissance du visage humain lors des lésions hémisphériques unilatérales. *Neuropsychologia, 8,* 403–416.

Tzavaras, A., Hécaen, H., & LeBras, H. (1971). Troubles de la reconnaissance du visage humain et latéralisation hémisphérique lésionnelle chez les sujets gauchers. *Neuropsychologia, 9,* 475–477.

Tzavaras, A., Mérienne, L., & Masure, M. C. (1973). Prosopagnosie, amnésie et troubles du langage par lésion temporale gauche chez un sujet gaucher. *L'encéphale, 62,* 382–394.

Tzavaras, A., Luauté, J. P., & Bidault, E. (1986). Face and psychopathology. In H. D. Ellis, M. A. Jeeves, F. Newcombe, & A. W. Young (Eds.), *Aspects of face processing.* Dordrecht: Martinus Nijhoff.

Vinter, A., Mounoud, P., & Husain, O. (1983). Accuracy and stability of self-image of mentally retarded adults. *American Journal of Mental Deficiency, 87,* 583–590.

Waghray, S. (1978). Capgras' syndrome and cerebral dysfunction. *British Journal of Psychiatry, 133,* p. 285.

Wallon, H. (1959). Kinesthésie et image visuelle du corps propre chez l'enfant. *Enfance, 3–4,* 252–263.

Weston, M. J., & Whitlock, F. A. (1971). The Capgras syndrome following head injury. *British Journal of Psychiatry, 119,* 25–31.

Whiteley, A. M., & Warrington, E. K. (1977). Prosopagnosia: a clinical, psychological, and anatomical study of three patients. *Journal of Neurology, Neurosurgery, and Psychiatry, 40,* 395–403.

Zazzo, R. (1948). Images du corps et conscience de soi. *Enfance,* 29–43.

Zazzo, R. (1975). *Psychologie de la connaissance de soi.* Paris: Presses Universitaires de France (pp. 145–198).

Zazzo, R. (1977a). Image spéculaire et conscience de soi. In *Psychologie expérimentale et comparée. Hommage à Paul Fraisse* (pp. 325–338). Paris: Presses Universitaires de France.

Zazzo, R. (1977b). Image spéculaire et image anti-spéculaire. Expérience sur la construction de l'image de soi. *Enfance,* 223–229.

Zazzo, R. (1979). Des enfants, des singes et des chiens devant le miroir. *Revue de Psychologie Appliquée, 29,* 235–246.

1 Introduction: Processes Underlying Face Recognition

Hadyn D. Ellis

It was no accident that the first postage stamps, introduced in 1840, bore the features of Queen Victoria. This facial pattern was chosen in preference to others, partly at least, in order to reduce the risk of forgery: small changes in detail to a familiar face, it was assumed, would be readily noticed and thereby the counterfeiter would be foiled (Rose, 1980). Benjamin Cheverton, whose design was accepted wrote, "Now it so happens that the eye being used to the perception of differences in the features of the face, the detection of any deviation in the forgery would be more easy . . . although (the observer) may be unable to point out where the differences lie."

The assumption of the early postage stamp designers was that our ability to discriminate and retain facial information probably represents the acme of nonverbal perceptual skills. Indeed, not only can we distinguish among an infinity of faces, but we seem to be relatively good at recognizing large numbers of strangers' faces following just a brief exposure to them. Moreover, familiar faces can be identified reliably from quite small fragments or under fairly poor viewing conditions (Ellis, 1981). It is difficult to ascertain just how many faces we can store together with other information about the person, but preliminary work by a group of my students indicated that on average we are able to name around 700 people who are known personally. The number of faces we can recognize, however, must double, triple, or even quadruple that figure—a "vocabulary" of faces that is, admittedly small compared with that which exists for words but which is nonetheless impressive.

The primary object of this chapter is to examine the likely stages involved in and leading up to final facial recognition. The ways in which these stages may be interconnected also are explored in an attempt both to review relevant,

1

particularly recent, literature and to see how well these various studies can be integrated within an information-processing framework.

INTRODUCTION

Research into the processes underlying face perception and memory for individuals has accumulated at a very rapid pace during the last 2 decades. Work published before the mid 1970s was largely atheoretical and, although nonetheless of interest to cognitive and social psychologists, lacked any cogent explanatory ideas that might have guided research toward an understanding of the mechanisms underlying physiognomic processing (Bruce, 1979; Ellis, 1975).

Since then there have been a number of attempts at establishing the likely cognitive stages involved in identifying people by their faces (Baddeley, 1982; Bruce, 1979, 1983; Ellis, 1981, 1983; Hay & Young, 1982). The various models that have been advanced usually involve the implicit assumption that these stages are functionally modular and that they are largely independent of one another. This assumption seems warranted in the light of evidence that I review shortly and is one that has been considered essential in other areas of cognitive psychology (Fodor, 1983; Morton, 1981).

In order both to structure the present chapter and to focus attention upon specific modules preceding facial identification I have constructed the model shown in Fig. 1.1. This model is a hybrid of those already in existence and is offered as a heuristic rather than a definitive explanation. The emphasis of this chapter is on cognitive psychological research but, because much of the evidence for the particular model arises from the neuropsychological literature, it would be inadvisable if not impossible not to make some references to clinical cases of prosopagnosia. (These are considered at greater length in Damasio and Damasio and Tiberghien and Clerc's chapters). The literature on brain-damaged patients provides evidence about face processing from cases where part of the system is impaired and, as such, offers some of the strongest evidence for functional modularity. The cognitive literature, on the other hand, tends to dwell on experimental evidence concerning the speed and accuracy of face processing and retention under various viewing and post-viewing conditions. Recently, however, Young, Hay, and A. Ellis (1985) showed that investigations of normal, everyday errors in face recognition can provide quite powerful information from which inferences concerning likely mechanisms underlying face processing may be drawn.

Inasmuch as I refer to the Young et al. findings throughout the chapter some indication of the nature of their investigation is appropriate here. They asked 22 people to keep a record of any difficulties or errors they experienced over a 7-week period in recognizing people. From the 1,000 or so incidents recorded, Young et al. identified seven main categories of commonly occurring slips in

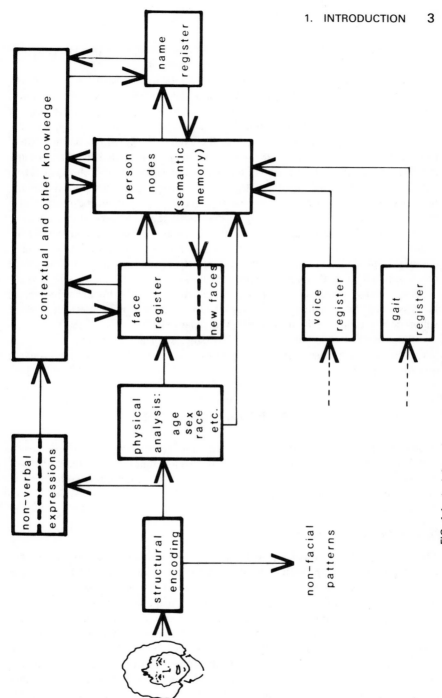

FIG. 1.1. An information processing model of fact recognition that is used to structure the literature review contained in this introductory chapter.

person recognition, details of which are cited at appropriate points in the following text.

The model shown in Fig. 1.1, although complicated enough for present purposes, is undoubtedly an oversimplification: it depicts excitatory pathways only, ignoring likely inhibitory ones; and the connections that are shown give only a hint of the likelihood that some subprocesses proceed in a serial fashion whereas others operate in parallel. Furthermore, the system is shown as being vertical rather than horizontal (Fodor, 1983). No account of possible sharing of processing modules with other classes of stimuli has been shown but such cooperation cannot be excluded at this stage. Finally, the model indicates no exit points, but, of course, any processing system must have an output. In the present case it is possible that an output leading to conscious representation could occur at any point in the system but that normally our awareness is confined to the final state of knowing who a person is. Only under unusual conditions or in specific cases of brain damage, are we conscious merely of seeing a face, a female face or a familiar face that cannot be specified further.

There are two principal areas to the model, roughly involving early perceptual processes and later memory processes. Within each area there are a number of subprocesses each of which is considered separately.

Metaprocesses involving extra-facial factors such as environmental context and expectations are also important attributes of an overall face-processing system and these are also reviewed.

PERCEPTUAL PROCESSES

Although any sharp division between perception and memory is a gross oversimplification, it is certainly convenient to discuss them apart. Under the perception rubric I briefly describe putative modules for structural encoding; gross physical categorization; and detection of emotional expression.

Structural Encoding

The initial categorization of a visual pattern as being that of a face is a necessary preliminary stage to the rich processing capacity of what might be termed the *general face schema*. It is probably based upon an automatic analysis in which the essential "facedness" of the stimulus input—or the recognition that a pattern corresponds to what might be termed the *facial syntax* governing the arrangement of features—may be extracted, possibly through some mechanism like the "primal sketch" stage in Marr's (1982) theory of perception.

Indeed, so biologically important is the identification of facial stimuli that some have argued that the facility is at least to some extent innate. In a rather obscure study by Goren, Sarty, and Wu (1975), for example, persuasive evidence was discovered for the attention-holding capacity of face-like stimuli shown to human neonates, which does not extend equally to faces with jumbled features. In fact, according to Meltzoff and Moore (1977) not just attention to faces but actual facial discrimination also may take place shortly after birth. Evidence for this claim centers on their observations that an infant will mimic certain facial expressions displayed by an adult. This capacity, they argue, normally may be important in the social bonding process between mother and baby. I do not wish to dwell on this line of evidence: it is contentious and not everyone has been able to replicate the observations of neonatal interest in faces (Hayes & Watson, 1981). The possibility remains, however, that facial configurations are such biologically significant stimuli for primates that a degree of hard wiring may be present that enables the early stage of face perception to occur without a learning stage being required (Ellis, 1981). One advantage of such a system may be that it is unlikely to malfunction. Indeed, it is most improbable that anyone viewing a face will erroneously encode it as some other object. The 1,000 slips in person recognition collected by Young et al., for example, did not contain any such instances. Similarly, in the literature on cases of prosopagnosia it is striking that, in the vast majority of cases, faces are correctly categorized, though, of course, usually not specifically identified. For such patients facial features usually seem reasonably normal but they cannot be processed further to a state of complete recognition. In Bodamer's (1947) third case, however, a degree of feature distortion was reported as was the case with the first patient described by Shuttleworth, Syring, and Allen (1982). Further exceptions to the rule are to be found in cases where pronounced metamorphopsia occurs. Here faces may appear entirely distorted as in one of the cases reported by Whiteley and Warrington (1977), where the patient described faces as looking like fish heads. Psychotropic drugs also may produce distortions in face perception (Ellinwood, 1969). McKellar (1957) for example, reported that mescaline may alter perception of the size of objects, including faces, and that distortions in shape also may occur.

Generally, however, distortions in facial features leading to an inability to assign correctly a face to the face category are rare, and even here they lead to perception of associated objects, like fish heads. More commonly, it would seem that the system actively selects ambiguous configurations such as those found in clouds and flames to interpret them as faces. By the same token, visual hallucinations and hypnagogic images, sometimes called "faces in the dark," frequently involve faces (McKellar, 1957). In other words, such a strong perceptual bias exists toward seeing patterns as faces that failures to assign a face correctly to the appropriate processing system are most unlikely.

Physical Analysis

When an object has been classified as a face rather than something else there then follows a process whereby it is categorized along a number of dimensions based upon physical features. It is not possible to establish at this juncture just how many dimensions there might be, but a cursory examination of the proso-pagnosia literature suggests that the major ones may include sex, age, and complexion. Bornstein (1963) examined two prosopagnosic patients who were unable to distinguish male from female faces, and the patient described by Cole and Perez-Cruet (1964) had similar difficulties. Another of Bornstein's cases involved a prosopagnosic patient who misclassified ages, being quite wrong when telling age from facial clues. Whiteley and Warrington's (1977) second case of prosopagnosia thought all faces looked younger than they were. Their first case had difficulties in distinguishing white from black faces—an impairment also shown by patients described by Cole and Perez-Cruet (1964) and Shuttle-worth, Syring, and Allen (1982).

Although each of these examples may reflect difficulties in the operation of specific detection processes tuned to select various distinguishing features, it also is possible that they are the result of a fault in some mechanism common to the processing of all objects. This particular mechanism, for example, could involve the analysis of both the high and the low spatial-frequency information contained within complex patterns. Faces contain a range of spatial frequencies and, whereas it was once thought that the lower ones alone were entirely adequate for face recognition (e.g., Tieger & Ganz, 1979), it now seems clear that higher frequencies are equally useful for face discrimination (Fiorentini, Maffei, & Sandini, 1983). Under conditions of low contrast, facial discrimination may become particularly difficult because higher frequencies are not detected so easily and therefore only low frequency information may be effectively available. Indeed, Owsley, Sekuler, and Boldt (1981) demonstrated that a group of 74-year-olds were significantly less able than a group of 20-year-olds, with equiv-alent visual acuity, to detect and discriminate faces largely because of a dimin-ished ability to detect lower spatial frequencies at low contrast levels (when high frequency information had all but disappeared for all subjects). Many proso-pagnosics complain that the world looks foggy or grey and that colors seem faded (Bornstein, 1963; Pallis, 1955), which may imply that they have lost high frequency facial information conveying details of complexion and so on, and this, in turn, could impair discrimination of age and sex as well as fine details of other objects. It is worth noting that Newcombe's (1979) prosopagnosic patient, for example, could not solder pipes because he was unable to detect surface changes; and the patient described by Bruyer et al. (1983) found diffi-culties when inspecting potatoes for bruises. Any further loss in ability to pick up low spatial frequency information, of course, could also reduce subsequent ability to identify faces.

One patient described by Shuttleworth et al. (1982) was initially able to distinguish both faces and face-like representations in abstract paintings. But he saw all faces simply as a 'glob,' with two dark holes for eyes and identical hairstyles. Only later was he able to perceive more detailed facial structure, though even then faces seemed like cartoon representations.

Expression Analysis

Figure 1.1 indicates the analysis of facial expressions as an early perceptual process but one which is carried out by a separate mechanism from those involved in the gross categorization of other physical features. Once again the evidence for this inference arises mainly from the clinical field (Ellis, 1983).

Bodamer's (1947) first case of prosopagnosia complained that as well as being unable to recognize faces he found it difficult to interpret facial expressions. Bornstein (1963) reported three cases in which symptoms of prosopagnosia receded but in which the patients were subsequently unable to interpret facial expressions. As one patient explained: "Today, faces say nothing to me."

A dissociation between facial identification and ability to interpret expressions also has been reported in patients with chronic organic brain syndrome (Kurucz, Feldmar, & Werner, 1979). These patients were later found to be quite able to identify famous faces (Kurucz & Feldmar, 1979), which again implies that different mechanisms may underlie recognition and emotional interpretation (Ellis, 1983). Experiments with normal subjects using tachistoscopic exposure methods also have indicated that recognition and emotional analysis may proceed independently. Ley and Bryden (1979), for example, presented schematic faces in the left or right visual field and found *inter alia* that identification of the faces did not covary with categorization of the expressions they bore. Further details of the experimental literature on facial expressions is given in later chapters of this volume.

I return to this part of the model later when discussing a suggested distinction between initial face processing and that involved during a prolonged encounter where attention to expression and other nonverbal cues become dominant.

FACE REGISTER

Familiar Faces

At the center of the face model is the face register containing what Hay and Young (1982) refer to as "face recognition units." These units may be likened to those in Morton's (1969) logogen model of word recognition (Ellis, 1981; Hay & Young, 1982). Thus it is suggested that for every face that a person knows there exists a unit that registers or acknowledges its familiarity, operating across a range of transformations, distances, lighting, and so on. New faces gradually are incorporated into the corpus of known faces, and, presumably, the more familiar a face becomes the less evidence is required to fire its corresponding recognition unit (Ellis, 1981). The nature of these units and their organization is largely unknown. Whether they involve analytic or wholistic processing and whether they respond most readily to some particular canonical face form are issues yet to be resolved (Ellis, 1981). It is evident, however, that familiar faces, perhaps as a result of repeated attention to the expressive features, are recognized more readily by internal than external facial features, whereas for newly encountered faces the two facial areas are equally salient (Ellis, Shepherd, & Davies, 1979).

Ellis et al. (1979) also observed that episodic recognition memory was superior for famous faces compared with unknown faces. Klatzky and Forrest (1984) have greatly extended this finding. First they replicated the advantage for recognizing famous faces. Then they proceeded to explore possible reasons for this superiority. In one experiment subjects were shown a set of faces and later were presented with the faces masked to occlude mouth or ears. Their task was not only to recognize the target faces but also to say whether the mouth was open or closed or whether the ears were showing or covered by hair when initially presented. Although the famous face superiority was again found, this did not seem to depend on better encoding of specific facial details because there was no equivalent advantage for reporting whether the mouth was open or the ears covered.

Having satisfied themselves that the famous faces superiority effect is not due to better pick-up of specific features, Klatzky and Forrest (1984) then turned their attention to the possibility that it may be attributable to easier verbal labelling. They did find that famous faces elicited more verbal labels than unknown faces when subjects at initial presentation were invited to volunteer as many descriptions as possible; but, within the set of famous faces, ease of labelling appeared not to influence recognizability in a subsequent episodic memory test.

Interestingly, Klatzky and Forest (1984) found that unknown faces erroneously judged to be famous also were better recognized later than those not thought to be famous. As they point out, this result may be due to factors such as distinctiveness or attractiveness; but whatever the reason it is clear that the advantage in recognizing faces that either are thought to be or that are famous is due neither to any improvement in storing specific facial features nor to ease of verbal labelling. Instead, some more abstract attribute must be sought.

It could be argued that when confronted with a familiar face we simply have to tag its representation with the surrounding contextual information, whereas with unknown faces there is, in addition, some cognitive effort required to form a new face unit. Furthermore, it seems reasonable to suggest that any directly conscious output from a face recognition unit is better considered as simply serving to indicate a sense of familiarity without any information about who in particular the person is. Young et al. (1985) found that all of their diarists at some time reported errors whereby they encountered individuals who seemed familiar but who remained unidentified for a while. Occasionally, similar feelings of familiarity without identification have been reported by prosopagnosic patients (Bodamer, 1947; Bornstein, 1963), but usually, of course, there is a complete absence both of a recognition and a sense of familiarity. It therefore seems reasonable to distinguish between a feeling of knowing and knowledge itself

(Klatzky, 1984; Mandler, 1980). Moreover it should be acknowledged that memory for familiar faces arranged in a sequence differs from that where entirely novel faces are presented. In the latter case any sense of familiarity may serve as a basis for responding "old" at recognition test, but such a crude criterion could not be used when the stimuli are already familiar.

Unfamiliar Faces

Before leaving the face register it is worthwhile indicating that an adjunct to it must involve the ability to incorporate new units of information. It is perhaps a regrettable fact that we know so much about the acquisition of new faces for the vast majority of experimental work on face memory has exclusively concerned memory for unknown faces and very little has been concentrated on the processing of familiar faces (Bruce, 1983).

As has been indicated already, in a typical face memory experiment a set of target faces is shown and later they are mixed with a set of distractor faces: subjects are then required to discriminate "old" from "new" faces. Thus faces do not need to be recognized as such, rather it is sufficient that they evoke a sense of familiarity, based partly upon structural information and partly upon "pictorial" information specific to a particular portrait (Bruce, 1983). The ability to make a correct response depends on many factors including duration of initial exposure and intervening interval; changes in pose or expression between exposure and test, etc. (Bruce, 1982; Ellis, 1984). It is also true that some faces are more memorable than others. These may be pleasant or unpleasant (Peters, 1917), attractive or unattractive (Shepherd & Ellis, 1973), judged to be unusual (Light, Kayra-Stuart, & Hollander, 1979), or rated as unique (Goldstein & Chance, 1981). It is possible that in all cases it is the inter-face similarity that determines later recognition (Light et al., 1979). Faces on any extreme dimension perhaps are encoded easily and incorporated into the face register. Less distinctive faces also may be more susceptible to retroactive interference from subsequent faces. John Shepherd and I have recently completed an experiment showing that, whereas retroactive interference effects in face recognition normally may be relatively small and affect decision criteria rather than sensitivity (Davies, Shepherd, & Ellis, 1979), when target faces are followed by others judged to be physically similar there can be a fairly pronounced reduction in face recognition accuracy compared with the situation where dissimilar faces or no faces intervene (see Table 1.1). It can be concluded, therefore, that newly formed face recognition units may be upset by exposure to faces bearing a degree of physical likeness to them.

Recent work by Bartlett, Hurry, and Thorley (1984) has extended our understanding of the ways in which new typical and untypical faces are processed. They point out that Light et al. (1979) not only found unusual faces to be better recognized than typical faces but also observed them to be less likely to be falsely

TABLE 1.1
Number of Subjects Making Correct and Incorrect Choices
on a Target Face Following Different Interpoleted
Experiences

	Similar	Dissimilar	Control
Hits	18	27	19
Misses	14	5	6

Note: Chi squared $= 6.55$, $df = 2$, $p = 0.05$ (Shepherd & Ellis, 1983).

recognized when in the distractor set. Following Mandler's (1980) suggestions Bartlett et al. (1984) postulated that: (a) all new faces have "non-zero levels of perceived familiarity"; (b) new typical faces produce a stronger impression of familiarity than do unusual faces; and (c) any increment in a sense of familiarity following a single exposure to a face is greater for unusual than for typical faces.

Bartlett et al. were able to confirm the first and second postulate by asking one group of subjects to rate a set of faces for typicality and another group to rate them for any sense of familiarity each face may evoke. As predicted, the faces rated as being typical were also the ones that seemed familiar. In another experiment faces were presented to some subjects before being shown to them for judgments on friendliness or to provide a verbal description. Other subjects made the same judgments without prior exposure. All subjects then received a surprise recognition test, the results of which revealed a greater accuracy for unusual compared with typical faces under the "normal" conditions where subjects had no previous knowledge of the faces. For those subjects who had previously seen all of the faces used in the study, however, the results were slightly different: they made relatively more false alarm responses to unusual faces. Bartlett et al. infer from this result some support for their third postulate (i.e. that unusual faces seen once produce a strong impression that may subsequently lead to erroneous "recognition" in an episodic memory task—they may produce an incorrect feeling that they were part of the subsequent stimulus set).

Earlier, when describing the initial classification of a pattern as a face because it corresponds to some abstract prototypical criteria of facedness, I added that at the next stage there is some tentative evidence that the system may be capable of extracting further information concerning the specific categories of faces. Obvious examples of such sub-divisions include male–female, Caucasian–Negro–Oriental, and young–middle-aged–old. Klatzky (1983) has argued that occupational categories such as "movie actress," "undertaker," and "football player" may also be of importance in face processing—though whether at an early or later stage is unclear.

In one experiment, faces were assigned to various occupational categories and those that best fit such stereotypes were subsequently found to be remembered with greatest ease. In a related experiment, Klatzky, Martin, and Kane (1982) presented either normal faces or composite faces made from the left half of one face together with the right half of another face and subjects had to report whether the photograph was made from one or two individuals. Each stimulus was preceded either by the word "blank" or by one of 13 occupational titles ("accountant," "athlete," "farmer," etc.) which, on the basis of independent ratings, were either congruent or incongruent with the faces. The results indicated some support for the prediction that congruent labels would reduce response latency by facilitating processing in some way, for three of the labels did significantly reduce RTs. Similarly, a few of the incongruent labels significantly increased response latencies perhaps by a process of inhibition. Klatzky et al. (1982) discuss these data in terms of *priming effects* whereby occupational categories provide "somewhat abstract fuzzy facial information, rather than perceptual features" (p. 107). If the work of Klatzky and her associates proves reliable it suggests that the processing of novel faces involves more than extraction of physical information to be used as a basis for future recognition. Instead it implies that new faces are also categorized according to existing stereotypes, which are not necessarily very distinct pigeon-holes but which may nonetheless assist us in processing the faces of strangers.

A similar interpretation may be applied to the work showing that, when initially viewing faces subjects are forced to make abstract classifications of character traits such as pleasantness and honesty an improvement in their subsequent recognition is usually found (Bower & Karlin, 1974; Patterson & Baddeley, 1977; Winograd, 1978). Mueller and his associates (e.g. Mueller, Heesacker, Ross, & Nicodemus, 1983) also have shown that rated emotionality associated with such classifications may further improve recognition performance. It would be of interest to know whether those faces that are rated at the extreme ends of any dimension during initial viewing are the ones that are best subsequently recognized. One might predict such a result on the basis of Klatzky's work for those faces presumably more closely correspond to idealized or stereotypical notions of pleasantness, honesty, and so on. The notion of priming is raised again when dismissing semantic associates of familiar faces.

Yet another aspect of encoding a new face and constructing a face unit from it is the question as to which facial features are most important to the process and to what extent their spatial arrangement is significant? The saliency of facial features decreases roughly from top to bottom with hair and eyes commanding most attention (Shepherd, Davies, & Ellis, 1981). One of the many lines of evidence converging on this conclusion comes from an experiment by Davies, Ellis, and Shepherd (1977) in which a series of target Photofit faces was shown and each face was embedded among other faces that differed by a different single feature from the target. Subjects rarely erroneously selected distractor faces that differed in hairstyle or eyes from the target: changes to nose, mouth and chin, however, did lead to some confusion. This findings has been partly replicated by Endo (1982), who also demonstrated that the result holds for inverted as well as upright faces.

Although a great deal of work on feature saliency has been published, involving both normal and clinical populations, relatively little attention, until recently, had been paid to their spatial relationships. Clearly, faces contain information about both features and configurational arrangements and when examining a face we extract each type of information (Bradshaw & Sherlock, 1982). Recent work involving a new method of stimulus presentation in one case and quite powerful statistical and mathematical analyses in another case are worth looking at in some detail for the insights they give into the role of the arrangements of features as opposed to the significance of the features themselves.

First some rather remarkable demonstrations of significance of configurational information in face recognition are provided by Haig (1984).

Using a very sophisticated computer-driven display system, Haig was able to present faces that had been altered configurationally as shown in Fig. 1.2. The eyes were shifted up, down, in and out; the nose was moved up or down, and made narrow or wider; all internal features were moved up or down in relation to the head; and, finally, the whole head was made narrower or wider. In each case the degree of change required to be noticed was fairly small. It is evident from the example in Fig. 1.2, the effects of such configurational changes on recognizability are quite striking. This is particularly true for the conditions where the interocular distance was reduced and where the vertical positioning of the mouth was altered—a finding that extends and to some extent modifies Benjamin Cheverten's idea that a forger's mistake on any of Queen Victoria's face would be equally discernible.

A second new line of evidence on the importance of configurational information in face perception has recently been put forward by Sergent (1984). She employed the eight schematic faces, shown in Fig. 1.3, for both a simultaneous matching task (pairs of faces presented for "same–different" decision) and a dissimilarity judgment task (subjects required to give a numerical indication of dissimilarity between all possible pairs of faces). The faces differed in spatial arrangements of features as well as in the features themselves, and they were used both in upright and inverted orientation.

From the stimulus matching data, regression analyses on both latency and error data from the initial same–different decision task revealed a significant interaction between feature and configurational information. Interestingly, this evidence for the joint importance of feature and configurational information when processing upright faces did not extend to inverted faces. Here, Sergent found that decisions principally relied upon feature differences.

Sergent then analyzed data derived from dissimilarity judgments made to all possible pairs of the eight faces by multidimensional scaling (MDS). Half the subjects revealed the two-dimensional solution shown in Fig. 1.4. This indicates that for the particular set of faces employed, chin and internal configuration are

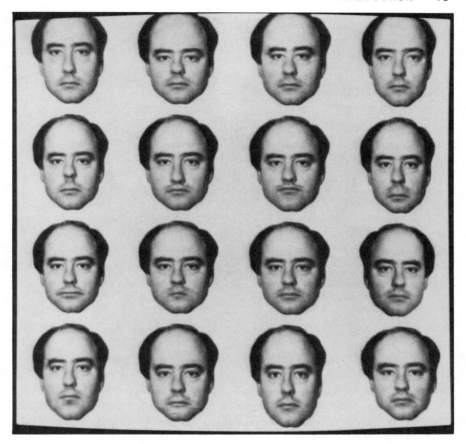

FIG. 1.2. An example of the stimulus distortions introduced in Haig's experiment, showing how fairly small changes in feature configurations can alter a person's appearance. (Reproduced with the permission of Nigel Haig).

separate salient facial characteristics. For the other subjects, who had already completed the RT matching part of the experiment and therefore were relatively familiar with the stimuli, a three-dimensional MDS solution provided the best solution because in addition to chin and internal space, eyes formed another dimension. According to Sergent (1984), the fact that the solution in Fig. 1.5 does not form a perfect cube suggests that "the features were not processed independently of one another, and that each value of a particular feature had a different influence on the perception of each other" (p. 235). Thus, the perception of faces appears to involve both an overall analysis of features and the extraction of their configurational arrangement; moreover, these facial aspects are modified by the general context in which they occur. Once again increased familiarity

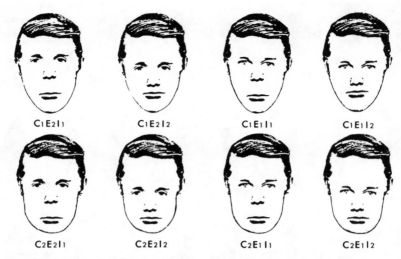

FIG. 1.3. The eight faces used by Justine Sergent (1984). C = chin, E = eyes, and I = internal space. (Reproduced with the permission of the author and the *British Journal of Psychology*).

with the faces appears to alter the manner in which they are processed (cf. Ellis et al., 1979).

The fairly novel techniques used by Haig and Sergent have provided interesting data on the obvious importance of both the feature and the configurational properties of faces in determining their individuality. Any detailed account of the mechanisms by which faces are perceived must take full cognizance of these findings and in future, there must be emphasis on both of these aspects of faces when designing experiments or examining patient populations.

Getting back to the face-processing model, I move on now to the stage of processing that follows the gross categorization of a facial percept as being familiar or unfamiliar. The identification of a face as someone known from previous encounter(s) usually involves accessing semantic information that seems to involve a complex associative network of person nodes. Here the work of Bruce (1979, 1983) provides us with most of the information currently available.

LONG-TERM SEMANTIC STORE

Earlier, I drew attention to Bruce's (1983) distinction between the structural and pictorial codes that may be simultaneously constructed when viewing a picture of a familiar person. She illustrated the difference between these codes and their differential importance when remembering familiar and unfamiliar faces by an experiment in which subjects were shown either familiar or unfamiliar faces,

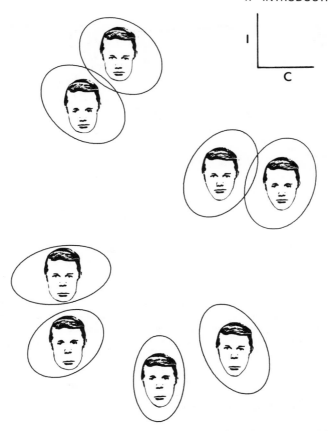

FIG. 1.4. Two-dimensional solution to the MDS analysis from Sergent (1984) along with the 95% confidence regions for the group of subjects relatively unfamiliar with the faces. (Reproduced with the permission of the author and the *British Journal of Psychology*).

some of which were altered in pose between study and test (Bruce, 1982). Both accuracy and latency to make a decision "old" or "new" were measured. Accuracy in deciding whether a familiar face had been presented was unaffected by change of pose, whereas the same transformation applied to unfamiliar faces did disrupt recognition performance. The importance of such pictorial information is even more marked when identifying not only unfamiliar faces but unfamiliar types of faces (black faces for white subjects and white faces for black subjects; Ellis & Deregowski, 1981). Bruce (1982) found, however, that latencies were affected by change of pose for both types of face, indicating, perhaps that the structural information requires longer time to access than does pictorial information.

The significance of pictorial information, when remembering familiar faces, is underlined by an unpublished study of my own. Forty-four subjects were

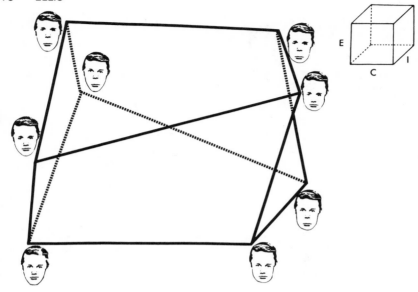

FIG. 1.5. Three-dimensional solution for Sergent's (1984) Group of subjects who were familiar with the eight stimulus faces. The shape of the solution departs from the cube expected if all three features had been processed independently. (Reproduced with the permission of the author and the *British Journal of Psychology*).

TABLE 1.2
Mean Percentage Errors in Deciding Whether or Not Previously
Presented Celebrities Were Shown in the Same or Different
Photographs Made by 22 Subjects Following a 1-hour Delay and 22
Subjects Following a 1-week Delay

	Delay	
	One Hour	One Week
Percentage Errors	19.5	30.9

Note: $t = 3.65$, $df = 42$, $p < 0.001$ (Ellis, 1984).

shown and asked to rate for famousness, the faces of 24 celebrities. They were then shown all 24 individuals again but their task now was to state for each picture whether or not it was the same portrait of the celebrity as was shown earlier. For half of the stimuli a different picture from that initially shown was presented (varying in pose, size, etc.). Half of the subjects completed the second stage of the experiment 1 hour later and the other half did so after an interval of 1 week.

Table 1.2 summarizes the results of this experiment. In view of Bruce's findings that people's ability to recognize familiar faces shown 15 minutes earlier is relatively unaffected by pictorial changes between study and test the data in

Table 1.2 are quite interesting. It is clear that after an interval of 1 hour more than 80% of pictures are correctly observed either to be altered from or to be identical to the original. After 1 week the accuracy drops but remains around 70% correct. Thus, although pictorial information may not play a very important role when recognizing familiar faces as having been members of an experimental target set, information about the particular portrait shown is available for some time afterwards. The same appears to be true for what can be termed *unfamiliar faces*. An analysis of the accuracy with which subjects reported change/no change on the relatively few occasions that they did not know a particular celebrity's face was actually slightly better than for familiar faces (familiar: 17% errors; unfamiliar; 11% errors).

Bruce (1983) makes the obvious point that familiar faces may enjoy dual coding in both visual and name codes, whereas unfamiliar faces are not nameable (though other verbal labels may on occasion be attached to them). She then argues that not only can familiar faces be named but they may trigger other representations associated with them, held in semantic memory.

The model outlined in Fig. 1.1 shows that semantic information may be accessed while logically earlier processes are still proceeding. The reason for including such a paradoxical pathway springs from the empirical work on searching for faces by Bruce (1979). She found that subjects' ability to decide whether or not a stimulus face belonged to a small set of target faces (four politicians) was influenced both by the physical and semantic similarity of distractors to targets. Thus, as one might have expected, visually similar distractors took longer to reject than dissimilar ones but also semantically related distractors (politicians) took longer to reject than distractors drawn from a different category (actors). The two sources of interference were statistically unrelated from which Bruce concluded that a physical analysis and a semantic analysis may take place simultaneously.

Bruce (1983) has speculated that such semantic effects may arise from the priming of specific face recognition units (i.e., top-down processing) rather like that found for word processing whereby previous associated words improve ability to make word/non-word decisions (Meyer & Schvanaveldt, 1976).

An experiment aimed at examining priming effects between faces was carried out by Bruce (1983), who presented a series of faces some of which were familiar and some unfamiliar to her subjects. Among the familiar items were a few pairs of related faces (e.g., a comedy duo, two well-known TV newscasters). Taking latency of decision "known" or "not known" as her dependent variable, Bruce found shorter RTs to faces preceded by a related face than when following an unrelated face. This result was not replicated with a second group of subjects but, ignoring that failure, it is tempting to invoke the idea that semantic priming may automatically occur for faces, much as it does for words. Bruce (1983) is anxious to push the analogy between word and face processing as far as possible. At present, her data tend to speak for themselves but, although I share her fascination with the analogy, I must confess to one or two nagging doubts as to how far we can pursue the similarities. My principal worry is that Bruce is happy to see a parallel between the word/non-word distinction and that between familiar faces and unfamiliar faces. It seems to me however, that whereas non-words are more or less meaningless, not to say strange and unexperienced outside the very circumscribed context of looking at words written in an unknown language, unfamiliar faces are commonly encountered and are anything but meaningless. Having said that, though, I must admit to sharing her belief that face recognition units are linked to associatively interconnected nodes in semantic memory corresponding to individuals and perhaps categories of individuals and that, therefore, spreading activation among nodes is possible and may assist us in face recognition in a manner not so very different from that provided by contextual information which, as in the work of Klatzky and her associates, may also involve verbal priming of categorical information.

Access to these nodes, of course, may be made from more than route. Facial information is probably the most reliable one but, as is well documented in the prosopagnosia literature, when this particular avenue is blocked personal identity can be established on the basis of voice, gait, clothing, and so on (Damasio, Damasio, & Van Hoesen, 1982). There has therefore always been the possibility that specific brain damage, or other means of cognitive disruption, may prevent person identification from voice or gait alone. This hypothetical possibility recently has been demonstrated for voice recognition by Van Lancker and Canter (1982) who investigated a group of unilaterally damaged neurological patients and found that problems in identifying both faces and voices were largely associated with right hemisphere damage. They coined the term *phonagnosia* to denote inability to identify familiar people from their voices. A few patients displayed difficulties with both faces and voices implying either some more general cognitive impairment or that the two systems of accessing the long-term semantic store concerned with person information are anatomically fairly close and therefore liable to joint damage. The fact that not all phonagnosics suffer from prosopagnosia, however, suggests that the conditions are dissociable. No accounts of pure phonagnosia or "gaitagnosia" have been published indicating their rarity and/or the fact that these may be clinically and phenomenologically trivial complaints because compared with faces they are less commonly used as person identification cues in isolation.

It seems reasonable to predict that once a personal identity node has been activated by whatever route then the rich semantic knowledge concerning the individual becomes available. Sometimes, however, the actual name of the person is elusive (Yarmey, 1973; Young et al., 1985) implying that, as the model in Fig. 1.1 indicates, the name store may constitute a separate means of accessing personal semantic memory. A clue to the manner in which this may be achieved is provided by some very recent experiments by Young, A. Ellis, McWeeny, and Hay (1984). They presented subjects with either photographed faces or written names and required them to either vocalize the names of the individuals or to classify them as familiar or unfamiliar. Faces were more quickly categorized as familiar/unfamiliar and written names were more quickly named. Young et al. argue that these observations support the notion that faces can only access the name store via the intervening semantic store and cannot do so directly as is the case with written names. The fact that written names can be vocalized faster than they can be categorized as familiar or unfamiliar, however, implies that the name code may be accessed directly without first passing through any system extracting information concerning familiarity.

Before leaving the topic of name and face routes to personal identity nodes I mention briefly some work of mine that is not yet completed but that has already produced some interesting data. The investigations concern memory for familiar faces and names. In one experiment subjects were given a mixture of famous names and famous faces to rate for familiarity. A surprise recall test was then given either 1 hour or 1 week later. After the short interval significantly more individuals initially presented as names were recalled than those seen first as faces. After a week, however, the trend was significantly reversed. Furthermore, when subjects were asked to state whether each recalled celebrity was initially seen as name or face they made errors, amounting to 20% of misattributions following 1 week's delay. Clearly, then, the mode of accessing a semantic node corresponding to a known individual is not immaterial. Presumably, multiple codes are established and those concerned with the visual analysis of faces are more resilient than those involved in triggering nominal codes. Information concerning access mode is mostly preserved but does tend to disappear over time, again suggesting the operation of multiple codes each with its own temporal parameters.

Context

It is occasionally apparent from the diary study of Young et al. (1985) that contextual information is sometimes important in person recognition. Indeed it is not an uncommon observation that familiar individuals seen out of context are identified with difficulty or only produce a sense of familiarity without activation of the corresponding semantic information.

Various studies have been published to show that context effects may even operate, albeit in a small way, when recognizing relatively unfamiliar faces (Tiberghien, 1983; Watkins, Ho, & Tulving, 1976; Winograd & Rivers-Bulkeley, 1977). Whether this is due to any change in recognition sensitivity or instead reflects a shift in response criterion, however, is open to question (Ellis, 1981). Baddeley (1982) is firmly convinced that a criterion shift is the answer. He presented faces together with what he termed a *contextual statement* such as "diver on an oil rig" or "barman in a village pub." The faces were subsequently mixed with new faces and subjects required to recognize them from one of four formats: no context, with original context, with the "wrong" context, or with an entirely new context. The results revealed that appropriate context did improve hit rate compared with no context, but that a mismatched context also improved performance, (e.g., a face originally seen in the context "diver" shown at test with the "barman" description). Because the original contextual information when paired with new faces caused an increase in false alarms Baddeley concluded that: "Context has no reliable effect on sensitivity but does affect bias" (p. 715).

Although I would not quarrel with Baddeley's conclusions, I feel that they should be qualified in two ways. First, as I mentioned earlier, his experiment involved only unfamiliar faces for which no strong contextual association would have formed. Second his "contexts" were rather different from those involved when normally seeing people in specific situations, such as the local postmistress in her post office, and then encountering her in unusual surroundings, such as meeting the same postmistress at a football match.

These qualifications were partly taken into account in experiments performed by Davies and Milne (1982). In one section of their first experiment subjects were shown unfamiliar faces photographed against one of two different back-drops. Shortly afterwards the subjects were given a recognition test at which the backdrop was the same or different from that at presentation. Changed background significantly reduced sensitivity to target faces as measured by A' (a nonparametric index of sensitivity as opposed to response bias).

In their second experiment Davies and Milne used famous faces as stimuli. Here, similar contextual changes to those employed in their first experiment had no significant influence on A'.

At first glance the result of Davies and Milne's second experiment seems unexpected because common experience tells us that failures to recognize familiar people out of context are not uncommon. But in real life, the associations between person and context are themselves highly overlearned, and, to use Baddeley's (1982) terminology, the face and context are related in an "interactive way." It seems to me that typical laboratory experiments on context effects in face rec-ognition are unlikely to be very informative about real-life face recognition as they do not allow sufficient opportunity for prolonged interaction among subjects, target and context. Future work could best employ the kind of methodology pioneered by Young and his associates involving records of everyday errors in face identification. Alternatively, efforts could be directed toward establishing experimentally–controlled target—context associations, involving more than the single presentation normally used.

Before leaving the topic of contextual influences on face recognition I briefly consider where in the overall process context might play a role. There presently is no strong evidence on this. Baddeley (1982) analyzes the problem within his more general theory concerning "processing domains" by which he means areas of memory that are characterized by extensive associative links. It is possible, perhaps, to map this notion on to the face processing model in Fig. 1.1 by simply substituting the terms *physical domain* and *semantic domain* for the *face register* and *associative store*. According to Baddeley, context is an aspect of the semantic domain and can perhaps only influence this stage of processing. One might expect, therefore, that the earlier stage, producing only a conscious impression of familiarity, is not directly influenced by contextual information.

A recent experiment with at least an indirect bearing on this issue was conducted by Péris and Tiberghien (1984). They presented faces along with names spoken by different voices. At recognition test these faces were presented alongside new faces and the "context" was either the same (same name, same voice) or different (different name, same voice; same name, different voice; or different name and different voice). An analysis of hit rates revealed a small but significant context effect, but of even greater interest was the finding that when decision latencies were short no context effect occurred. The context effect was confined to slow decisions. Unfortunately, Peris and Tiberghien do not present RT distributions that would allow us to see whether the responses conform to a distinctly bimodal pattern, but, assuming that there are two definite underlying distributions, one interpretation of these data might be that a face that easily triggers its representation in the face register is free of contextual influence. When the percept does not produce an immediately strong response, however, information concerning context is processed before arriving at a decision familiar or unfamiliar. On this analysis contextual effects occur rather late in the system and this seems to fit Baddeley's interpretation that they operate at the semantic level.

What happens, however, for faces that are very well known in specific contexts (as opposed to being simply associated with a backdrop, a name, or an occupational description) remains unknown. It is conceivable that in these circumstances the units within the face register may actually be primed in some way by more meaningful contextual information. Such a process would affect readiness to respond with a signal of familiarity to particular faces especially in specific places (i.e., the threshold for responding may be partly governed by context). This theoretical possibility is allowed for within the proposed model but requires empirical support. One way to achieve this may be to adopt Peris and Tiberghien's (1984) latency technique for use with familiar faces situated either in predictable or in unpredictable contexts.

Means of priming face recognition units other than by environmental context also are suggested by the model in Fig. 1.1. These may be grouped under the heading *cognitive knowledge* by which is meant any non-facial cue other than specific context that may influence face recognition. Expectations, hypotheses, and so on, about who a person could influence the threshold or rate of firing for particular units. Emotional factors also could exert an influence at either this level or the level of the semantic store.

A possible example of such a process is to be found in a case described by Gudjonsson and Mackeith (1983). They described an elderly man who battered his wife to death and who displayed amnesia for the event. Upon further investigation it was found that he made some interesting errors on Milner's (1968) face recognition test. This test comprises 6 male and 6 female target faces that are shown together for 45 seconds. The recognition set contains 25 faces (12 males and 13 females). The subject made no errors with male faces and yet only correctly recognized one of the female faces. Gudjonsson and Mackeith (1983) interpret these and other findings as indicating that the patient demonstrated the powerful effects of repressive and/or dissociative mechanisms on female face recognition as a result of repressing the memory of the homicide. It would be as well not to put too much emphasis on results obtained from a single case but it is tempting to speculate that recognition of whole classes of faces may be inhibited by emotional/cognitive intervention at a level beyond perception (there was no suggestion that the patient failed to perceive female faces) but before any familiarity information could be obtained. We do not know whether any problems of a selective prosopagnosic kind occurred for recognizing familiar female faces but we may conjecture that, as Gudjonsson and Mackeith make no reference to such difficulties, the patient's impairment was confined to storing and/or accessing information concerning novel female faces. The fact that he could not very easily recognize female faces, however, may reflect a relatively limited amount of attention paid to them at initial viewing. A sequential presentation of stimuli might have avoided this possibility.

OVERVIEW

This chapter was designed not to act as a direct introduction to the remainder of the book that is largely concerned with the neuropsychology of face recognition and facial expressions, but to provide a commentary on contemporary cognitive investigations into related problems.

The cognitive theories that are now emerging should provide clues that neuropsychologists can pursue in their own investigations of people with brain damage. This is not a one-way process, of course. Many of the theoretical ideas have come from clinical observations and anatomical evidence (e.g., Bruyer et al., 1983; Damasio et al., 1982).

A particularly knotty problem where the evidence from experiments on research and observations of prosopagnosics often has been seen as providing converging evidence concerns the possibility that face processing is a special process, qualitatively different from that involved in perceiving and remembering other classes of material (Ellis, 1975). Comparisons are difficult, however, for, as Damasio et al. (1982) point out, faces are unusually "ambiguous" in that each exemplar is entirely unique and that it is normally insufficient to make a general identification as with most other object classes. The whole topic of the possible uniqueness of faces is addressed by Davidoff (this volume) so I shall not dwell upon the issue here. The model that has provided the framework to this review, however, does imply face specialness in the sense that, following initial allocation to the category faces a stimulus pattern is shown as being processed through a series of stages or modules that are face specific. In this regard the model assumes that faces are to some extent "special." However, there is nothing in the cognitive or neuropsychological literature to refute the possibility that parallel systems exist for the processing of other classes of object (cf. Konorski, 1967). To what extent such systems are autonomous and to what extent they share resources is difficult to establish. Similarly it is not yet possible to define the ways in which they may be different in detail. For example, the various priming effects identified in the work of both Klatzky and Bruce are clearly akin to those found for word processing and it may be possible to establish similar ones for the recognition of other classes of object, but it is equally likely that the special interactive, social and communicative properties of faces render such top-down influences in recognition more likely.

The model shown in Fig. 1.1 is necessarily static. Faces and face perception, however, are not. The model, if it tells us anything, is only able to account for initial categorization and recognition of a face. Yet once we have identified an individual and interaction proceeds it seems likely that the balance of the system must shift toward the analysis of facial expression and extraction of the person's meaning and intention. We have to know, of course, that the person before us remains the same during our encounter but our primary facial concern must be to derive nonverbal information. One prediction follows directly from this argument. Changes applied to a known face, say using Haig's computer graphics techniques, may be detected when they occur before an encounter: If they are made during an interaction they will be less likely to be noticed because processing capacity will be concentrated upon the extraction of other kinds of information and therefore less sensitive to structural abnormalities. This prediction remains to be tested but the idea of shifts over time in the balance between recognition and communication is probably worth pursuing.

The face processing system must also be dynamic in another sense. The faces with which we are familiar are themselves undergoing gradual change yet we are usually unaware of any alteration. In other words, the units within the face register must be constantly updated. An interesting question here is whether we effectively discard old templates or whether we keep some record of how people used to look? Perhaps the more parsimonious scheme would be the former coupled with the use of transformation rules, say, when comparing old film or photographs with the updated unit (cf. Pittenger & Shaw, 1975). Semantic information, of course, also will be subject to change as we learn more and more about individuals we know.

The questions raised throughout this chapter are indicative, at the same time, of how little we know about face processing and how far our understanding has progressed. We can now ask more pertinent questions than ever before and, in time no doubt, will discover the answers to many of them. The search has been and, I am sure, will continue to be conducted in a spirit of fruitful interaction among psychologists, neurologists, neuroanatomists, and computer scientists.

At the same time, questions of a practical nature will continue to be asked, many of which will address face and name recall rather than face recognition. I have largely avoided this aspect of gaining access to person information but, clearly, it is imperative that we discover not only how the system operates when confronted with a facial input but also how it manages to perform the biologically less significant task of recalling an image of a face. Here the diary techniques used by Young and his associates at Lancaster University may prove suitable for examining the kinds of errors that are made when we try to retrieve facial information for visual or verbal transmission to someone else.

Other practical questions such as how one might improve people's memory for faces—especially in those who are impaired as a result of organic brain damage—and how to aid witnesses to a crime to share his or her recollection of the culprit's face provide not only socially important practical problems but also may stimulate interesting theoretical ideas.

ACKNOWLEDGMENT

I should like to thank John Shepherd and Andy Young for their help in writing this review.

REFERENCES

Baddeley, A. D. (1982). Domains of recollection. *Psychological Review, 89,* 708–729.

Bartlett, J. C., Hurry, S., & Thorley, W. (1984). Typicality and familiarity of faces. *Memory and Cognition, 12,* 219–228.

Bodamer, J. (1947). Die prosop-agnosie (Die agnosie des physiognomieerkennens). *Archives Psychiatrie Nevenkrante, 179,* 6–53.

Bornstein, B. (1963). Prosopagnosia. In L. Halpern (Ed.), *Problems of dynamic neurology* (pp. 283–318). Jerusalem: Hadessah Medical Organization.

Bower, G. H., & Karlin, M. B. (1974). Depth of processing pictures of faces and recognition memory. *Journal of Experimental Psychology, 103,* 751–757.

Bradshaw, J. L., & Sherlock, D. (1982). Bugs and faces in the two visual fields: The analytic/wholistic processing dichotomy and task sequencing. *Cortex, 18,* 211–226.

Bruce, V. (1979). Searching for politicians: An information-processing approach to face recognition. *Quarterly Journal of Experimental Psychology, 31,* 323–395.

Bruce, V. (1982). Changing faces: Visual and non-visual coding processes in face recognition. *British Journal of Psychology, 73,* 105–116.

Bruce, V. (1983). Recognizing faces. *Philosophical Transactions of the Royal Society London (Series B), 302,* 423–436.

Bruyer, R., Laterre, C., Seron, X., Feyereisen, P., Strypstein, E., Pierrard, E., & Rectem, D. (1983). A case of prosopagnosia with some preserved covert remembrance of familiar faces. *Brain and Cognition, 2,* 257–284.

Cole, M., & Perez-Cruet, J. (1964). Prosopagnosia. *Neuropsychologia, 2,* 237–246.

Damasio, A. R., Damasio, H., & Van Hoesen, G. W. (1982). Prosopagnosia: Anatomic basis and behavioural mechanisms. *Neurology, 32,* 331–341.

Davies, G., & Milne, A. (1982). Recognizing faces in and out of context. *Current Psychological Research, 2,* 235–246.

Davies, G. M., Ellis, H. D., & Shepherd, J. W. (1977). Cue saliency in faces as assessed by the Photofit technique. *Perception, 6,* 263–269.

Davies, G. M., Shepherd, J. W., & Ellis, H. D. (1979). Effects of interpolated mugshot exposure on accuracy of eyewitness identification. *Journal of Applied Psychology, 64,* 232–237.

Ellinwood, E. H. (1969). Perception of faces. *Psychiatric Quarterly, 43,* 622–646.

Ellis, H. D. (1975). Recognizing faces. *British Journal of Psychology, 66,* 409–426.

Ellis, H. D. (1981). Theoretical aspects of face recognition. In G. M. Davies, H. D. Ellis, & J. W. Shepherd (Eds.), *Perceiving and remembering faces* (pp. 171–197). London: Academic Press.

Ellis, H. D. (1983). The role of the right hemisphere in face perception. In A. W. Young (Ed.), *Functions of the right cerebral hemisphere* (pp. 33–64). London: Academic Press.

Ellis, H. D. (1984). Practical aspects of face memory. In G. L. Wells & E. F. Loftus (Eds.), *Eyewitness testimony: Psychological perspectives* (pp. 12–37). New York: Cambridge University Press.

Ellis, H. D., & Deregowski, J. B. (1981). Within-race and between-race recognition of transformed and untransformed faces. *American Journal of Psychology, 94,* 27–35.

Ellis, H. D., Shepherd, J. W., & Davies, G. M. (1979). Identification of familiar and unfamiliar faces from internal and external features: Some implications for theories of face recognition. *Perception, 8,* 431–439.

Endo, M. (1982). Cue-saliency in upside down faces. *Tohoku Psychologica Folia, 41,* 116–122.

Fiorentini, A., Maffei, L., & Sandini, G. (1983). The role of high spatial frequencies in face perception. *Perception, 12,* 195–201.

Fodor, J. A. (1983). *The modularity of mind: An essay in faculty psychology.* Cambridge, MA: MIT Press.

Goldstein, A., & Chance, J. (1981). Laboratory studies of face recognition. In G. M. Davies, H. D. Ellis, & J. W. Shepherd (Eds.), *Perceiving and remembering faces* (pp. 81–104). London: Academic Press.

Goren, C. C., Sarty, M., & Wu, P. (1975). Visual following and pattern discrimination of face-like stimuli. *Pediatrics, 56,* 544–545.

Gudjonsson, G. H., & Mackeith, J. A. C. (1983). A specific recognition deficit in a case of homicide. *Medicine, Science and Law, 23,* 37–40.

Haig, N. D. (1984). The effect of feature displacement on face recognition. *Perception, 13,* 505–512.

Hay, D. M., & Young, A. W. (1982). The human face. In A. W. Ellis (Ed.), *Normality and pathology in cognitive functions* (pp. 173–202). London: Academic Press.

Hayes, L. A., & Watson, J. S. (1981). Neonatal imitation: Fact or artifact? *Developmental Psychology, 17,* 655–660.

Klatzky, R. L. (1983, August). *Facial categories: How visual? How abstract?* Paper presented at the APA Convention.

Klatzky, R. L. (1984). *Memory and awareness.* New York: Freeman.

Klatzky, R. L., & Forrest, F. H. (1984). Recognizing familiar and unfamiliar faces. *Memory and Cognition, 12,* 60–70.

Klatzky, R. L., Martin, G. L., & Kane, R. A. (1982). Semantic interpretation effects on memory for faces. *Memory and Cognition, 10,* 195–206.

Konorski, J. (1967). *Integrative activity of the brain: An interdisciplinary approach.* Chicago: The University of Chicago Press.

Kurucz, J., & Feldmar, G. (1979). Prospo-affective agnosia as a symptom of cerebral organic disease. *Journal of the American Geriatrics Society, 27,* 225–230.

Kurucz, J., Feldmar, G., & Werner, W. (1979). Prosopo-affective agnosia associated with chronic organic brain syndrome. *Journal of the American Geriatrics Society, 27,* 91–95.

Ley, R. G., & Bryden, M. P. (1979). Hemispheric differences in processing emotions and faces. *Brain and Language, 7,* 127–138.

Light, L. L., Kayra-Stuart, F., & Hollander, S. (1979). Recognition memory for typical and unusual faces. *Journal of Experimental Psychology: Human Learning and Memory, 5,* 212–228.

Mandler, G. (1980). Recognizing: The judgment of previous occurrence. *Psychological Review, 87,* 252–271.

Marr, D. (1982). *Vision: A computational investigation into the human representation and processing of visual information.* San Francisco: Freeman.

McKellar, T. P. H. (1957). *Imagination and thinking: A psychological analysis.* London: Cohen & West.

Meltzoff, A. N., & Moore, M. K. (1977). Imitation of facial and manual gestures by human neonates. *Science, 198,* 75–78.

Meyer, D. E., & Schvanaveldt, R. W. (1976). Meaning, memory structure and mental processes. *Science, 192,* 27–33.

Milner, B. (1968). Visual recognition and recall after right temporal excision in man. *Neuropsychologia, 6,* 191–209.

Morton, J. (1969). Interaction and information in word recognition. *Psychological Review, 76,* 401–416.

Morton, J. (1981). Will cognition survive? *Cognition, 10,* 227–234.

Mueller, J. H., Heesacker, M., Ross, M. J., & Nicodemus, D. R. (1983). Emotionality of encoding activity in face memory. *Journal of Research in Personality, 17,* 198–219.

Newcombe, F. (1979). The processing of visual information in prosopagnosia and acquired dyslexia: Functional versus physiological interpretation. In O. J. Osborne, M. M. Gruneberg, & J. R. Eiser (Eds.), *Research in psychology and medicine.* London: Academic Press.

Owsley, C., Sekuler, R., & Boldt, C. (1981). Aging and low-contrast vision: Face perception. *Investigative Opthalmology, 21,* 362–365.

Pallis, C. A. (1955). Impaired identification of faces and places with agnosia for colours. *Journal of Neurosurgery and Psychiatry, 18,* 218–224.

Patterson, K. E., & Baddeley, A. D. (1977). When face recognition fails. *Journal of Experimental Psychology: Human Learning and Memory, 3,* 406–417.

Péris, J. L., & Tiberghien, G. (1984). Effet de contexte et recherche conditionelle dans la reconnaissance de visages familiers. *Cahiers de Psychologie Cognitive, 4,* 323–334.

Peters, A. (1917). Gufuhl and Wiedererkennen. *Fortschritte der Psychologie und ihrer Anwendurgen 4,* 120–133.

Pittenger, J. B., & Shaw, R. E. (1975). Aging faces as viscal-elastic events: Implications for a theory of non-rigid shape perception. *Journal of Experimental Psychology: Human Perception and Performance, 104,* 374–382.

Rose, S. (1980). *Royal Mail stamps: A survey of British stamp designs.* Oxford: Phaidon Press.

Sergent, J. (1984). An investigation into component and configurational processes underlying face perception. *British Journal of Psychology, 75,* 221–242.

Shepherd, J. W., Davies, G. M., & Ellis, H. D. (1981). Studies of cue saliency. In G. M. Davies, H. D. Ellis, & J. W. Shepherd (Eds.), *Perceiving and remembering faces* (pp. 105–131). London: Academic Press.

Shepherd, J. W., & Ellis, H. D. (1973). The effect of attractiveness on recognition memory for faces. *American Journal of Psychology, 86,* 627–633.

Shuttleworth, E. C., Syring, V., & Allen, N. (1982). Further observations on the nature of prosopagnosia. *Brain and Cognition, 1,* 307–322.

Tiberghien, G. (1983). La memoire des visages. *L'Année Psychologique, 83,* 153–198.

Tieger, T., & Ganz, L. (1979). Recognition of faces in the presence of two-dimensional sinusoidal masks. *Perception and Psychophysics, 26,* 163–167.

Van Lancker, D., & Canter, G. J. (1982). Impairment of voice and face recognition in patients with hemispheric damage. *Brain and Cognition, 1*, 185–195.

Watkins, M. J., Ho, E., & Tulving, E. (1976). Context effects in recognition memory for faces. *Journal of Verbal Learning and Verbal Behaviour, 15*, 505–517.

Whiteley, A. M., & Warrington, E. K. (1977). Prosopagnosia: A clinical, psychological and anatomic study of three patients. *Journal of Neurology, Neurosurgery and Psychiatry, 40*, 395–403.

Winograd, E. (1978). Encoding operations which facilitate memory for faces across the life-span. In M. M. Gruneberg, P. E. Morris, & R. N. Sykes (Eds.), *Practical aspects of memory* (pp. 255–262). London: Academic Press.

Winograd, E., & Rivers-Bulkeley, N. T. (1977). Effects of changing context on remembering faces. *Journal of Experimental Psychology: Human Learning and Memory, 3*, 397–405.

Yarmey, A. D. (1973). I recognize your face but I can't remember your name: Further evidence on the tip-of-the-tongue phenomenon. *Memory and Cognition, 3*, 287–290.

Young, A. W., Ellis, A. W., McWeeny, K. H., & Hay, D. C. (1984). *Naming and categorization latencies for faces and written names.* Unpublished manuscript.

Young, A. W., Hay, D. C., & Ellis, A. W. (1985). The faces that launched a thousand slips: Everyday difficulties and errors in recognizing people. *British Journal of Psychology, 76*, 495–523.

I

BRAIN DAMAGE AND
FACE PERCEPTION

2 The Anatomical Substrate of Prosopagnosia

Antonio R. Damasio
Department of Neurology (Division of Behavioral Neurology)

Hanna Damasio
University of Iowa College of Medicine Iowa City, Iowa

The post-mortem study of the very first cases of prosopagnosia, those of Wilbrand (1892) and Heidenhain (1927), revealed bilateral lesions of the central visual system. By then, the term *prosopagnosia* had not been coined (it was introduced by Bodamer only in 1947) and, for numerous reasons, the concept of a visual agnosia predominantly involving the recognition of familiar faces was not accepted and not incorporated in the scientific literature. The pathological correlates of the disorder were just as neglected. The defect appeared bizarre and many investigators found it difficult to believe it could indeed occur. Was it not possible that such patients were malingering, or hysterical, or psychotic, or merely demented? The rarity of the description cast doubt on the probability of similar cases surfacing again. Sir Gordon Holmes' work on the organization of the visual system, by focusing on surviving patients with gunshot wounds of the occipito-parietal region, failed to identify cases of prosopagnosia and thus, by default, further strengthened the reluctance in accepting the complaint as real or, if real, as truly neurological (Holmes, 1918a, 1918b, 1919). In the past 2 decades, however, there has been a resurgence of interest on prosopagnosia. The first new contributions on the problem appeared at a time when the neuropsychological study of patients with right hemisphere lesions and of surgical callosal section had uncovered the right hemisphere's special endowment for visuo-spatial processing. Under the weight of such evidence, facial recognition came to be conceptualized as a typical right hemisphere ability and, naturally, it was hypothesized that prosopagnosia was the result of exclusive right hemisphere damage.

Hécaen's clinical descriptions of prosopagnosia in the 1950s supported the right hemisphere hypothesis (Hécaen, Angelergues, Bernhardt, & Chiarelli, 1957), but the post-mortem study of the only patient of his to come to autopsy showed that the lesions were bilateral (Hécaen & Angelergues, 1962). In 1974, when Meadows prepared a thoughtful review on prospoagnosia, he noted the prevalence of left visual field defects in the few patients with prosopagnosia that had been reported until then. He used the finding as an indicator that the right hemisphere might be the one primarily involved in the causation of prosopagnosia (Meadows, 1974). One decade later, however, the views on the subject have changed remarkably and the questions of whether the right hemisphere lesion is sufficient to cause prosopagnosia, or indeed if a unilateral lesion can cause prosopagnosia, have been largely clarified. The arguments accumulated in recent years are as follows:

The Use of Visual Field Data in the Prediction of Lesion Sites.   In the days that preceded the availability of *in vivo* imaging techniques with reliable localizing capability, the localization of lesions was carried out mostly on the basis of inference from neurological signs. The presence, absence, and type of visual fields was one of the most utilized forms of neurological data. There were, however, numerous pitfalls in the interpretation of such data. Although it is true that the presence of certain types of visual field defect can be indicative of damage in the central visual system, the absence of a visual field defect does not rule out the presence of a major cerebral lesion. As far as the posterior (i.e., post-geniculate) sector of the visual system is concerned, in fact, lest the lesion involve optic radiations or primary visual cortex, no field defect for form vision will ensue. A large unilateral lesion confined to the visual association cortices generally does not cause basic visual field defects for form vision. Such a lesion may, on the other hand, produce other forms of disturbance of visual processing, for instance, a defect in the visual fields for color, or an impairment of movement perception, or of spatial analysis (Damasio, 1985). Many of these complex defects are commonly undetected in routine observations and such unilateral lesions may thus be silent. The autopsy of Hécaen's patient (Hécaen & Angelergues, 1962) proved precisely this point by showing that the patient had a bilateral lesion although only the one in the right occipital lobe had given rise to a visual field cut. The same happened with the patient of Benson and associates whose visual fields might have led one to believe he had a right hemisphere lesion only (Rubens & Benson, 1971). Post-mortem study revealed bilateral damage of the occipital of the visual system (Benson, Segarra, & Albert, 1974).

More often than not, patients who develop bilateral lesions in the occipital lobe do so as a result of double lesions of vascular origin, often acquired at different epochs. Such infarctions are generally the result of disease in the vertebral or basilar arteries. Although these lesions are functionally symmetric, in the sense that they occur within the same functional system of the brain, they are always asymmetric in terms of precise placement and size, a feature that is largely the consequence of slight but by no means insignificant asymmetries of cortical structure and of cerebral vascular supply. Thus, it is possible for nature to produce bilateral lesions in the same system and not produce bilateral visual field defects because a minor shift in the exact position of the lesion may well lead to the sparing or involvement of optic radiations or primary visual cortex (i.e., to the sparing of one side and the involvement of the other). It is almost surprising how these bilateral lesions indeed produce bilateral visual field defects at all. In short, although it is of the highest importance to have the minute plotting of visual fields of form and color in patients with visual agnosia (the interpretation of patients' performance must take visual field data into account), it is not possible to use visual field data for precise lesion localization.

In retrospect, perhaps investigators ought to have been more skeptical of utilizing visual field information in the understanding of the anatomical basis of prosopagnosia, for both methodological and theoretical reasons. Although most patients with unilateral field defects had left-sided defects, a sizeable number of subjects had exclusively right visual defects (i.e., would have had lesions exclusively in the left hemisphere). Those cases would have been difficult to reconcile with the notion that prosopagnosia was caused by right hemisphere damage.

Post-Mortem Analysis of Patients with Prosopagnosia. Some years ago we undertook to analyze all the post-mortem reports of patients with prosopagnosia (Damasio, Damasio, & Van Hoesen, 1982). There were, as of 1982, 11 cases of prosopagnosia studied at autopsy, a surprisingly high number considering the rarity of the condition. For most of the patients, the post-mortem information was of good quality and showed, quite unequivocally, that the lesions were (a) bilateral in all cases; and (b) functionally symmetric in all cases but one (i.e., located in such a way as to impair the operation of the central visual system both in the right and in the left hemispheres). But those data were revealing in yet another way. It was apparent that one could define more precisely the necessary and sufficient component of damage associated with prosopagnosia. Not only did the lesion have to be in the central visual system but in the inferior (ventral) component of that system (i.e., in the occipito-temporal region as opposed to the occipito-parietal). The same review uncovered one case of damage in this same location, in the right hemisphere alone, without prosopagnosia (Lhermitte, Chain, Escourolle, Ducarne, & Pillon, 1972). One additional case has since been reported (Nardelli et al., 1982), also with similar bilateral lesions.

The neuropathological evidence available for this rare condition is thus quite substantial and unequivocally indicates that in 100% of autopsied cases with prosopagnosia the lesions were bilateral.

Computed Tomography (CT), Magnetic Resonance (MR) and Emission Tomography (ET) Studies in Prosopagnosia. To the best of our knowledge, with only one exception, all patients who have been studied with CT also have shown bilateral lesions of the central visual system (cf. Brazis, Biller, & Fine,

1981; Bruyer et al., 1983; Damasio et al., 1982; Nardelli et al., 1982; Newcombe, 1982). It is, of course, entirely possible that patients with a less standard form of anatomophysiological organization, may develop prosopagnosia on the basis of a unilateral lesion. This may have been the explanation for the findings reported by Whiteley and Warrington (1977) who noted, in their study, that one of three cases had bilateral lesions but that two did not. In one of the negative cases the patient had a right occipital glioma compressing the left hemisphere and had, in all likelihood, invasion of the contralateral visual system through the splenium of the corpus callosum even if that was not apparent on CT. The patient's prosopagnosia improved, thus rendering the condition compatible with a primary unilateral lesion (it should be noted that in all patients with prosopagnosia found to have bilateral lesions the defect remains stable). But, the other patient had a right occipital hemorrhage in the setting of hypertension. Although a second small lesion in the opposite hemisphere may have gone undetected, clinically or by CT, the possibility remains that the lesion was indeed unilateral.

In the prosopagnosic patients studied thus far by Magnetic Resonance, the lesion was found to be bilateral and occipito-temporal (Damasio, 1985). In the two cases studied by Single Photon Emission Tomography, the functional defect also was shown to be bilateral (Damasio, 1985).

CT has been crucial in adding evidence on the result of bilateral lesions located in the occipito-parietal sector of the brain (i.e., bilateral lesions just as in the instance of prosopagnosia but located in the dorsal aspect of the brain). Patients with lesions in such a location develop visual disorientation (*simultan-agnosia*), and often ocular apraxia and optic ataxia (i.e., the triad that constitutes the Balint syndrome; Damasio, 1985). If the lesion does not extend downward into the occipito-temporal region, none of those patients develop prosopagnosia, although many of them, because of their disturbance of the ability to analyze visual space properly, may appear to be agnosic or alexic on a casual observation. When their gaze can be directed to the stimuli for which recognition is requested, they can recognize faces and letters normally. It is likely that some of the patients with what was described in the classic literature as visual *apperceptive* agnosia, did have a Balint syndrome that was not properly diagnosed. The impairment of such patients is not one of recognition, primarily, but rather one of the ability to analyze the placement of stimuli in space and of gathering the appropriate amount of information so that recognition can take place. By the same token, patients with significant lesions of the right occipito-parietal region, often show severe visuo-spatial disturbances that may, at least acutely, preclude appropriate analysis of visual stimuli and thus impair recognition. Careful analysis of those patients reveals their defect as one of perception primarily (see the work of Benton, 1980 for a comprehensive review of the perceptual issue in prosopagnosia). Those patients have the kind of defect that is incompatible with recognition of almost any visual stimulus and certainly incompatible with matching of stimuli, or reproduction of the stimulus by drawing, both tasks that patients with true prosopagnosia (i.e., with a visual "associative" agnosia, carry out without difficulty).

Evidence from Unilateral Lesions.   Evidence regarding the result of unilateral lesions in either the left or the right occipito-temporal region is now abundant, and based on both post-mortem and CT evidence. Unilateral left lesions commonly give rise to the syndrome of pure alexia, to defects in color processing in the right visual field, to right hemianopia or to right upper quadrantanopia. Similar lesions on the right cause left hemiachromatopsia, left hemianopia, left upper quadrantanopia, or defects in visual perceptive ability that can be detected in such procedures as the Judgment of Line Orientation Test (Damasio, 1985; Damasio, Yamada, Damasio, Corbett, & McKee, 1980; Damasio et al., 1982). Chronic and stable prosopagnosia has never been described with one of these unilateral lesions, of the left or of the right. As stated earlier, we would not be surprised to learn about exceptional cases in which such a unilateral lesion would cause prosopagnosia. Indeed, we are rather surprised that such non-standard cases have not yet been identified and published save for Whiteley and Warrington's.

Evidence from Hemispherectomy and from the Surgical Callosal Section.   If lesions of the right hemisphere alone would normally cause prosopagnosia one would expect patients subject to right hemispherectomy to become prosopagnosic. Right hemispherectomy was once widely used for the treatment of seizures but we are not aware of a single report of prosopagnosia in the hundreds of patients subject to that treatment. In patients with right hemispherectomy studied personally (see Damasio, Lima, & Damasio, 1975), it was apparent that the ability to recognize familiar faces and to learn new ones was perfectly intact despite a major left visual field defect and despite the absence of the hemisphere known to have visual perceptive advantage. It might be argued that the congenital lesions of the right hemisphere, which caused the seizures and motivated the hemispherectomy in the first place, would have led to a compensatory functional shift to left hemisphere structures. That, in turn, might explain the absence of prosopagnosia. Although such an explanation might obtain, in selected cases, we doubt it applies to most instances of right hemispherectomy, especially because the lesions in question tended to spare the posterior sectors of the brain.

Similar conclusions can be reached from the study of facial recognition performance in patients with surgical callosal section. Commissurotomized patients recognize faces presented in the left or right visual fields (i.e., with either of their isolated hemispheres, as Levy has demonstrated; Levy, Trevarthen & Sperry, 1972). This effect has been noted once again in a recent study by Gazzaniga and Smylie (1983). These authors showed that both hemispheres are capable of facial recognition, and that, in all likelihood, each carries out the job with a different cognitive strategy. A similar conclusion was reached by Sergent and Bindra (1981) in a tachistoscopic study of facial recognition in normals.

   Evidence from Amnesic Syndromes.   Patients with global amnesic syndromes also have prosopagnosia. For instance, it is apparent that patient HM has not been able to learn new faces since the time of his operation and is thus unable to recognize the faces of people that have come into contact with him since then (Corkin, 1984). Prosopagnosia is thus embedded in the global amnesic syndrome, one of the many forms of recognition defect that such patients exhibit. Patient DRB provides an even better illustration of this point (Damasio, Eslinger, Damasio, Van Hoesen, & Cornell, 1984). DRB has a pervasive retrograde as well as anterograde amnesia. His defect of facial recognition encompasses all of his friends and relatives as well as all of the persons that have come into contact with him since the onset of his illness. These patients have bilateral damage in the temporal lobe, in structures of the limbic system to which the occipito-temporal cortices project powerfully and from which they receive important projections as well. It is of special interest that patients with partial amnesic syndromes caused by unilateral temporal lobe involvement do not develop prosopagnosia (Milner, 1968). For instance, if the lesion is located in the left temporal lobe structures, they develop a pervasive anomia for familiar faces, but they still give ample evidence of recognition at a nonverbal level.

CONCLUSION

In conclusion, it can be said that all avenues of available evidence indicate that chronic and stable prosopagnosia is caused by bilateral lesions. Those lesions generally respect two criteria: (a) they fall in one specific region of the brain, the central visual system, and (b) they involve the occipito-temporal sector of that system.

   The fact that no single exception to the aforementioned rule has been found in the documented autopsy cases of prosopagnosia (incidentally, an unexpected large number of autopsies considering the relative rarity of the condition), certainly gives weight to the bilateral lesion concept. Nonetheless, it should be clear that exceptions to such rules are common in neurology and are to be expected. Furthermore, when and if such exceptions surface, they should not be construed as evidence that prosopagnosia is not generally caused by bilateral lesions, or that facial recognition is not generally operated by both hemispheres. Such a line of reasoning, unfortunately all too common, would be the equivalent of denying that cerebral dominance for language is generally a left hemisphere affair, every time we find a case of crossed aphasia (aphasia with a right hemisphere lesion in a right hander). Natural exceptions of that sort clearly do not invalidate the more general observation they depart from.

But perhaps the greatest weight for the bilateral lesion concept comes from the conceptualization of what the process of facial recognition means, psychosocially, and of how it must be specified cognitively and neurophysiologically.

Prosopagnosia is not confined to human faces but rather encompasses any stimulus that, as human faces, (a) requires *specific* and *context-related* recognition (as opposed to non-specific, generic recognition only), and (b) is visually ambiguous, (i.e. a stimulus that is part of a group that has numerous *different* members with *similar* visual structure, Damasio et al., 1982).

The environment is rich in visually ambiguous stimuli for which a specific recognition is mandatory. Lack of precise recognition of such stimuli is socially unacceptable and virtually incompatible with normal activity in a human environment. The type of recognition impaired in prosopagnosia has important survival value and is present in numerous other species—it is difficult to conceive the social life of most higher mammals without it. It would be unlikely that nature would have maintained this old and fundamental ability in relation to one hemisphere only. That is certainly not the case with memory in general and facial recognition is nothing but visually triggered episodic memory. It would appear more sensible that nature has endowed the right and the left hemispheres with the ability to encode, store, and both recall and recognize visually ambiguous stimuli. It is apparent that the mechanisms utilized for both learning and recall/recognition are different in each side, in keeping with the different anatomical, physiological, and cognitive specialization characteristic of each hemisphere, at least in humans. It is also probable that the mechanisms used by the right hemisphere are more efficient than those of the left (Ellis, 1983; Gazzaniga & Smylie, 1983; Warrington & James, 1967).

ACKNOWLEDGMENT

This chapter was supported by NINCDS Grant PO NS 19632.

REFERENCES

Benson, D., Segarra, J., & Albert M. L. (1974). Visual agnosia-prosopagnosia. *Archives of Neurology, 30,* 307–310.

Benton, A. (1980). The neuropsychology of facial recognition. *American Psychologist, 35,* 176–186.

Bodamer, J. (1947). Die Prosop-Agnosie. *Archiv Fur Psychiatrie Und Nervenkrankheiten, 179,* 6–54.

Brazis, P. W., Biller, J., & Fine, M. (1981). Central achromatopsia. *Neurology, 31,* 920.

Bruyer, R., Laterre, C., Seron, X., Feyereisen, P., Strypstein, E., Pierrard, E., & Rectem, D. (1983). A case of prosopagnosia with some preserved covert remembrance of familiar faces. *Brain and Cognition, 2,* 257–284.

Corkin, S. (1984). Lasting consequences of bilateral medial temporal lobectomy: Clinical course and experimental findings in HM. *Seminars in Neurology, 4,* 249–259.

Damasio, A. R. (1985). Disorders of complex visual processing: agnosias, achromatopsia, Balint syndrome and related difficulties of orientation and construction. In M. M. Mesulam (Ed.), *Principles of behavioral neurology.* Philadelphia: F. A. Davis.

Damasio, A. R., Damasio, H., & Van Hoesen, G. W. (1982). Prosopagnosia: Anatomical basis and behavioral mechanisms. *Neurology, 32,* 331–41.

Damasio, A. R., Eslinger, P. J., Damasio, H., Van Hoesen, G. W., & Cornell, S. (1985). Multimodal amnesic syndrome following bilateral temporal and basel forebrain damage: The case of patient DRB. *Archives of Neurology, 42,* 252–259.

Damasio, A. R., Lima, P. A., & Damasio, H. (1975). Nervous function after right hemispherectomy. *Neurology, 25,* 89–93.

Damasio, A. R., Yamada, T., Damasio, H., Corbett, J., & McKee, J. (1980). Central achromatopsia: Behavioral, anatomic and physiologic aspects. *Neurology, 30,* 1064–1071.

Ellis, H. D. (1983). The role of the right hemisphere in face perception. In A. W. Young (Ed.), *Functions of the right cerebral hemisphere* (pp. 33–64). London: Academic Press.

Gazzaniga, M. S., & Smylie, C. S. (1983). Facial recognition and brain asymmetries: Clues to underlying mechanisms. *Annals of Neurology, 13,* 537–540.

Hécaen, H., & Angelergues, R. (1962). Agnosia for faces (prosopagnosia). *Archives of Neurology, 7,* 92–100.

Hécaen, H., Angelergues, R., Bernhardt, C., & Chiarelli, J. (1957). Essai de distinction des modalités cliniques de l'agnosie des physiognomies. *Revue Neurologique* (Paris), *96,* 125–144.

Heidenhain, A. (1927). Beitrag zur Kenntnis der Seelenblindheit. *Monatschrift Psychiatrische Neurolojische, 66,* 61–116.

Holmes, G. (1918a). Disturbances of vision by cerebral lesions. *British Journal of Ophthalmology, 2,* 353–383.

Holmes, G. (1918b). Disturbances of visual orientation. *British Journal of Ophthalmology, 2,* 449–468.

Holmes, G. (1919). Disturbances of spatial orientation and visual attention with loss of stereoscopic vision. *Archives of Neurology and Psychiatry, 1,* 385.

Levy, J., Trevarthen, C., & Sperry, R. W. (1972). Perception of bilateral chimeric figures following hemispheric disconnection. *Brain, 95,* 61–78.

Lhermitte, J., Chain, F., Escourolle, R., Ducarne, B., & Pillon, B. (1972). Etude anatomoclinque d'un cas de prosopagnosie. *Revue Neruologique* (Paris), *126,* 329–346.

Meadows, J. C. (1974). The anatomical basis of prospagnosia. *Journal of Neurology, Neurosurgery and Psychiatry, 37,* 489–501.

Milner, B. (1968). Visual recognition and recall after right temporal lobe excision in man. *Neuropsychologia, 6,* 191–209.

Nardelli, E., Buonanno, F., Coccia, G., Fiaschi, A., Terzian, H., & Rizzuto, N. (1982). Prosopagnosia: Report of four cases. *European Neurology, 21,* 289–297.

Rubens, A. B., & Benson, D. F. (1971). Associative visual agnosia. *Archives of Neurology, 24,* 305–316.

Sergent, J., & Bindra, D. (1981). Differential hemispheric processing of faces: Methodological considerations and reinterpretation. *Psychological Bulletin, 89,* 541–554.

Warrington, E. K., & James, M. (1967). An experimental investigation of facial recognition in patients with unilateral cerebral lesions. *Cortex, 3,* 317–326.

Whiteley, A. M., & Warrington, E. K. (1977). Prosopagnosia: a clinical, psychological, and anatomical study of three patients. *Journal of Neurology, Neurosurgery and Psychiatry, 40,* 395–403.

Wilbrand, H. (1892). Ein Fall von Seelenblindheit und Hemianopsie mit Sectionsbefund. *Deutsche Z Nervenheik, 2,* 361–87.

3 The Cognitive Locus of Prosopagnosia

Guy Tiberghien
University of Grenoble

Isabelle Clerc
Rouen Hospital

The inability to recognize faces, especially the most familiar, is a pathological disorder that has not received systematic attention for a very long time, although in recent years it once again has aroused strong theoretical interest. The clinical picture usually given of face agnosia is, unfortunately, most complex, especially because of various associated disorders that make it difficult to grasp clearly (defects in body schema and color perception, for example). The fact is that Bodamer (1947) made a remarkably daring, almost rash, move in isolating the syndrome of prosopagnosia. The theoretical problem is complicated even further by the fact that "pure" cases of prosopagnosia are extremely rare and to date fewer than 100 detailed case records are available for study. Finally, though prosopagnosia is predominantly associated with lesional damage to the occipito-temporal area of the right hemisphere, there exist anatomical variations determined by whether, for instance, damage is bilateral or not or whether the integrity of the visual field is preserved or not (Bruyer, 1983; Bruyer & Velge, 1980; Hécaen, 1981; Rondot & Tzavaras, 1969). Such neurological observations are, moreover, consistent with various experimental evidence of the importance, if not the exclusive role, of the right hemisphere for the recognition of faces in normal subjects (Bradshaw & Nettleton, 1981; Bruyer, 1980a, 1980b; Bruyer & Gadisseux, 1980; Ellis, 1983; Hay, 1981; Versace & Tiberghien, 1985), or subjects that have undergone right temporal lobotomy (Milner, 1968), or a cerebral commisurotomy (Gazzaniga & Smylie, 1983).

Almost 40 years after Bodamer's etiological account, we have to admit that no satisfactory explanatory theory of prosopagnosia has been worked out or formulated. Worse still, certain very general and basic questions have not received unequivocal answers and we still do not know whether the inability to recognize faces should be considered genuine agnosia or merely as a malfunctioning of memory. It is not known, either, whether we are dealing with a highly specific defect or a more general complaint possibly affecting other classes of objects in addition to human faces (Baddeley, 1976). It is true that some interesting hypotheses have been advanced (defect of body schema; defect in perceptual analysis and/or synthesis; defect in individualization), but they are often contradictory and none has so far managed to become generally accepted (Bruyer et al., 1983; Damasio, Damasio & Van Hoesen, 1982; Faust, 1955; Hécaen, 1981; Pallis, 1955; Rondot & Tzavaras, 1969).

This state of affairs is probably due at least partly to a certain degree of compartmentalization of research in this field. Few durable functional connections have been made between the neurological approach, clinical investigation, and experimental research in cognition. The possibility of a theoretical breakthrough most likely depends on a real intensification of interaction between these three levels of analysis and explanation. The association between neuro- and cognitive psychology could provide the former with more precise models of cognitive functioning and the latter with actual "natural" experimental material for the testing of certain of its theoretical predictions (Baddeley, 1982a; Hay & Young, 1982; Richardson, 1982; Schacter & Tulving, 1982).

With this in mind we present the clinical and neurological account of a case of prosopagnosia we followed regularly for 2 years at the Centre Hospitalier Universitaire of Rouen. We also used systematic experimentation in order to ascertain the exact place of memory processes in prosopagnosia. Our research reveals the apparently decisive role of the factors, familiarity and context. This leads us to consider their psychological significance and to examine the question of how they might be accounted for in a general theory of amnesia. We conclude that prosopagnosia probably corresponds imperfectly to the generic category of agnosia and might be more relevantly described as prosopamnesia.

FAMILIARITY, CONTEXT AND PROSOPAGNOSIA: THE CASE OF A. H

Neurological and Neuropsychological History

A.H., aged 53, was hospitalized in 1982 in the Centre Hospitalier Universitaire in Rouen for acute headaches accompanied by visual clouding. Clinical examination revealed a meningeal syndrome associated with a left lateral homonymous hemianopsia. Tomodensitometric examination revealed a large right occipitotemporal hematoma. Arteriography showed up an arteriovenous fistula irrigated by a posterior branch of the Sylvian vein (Fig. 3.1). A. H. then underwent a surgical operation that consisted of the removal of the hematoma and of the

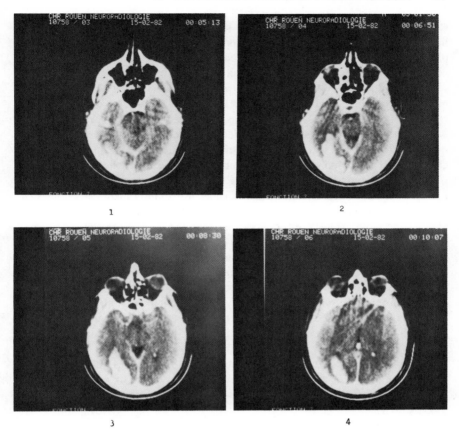

FIG. 3.1 CT scan: horizontal sections with 15° extension from the orbitome line. (1) 20mm, (2) 29mm, (3) 38mm and (4) 47mm above the external acoustic meatus. The hematoma was located in four slices from 20mm to 47mm. It involved the white matter axis of the right occipital lobe and occipitotemporal junction. It reached into the calcarine cortex and compromised optic radiations. It extended to the temporal horn and parahippocampal gyrus. The forceps major and lingual gyrus appeared intact.

arteriovenous aneurism and thrombosis. After the operation, A. H. declared he did not recognize any of the nursing staff. On returning home, he declared that familiar persons had the same face as the nursing staff. Some time later he declared that all had "an Asiatic look." After 2 weeks all faces seemed strange and he had a feeling they were all the same.

Eight months later this feeling remained and he found most familiar faces impossible to identify. The neuropsychological assessment that led to the conclusion of prosopagnosia showed an excellent intellectual level (PM 38 = 55), no memory deficiency in classical clinical tests (Battery 144, Benton, test of

Rey, learning test of Violon & Seyll), and, finally, no language disorder. An in-depth investigation revealed no perceptual deficiency, no agnosia of colors, pictures, objects, voices, or melodies. Nor did there seem to be any deficiency of topographical vision or loss of mental imagery.

The diagnosis of prosopagnosia led to investigations based on more specific material: faces, cars, and animals. With faces, A. H. showed no defect in mental representation (recall of familiar famous faces, reconstructions, drawings); he was able to match identical faces; he identified emotional face expressions correctly, and, finally, he succeeded in identification tests (in forced and free choice). On the other hand, he had trouble identifying the sex and the age of persons from their faces, and trouble identifying famous faces (on photos) and familiar faces. With cars, A.H. was perfectly capable of matching identical vehicles (in similar position or in a front view/side view relation). However, he failed to identify the same vehicles, errors almost always showing, moreover, a tendency to enlargement (example: a little Simca 1000 was mistaken for a large American car; and a Renault 4 for a Lada). With animals it was noted that A.H. had great trouble identifying races within a given species and there was the same tendency to exaggerate size as was the case with cars.

Clinical examination of the case clearly showed that the perturbations observed did not concern representation or perception. Indeed, A.H. is perfectly capable of recalling faces and assessing similarities and differences. It seems that in his case the problem is rather one of memory, because what gives him the most trouble is memory recognition and placing a name on faces. Moreover, the more familiar the face, the stronger the perturbation is, and it is likely that the factor familiarity of information to be recognized plays a crucial and decisive role in this disorder.

Furthermore, A.H. used three modes of recognition. In ascending order of frequency of use: (a) a rapid identification with a feeling of confidence; (b) slow identification based on analysis of details of the face or objects (nose, mouth, radiator grill, headlights, coat, head shape); (c) very slow identification based on a highly complex activity of categorical search. (Thus, confronted with the face of Mr. Badinter, the preceding "Garde des Sceaux" and Minister for Justice in France, A.H. stated, " an austere person, definitely a politician, maybe Badinter?") *"Everybody is the same"* is a leitmotif in A.H.'s own commentary on his case. He complains, too, that he can't distinguish familiar faces from unknown ones. Yet he consistently uses contextual cues in order to reconstruct the faces of people he encounters ("I try to get to the bottom of my analysis, I try to see who it might be in respect of the place, the hair . . ."). Certain context effects are particularly striking and psychologically intriguing. Thus, when A.H. hears a politician on TV without seeing him, he can identify him; but if he sees and hears him at the same time, he can no longer recognize him. On coming across soldiers on leave in a railway station, A.H. thinks he recognizes in every one of them an old Army friend of 20 years ago. However he immediately recognizes a friend he has not seen for more than 10 years when he encounters him in the familiar setting of his office.

Taken as a whole these observations seem to imply that A.H. is affected by contextual variations in his environment and that these can improve or perturb face recognition. Thus context also is a critical factor in A.H.'s pathological condition. Further, it is not impossible that the context factor and the familiarity factor are associated within a pattern of complex interaction.

The neuropsychological examination of the case of A.H. enabled us to identify two factors which, we know from other evidence, play an important part in the functioning of memory (Tulving, 1983). But mere clinical examination obviously cannot suffice to bring out their full theoretical significance. So we had A.H. undergo a classical, but in-depth, experimental investigation that made it possible for us systematically to control the critical factors brought to light in the neuropsychological and clinical examination.

Experimental Study

We submitted A.H. to a series of 37 experiments based on differing material (words, objects, faces), but here we detail only the data gathered on face recognition. The same experiments were carried out with a group of 20 normal subjects (control group) comprising 13 women and 7 men of an average age of 60. In a first type of experiment we manipulated only the degree of familiarity of the faces to be memorized and recognized. Under the conditions of the experiment, faces to be memorized and faces to be recognized, old or new, could be familiar or unfamiliar. Face familiarity was experimentally induced by a perceptual pre-exposure to faces to be memorized later. The faces whose familiarity we wanted to increase were presented simultaneously among others with short biographical descriptions, the familiarization phase lasting about 10 minutes. Four different experimental conditions were decided upon: (a) None of the faces—old or distractor—was submitted to the phase of perceptual pre-familiarization; (b) all faces to be recognized were submitted to the pre-familiarization phase but none of the distractor faces used later in the recognition task was given pre-familiarization; (c) none of the faces to be recognized was given pre-familiarization, but all the distractor faces were; (d) half of the recognition and half of the distractor faces were given pre-familiarization. The study of the critical faces immediately followed the familiarization phase. Each face was studied for 5 seconds. There was no retention interval between study and the yes-no recognition test in which the "old" faces were mingled with new ones in random order.

In the first class of experiments, faces were to be memorized in isolation; in a second series of experiments, along the same general lines, we had A.H. and the control-group subjects memorize faces that could be accompanied by various associated contexts (landscapes, other faces, words). The faces could be completely unknown to the subjects or on the contrary have been given pre-experimental familiarization. In the recognition test, some of the faces were presented in an identical context to that of study, some in a new context similar to the study context and others, finally, in a completely different context.

We established the index d' for discriminability between old and new faces and the decision index β from signal detection theory applied to memory recognition (Lecocq & Tiberghien, 1981; Swets, 1964; Tiberghien, 1984b). Variations in decision criterion β are parallel to those in discriminability index d'. We therefore analyze in detail only index d', given that the inferential conclusions applicable to this parameter are also applicable to index β. In other words, the results obtained show that the experimental factors affecting memory discriminability likewise affect the decision criterion.

Figure 3.2 presents the variations of d' according to type of face prefamiliarization. We can see that this factor has a striking effect on A.H. but only a very moderate one on the control group. A.H.'s performance is definitely poorer than that of normal subjects when no face is familiar. On the other hand, when half of the old and new faces have been given pre-experimental familiarization, we see no difference between A.H. and the control group. It is clear,

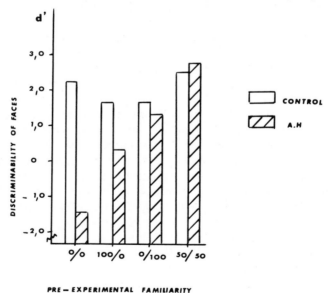

PRE — EXPERIMENTAL FAMILIARITY

FIG. 3.2 Effect of pre-experimental familiarity of faces on the discriminability parameter d' between old and new faces in recognition memory for normal control (N = 20) and a prosopagnosic patient (A.H.): 0/0 (no face is familiar): 100/0 (old faces are familiar): 0/100 (new faces are familiar): 50/50 (half of new and old faces are familiar).

then, that in the absence of associative context A.H. is affected by variations in perceptual familiarity of the faces and his performance is strikingly better when the contrast between list context associated with old and new faces is increased.

When, in the second type of experiments, pre-experimental familiarity of faces and the context in which they have to be memorized are varied simultaneously, the pattern of results is quite different (Fig. 3.3 and Fig. 3.4). Whereas the pre-experimental familiarization of faces has a significantly positive overall effect on the recognition of the normal subjects, it has no effect on A.H.'s (normal: $d' = 1.08$ for nonfamiliar faces and $d' = 2.08$ for familiar faces; A.H.: $d' = 1.02$ for nonfamiliar faces and 1.05 for familiar faces). It may be noted here that there is no difference between A.H. and normal subjects for the recognition of unfamiliar faces. On the other hand, whereas context modification between study and recognition did not affect the overall memory performance of normal subjects, it had a striking effect on A.H.'s (normal: $d' = 1.65$ when context unchanged; $d' = 1.58$ when context modified but similar; $d' = 1.38$ when different; A.H.: $d' = 0.00$ when context identical; $d' = 1.12$. when different and without relation to original; $d' = 2.35$ when context different but similar to study context).

Finally, we can see a significant interaction between face familiarity and change of context for normal subjects as well as for A.H. However, the pattern of this interaction is very different in the two cases. For our prosopagnosic patient, familiarity has a facilitating effect only when the memorization context

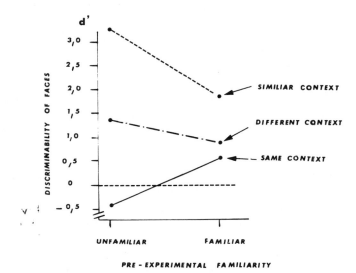

FIG. 3.3 Effect of pre-experimental familiarity and contextual changes on the discriminability parameter d' between old and new faces in recognition memory for a prosopagnosic patient (A.H.).

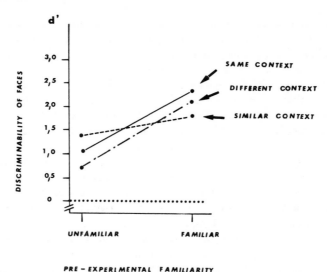

FIG. 3.4 Effect of pre-experimental familiarity and contextual changes on the discriminability parameter d′ between old and new faces in recognition memory for normal control.

is unchanged between study and test—the effect does not, however, reach the significance threshold on the test of Pollack and Norman (1964). The tendency is completely reversed when the context is modified. In this case recognition is significantly better when there is no perceptual pre-familiarization of faces to be memorized. It can be noted finally that *A.H.'s performance is definitely poorer than that of normal subjects only if study and test take place in exactly the same context*. When the context is modified, A.H.'s performance is comparable to that of the controls. It is even better when the recognition context is modified but retains a similarity relation to the study context. The interaction found for normal subjects is much more classic. When there is no pre-experimental familiarization of the face, a complete change of context significantly perturbs recognition.

However, if the change preserves intercontextual similarity, recognition is facilitated. If the face has received pre-familiarization, any context change has an inhibiting effect on recognition and there is no significant difference between a complete change of context and one which preserves semantic similarities with the original context.

Experimental comparison of this case of prosopagnosia with normal subjects enables us therefore to draw the following conclusions: (a) The lesion A.H. suffers from has obvious effects on memory. These very largely concern A.H.'s episodic memory. (b) When the associative context effect on recognition is neutralized, A.H. seems affected by pre-experimental perceptual exposure to faces he will later have to discriminate. His performances then vary in direct relation to the previous familiarity of the faces: they are poor with unfamiliar faces and improve if the faces he is later asked to recognize or reject have been presented to him earlier. Discriminability is maximum when old and new faces presented differ in degree of familiarity. In other words, A.H. seems affected mainly by combinations of faces of different familiarity. (c) A.H. is capable of using context cues to recognize faces. He is highly disturbed when study and recognition involve identical associated context. Any change of context between study and recognition improves his performance notably, especially if a similarity relation is preserved between study and test contexts. The pattern of this inter-action between face familiarity and context is however very different for A.H. and normal subjects. For normal subjects, context effects differ according to the degree of familiarity of the face to be recognized: a recognition context totally different from the study one is disturbing, whatever the degree of familiarity, and a recognition context that is different from, but similar to, the study context facilitates recognition of an unfamiliar face but inhibits that of a familiar face. On the contrary, for A.H., whatever the degree of familiarity of the face to be recognized, a similar context is always superior to a totally different one and the latter is again superior to an identical context for study and test.

In the end, both the experimental and the clinical studies of A.H. confirm the apparently crucial importance of the interaction between the factors of famil-iarity and context association in the disorder we are considering here. The impor-tance of these factors is also recognized in the general economy of the functioning of the human memory (Horton & Mills, 1984). The picture that emerges from this in-depth study is, however, especially complex and likely to bring into question certain theoretical analyses proposed to account for this inability to identify faces. What then are the theoretical implications of this observation of the case of A.H.?

TOWARD A COGNITIVE THEORY OF THE
AGNOSIA OF FACES

General Framework

Where should the psychological origin of prosopagnosia be located? Are we dealing with agnosic deficiency in representation of face information? Or with a disorder in the functioning of episodic memory, manifest in one class of objects, in this case faces, objects of quite obvious complexity and variety, the social significance of which makes it obvious that they may be difficult to process (Ellis, 1975; Tiberghien, 1983)? The question has received varying answers since Bodamer (1947), Stollreiter-Butzon (1950), Faust (1955) first opted for the former hypothesis, putting forward either a perceptual disorder affecting a specific category of objects or a "general disorder in psychic synthesis" or, finally, an incapacity to abstract specific features defining a class of facial resemblances and the individuality of some of them. However, other researchers (Bruyer, 1983; Hecaen, 1981) favor a memory explanation of the disorder. Hecaen (1981) following the observations of Warrington and James (1967) even proposed a combined hypothesis according to which certain forms of prosopagnosia are mainly perceptual (when the damage involved is parietal) and others mainly concern memory (when damage is temporal). The account just given definitely favors an interpretation of prosopagnosia in terms of memory. Clinical observation and experimental investigation did in fact clearly reveal definite defects and overcompensation in comparison with normal functioning of episodic memory in a situation of occurrence recognition obviously involving memory. This finding, however, is not necessarily in complete contradiction to a combined interpretation, for we must not forget that in A.H.'s case the lesion concerned the occipito-temporal region. If we wish to advance in our understanding of the problem it will be essential to confront the data collected with the various explanations of the functioning of memory and in particular with the theories that have gone so far as to propose explanations of memory malfunctioning (for an overview, see Mayes & Meudell, 1983).

Theories of amnesia that have attempted to account for memory deficiencies have looked for the origin of the observed disorder at the level of encoding processes (Cermak & Butters, 1972; Cermak, Butters, & Gerrein, 1973) or consolidation processes (Milner, 1970). Here we renounce recourse to either type of theory for they do seem unable satisfactorily to account for prosopagnosia. For example, results of the neuropsychological examination of A.H. give no real evidence of any defect in short-term memory. It would be tempting to try to interpret the data in the light of theories advancing the idea that memory difficulties can result solely from malfunctioning of information-retrieval procedures (Warrington & Weiskrantz, 1970; Winocur, 1982; Winocur & Kinsbourne, 1978; Winocur & Weiskrantz, 1976). However, for many researchers in human memory it seems obvious that full understanding of the latter is impossible unless the circumstances in which encoding took place are related with precision to those concerned in the retrieval phase. The work of the Toronto School (Tulving, 1983) has contributed varied and convincing experimental evidence in support of this theoretical necessity. Information retrieval indisputably results from ecphoric interaction between environmental features and the properties of memory representation resulting from their encoding and later modification (Hars, 1980; Kinstbourne & Wood, 1982; Schacter, Wang, Tulving & Freedman, 1982; Winocur & Olds, 1978; Wood, Ebert, & Kinsbourne, 1982).

We can see, then, the full importance of theories of human memory and its disorders based on this methodological principle. We can apply to them the general term of contextualist theories (Carrillo, 1985; Hirsch, 1974; Jenkins, 1974; Pribram, 1969; Stern, 1981). One particular class of such contextualist theories that probably have their origin in the theoretical propositions of Mandler, Pearl-stone, and Koopmans (1969) and in the experimental work of Atkinson and Juola (1974) assumes that access to information in the memory can take place in two different ways: (a) through sheer associative force, in recall, or sheer familiarity, in recognition; (b) through intentional activity of search for concep-tual, categorical, and contextual links between information to be recorded or recognized and other memory representations. In this way Mandler (1976, 1980) makes a distinction between two types of memory access code: a directly and automatically accessible presentation code inducing the familiarity of information to be recognized and a conceptual code giving rise to the contextual relation of slower and intentional access. Jones (1978) also suggests that recall can be produced through intrinsic knowledge of the association between information to be recalled and the context, or through extrinsic knowledge, which reactivates critical association by means of associative reconstruction. Following Hewitt, who made a distinction between extrinsic and intrinsic contexts, Baddeley (1982b) opposes the context that is independent of the representation to be recalled or recognized (and that can act as association clue for retrieval) and the interactive context that modifies the encoding of the information itself. Baddeley is in fact led to distinguish a process of automatic retrieval from a process of intentional retrieval analogous to problem solving that he calls "recollection." Tiberghien (1976, 1980a, 1980b, 1984a) also made the distinction in memory recognition between a rapid and automatic predecision mechanism based on the familiarity of information to be recognized and a slow and deliberate intentional search mechanism based on the system of associations between the recognition and the study contexts. Finally, it appears from these theoretical and experimental studies that there is a strong consensus on the existence of two types of retrieval proc-esses, one automatic and the other deliberate, and that they are affected by different situational elements, because the former seems to depend mainly on fluctuations in familiarity and the latter is affected chiefly by the system of contextual and categorical associations stored in permanent memory (Fig. 3.5).

Familiarity, Context, and Amnesia

If we accept this general theoretical framework, it is, then, possible to explain memory disorders with reference either to a perturbation of the mechanism of familiarity estimation, a perturbation of the contextual and categorical search process, or as an interactive combination of both classes of malfunctioning. Most hypotheses advanced so far attribute most memory deficits to a disturbance of processes of intentional search, and specifically to difficulty in encoding, retrieval, or utilization of contextual information. Thus, for example, Huppert and Piercy (1976, 1978) assumed that in the amnesic syndrome familiarity-estimation capac-ities remained intact but the subject proved incapable of recalling contextual elements associated with the event to be recognized or recalled. Wickelgren's

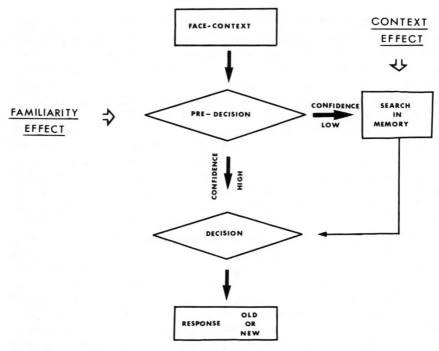

FIG. 3.5 Signal flow diagram for long-term recognition memory and the hypothetical cognitive locus of two critical factors—context and familiarity.

(1979) theoretical formulations are fundamentally the same because he postulates a double system of associations: horizontal associations of the S.R. type and vertical associations of a categorical type. Amnesic syndromes might then, in his view, be explained by the inability to constitute or retrieve vertical associations, whereas the horizontal associations are not particularly affected (see also Moscovitch, 1982). Similar theoretical views have been put forward by O'Keefe and Nadel (1978). They make a distinction between a system of "local" episodic representation and a "taxon" (categorical and semantic) system; amnesic conditions might be explained, he thinks, by defects in the working of the local system that cause difficulty in processing spatio-temporal contextual information. Jacoby and Witherspoon (1982) give a very similar account. According to them, amnesia results from disturbance of episodic memory, which is much more easily affected by contextual fluctuations than semantic memory (see also Tulving, Schacter, & Stark, 1982).

Whatever the type of the formal presentation, all the aforementioned theories take it that the cause of memory disorders is to be looked for in the perturbation of deliberate search mechanisms, especially as applied to contextual associations.

The importance of such contextual associations has been amply proved in connection with normal subjects and in particular in situations of recognition of unfamiliar faces (for an overview: Ellis, 1981; Goldstein & Chance, 1981; Tiberghien, 1983). Thus Watkins, Ho, & Tulving (1976) showed that unfamiliar faces are more easily recognized when the verbal description accompanying them at the moment of recognition is the same as that associated with them at the time of study. A change in angle of view (front/profile) or in physical appearance between study and testing also affects face recognition (Patterson & Baddeley, 1977). These results are confirmed by Baddeley and Woodhead (1982) and generally applied to "independent" visual contexts (for instance landscapes) or "interactive" ones (for instance head-wear) by Brutsche, Cisse, Deleglise, Finet, & Tiberghien (1981) and by Klee, Leseaux, Malai, and Tiberghien (1982). The modification in contextual situation between study and recognition also has an inhibiting effect on the recognition of faces (Baddeley, 1979; Davies & Milne, 1982, 1983; Deffenbacher, Carr, & Leu, 1981; Ellis, Davies, & Shepherd, 1977; Godden & Baddeley, 1980; Thomson, Robertson, & Vogt, 1982). In all these cases it appears that the modification of an interactive context has a much more disturbing effect on recognition than that of an independent context (Baddeley, 1982; Baddeley & Woodhead, 1982; Davies & Milne, 1983). It should be noted that these context effects are much more wide reaching for unfamiliar faces than for familiar faces (Bruce, 1982; Klatzky & Forrest, 1984). Finally, experimental data obtained by Péris & Tiberghien (1984) show that context effects occur only in slow recognition and disappear in rapid recognition, which obviously constitutes a strong experimental argument in favor of a double recognition mechanism.

Familiarity, Context, and Prosopagnosia

It is therefore understandable that, taken as a whole, data obtained from normal subjects and the elaboration of contextualist theories suggest appealing to a deficiency in the processing of contextual information as a plausible explanation of prosopagnosia. This hypothesis was systematically developed by Damasio et al. (1982). For these researchers prosopagnosia results from dissociation betweeen the mechanism of generic recognition of a conceptual class and the mechanism of recognition of the singular historical context of the face. It thus is supposed to be a memory disturbance of retrieval processes resulting from an incapacity to recall an appropriate context in the presence of a given face. This disturbance, though it affects faces in the case of the prosopagnosic patient, is taken to be more general and could be defined as a deficit of contextual recall affecting stimuli belonging to ambiguous multidimensional categories.

Damasio et al.'s explanation of prosopagnosia obviously belongs, then, to the contextualist type of theory of normal or pathological forgetting. It does, however, raise a certain number of problems if we examine it in connection with the observations made on the case of A.H. It is certain that the patient was affected by quite manifest memory disturbance, and memory malfunctioning was part of the clinical picture. However, with normal subjects context effects do not affect the recognition of familiar faces very much, which suggests that the latter is relatively independent of context fluctuations. Now it is precisely recognition of familiar faces that is mainly perturbed in the majority of prosopagnosic patients. Furthermore, the clinical examination of A.H. showed him to be perfectly capable of using contextual information to improve his recognition; we even saw that it was the strategy he most relied on. The fact is not unique since it is confirmed for example by the observation of a case of prosopagnosia described by Assal & Lanares (1981). The patient they studied produced a veritable self-analysis of his difficulties in the following excerpt of dialogue: "*Neuropsychologist*: When you see a photo (famous face) you don't recognize it? *patient*: No, unless it's in a definite setting (. . .) if it's in a newspaper, there's a title and a photo underneath, there's some chance I might recognize it. *Neuropsychologist*: When you see a politician, do you have a feeling of familiarity? *Patient*: No, not at all. *Neuropsychologist:* The face doesn't mean anything at all to you? *Patient*: No; unless I see it in a context." This short dialogue clearly shows that certain prosopagnosic patients can process context information and we can only consider that at most in a contextless situation the patient is unsuccessful in recalling the initial encoding context. We also know, moreover, that elimination of context between study and testing also brings about a definite lessening in memory performance for a normal subject (Tulving, 1983).

We are therefore inclined to think that it is not fully proved that prosopagnosia is a result of the destruction of contextual memory representation or its inaccessibility. This feeling is reinforced by the study of the case of A.H. which, by the way, we originally thought would show the validity of the contextualist theories. We see, indeed, that if study and recognition of a face are to be done without context, A.H. is greatly affected by the preexperimental familiarity of the faces involved. On the basis of these results alone we could obviously conclude that the mechanism of estimation of the familiarity of faces is not affected in A.H. But this conclusion proves mistaken when A.H. has to study and recognize faces in a definite contextual situation. Indeed, under these conditions, we do not see an overall familiarity effect but a complex interaction between familiarity and the type of context modification. Which leads us to think that A.H.'s memory difficulties result more from a perturbation of his mechanism of familiarity estimation than from his ability to use context information, and that it may be not so much the absolute as the relative estimation of familiarity that has been rendered more difficult for A.H. The fact is that in a complex everyday situation various elements contribute to the overall feeling of familiarity: for instance, faces can be familiar or not in a context which itself is familiar or not. We deduce from this observation that a mechanism of estimation of face familiarity must be capable of dissociating what, in the overall feeling of familiarity, concerns the face from what concerns the various context elements accompanying it (McDougall, 1923; Tulving, 1982). Thus, when there is no accompanying context, recognition of a face probably depends solely on the absolute familiarity of the face that in such a case is virtually the same thing as overall sense of familiarity. In such cases it can be seen that an increase in the degree of familiarity of a face increases the probability of recognition at the same time; also, an increase in relative discriminability in the familiarity of different faces should facilitate resulting memory performance. And, in effect, this is seen to be the case, because A.H.'s face-recognition capacity increases in proportion to relative discriminability of pre-experimental familiarity of faces to be recognized.

The presence of a context associated with faces to be recognized thus notably modifies A.H.'s performance. In this particular case the overall familiarity effect disappears but a very strong context effect makes itself felt. The context effect is quite different from what is usually seen in normal subjects, for A.H.'s performance is poorest under the condition of unchanged context. Now under this particular experimental condition the degree of context familiarity is as high as the familiarity of the face to be recognized (if there was no pre-experimental familiarization of the face) and somewhat lower (in the opposite case). Consequently, A.H. has to decide whether his overall feeling of familiarity is due to the face to be recognized or the accompanying context. And, we think, this differential estimation is precisely what is strongly perturbed in his case. The poor performance is improved, though not significantly, by an increase in pre-experimental familiarity. In other words, it seems to be the absence of contrast between familiarity of different origins which causes trouble for A.H. A change in context between study and testing would therefore have the effect of intensifying the contrast, thus making it possible to decide whether the overall familiarity of the situation is due to the faces and not to the context since the latter is in fact different. A.H.'s memory performance reaches a maximum if, on the one hand, context is modified between study and recognition and, on the other, there is a relation of similarity between the new recognition context and the old study context. In this case the change of context increases the contrast between face familiarity and context familiarity and increases the probability of correct recognition resulting from a simple predecision mechanism based on face familiarity alone; further, the intercontextual relationship makes it possible, if this mechanism fails to operate, to retrieve from permanent memory additional information on the relation between contexts. The fact that familiarity has a facilitating effect when the context is unchanged and an inhibiting one when the context is modified is much more difficult to interpret. We could advance the hypothesis that when an unfamiliar face is presented for recognition in a familiar context there arises a conflict in discriminability between two of the basic sources that contribute to the overall sense of familiarity. This discriminability contrast also seems to occur, symmetrically, when a familiar face is presented in an unfamiliar context.

In conclusion, our investigation of this case of prosopagnosia does not support the theoretical interpretation proposed by Damasio et al. (1982). Contrary to their theoretical proposition, a prosopagnosic subject is perfectly capable of using contextual information in occurrence memory recognition. It even appears that, compared to normal subjects, A.H. is particularly strongly affected by contextual modifications intervening between study and recognition testing. It would be tempting to conclude that A.H.'s deficiency originates in a malfunctioning of familiarity-analysis mechanisms. Such a conclusion might be based on the obvious absence of a significant overall familiarity effect. It should be noted that such a conclusion would be consistent with the theoretical arguments put forward by Gaffan (1976), according to which certain memory disturbances could be explained by inability to estimate the familiarity of a situation. Familiarity would thus constitute a "universal association" making it possible to retrieve and recognize information no matter what the contextual variability in its occurrences. However this conclusion is inconsistent with A.H.'s being affected by variations in face familiarity in the absence of any associated context and with the complex inter- action, different from that observed in normal subjects, between familiarity and context. There would seem to be no solution to this theoretical puzzle if we do not take into account the interaction between context and familiarity. We think Gaffan is probably correct in explaining certain forms of amnesia by the subject's inability to estimate or recall familiarity (Blanc-Garin, 1984). This hypothesis, which has not be given as full an examination as it should have (Baddeley, 1982), seems nevertheless more plausible than that of Damasio et al. To be precise, we could consider that it is not absolute familiarity-estimation ability that is affected in A.H. but his capacity for differential estimation. In order to recognize a particular feature in a situation on the basis of familiarity an individual must in point of fact be able to evaluate the relative share of the various elements of the situation in his overall sense of familiarity, including, moreover, their temporal characteristics as shown in the possibility of "source" amnesia (Schac- ter, Harbluk, & MacLachland, 1984). This is the evaluation that seems to be disturbed in A.H.'s case. Just as it was in the case of the patient with Capgras's syndrome (illusion of double) for whom tests showed a "perturbation in percep- tual hierarchy," each detail proving to have the same value as the other points in the perceptual field (Luauté, Bidault, & Thionville, 1978, p. 808). Recent observations moreover lead us to think that such difficulty in differential proc- essing of familiarity can be seen in certain amnesic patients (Carrillo, 1985; Huppert & Piercy, 1982). But we must point out before going any further that this mechanism of differential estimation cannot be conceptualized independent of context. It is in fact the specific familiarity of context in relation to the specific familiarity of the face that either presents or not a contrast sufficient to make recognition possible. In other words, it is probable that the mechanism of differential estimation of familiarity may be disturbed in prosopagnosia, the ability to store and use context remaining relatively intact. What makes observed data so difficult to interpret is probably the fact that the constitution of the feeling of familiarity of a face is not independent of the context it is associated with, nor perhaps of their degree of association and integration. Besides, interaction between familiarity and context has been observed in many investigations of normal subjects: the change of viewing angle, for instance, between study and test has an inhibiting effect on the recognition of unknown faces but not on that of famous faces (Bruce, 1982; Klatzky & Forrest, 1984, experiment 1); furthermore, a change in situational context only perturbs recognition of unfamiliar persons (Thomson et al., 1982, experiment 5). It is also quite probable that the familiarity feeling has at least two possible sources according to whether it is due to numerous repetitions of an event in the same context or numerous repetitions of an event in different contexts (Donaldson, 1981). Besides, Lamon (1982) showed that repetition of a verbal item in modified list contexts was more favorable to recognition than repetition in the same context. We have ourselves observed that in a face-recognition situation with normal subjects the disturbing effect of a change of context was highly significant when the face had been examined only once (unfamiliar face) and that it was reduced when the face received four study trials (familiar face). Furthermore under the latter condition the inhibiting effect of context change between study and recognition testing was present only if the faces had been examined four times in an identical context, and disappeared when faces had been examined four times in different contexts (Paturle, Morens, Hullard, & Tiberghien, 1984; Seamon, 1982; Smith 1979; Tiberghien, in press). Such experimental data, classic with normal subjects, point up the importance of the interaction between context and familiarity for the understanding of memory functioning in the prosopagnosic subject. To explain prosopagnosia either by a deficiency in familiarity alone or a deficiency in contextual information processing only can yield no more than a partial explanation of the memory characteristics of the case we have described.

To sum up, it first of all appears quite clear that very definite disturbances of recognition memory are correlated with the clinical picture of prosopagnosia presented by A.H. Viewed in this way, the prosopagnosia is doubtless also a prosopamnesia and the malfunctioning of recognition memory probably constitutes the basic cause of the face-identification difficulties A.H. encounters. This confirms other earlier observations and in particular the in-depth study of the case of W. done by Bruyer et al. (1983), but it differs from the interpretation of evidence gathered in the case of C.F. by Dumont, Griggio, Dupont, and Jacquy (1981). Secondly, thanks to the experimental data collected, we can consider that the observed subject's basic problem consists in his inability to estimate the respective familiarity of component elements of a situation. This relative, not absolute, inability accounts for the fact that A.H. is affected by variations in the familiarity of faces when they are presented alone but that the overall familiarity effect disappears when faces have to be recognized in a definite context. Whereas, with normal subjects, familiarity is the main determinant of face recognition, in A.H.'s, recognition context is the decisive factor. This observation means we can eliminate any strictly contextualist hypothesis which explains prosopagnosia solely by the inability to process contextual information. Not only can A.H. use contextual information in recognition tasks, but it has a much more important psychological role with him than with normal subjects.

Nevertheless, to admit that in our case of prosopagnosia the problem results from a difficulty in the estimation of familiarity does not mean we can accept so simple a hypothesis as that put forward by Gaffan. Indeed, if familiarity is a critical factor with normal subjects, and with A.H. the contextual relation is, in both cases they interact, and the interaction is not the same for A.H. and for normal subjects. The key to the problem of prosopagnosia is probably in this double interaction. First, it is obvious that contextual constancy between encoding and recognition seriously perturbs A.H.'s memory performance. Indeed it is under these conditions that the degree of face familiarity and of context familiarity are closest, and it is doubtless most difficult for A.H. to evaluate the origin of his overall feeling of familiarity, context, or face. The modification of the context, by increasing the contrast between the two sources of familiarity, makes differential estimation of familiarity easier. This increased ease of use of the familiarity estimation mechanism may moreover be associated with greater ease of use of the mechanism for processing contextual associations, if the new context presented at the moment of recognition is associated with the initial study context. In both cases, not only is A.H.'s memory performance not adversely affected, but it proves to be superior to that of normal subjects.

CONCLUSION

In conclusion, prosopagnosia might well result from a perturbation of retrieval of the "universal association" mentioned by Gaffan (1976, p. 238) which is no more than familiarity constituted on the basis of the frequency of event occurrence in different contexts. This familiarity makes possible both recognition of occurrences and rapid perceptual identification of the event concerned. Deprived of this universal association, the prosopagnosic patient becomes highly dependent on contextual information that alone makes it possible to differentiate the familiarity of the test context, acting therefore on the familiarity estimation mechanism. Such contextual information also makes it possible for him to reconstruct the original conditions of study of the face to be recognized, acting therefore on the memory search process. With a normal subject, on the other hand, the availability of the universal association makes the subject less dependent on the contextual information, and in particular for familiar faces of frequent occurrence. In his case contextual information would not seem to act on the process of familiarity estimation but only the process of search in memory or reconstruction; that is to say, mainly in the presence of unfamiliar faces. Prosopagnosia could therefore result from a deficiency that may be situated at different levels of a hierarchy of hypothetical processes. If we take this view, it would be possible to explain prosopagnosia as a breakdown in the process of storage and/or retrieval of contextual information associated with the face, which leaves relatively intact the possibility of access to memory representations of faces and to the estimation of their familiarity. But if this be so, the difficulties of prosopagnosic patients should concern above all the recognition of unfamiliar faces because these are, in normal subjects, the ones most affected by context effects. But this is obviously not what we have seen. It seems, then, more plausible to assume that the trouble stems from a disturbance in the mechanism of estimation of familiarity which can both be compensated for by access to specific contextual cues and also disturbed by the very familiarity of contextual aspects of the recognition situation. It is, moreover, possible that depending on the localization and extent of the lesions, one or other, or both, of these processes may be perturbed, which would make it possible to explain the variability of clinical observations. It is true that this diversity of symptoms may be partly due to the lack of systematic comparison of different cases of prosopagnosia and a relative underestimation of the interaction between familiarity and context, which we believe to be of crucial importance.

In-depth study of the hypothetical views we have just presented will require even more careful control of a certain number of factors. Control of familiarity, first of all, needs to be much more operationally exact. In particular, in order to answer certain theoretical questions we have formulated earlier, we need, on the one hand, to define a type of familiarity resulting from multiple occurrences of a face in the same context and, on the other, a type resulting from multiple occurrences of the same face in varying contexts. Furthermore, it is most probable that contexts do not have the same effect when they are independent of the target face they are associated with (extrinsic, independent context) and when they are strongly integrated with it in a perceptual gestalt (intrinsic, interactive context). This distinction proposed by Baddeley (1982) and examined by Baddeley and Woodhead (1982) is absolutely crucial and should be taken into careful account in future research. It is also clear that more exact control of ecphoric similarity relations between the face and the representation stored in memory beforehand and also of relations of perceptual similarity between the various possibilities among which recognition choice is made can help to produce experimental data that are easier to interpret (Tulving, 1981). Finally, neuropsychological and psychological investigation should at some point examine the exact relation between their theories and hypotheses and the neurological data as such. From this point of view, in order to understand prosopagnosia, which perhaps stems basically from the difficulty in determining psychologically "where the person begins and the context ends" (Thomson et al., 1982), we need to explain the role played by the right hemisphere and the limbic structures in mechanisms of computation of familiarity and in the processing of contextual information. (Sergent & Bindra, 1981; Versace & Tiberghien, 1985; Warren, 1980). Be that as it may, the complexity of the data requiring interpretation and the increasing sophistication of competing theories will of necessity impose an ever closer collaboration between different specialists of the cognitive sciences (neurologists, neuropsychologists, psychophysiologists, cognitive psychologists).

ACKNOWLEDGMENTS

We wish to thank those who have contributed in various ways to the completion of this paper: Marie Guillet-Caillau, Magdeleine Fasola, Patricia Fogarty, D. Hannequin, L. Magne, Christine Mazo, and Viviane Mendelsohn.

This work also owes a great deal to discussion and exchange over recent years with Mercedes Carrillo, J. Pellat, J-L. Peris, E. Tulving and R. Versace to whom we express our sincere gratitude.

REFERENCES

Assal, G., & Lanares, J. (1981). *Un cas de prosopagnosie.* Lausanne: videotape.

Atkinson, R. C., & Juola, J. F. (1974). Search and decision processes in recognition memory. In D. H. Krantz, R. C. Atkinson & P. Suppes (Eds.), *Contemporary developments in mathematical psychology* (pp. 243–293). San Francisco: Freeman.

Baddeley, A. D. (1976). *The psychology of memory.* London: Harper & Row.

Baddeley, A. D. (1979). Applied cognitive and cognitive applied psychology: The case of face recognition. In L. G. Nilsson (Ed.), *Perspectives in memory research* (pp. 367–388). Hillsdale, NJ: Lawrence Erlbaum Associates.

Baddeley, A. D. (1982a). Amnesia: A minimal model and an interpretation. In L. S. Cermak (Ed.), *Human memory and amnesia* (pp. 305–336). Hillsdale, NJ: Lawrence Erlbaum Associates.

Baddeley, A. D. (1982b). Domains of recollection. *Psychological Review, 89,* 708–729.

Baddeley, A. D., & Woodhead, M. (1982). Depth of processing, context and face recognition. *Canadian Journal of Psychology, 36,* 148–164.

Blanc-Garin, J. (1984). Perception des visages et reconnaissance de la physionomie dans l'agnosie des visages. *L'Année Psychologique, 84,* 573–598.

Bodamer, J. (1947). Die Prosop-agnosie. *Archiv für Psychiatrie und Nervenkrankheiten, 179,* 6–53.

Bradshaw, J. L., & Nettleton, N. C. (1981). The nature of hemispheric specialization in men. *The Behavioral and Brain Sciences, 4,* 52–91.

Bruce, V. (1982). Changing faces: Visual and non visual coding process in face recognition. *British Journal of Psychology, 73,* 105–116.

Brutsche, J., Cisse, A., Deléglise, D., Finet, A., & Tiberghien, G. (1981). Effets de contexte dans la reconnaissance de visages non familiers. *Cahiers de Psychologie Cognitive, 1,* 85–90.

Bruyer, R. (1980a). Perception du visage humain et différences cérébrales hémisphériques chez le sujet normal. *L'Année Psychologique, 80,* 631–653.

Bruyer, R. (1980b). Lésion cérébrale et perception du visage: étude de la symétrie faciale. *Journal de Psychologie, 77,* 85–98.

Bruyer, R. (1983). *Le visage et l'expression faciale: approche neuropsychologique.* Bruxelles: Mardaga.

Bruyer, R., & Gadisseux, C. (1980). La reconnaissance du visage chez l'enfant normal: comparaison avec l'adulte cérébrolésé. *Enfance, 3,* 95–106.

Bruyer, R., & Velge, V. (1980). Lésions cérébrales et reconnaissance visuelle du visage humain: une étude préliminaire. *Psychologica Belgica, 20,* 125–139.

Bruyer, R., Laterre, C., Seron, X., Feyereisen, P., Strypstein, E., Pierrard, E., & Rectem, D. (1983). A case of prosopagnosia with some preserved covert remembrance of familiar faces. *Brain and Cognition, 2,* 257–284.

Carrillo, M. (1985). *Contexte et amnésie.* Unpublished thesis, University of Grenoble, Grenoble.

Cermak, L. S., & Butters, N. (1972). The role of interference and encoding in the short-term memory deficits of Korsakoff patients. *Neuropsychologia, 10,* 89–95.

Cermak, L. S., Butters, N., & Gerrein, J. (1973). The extent of the verbal encoding ability of Korsakoff patients. *Neuropsychologia, 11,* 85–94.

Damasio, A. R., Damasio, H., & Van Hoesen, G. W. (1982). Prosopagnosia: Anatomic basis and behavioral mechanism. *Neurology, 32,* 331–340.

Davies, G. M., & Milne, A. (1982). Recognizing faces in and out of context. *Current Psychological Research, 2,* 235–246.

Davies, G. M., & Milne, A. (1983). *Eyewitness recall and recognition of persons in and out of context.* Unpublished paper, University of Aberdeen, Aberdeen.

Deffenbacher, K. A., Carr, T. H., & Leu, J. R. (1981). Memory for words, pictures and faces: Retroactive interference, forgetting and reminiscence. *Journal of Experimental Psychology: Human Learning and Memory, 7,* 299–305.

Donaldson, W. (1981). Context and repetition effect in recognition memory. *Memory and Cognition, 9,* 308–316.

Dumont, I., Griggio, A., Dupont, H., & Jacquy, J. (1981). A propos d'un cas d'agnosie visuelle avec prosopagnosie et agnosie des couleurs. *Acta Psychiatrica Belgica, 81,* 25–45.

Ellis, H. D. (1975). Recognizing faces. *British Journal of Psychology, 66,* 409–420.

Ellis, H. D. (1981). Theoretical aspects of face recognition. In G. M. Davies, H. D. Ellis, & J. W. Shepherd (Eds.), *Perceiving and remembering faces* (pp. 17–97). London: Academic Press.

Ellis, H. D. (1983). The role of the right hemisphere in face perception. In A. W. Young (Ed.), *Functions of the right cerebral hemisphere* (pp. 33–64). London: Academic Press.

Ellis, H. D., Davies, G. M., & Shepherd, J. W. (1977). Experimental studies of face identification. *Journal of Criminal Defense, 3,* 219–234.

Faust, C. (1955). *Die zerebralen Herdstorungen bei Hinterhauptverletzungen und ihre Beurteilung.* Stuttgart: George Thieme.

Gaffan, D. (1976). Recognition memory in animals. In J. Brown (Ed.), *Recall and recognition* (pp. 229–242). New York: Wiley.

Gazzaniga, M. S., & Smylie, C. S. (1983). Facial recognition and brain asymmetries: Clues to understanding mechanisms. *Annals of Neurology, 13,* 536–540.

Godden, D., & Baddeley, A. D. (1980). When does context influence recognition memory? *British Journal of Psychology, 71,* 99–104.

Goldstein, A., & Chance, J. (1981). Laboratory studies of face recognition. In G. M. Davies, H. D. Ellis, & J. W. Shepherd (Eds.), *Perceiving and remembering faces* (pp. 81–104). London: Academic Press.

Hars, B. (1980). Consolidation, rappel et réactivation. *L'Année Psychologique, 80,* 237–265.

Hay, D. C. (1981). Asymmetries in face processing: Evidence for a right hemisphere perceptual advantage. *Quarterly Journal of Experimental Psychology, 33A,* 267–274.

Hay, D. C., & Young, A. W. (1982). The human face. In A. W. Ellis (Ed.), *Normality and pathology in cognitive functions* (pp. 173–202). London: Academic Press.

Hécaen, H. (1981). The neuropsychology of face recognition. In G. M. Davies, H. D. Ellis, & J. W. Shepherd (Eds.), *Perceiving and remembering faces* (pp. 39–54). London: Academic Press.

Hirsch, R. (1974). The hippocampus and contextual retrieval of information from memory. *Behavioral Biology, 12,* 421–444.

Horton, D. L., & Mills, C. B. (1984). Human learning and memory. *Annual Review of Psychology, 35,* 361–374.

Huppert, F. A., & Piercy, M. (1982). In search of functional locus of amnesic syndromes. In L. S. Cermak (Ed.), *Human memory and amnesia* (pp. 123–137). Hillsdale, NJ: Lawrence Erlbaum Associates.

Jacoby, L. L., & Witherspoon, D. (1982). Remembering without awareness. *Canadian Journal of Psychology, 36,* 300–324.

Jones, G. V. (1978). Recognition failure and dual mechanism in recall. *Psychological Review, 85,* 464–469.

Kinsbourne, M., & Wood, F. (1982). Theoretical considerations regarding the episodic-semantic memory distinction. In L. S. Cermak (Ed.), *Human memory and amnesia* (pp. 195–217). Hillsdale, NJ: Lawrence Erlbaum Associates.

Klatzky, R. L., & Forrest, F. H. (1984). Recognizing familiar and unfamiliar faces. *Memory and Cognition, 12,* 60–70.

Klee, M., Leseaux, M., Malai, C., & Tiberghien, G. (1982). Nouveaux effets de contexte dans la reconnaissance de visages non familiers. *Revue de Psychologie Appliquée, 32,* 109–119.

Lamon, M. (1982). *The effects of context on recognition learning.* Unpublished thesis, University of Toronto, Toronto.

Lecocq, P., & Tiberghien, G. (1981). *Mémoire et décision.* Lille: Presses Universitaires de Lille.

Luauté, J., Bidault, E., & Thionville, M. (1978). Syndrome de Capgras et organicité cérébrale. *Annales Médico-Psychologiques, 5,* 803–815.

Mandler, G. (1976). *Memory research reconsidered: A critical view of traditional methods and distinctions.* San Diego: Center for Human Information Processing.

Mandler, G. (1980). Recognizing: The judgment of previous occurrence. *Psychological Review, 87,* 252–271.

Mandler, G., Pearlstone, F., & Koopmans, H. S. (1969). Effects of organization and semantic similarity on recall and recognition. *Journal of Verbal Learning and Verbal Behavior, 8,* 410–423.

Mayes, A., & Meudell, P. (1983). Amnesia in humans and other animals. In A. Mayes (Ed.), *Memory in animals and humans* (pp. 203–252). London: Van Nostrand Reinhold.

McDougall, W. (1923). *An outline of psychology.* London: Methuen.

Milner, B. (1968). Visual recognition and recall after right temporal lobe excision in man. *Neuropsychologia, 6,* 191–209.

Milner, B. (1970). Pathologie de la mémoire. In D. Bovet, A. Fessard, C. Florès, N. H. Frijda, B. Inhelder, B. Milner, & J. Piaget (Eds.), *La mémoire* (pp. 184–212). Paris: Presses Universitaires de France.

Moscovitch, M. (1982). Multiple dissociations of function in amnesia. In L. S. Cermak (Ed.), *Human memory and amnesia* (pp. 337–370). Hillsdale, NJ: Lawrence Erlbaum Associates.

O'Keefe, J., & Nadel, L. (1978). *The hippocampus as a cognitive map.* London: Oxford University Press.

Pallis, C. A. (1955). Unpaired identification of faces and places with agnosia for colours. *Journal of Neurology, Neurosurgery, and Psychiatry, 18,* 218–224.

Patterson, K. E., & Baddeley, A. D. (1977). When face recognition fails. *Journal of Experimental Psychology: Human Learning and Memory, 3,* 406–417.

Paturlé, I., Morens, V., Hullard, V., & Tiberghien, G. (1984). *Familiarité, contexte et reconnaissance de visages.* Unpublished paper, University of Grenoble, Grenoble.

Péris, J-L., & Tiberghien, G. (1984). Effet de contexte et recherche conditionnelle dans la reconnaissance de visages non familiers. *Cahiers de Psychologie Cognitive, 4,* 323–333.

Pollack, I., & Norman, D. A. (1964). A non parametric analysis of recognition experiments. *Psychonomic Science, 1,* 125–126.

Pribram, K. H. (1969). The amnesic syndromes: Disturbances in coding. In G. A. Talland & N. C. Waugh (Eds.), *The pathology of memory* (pp. 127–157). New York: Academic Press.

Richardson, J. T. E. (1982). Memory disorders. In A. Burton (Ed.), *The pathology and psychology of cognition* (pp. 48–77). London: Methuen.

Rondot, P., & Tzavaras, A. (1969). La prosopagnosie après 20 années d'études cliniques. *Journal de Psychologie, 66,* 133–165.

Schacter, D. L., & Tulving, E. (1982). Amnesia and memory research. In L. S. Cermak (Ed.), *Human memory and amnesia* (pp. 1–32). Hillsdale, NJ: Lawrence Erlbaum Associates.

Schacter, D. L., Wang, P. L., Tulving, E., & Freedman, M. (1982). Functional retrograde amnesia: A quantitative case study. *Neuropsychologia, 20,* 523–532.

Schacter, D. L., Harbluk, J. L., & MacLachland, D. R. (1984). Retrieval without recollection: An experimental analysis of source amnesia. *Journal of Verbal Learning and Verbal Behavior, 23,* 593–611.

Seamon, J. G. (1982). Dynamic facial recognition: Examination of a natural phenomenon. *American Journal of Psychology, 95,* 363–381.

Sergent, J., & Bindra, D. (1981). Differential hemispheric processing of faces: Methodological considerations and reinterpretation. *Psychological Bulletin, 89,* 541–554.

Smith, S. M. (1979). Remembering in and out of context. *Journal of Experimental Psychology: Human Learning and Memory, 5,* 460–471.

Stern, L. D. (1981). A review of theories of human amnesia. *Memory and Cognition, 9,* 247–262.

Stollreiter-Butzon, L. (1950). Zur Frage der Prosopagnosie. *Archiv für Psychiatrie und Nervenkrankheiten, 184,* 1–27.

Swets, J. A. (1964). *Signal detection and recognition by human observers.* New York: Wiley.

Thomson, D. M., Robertson, S. L., & Vogt, R. (1982). Person recognition: The effect of context. *Human Learning, 1,* 137–154.

Tiberghien, G. (1976). Reconnaissance à long terme: Pourquoi ne pas chercher?. In S. Ehrlich & E. Tulving (Eds.), *La mémoire sémantique* (pp. 188–196). Paris: Bulletin de Psychologie, special issue.

Tiberghien, G. (1980a). Reconnaissance à long terme: comment chercher? *Bulletin de Psychologie, 33,* 815–830.

Tiberghien, G. (1980b). Rappel et reconnaissance: les processus d'encodage et de recherche. *L'Année Psychologique, 80,* 501–521.

Tiberghien, G. (1983). La mémoire des visages. *L'Année Psychologique, 83,* 153–198.

Tiberghien, G. (1984a). Just how does ecphory work? *The Behavioral and Brain Sciences, 7,* 255–256.

Tiberghien, G. (1984b). *Initiation à la psychophysique.* Paris: Presses Universitaires de France.

Tiberghien, G. (in press). Context effects in recognition memory of faces: some theoretical problems. In H. D. Ellis, J. W. Shepherd, & A. W. Young (Eds.), *Aspects of face processing.* Dordrecht: Nijhoff.

Tulving, E. (1981). Similarity relations in recognition. *Journal of Verbal Learning and Verbal Behavior, 20,* 470–496.

Tulving, E. (1982). Synergistic ecphory in recall and recognition. *Canadian Journal of Psychology, 36,* 130–147.

Tulving, E. (1983). *Elements of episodic memory.* New York: Oxford University Press.

Tulving, E., Schacter, D. L., & Stark, H. A. (1982). Priming effects in word fragments completion are independent of recognition memory. *Journal of Experimental Psychology: Learning, Memory and Cognition, 8,* 336–342.

Versace, R., & Tiberghien, G. (1985). Spécialisation hémisphérique et fréquences spatiales. *L'Année Psychologique, 85,* 249–273.

Warren, L. R. (1980). Evoked potential correlates of recognition memory. *Biological Psychology, 11,* 21–35.

Warrington, E. K., & James, M. (1967). An experimental investigation of facial recognition in patients with unilateral cerebral lesions. *Cortex, 3,* 317–326.

Warrington, E. K., & Weiskrantz, L. (1970). Amnesic syndrome: consolidation or retrieval. *Nature, 228,* 628–630.

Watkins, M. J., Ho, E., & Tulving, E. (1976). Context effects in recognition memory for faces. *Journal of Verbal Learning and Verbal Behavior, 15,* 505–517.

Wickelgren, W. A. (1979). Chunking and consolidation: A theoretical synthesis of semantic networks, configuring in conditioning, S-R versus cognitive learning, normal forgetting, the amnesic syndrome, and the hippocampal arousal system. *Psychological Review, 86,* 44–60.

Winocur, G. (1982). The amnesic syndromes: A deficit in cue utilization. In L. S. Cermak (Ed.), *Human memory and amnesia* (pp. 139–166). Hillsdale, NJ: Lawrence Erlbaum Associates.

Winocur, G., & Weiskrantz, L. (1976). An investigation of paired-associate learning in amnesic patients. *Neuropsychologia, 14,* 97–110.

Winocur, G., & Kinsbourne, M. (1978). Contextual cueing as an aid to Korsakoff amnesics. *Neuropsychologia, 16,* 671–682.

Wood, F., Ebert, V., & Kinsbourne, M. (1982). The episodic-semantic memory distinction in memory and amnesia: Clinical and experimental observations. In L. S. Cermak (Ed.), *Human memory and amnesia* (pp. 167–193). Hillsdale, NJ: Lawrence Erlbaum Associates.

4 Face Processing and Brain Damage: Group Studies

Raymond Bruyer
*University of Louvain, School of Medicine, Unité de
Neuropsychologie Expérimentale de l'Adulte*

Like other gnosic, mnemonic, and praxic cognitive activities, the visual processing of human faces by brain-damaged subjects often has been studied. The purpose of such research either was to define more precisely the differential functional properties of hemispheric structures (by both within- and between-hemisphere comparisons), or to search for dissociations in the cognitive mechanisms in order to test hypotheses issuing from experimental psychology.

Two types of pathological populations have been analyzed in this field: single case studies of patients suffering from prosopagnosia, and matched groups of brain-injured patients tested for perception or recognition of familiar or unknown faces. As prosopagnosia has been reviewed by Damasio and Damasio, and by Tiberghien and Clerc (Chapters 2 & 3, this volume), this chapter deals only with the group studies.

It is useful to consider these studies from a historical point of view. On the one hand, studies of groups of brain-damaged subjects have been inspired by clinical reports of prosopagnosia. Initially, researchers speculated that face processing occurred in the right cerebral hemisphere, and sought "subclinical" forms of prosopagnosia among right brain-damaged patients, as the usual clinical examination was not deemed sensitive enough. On the other hand, the most significant data were not collected until a later, short period, roughly from 1966 to 1971, so that these observations had been made before the lateralized-face studies were conducted with normal subjects. These studies (reviewed in chapters 5–9 of this volume) have greatly increased our knowledge about the neuropsychology of face processing. Therefore, the old interpretations should be reexamined in the light of more recent theoretical propositions, and a new wave of studies with groups of brain-lesioned subjects should be conducted.

Before listing the data, we ask the reader to keep in mind the epistemological difficulties inherent in theoretical inferences from studies of brain-damaged groups: These analyses are necessarily made on between-subjects comparisons, so the matching of the compared groups always has to be considered cautiously (mainly as regards the lesional variables, given that groups are adequately matched for age, sex, etc.), and the cognitive tasks used are often "easy" given the pathological nature of the tested system (in some cases, the task is assumed to be error free for normal subjects).

As the earliest study in the field was on the processing of face memorization and recognition (De Renzi & Spinnler, 1966), we first review the publications concerning these mechanisms, and then the studies dealing with perception or discrimination of faces by groups of brain-injured subjects. A general discussion follows this review of the literature.

MEMORY

In this section, we discuss the paradigms where the subject is shown a given stimulus and has to make a decision by using information stored in memory. Four kinds of experiments are reviewed.

Recognition

By *recognition designs,* we mean those where the subject has to store in memory a limited number of previously unknown faces in order to recognize them in a subsequent phase. Note that the number of unknown faces is a potentially infinite set before the experiment, but it becomes very limited after the inspection phase.

In one condition of the study by De Renzi, Faglioni, and Spinnler (1968), left and right brain-damaged subjects (LBD and RBD), with and without visual field defect (VFD), first carefully studied a set of eight front-view faces for 30 sec. The board was then removed, and an informal conversation followed for 60 sec. The subject was then shown 60 faces, one at a time, among which each studied face appeared three times; old-new decisions were made. A significant defect of the RBD subjects appeared, and the VFD had no effect.

Milner (1968) designed an experiment in which the subject inspected a board of 12 faces for 45 sec and then tried to recognize them on a board of 25 faces. The test was given to subjects who had sustained a unilateral cortical excision for the relief of focal epilepsy and to neurologically intact subjects. Three conditions were used, with three sets of subjects. In the first condition, there was no delay between the inspection stage and the recognition phase. Three groups were tested: normals, left-temporal lobe excisions, and right-temporal lobe excisions. The RBD subjects scored lower than the normals, the LBD subjects not differing from the other two groups. The scores were not affected by the extent of the excision (sparing vs. hippocampus inclusion). In the second condition, a delay of 90 sec was inserted between inspection and recognition, during which the subject sat quietly without talking. In this condition, the right-temporal damaged group performed more poorly than the other groups (left-temporals, frontals, normals); the left-temporal subjects differed neither from the frontals nor from the normals, but the frontals were impaired relative to the normals. Again, the extent of surgical removal had no effect on the scores. Finally, the right-temporals scored the same as the right-temporals of the first condition, but the left-temporals and the normals scored lower than the corresponding groups of the no-delay condition. In the third condition, the 90-sec delay was filled by a visual task. Again, the right-temporals performed more poorly than the other groups (left-temporals, parietals, frontals). Moreover, this defect was not due to the extent of the lesion per se, but rather to the extent of hippocampal involvement.

Thus, the subjects with right-temporal damage were slightly impaired in an immediate recognition task, and this impairment was more pronounced when delayed recognition was used. Moreover, the RBD subjects, unlike the normal or the LBD subjects, were unable to take advantage of the delay to consolidate the retention of the material. Note, however, the defect even at the zero-delay condition, which suggests the possibility of troubles as early as the preliminary stages of memory processing: The memory deficits of RBD subjects could be superimposed upon difficulties of perceptual mechanisms or of encoding. Finally, the left-temporal subjects never differed from the normals, but the frontally damaged subjects did in the free-delayed condition, perhaps because of unspecific attentional or motivational disturbances, which are frequently noted with the frontal syndrome.

A variation of the third condition (delay of 150 vs. 90 sec, and use of various facial series) was included in a larger battery of cognitive tests designed to examine the effects of unilateral ventrolateral thalamotomy or pulvinotomy, both pre- and postoperatively, by Vilkki and Laitinen (1974: 25 cases of thalamotomy; 1976: 38 cases of thalamotomy including the previous 25 cases, and 24 cases of pulvinotomy). The subjects had been operated upon for motor deficiencies or chronic intractable pain. Preoperative investigations revealed no differences between left- and right-operated subjects; similarly, left and right operations did not differ in their effects on the performance in the task.

Yin (1970) administered to normals, as well as to various kinds of brain-damaged subjects, a recognition test in which the inspection of 40 stimuli (3 sec per picture) was followed by a recognition phase in which 24 pairs of stimuli were presented, the subject indicating the old picture of each pair. Unknown faces and houses were used under two conditions: inspection and recognition of right-side-up versus inspection and recognition of upside-down stimuli. The RBD subjects with a posterior lesion appeared to be specifically impaired as they scored lower for right-side-up faces, but higher for inverted faces, than the other brain-injured subjects, with no group effect for upright or inverted houses. Moreover, the RBD subjects with a nonposterior lesion scored higher for upright faces than for upright houses, and lower for reversed faces than for reversed houses— a pattern not observed for the RBD subjects with a posterior lesion. Finally, the difference between houses and faces was least in the posterior RBD subjects for right-side-up material, but these subjects performed more poorly for houses than for faces with the inverted stimuli. The RBD subjects with a nonposterior lesion also performed less well than did the normals on the upside-down faces test. Because inversion modifies neither the physical properties nor the complexity of stimuli, it therefore appeared that posterior RBD subjects had a specific defect for the recognition of previously unknown, normally presented (upright) faces.

Grüsser and Kirchoff (1982) also studied specific right-hemisphere mechanisms for the recognition of human faces but obtained different results than the study of Yin. These authors submitted LBD, RBD, and normal subjects to tests of recognition of faces and vases with delays of one hour and one week between inspection and recognition. Although they give no details, the authors suggest there were neither hemispheric nor material effects as concern memory deficiencies.

Cancellière and Kertesz (1984) engaged normals, as well as LBD and RBD subjects, in various tests dealing with the processing of emotions and with face recognition as a control for the processing of emotional facial expressions. The subjects were asked to recognize, among 16 faces, a series of eight faces previously seen in a test dealing with facial emotions. The authors noted a defect for the RBD but not for the LBD subjects. In the tests dealing with emotional expression and comprehension, both samples were impaired but did not differ from each other. The impairment for emotional speech was not secondary to language disabilities (LBD) or to impairment in the processing of complex patterns (RBD). Finally, the impairment in the identification of affective situations in LBD subjects was partially dependent on their disturbed language, and the impairment in the identification of emotional facial expressions in RBD subjects was partially dependent on their disturbed facial processing.

Dricker, Butters, Berman, Samuels, and Carey (1978) enrolled alcoholics with Korsakoff's syndrome, chronic alcoholics without Korsakoff's syndrome, RBD, and normal subjects for the second condition of the test of Milner (1968). The RBD and Korsakoff subjects were found to be impaired relative to the normals (with no difference between the two defective groups), and the chronic alcoholics did not differ from the normals and RBD. Also in the area of amnesia studies, Warrington and Taylor (1973) tested amnesic and normal subjects for the recognition of faces and surnames. In the first experiment, the task was to recognize n faces on a board of $3n$ faces, with $n = 1$ to 4; the same experiment was run with surnames ($n = 2$ to 5); in each case, the targets were displayed one at a time for 3 sec, and the recognition trial followed immediately. For faces, both groups performed perfectly with one target; the scores decreased when the number of targets was increased with more reduction for the amnesics.

This difference did not appear with surnames. In the second experiment, the $n = 3$ condition was repeated with the same subjects, with no interval versus a filled delay of 30 sec. For faces, the amnesics were slightly inferior to the normals, who were unaffected in the two delays. For surnames, the two groups did not differ and were similarly affected by the delays.

As a bridge from the recognition studies to the research dealing with storage and identification processes (the next two points of the present section), note the second task of Bruyer's (1981a) paper. Normal, LBD, and RBD subjects first studied a board of 10 famous faces for 20 sec, for later recognition. The board was then removed, and a new board of 10 famous faces followed immediately including six from the first board to which the subject was asked to point. During the inspection, four faces had been "incidentally" named by the experimenter as "examples," and they were included in the six retained faces. The same experiment was also run with well-known flowers and famous buildings. An advantage of normal over brain-injured subjects, of RBD over LBD subjects, and of buildings over faces appeared for the number of correct recognitions and the facilitative effect of the incidental naming. Moreover, the performance for faces never correlated with that for buildings, but it did correlate positively with the performance for flowers in normals and brain-damaged subjects with no VFD, and negatively in RBD subjects with a VFD. Finally, flowers and buildings were positively correlated in the various subgroups, except for the normal, the RBD without VFD, and the aphasic LBD subjects.

Storage Processes

Some authors have examined brain-damaged subjects for the way in which the to-be-memorized new faces are stored, rather than for the recognition performance per se.

Mayes, Meudell, and Neary (1980) asked Korsakoff and normal subjects to inspect a set of 60 faces and then to try to recognize them in 60 pairs, each consisting of one old and one new face. The faces for inspection were presented one at a time under three conditions: In one condition, the subject evaluated the hair of the displayed face; in the second condition, the subject judged the picture as friendly or unfriendly; the third condition was a neutral control (learn). In the recognition phase, the scores for deeply encoded faces (friendship) were higher than the scores for the neutral encoding, which, in turn, were higher than those for physically encoded faces (hair). This effect did not interact with the groups, and the groups did not differ from one another.

Biber, Butters, Rosen, Gerstman, and Mattis (1981) enlisted demented, RBD, Korsakoff alcoholic, and control subjects for a test in which the inspection of 72 unknown faces, displayed one at a time for 7 sec, was immediately followed by the presentation for recognition of 72 pairs of an old and a new face. During the inspection, by means of 4-point scales, the subject evaluated the likeability of 24 of these faces and the size of the nose of 24 other faces; the remaining 24 faces were inspected with no particular instructions. Normal subjects recognized more faces than the other three groups, which did not differ from each other, and the faces judged for likeability were recognized more often than those under the remaining two conditions, for which no differences appeared. But these two factors interacted significantly, and two important lessons resulted from this interaction. The advantage of the normals, together with the lack of difference between the three pathological groups, was observed for the neutral and the physical conditions of encoding, but not for encoding by likeability, where the alcoholics matched the high scores of the normals. On the other hand, the superiority of the "deep" encoding (likeability), with no differences between the other two kinds of encoding, was noted for alcoholics only: Normals recognized fewer faces when encoded physically (size of the nose) than in the remaining two conditions (with no difference between these two), whereas the RBD, as well as, likely, the demented subjects, were not affected by the kind of encoding. Thus, the normal subjects were negatively affected by a physical encoding; the alcoholics (amnesics) attained a normal score when deep encoding was used; and the RBD subjects did not benefit from deep encoding when memorizing faces.

The normal and demented aged subjects enrolled by Wilson, Kaszniak, Bacon, Fox, and Kelly (1982) were tested for the recognition of faces. Forty-eight faces were inspected one by one and were then presented for recognition in a set of 96. During the inspection, the subjects made judgments about the sex and the personality of the perceived person. The recognition rate of the demented subjects was lower than that of the normals, even when scores were weighted by a perceptual score (in which the same group effect was observed; See the section on perception following). Moreover, the results were not influenced by the kind of encoding in either group. A similar test was made with words (judgments about phonological vs. semantic properties), which again indicated an inferiority of the demented subjects, who appeared to be unable to benefit from the semantic cues.

In daily life conditions, meta-facial or contextual information is also registered when a new face is stored in the memory. These additional data concern, for example, the spatial and temporal environmental conditions of the encounter; the subject of a conversation; the likeability or physical appearance of the person; the person's business, name, and so forth. But we do not know if the recognition of a face results from or gives access to the recognition of the meta-facial data (for some discussion of this point about a case of prosopagnosia, see Bruyer et al., 1983).

Becker, Butters, Hermann, and D'Angelo (1983) examined the association of names and faces in detoxified chronic alcoholics and compared it with the performance of control subjects. In the first step, the subjects tried to learn, in a nine-trial sequence, the association of 12 surname-face pairs. After a delay of

1 hour with interpolated tasks, the 12 names had to be recognized on a board of 24, and the 12 faces on another board of 24. Finally, the 12 faces were displayed one at a time, and the subject tried to give the associated name. The normals learned the 12 associations more rapidly and more accurately than the alcoholics, but the two groups no longer differed either in the delayed recognition of names or faces or in the recall of names when the faces were presented. Gazzaniga and Smylie (1983) tested a split-brain subject for learning of name-face associations. Two sets of three faces were employed, the stimuli being highly similar or highly dissimilar. No difficulty appeared for the dissimilar set whatever the hemisphere tested; for the similar faces, the right hemisphere performed adequately, but the left was at chance level. Lewinsohn, Danaher, and Kikel (1977) engaged normal and brain-damaged subjects in a three-stage experiment of name-face pair learning. The first phase served as base line: The subjects tried to learn 10 pairs, and a recognition test was given after a 30-min delay. The second phase took place the next day: New learning was done in which the names used readily suggested visual imagery. The third phase of the experiment followed after 1 week and consisted of recalling the pairs of the second phase. Neither group differed as regards the effective benefit of imagery, and this imagery effect was no longer apparent after the 1-week interval.

Identification

In our operational, nonnormative catalogue of cognitive operations, the identification process represents a particular, deeper form of recognition. Identification refers to the individualization of the perceived face in what constitutes the personal, individual characteristics by which this object has become unique. Therefore, identification generally, but not necessarily, refers to (a) material stored in the long-term memory, that is, familiar or famous faces; (b) a finite but broad set of candidates; (c) the recognition, together with the face, of meta-facial information (see foregoing); (d) experimental paradigms in which only one stimulus is presented for each response, this response not being made in a multiple-choice manner. Of course, our distinctions are made only for purposes of analysis; there are situations on the frontier between "recognition" and "identification," as well as between "memory" and "perception" (see the next section of this chapter).

Warrington and James (1967) asked LBD, RBD, and control subjects to identify 10 well-known public faces. For each stimulus, the subject had to name or give unequivocal information to indicate a correct identification. For naming, the LBD subjects produced more errors than the other two groups, between which there were no differences, and the impairment of the LBD subjects resulted from those with a temporal lesion. For identification by giving unequivocal information, the RBD subjects performed more poorly than the LBD subjects. This impaired functioning was not related to a particular lesion localization or to a VFD, and the control subjects did not differ from the LBD or the RBD subjects. As a preliminary test for a study presented later in this chapter, Bruyer (1982) submitted LBD, RBD, and normal subjects to a task involving identification of famous faces (naming or, in cases of defective naming, pointing). An advantage of normals over brain-damaged subjects was revealed, with no group effect among the patients except that the non-aphasic LBD were superior to the aphasic LBD subjects.

In the study of Bruyer (1981a) cited earlier, the subjects had been presented with a board of 10 famous faces and asked to identify them. The test followed a preliminary discussion in which the experimenter had an anecdotal conversation with the subject about 5 of the 10 celebrities. An advantage of normals over brain-injured subjects and of RBD over LBD subjects appeared in the number of correct identifications and the positive effect of the preliminary conversation.

Van Lancker and Canter (1982) examined the identification of famous faces by LBD and RBD subjects submitted to seven items. In each item, a face was presented together with four names to elicit a multiple-choice response. The RBD subjects performed more poorly than the LBD subjects. The RBD subjects were tested after a shorter time since onset than the LBD subjects, but the authors showed that this variable did not affect the difference. The RBD subjects, however, were older than the LBD subjects. The same subjects were also tested for the identification of famous voices (seven items): The subjects heard a neutral recorded passage and selected the response on a board of four name-face pairs. Again, a significant defect appeared for RBD subjects. Note that, in the LBD group, the subjects with a defect for voices were not those who had a defect for faces, but, in the RBD group, 75% of patients with defect had a pathological score in both tests. We observe, however, that the voice identification test needed a face-name recognition.

In this field of identification of human beings after brain damage, we note two additional studies concerning the amnesic syndrome. The first one, like that of Van Lancker and Canter (1982), deals with the identification of famous voices. Meudell, Northen, Snowden, and Neary (1980) enrolled chronic alcoholic patients with Korsakoff's syndrome and matched normals for a test of identification of famous voices (80 items) from various decades. In cases of failure to identify, a recognition procedure was used in which the subject selected the response, first among four faces, then, if failure occurred, among four written names. The main superiority of the controls over the amnesics resulted especially from the identification and the recognition among faces, particularly for the more recent celebrities, and the amnesics performed more like the normals for the recognition by names. The second study, by Marslen-Wilson and Teuber (1975), concerns the identification of 85 famous faces from various decades, first, by the well-known amnesic surgical case "H.M.," compared both with traumatic nonamnesic and with non-traumatic cases; second, by a sample of Korsakoff amnesics compared with non-Korsakoff alcoholic subjects. The subject had to decide *first* if the presented face was familiar or not; if yes, the name was asked, then the period and reason for celebrity; upon failure to identify, the subject was cued either by the naming of a pertinent event or by the first letter or letters of the name. The results of the H.M. experiment indicated a normal identification by H.M. for celebrities of periods preceding the surgery but a defect after it, with a better identification of "recent" celebrities in the control groups; on the other hand, the cuing was very useful for both H.M. and the control groups. The results of the "alcoholic's experiment" indicated a defect of identification of "recent" celebrities by Korsakoff's subjects, with no difference between the two groups when cues were given.

Finally, the identification of famous and familiar faces by matched groups of normals, patients with no cerebral damage, and disoriented subjects with diffuse cerebral damage was studied by Kurucz and Feldmar (1979). The disoriented subjects were significantly impaired, with no correlation between this test and a test of recognition of facial expressions. A similar dissociation was observed when the same tests were given by Kurucz, Soni, Feldmar, and Slade (1980) to subjects with focal brain damage (left, right, bilateral), subjects with bilateral diffuse lesions, and subjects without brain injury.

Categorization

Like identification, categorization refers to the use of information stored in the long-term memory and to items where a response is requested for individual faces. However, the information in the long-term memory is not the face or the person, but stoutly limited specific parameters. Generally, the displayed faces are unknown and thus members of a potentially infinite set of material. The parameters about which a decision has to be made are, for example, the sex or the age of the person. Included under this heading are face/non-face decisions ("facial decision," by analogy with lexical decision).

Newcombe and Russell (1969; see also Newcombe, 1974) gave normals, LBD, and RBD subjects a test in which drawings of human faces (40 items) with exaggerated shadows and highlights were displayed: The subject had to decide if the picture was a woman or a man, old or young. The LBD subjects did not differ from normals but were superior to the RBD subjects, with no effect of the intrahemispheric locus of lesion or of a VFD. The same sample was administered a maze test, with similar results and a specific defect for the RBD subjects with a VFD. In both cases, the lowest scores resulted from subjects with post-rolandic damage but with no overlap between these two subsamples.

In the study by Bruyer and Velge (1981) with normal, LBD, and RBD subjects, a pretest was given in which the subject was shown a board of 20 stimuli: 5 unknown human faces, 5 dog heads, 5 "faces" of motor vehicles, and 5 house fronts. A target was simultaneously presented displaying a stimulus not present on the board but of one of the four classes. The subject pointed to the category of the target. The analysis revealed that only the LBD subjects did not differ from the normals, and that these two groups performed better than the RBD subjects. This deficit was especially pronounced in the subjects with a VFD, and then only for human faces.

Wayland and Taplin (1982) gave brain-damaged subjects a test of categorization of faces. The sample was formed of fluent and non-fluent aphasics and of nonaphasic subjects (a majority of whom had right-brain damage). With feedback, the subjects learned to classify drawings of faces according to their similarity and then to classify the same and added drawings without feedback. The fluent aphasics showed a selective categorization impairment: They were unable to abstract a prototypical model and then to classify the stimuli in function of this model (see also Wayland & Taplin, 1985a, 1985b).

In the study of Marslen-Wilson and Teuber (1975) cited earlier, the subject first had to categorize the stimuli by indicating if the face was familiar or not. Unfortunately, the authors did not give the results of this pretest.

Pontius (1983) asked chronic alcoholic and normal subjects to draw a face from the frontal view without a model. Using criteria issued from previous studies, the author showed that alcoholics produced significantly more "neolithic" faces (i.e., with specific distortions of the spatial arrangement of facial features) than normals. According to the author, this observation indicates a specific defect in spatial relations on a representational level in alcoholics and relates with their difficulties in the encoding phase of memory processes.

FROM MEMORY TO PERCEPTION

In this section, we consider studies in which the subject keeps in memory (i.e., with at least a minimal delay) a single face not actually displayed in order to recognize it on a multiple-choice board or to compare it with another face in a same-different paradigm. Thus, there is a memory component, but it is limited to a single stimulus, and the procedure is also similar to perceptual tasks involving searching for a target on a board or making same-different judgments on pairs of stimuli.

The pioneer work of De Renzi and Spinnler (1966) was an attempt to clarify the nature of prosopagnosia. LBD and RBD subjects were recruited together with matched normal subjects. For the test of face recognition, the subject inspected an unknown face for 15 sec and was then immediately invited to recognize it—the target being drawn out—on a board of 20 faces; four items were run according to the sex (male-female) and the position (front view-profile) of the target. The multiple-choice board was composed of five men and five women, each pictured front and profile. A superiority of normal over brain-damaged and of LBD over RBD subjects appeared; these differences were maintained even with groups matched for simple reaction time, which was assumed to reflect the extent of the brain damage. The subjects were also submitted to similar tests with chairs and abstract figures. The scores for abstract figures replicated those for faces, even when weighted by the reaction time. For chairs, only a tendency for the RBD subjects to be impaired relative to the LBD subjects appeared, this trend being no longer present after the weighting. On the other hand, the pattern of distribution of the subjects was similar for faces and abstract figures, but not for chairs. Moreover, the performances for faces were positively correlated with the performances for abstract figures and uncorrelated for chairs in both damaged groups. Finally, the scores for faces were unaffected by aphasia or VFD in the LBD subjects, but the RBD subjects with a VFD scored lower than the other RBD subjects.

Thus, there was a specific defect in face recognition for (posterior) RBD subjects, whatever the severity or extent of the damage. On the basis of the three tests, the authors suggested that the defect did not concern a process of individualization (faces, chairs), but rather the processing of perceptually complex stimuli (faces, abstract figures), that is, in the detection of subtle formal differences in the absence of verbal mediation.

This study, conducted 20 years ago, has the merit of having been "the first one." Nevertheless, the paper of De Renzi and Spinnler leads us to suppose that the correct response in the face test was pointing towards the stimulus displaying the same face under the same orientation; now from a retrospective point of view (see part II of this volume), such a process is stimulus recognition, not necessarily face recognition. In terms of face recognition, the pointing to the same face under another orientation constitutes true recognition of the person or physiognomy and has to be scored as correct. It would be interesting to analyze the data from this perspective.

In the study of Warrington and James (1967) cited earlier, the normal, LBD, and RBD subjects tested for the identification of famous faces were also examined for the retention of unknown faces. The test comprised eight items. A face (man, woman) was shown for 10 sec, and the subject then pointed to it on a board of 16 faces (8 men, 8 women). The normal and the LBD subjects did not differ from each other but did score better than the RBD patients; the hemispheric effect was due to parietal-injured subjects. Moreover, there was no concordance between the RBD subjects who failed in this test and the RBD subjects who failed in the identification of well-known faces. In addition, as for famous faces, the scores were not affected by a VFD. Along a similar line, Whiteley and Warrington (1979) gave unilaterally damaged subjects a two-choice recognition test involving faces, country scenes, city scenes, and abstract art. A selective defect for faces in the RBD subjects with an occipito-temporal lesion, and for topographical features in the RBD subjects with parietal damage, appeared.

In another condition of the study of De Renzi et al. (1968) cited earlier, the LBD and RBD subjects were asked to study a front view face carefully for 10 sec. This target was then removed, and the subject was invited to retrieve it on a board of 12 front-view faces. The test contained 8 items. Only a significant effect of the VFD appeared, and the scores did not differ from the results of the delayed memory test. Nevertheless, these two tests were significantly more correlated in the RBD than in the LBD subjects.

Normal subjects, and LBD and RBD subjects (with anterior or posterior lesions) were tested by Murri, Arena, Siciliano, Mazzotta, and Muratorio (1984), using a procedure in which a schematic target face was retrieved on an imme-diately shown board (24 items). The results indicated a slight advantage of the LBD over the RBD subjects and, above all, an impairment of subjects with a posterior lesion in both groups. In addition, the LBD subjects with a language deficit (in both anterior and posterior subsamples) were particularly impaired. A similar pattern of results was observed with a nonfacial visual recognition test.

In the study of Gazzaniga and Smylie (1983), the split-brain subjects were also asked to detect on a board of 10 faces the face displayed in the right or left visual field for 120 msec (40 items). An advantage for stimuli of the left field appeared. The same was observed for a similar task involving line orientations, and the hemispheric effect remained unaffected by presenting defocused (increas-ing the low spatial frequencies) or smaller (increasing the high spatial frequencies) stimuli. In addition, when pairs of successive faces were displayed in the right visual field[1] with an interval of 1 to 3 sec, the subject performed adequately in same-different judgments (20 items), whatever the degree of similarity between the two faces.

In a study by Fried, Mateer, Ojemann, Wohns, and Fedio (1982), the subjects were asked to retrieve a target on a board of three faces after a filled delay of 8 sec (counting backwards). This test was administered with and without elec-trical stimulation of the right brain during an intracranial operation for treating epilepsy. For subjects meeting criteria of adequate perception (discussed later), a significant detrimental effect of electrical stimulation on memory appeared in particular conditions: in the superior temporal gyrus during the encoding phase and in the parieto-temporal zone during the recognition phase. Moreover, there was an overlap of sites where a memory defect for line orientation was observed but not for the identification of emotional facial expressions.

Berent (1977) administered a unilateral electroconvulsive treatment to depressed subjects who were tested for facial recognition 1 to 2 days before and 5 to 8 hours after the treatment. In the test (10 items), the subjects examined a target for 3 sec and, after a delay of 5 sec, had to retrieve the same person on a board of 3 different faces displaying a similar facial expression that was different from that of the target. A selective detrimental effect of the right electroconvulsive treatment was observed. A similar procedure was used for the recognition of

---

[1]Only the left hemisphere was tested, given it was deficient in the preceding task as well as (see foregoing) in the name association task when a set of similar faces was used.

facial expressions (on a board showing a given person with 3 different expressions, the subject pointed to the expression similar to that of the target, which was a picture of another person) and, this time, a selective detrimental effect of the left electroconvulsive therapy appeared.

DISCRIMINATION

In this last section, we consider the procedures in which the material to be processed is entirely available: Stimuli are simultaneously shown, so the subject does not need to keep information in his-her memory. We examine two kinds of methods.

Same-Different Comparisons

In this procedure, the subject decides if two simultaneously presented faces or persons are identical or not. Note that the subjects of Whiteley and Warrington (1979) were also given perceptual tasks including same-different judgments with the categories used for recognition. It could be that similar results appeared, but a detailed report is not available.

Jones (1969) introduced this paradigm with normals, RBD, LBD, and bilaterally injured subjects. The 80 pairs involved two front views, one front and one profile view, two front views with one member under reduced lighting, or two profile views with one member under reduced lighting. The brain-damaged subjects scored lower than the normals, with no difference appearing in function of lesion lateralization. With front view faces (16 items), DeKosky, Heilman, Bowers, and Valenstein (1980) showed that LBD subjects did not differ from normals, and that these two groups scored higher than the RBD subjects. Moreover, the effect of lesion laterality was almost entirely responsible for a similar effect on facial expressions (but see Bowers, Bauer, Coslett, & Heilman, 1985).

Christen and Landis (1984) displayed pairs of faces in the right tachistoscopic visual field of RBD subjects with a VFD, under different exposure durations. The subjects had difficulties in managing the task, but the scores were not affected by the exposure duration. These difficulties were not observed, and the lack of effect of duration was maintained for internal tangrams, objects, and words.

Bruyer and Velge (1980) used pairs of faces to test normal as well as LBD, RBD, and bilaterally injured subjects. Drawings of faces with seven features, each with two possible values, were employed. Eight subtests were devised by crossing two durations of exposure (5 vs. 10 sec) with two kinds of response (verbal vs. nonverbal) and with two conditions of verbal feedback (with vs. without reinforcement). In each subtest, the two members of the pairs differed by zero (same) to seven features. The results showed an advantage of the normal over the brain-damaged subjects and of the LBD over the RBD subjects, especially in the short exposure conditions with reinforcement. The increasing order of difficulty of the facial features was: ears and chin; mouth, nose, and forehead; then eyes and root of the nose. This series of tests was part of a battery submitted to four groups of normal children (5–6, 7–8, 9–10, and 11–12 years old) by Bruyer and Gadisseux (1980). When all the groups were compared for this series, the RBD subjects scored lower than the adult normals and the oldest children. These preliminary studies examined the effects of the exposure duration, the reinforcement, and the mode of response. Therefore, scores for the various degrees of similarity between the faces were pooled. For the present chapter, we have reanalyzed the data in function of the level of similarity by pooling the other variables. The results are given in Fig. 4.1[2]. Beyond the general deficit of the RBD subjects, the significant interaction, together with a qualitative observation of the curves, revealed a globally similar pattern for all groups, including an unexplainable effect of the condition with six different features, and that the difficulty for the "same" condition resulted largely from the children and the RBD subjects. With the same material but other subjects, and complete versus incomplete faces, a selective impairment of RBD subjects with a VFD for the internal facial features only was revealed (Bruyer, 1980a).

Multiple-Choice

In a sense, the simultaneous multiple-choice procedure is a generalization of the same-different paradigm: The subjects can proceed by successive paired comparisons of the target with each stimulus. Nevertheless, they have to make a choice, and thus can compare the stimuli of the board and decide by elimination.

In addition to the memory task, the subjects of De Renzi et al. (1968) performed two multiple-choice tests with simultaneous presentation of a target and a board of 12 complete front-view faces. In the first test (24 items), the target was a fragment of a face: the eyes, the mouth, or a lateral half-face. A significant impairment of the RBD subjects and of the subjects with a VFD appeared with no interaction, and these effects resulted from the subtest involving half-faces. In the second test (8 items), the target was a profile-view face, and a deficit of the RBD subjects was observed. Finally, these two tests were correlated with each other and with the two recognition tasks, especially for the RBD subjects.

---

[2]The proportion of errors (adults: scores out of 8; children: scores out of 16) was submitted to a mixed, two-way, 7 (groups) × 8 (levels of similarity) analysis of variance. First, a significant main group effect appeared ($F = 5.6$; $df = 6,173$; $p < .001$): post-hoc comparisons indicated that the RBD subjects scored more poorly than did the other samples. The main level of similarity was significant ($F = 91.3$; $df = 7,1211$; $p < .001$). The increasing ranking of errors was: maximal difference (7 features); then 4, 5, and 3 different features; then 2 features, then 6, finally 1 and 0 (same). Nevertheless, the two factors interacted significantly ($F = 2.76$; $df = 42,1211$; $p < .001$) as shown by Fig. 4.1. The details of the post-hoc comparisons cannot be presented here.

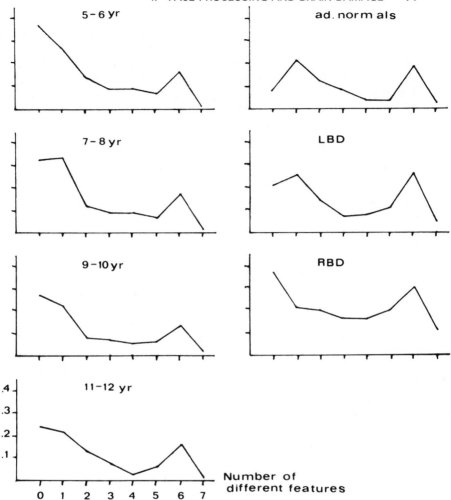

FIG. 4.1 Mean proportion of errors by subject in a paired comparison task according to the various samples and the number of different features (from 0 to 7). The samples are: 5–6 (*n* = 30), 7–8 (*n* = 30), 9–10 (*n* = 30), and 11–12 (*n* = 30) year-old children; and normal (*n* = 20), LBD (*n* = 20), and RBD (*n* = 20) adult subjects. Scores out of 8 for adults and out of 16 for children (from Bruyer & Gadisseux, 1980; Bruyer & Velge, 1980).

With a modified form of the second test (10 items and 10 front-view faces on the board), De Renzi and his colleagues noted a defect of the RBD subjects, particularly of those of a VFD. In addition, this test was correlated with two perceptual tests (Ghent test of overlapped figures and Farnsworth test of color discrimination) and the coefficients were higher for the RBD than for the LBD subjects. Finally, the perceptual defects were responsible for a deficit in an "associative" task (matching of a real object with the figure of a similar one), this phenomenon being predominant in the RBD subjects (De Renzi, Scotti, & Spinnler, 1969).

In the same year, Benton and Van Allen (1968) published their well-known test.[3] It consisted of three parts, and in each case the subject was simultaneously presented with a single, front-view face (target) and a board of six stimuli. In the first part, the board showed front-view faces, among which was the target (6 items); in the second, the board showed various three-quarter views including three representations of the target (8 items, 24 responses); in the third, the board displayed front-view faces under various lighting conditions (8 items, 24 responses). Using, unfortunately, a single combined score for the three parts, the authors examined normal as well as LBD and RBD subjects. The LBD subjects scored lower than the normals but better than the RBD. The results were affected neither by a VFD nor by aphasia, intrahemispheric locus of lesion, or etiology. In addition to the paired comparison task, the subjects of Jones (1969) were given the test of Benton and Van Allen. This time, the RBD performed worse than the LBD subjects, and the correlation between the two tests was weak. With this test, Hamsher, Levin, and Benton (1979) evidenced an impairment of RBD subjects (especially with a posterior lesion), and of aphasics with an auditory comprehension defect. There was no effect of a VFD. Blunk (1982) reported an impairment of RBD subjects with this test, the lateralization effect being no longer observed with a task of matching facial expressions. Bentin and Gordon (1979) included this test in a battery of cognitive asymmetries, but only combined scores were analyzed. On the other hand, the demented and normal subjects of Wilson et al. (1982) were also submitted to the test of Benton and Van Allen: Demented subjects were impaired, as with the recognition test, but the statistical analyses tended to show the independence of the two processes. Levin and Benton (1977) showed that the test could reasonably differentiate brain-injured from functional psychiatric cases. Finally, Levin, Hamsher, and Benton (1975) proposed a shortened form of the test (27 responses instead of 54) that preserved the psychometric properties of the full form. Levin, Grossman, and Kelly (1977) administered this revised version to subjects who had suffered a traumatic closed-head injury, and to normals. The groups differed, and the scores were affected by the severity of the trauma and correlated with the duration of the coma. Poizner, Kaplan, Bellugi, and Padden

---

[3]This test is now widely used and has been published for clinical use together with the shortened form presented later.

(1984) examined congenitally unilaterally brain-damaged deaf singers, fluent in American Sign Language before the stroke. The subjects were enrolled for various neuropsychological tests, including the test of Benton and Van Allen (LBD: full form; RBD: short form). The LBD subjects scored normally, but the RBD subjects were defective. One LBD subject was also given a facial closure test on which he gave a superior performance. On the other hand, the usual hemispheric dissociations were largely observed with this battery. Wasserstein, Zappulla, Rosen, and Gerstman (1984) gave RBD subjects the short version of the test, together with a closure test (to identify familiar objects from incomplete pictures). The subjects with frontal, rolandic, or temporoparietal lesions were impaired for faces but not for closure, whereas the reverse pattern was observed for subjects with parieto-occipital or temporal damage. In another study (Wasserstein, Zappulla, Rosen, & Thompson, 1983), LBD and RBD subjects were given these two tests, as well as a test of visual illusion and facial closure. The last task was positively correlated with visual illusion in the LBD subjects, with the object closure in both samples, but especially in the LBD subjects, and with the Benton and Van Allen test for the LBD subjects; the last correlation, again, was negative for the RBD subjects.

Tzavaras, Hécaen, and LeBras (1970) devised tests in which the subject had to retrieve the target on a board of six normal faces. The target was one of these faces, either normal or modified by means of accessories, lighting, or facial expressions. One subtest dealt with photographs, another with drawings of faces. Additional tests concerned famous buildings, blots, nonsignificant drawings, and normal versus modified coffee cups. The normals performed better than the brain-damaged, and the LBD better than the RBD subjects. This effect of the lesion laterality was specifically due to the tests involving faces, and the scores were affected neither by a VFD nor by intrahemispheric lesion localization. Moreover, the two tests with faces were highly correlated in the RBD sample only. Finally, the most difficult conditions in these tests were as follows: for the normals, the photographs modified by accessories or lighting; for the LBD subjects, the drawings with accessories; for the RBD subjects, the same condition and the photographs modified by expressions. The authors (Tzavaras et al., 1971) also submitted left-handed brain-damaged subjects to the same battery, but no group differences appeared. Kremin (1980) used a shortened form of the face subtests of Tzavaras et al. as a control in a study dealing with the processing of non-verbal signals (facial expressions and gestures). Her LBD aphasic and RBD subjects scored lower than her non-aphasic LBD subjects, this difference not being observed for facial expressions. Nevertheless, the two tests correlated with each other for the RBD subjects with a VFD or with hemineglect. Finally, the subjects with hemineglect scored lower than the other RBD subjects for faces and facial expressions.

Along a similar line, Cicone, Wapner, and Gardner (1980) employed a test of face perception as a control for the processing of emotional stimuli with normal and brain-injured subjects. A target face had to be retrieved from a board of four faces having a copy of the target or the target with a modified hair style (6 items). A selective deficit of the RBD subjects appeared, especially with items involving hair modification, but without an effect of the intrahemispheric lesion localization. These subjects were also impaired for emotional facial expressions (as well as for emotional drawings but not for emotional sentences), but the two scores did not correlate. Bruyer (1980b) enlisted LBD and RBD subjects for the matching of a target face with a board displaying nine different faces, with six levels of blurring (48 items): The RBD subjects (particularly with a VFD) were impaired, but not for the higher levels of defocusing. The same subjects were given an identical task involving facial expressions (72 items), and similar results were obtained (Bruyer, 1981b). Moreover, this last defect did not seem to depend on the deficit for faces (Bruyer, 1984).

In another condition of the study of Dricker et al. (1978), the matching of a target face with a board of 25 faces (12 items) was used. Again, the alcoholic Korsakoff and the RBD subjects were impaired. Finally, the same subjects performed a matching task in which a target had to be selected from a board of two faces; four kinds of problems were designed by manipulating either the expression or the paraphernalia or both. The alcoholic Korsakoff and the RBD subjects were impaired, especially when the wrong choice could be induced by paraphernalia.

The subjects of Bruyer and Velge (1980), tested with drawings of 7-feature faces, were also enlisted for the matching of a target with a board of eight faces (16 items). Unlike the paired comparison condition, this task was relatively insensitive to group differences, and the more difficult features were now the eyes, the forehead, and the nose. Beyond the pretest of classification, the subjects of Bruyer and Velge (1981) were given the task of matching (20 items) a target (photograph) with a board of 20 stimuli, 5 of each category (faces, dogs, houses, and motor vehicles). The test was run with the normal versus upside-down presentations, and a control condition was provided with boards displaying only one category of stimuli. Unlike the pretest of categorization, the control condition did not reveal differences between the two samples of brain-damaged subjects, but there was an advantage for the normals. Moreover, these two tests were correlated only in the RBD subjects for houses. For the main test, a deficit of the RBD subjects was first observed (with no difference between the LBD and the normal subjects), mainly due to the human faces and not interacting with the orientation. Second, the correlation between the two orientations was sig- nificant for motor vehicles in normals; for faces, dogs, and motor vehicles in the LBD subjects; and for the four categories in the RBD subjects. Third, the study revealed a significant linkage between the three non-face classes for the LBD subjects with the upside-down presentation, and a dissociation between living (faces, dogs) and artificial (houses, cars) right-side-up objects for the RBD subjects. In addition to the identification task, the subjects of Bruyer (1982) were given two tasks: The matching of a famous versus an unknown target with a board containing five famous and five unfamiliar faces revealed a defect in the RBD subjects (especially those with a VFD), which was due only to unknown faces; the remaining task was similar with 10 unknown faces among whom 5 were verbally described by the experimenter. The same task was also run with unfamiliar flowers and buildings: Whatever the kind of stimuli, a deficit appeared again in the RBD subjects (especially with a VFD), mainly due to the nondescribed stimuli.

The subjects of Fried et al. (1982), who received electrical right-brain stimulation, had to first match the to-be-memorized target with a board of three faces. Apparently, no site elicited specific deficits for faces: The defects noted for temporal posterior, temporoparietal, and inferior frontal zones concerned face and line orientation. In the studies by Vilkki and Laitinen (1974, 1976), the subjects were also tested pre- and postoperatively for the matching of 12 faces with a board of 25 faces[4]. The right pulvinotomized subjects were slightly impaired before the operation; the detrimental effect of the operation appeared only for the subjects operated on in the right brain; and this right-left difference disappeared in a long-term control. Finally, Benton and Gordon (1971) gave mentally retarded subjects a set of three tests: the matching of a target face with a board of nine faces (48 items), a similar test with nonmeaningful complex line drawings, and the matching of colored versus uncolored shading patterns. The battery also included left- and right-hemisphere neuropsychological tests. The test with faces correlated with shading patterns and right-hemisphere tests, but not with line drawings and left-brain tests.

Miscellaneous Tasks

In the recognition studies under various encoding conditions, the samples were also compared as regards the encoding itself. The amnesics examined by Mayes et al. (1980) did not differ from the normals for the judgments concerning the hair or the friendliness of the displayed faces. Similarly, the differential recognition deficits of RBD and alcoholic amnesic subjects tested by Biber et al. (1981) could be attributed to group differences, neither for the evaluation of the size of the nose, nor for the likeability of the faces.

The split-brain subject with a left-hemisphere deficit for face processing was asked by Gazzaniga and Smylie (1983) to verbally describe laterally displayed faces (20 items). Hemispheres differed neither in the number of spontaneous selected attributes nor in the accuracy of the responses.

Etcoff (1984) invited normal as well as LBD and RBD subjects to sort sets of 32 stimuli according to a given attribute. The stimuli were faces or geometric figures varying in two attributes: identity and expression for faces, shape and color for geometric figures. The sets varied in the linkage between the two

---

[4]In this procedure, the 12 target faces were shown at the same time.

attributes: strong correlation, in which a given person (shape) systematically displayed the same expression (color), versus null correlation, either by keeping constant one attribute or by crossing the two attributes orthogonally. The analysis of errors did not show group differences for the geometric figures; for faces, a deficit of the RBD subjects (with no differences between the LBD subjects and the normals) appeared, due to the condition in which identities had to be processed under the orthogonal condition. The speed of sorting geometric figures did not reveal interference between the attributes, whatever the group. For faces, the RBD subjects performed more slowly than the LBD subjects, and the latter more slowly than normals. The RBD subjects' deficits resulted from interferences between the two attributes (in both directions) in the orthogonal condition. In addition, there was a selective interference of expression over identity for the RBD subjects with posterior temporal damage, and of identity over expression for the RBD subjects with frontoparietal or temporoparietal lesion.

Using the 7-feature drawings of faces, Bruyer (1980c) presented 20 items to normal, LBD, and RBD subjects. Each item involved one complete target together with four half-faces: the upper, lower, left, and right hemifaces, which were derived from the target, except for one random half-face inserted as a distractor. The task was to point to the incomplete face that was the most similar to the target. It appeared that the RBD subjects tended to selectively avoid the lateral hemifaces. This observation could be linked with the results of De Renzi et al. (1968) on their subtest involving fragments of faces (see foregoing).

In a related area, Kolb, Milner, and Taylor (1983) submitted normal and unilaterally brain-damaged subjects to the procedure of the symmetrical chimeras (see part III of this volume): A target face was presented with the two symmetrical composites derived from the lateral hemifaces of the target. Asked to choose the chimera the most similar to the target or to the mirror-image of the target (19 items) under the normal versus upside-down conditions, the subjects performed as follows: (a) for the upright presentation, all subjects, except those with a retrorolandic or temporal right damage (no bias), evidenced the usual bias favoring the right portion of the face; (b) for the upside-down condition, all but the RBD subjects (no bias) again evidenced this "left field" bias.

DISCUSSION AND CONCLUSION

The empirical data to review were copious, and the length of this tour of the literature allows too little space for a detailed discussion. We focus on five main topics:

1. The first, robust result of the literature is that RBD subjects (particularly with posterior lesion inducing; a VFD) are specifically defective in the processing of faces (see Benton, 1980; or Yin, 1978, for reviews). We must, however,

take two qualifications into account. On the one hand, even though some studies did not reveal an RBD defect, a careful examination of the procedural characteristics of these paradigms could well provide valuable information on the mechanisms of face processing. On the other hand, there were experiments in which other populations were affected: demented, amnesic, and unilaterally LBD subjects. Again, a detailed study is needed to locate the critical variables related to the underlying operations.

2. Another conclusion is that defects were principally noted for recognition tasks. Nevertheless, it seems that the deficits could be attributed to difficulties as early as the perceptual stages of processing, as we have suggested earlier. Given the perceptual defects, it is risky to assert that a right hemispheric lesion impairs the recognition of faces, for it could simply be a consequence of defects during perception. However, we have to consider these conclusions prudently: Indeed, there is research showing a recognition deficit with no perceptual impairment at a within-group level, and other research has revealed lesion localization dissociations between the subjects with a memory deficit and those with a perceptual one.

3. This kind of research was initially developed on the basis of clinical reports of prosopagnosia that suggested a specific involvement of the right hemisphere in the processing of faces. It was assumed that a more subtle examination of patients with no clinical complaint would reveal "sub-clinical" deficits. On a superficial level, the results thus confirm this view, but, again, qualifications are needed. First, it is now largely recognized that prosopagnosia results from bilateral damage; second, it is probable that prosopagnosia is not a unitary syndrome; third, the data collected when prosopagnosic subjects were submitted to some of the foregoing-listed experiments are inconclusive.

4. A major current theoretical concern is the existence of specific (right-sided brain) mechanisms to process faces. Two points of view underlie this debate. On the one hand, one must distinguish between the stimulus and the face. In the great majority of the research reviewed earlier, the to-be-recognized material is identical to the target: The subject had to match stimuli, but not necessarily "faces" (however, this does not imply that faces were not recognized). We have nevertheless noted studies in which the task was to match various representations of a face differing by orientation, accessories, or expression. In this last situation, it is obvious that the comparison or recognition concerned the "person" or the "physiognomy," not the stimulus, which was, indeed, entirely modified. However, these studies, which almost exclusively focused on the perceptual stages, reiterated the defect of RBD subjects.

On the other hand, the problem concerns the specificity for human faces versus other stimuli, both "horizontally" and "vertically." The horizontal axis deals with faces compared, for similar task requirements, to other, functionally unrelated, materials. The few studies having taken such point into account are globally inconclusive. There is, however, a major methodological difficulty in asserting that structurally different materials are similar in "complexity." The vertical axis is related both to the possibility that deficits for faces result from unspecific defects in the processing of more rudimentary visuospatial stimuli, and to the possibility that the deficits for faces impair the processing of other, face-related, materials (such as facial expressions). Again, these two questions need further analysis.

5. Finally, we would like to suggest some areas for future research. It could be useful to examine the stimuli used in the experiments: When statistically significant effects are evidenced, they generally authorize inferences in terms of population (for example, the effect obtained with a particular sample of RBD subjects may reasonably be generalized to the entire, theoretical population of RBD patients). However, the (usually low number of) used faces are implicitly considered as representative of the population of "human faces." This factor is considered as random, but this is doubtful given the selection and construction of the stimuli. Therefore, it could be useful to apply to studies with faces the statistical procedure recommended by Clark (1973) for psycholinguistic studies dealing with words.

Furthermore, it is urgent that we design experiments with brain-damaged subjects on the basis of the actual state of the knowledge concerning the cognitive mechanisms involved in the processing of faces (Ellis, 1983; Hay & Young, 1982), as suggested by Blanc-Garin (1984). For example, it is becoming clear that faces cannot be dissociated from the "context" in which they are perceived. A psycho-cognitivist approach has to fill the place of the neurological point of view, the latter having virtually exhausted its potential. Nevertheless, we have to keep in mind the problems dealing with the inference from brain damage to the functioning of a normal system (Sergent, 1984).

REFERENCES

Becker, J. T., Butters, N., Hermann, A., & D'Angelo, N. (1983). Learning to associate names and faces. *Journal of Nervous and Mental Disease, 171,* 617–623.

Bentin, S., & Gordon, H. W. (1979). Assessment of cognitive asymmetries in brain-damaged and normal subjects: validation of a test battery. *Journal of Neurology, Neurosurgery, and Psychiatry, 42,* 715–723.

Benton, A. L. (1980). The neuropsychology of facial recognition. *American Psychologist, 35,* 176–186.

Benton, A. L., & Gordon, M. C. (1971). Correlates of facial recognition. *Transactions of the American Neurological Association, 96,* 146–150.

Benton, A. L., & Van Allen, M. W. (1968). Impairment in facial recognition in patients with cerebral disease. *Cortex, 4,* 344–358.

Berent, S. (1977). Functional asymmetry of the human brain in the recognition of faces. *Neuropsychologia, 15,* 829–831.

Biber, C., Butters, N., Rosen, J., Gerstman, L., & Mattis, S. (1981). Encoding strategies and recognition of faces by alcoholic Korsakoff and other brain-damaged patients. *Journal of Clinical Neuropsychology, 3,* 315–330.

Blanc-Garin, J. (1984). Perception des visages et reconnaissance de la physionomie, dans l'Agnosie des visages. *L'année Psychologique, 84,* 573–598.

Blunk, R. (1982). Recognition of emotion and physiognomy in right- and left- hemisphere damaged patients and normals. *Communication,* International Neuropsychological Society, Deauville, France.

Bowers, R., Bauer, R. M., Coslett, H. B., & Heilman, K. M. (1985). Processing of faces by patients with unilateral hemisphere lesions. *Brain and Cognition, 4,* 258–272.

Bruyer, R. (1980a). Lésion cérébrale et perception du visage: rôle des parties du visage. *Psychologie Médicale, 12,* 1261–1270.

Bruyer, R. (1980b). Lésion cérébrale et perception de visages flous: différences hémisphériques. *L'année Psychologique, 80,* 379–390.

Bruyer, R. (1980c). Lésion cérébrale et perception du visage: étude de la symétrie faciale. *Journal de Psychologie Normale et Pathologique, 77,* 85–98.

Bruyer, R. (1981a). Reconnaissance de visages célèbres et lésions cérébrales: effet du langage. *Le Langage et L'homme, 46,* 3–8.

Bruyer, R. (1981b). Perception d'expressions faciales émotionnelles et lésion cérébrale: influence de la netteté du stimulus. *International Journal of Psychology, 16,* 87–94.

Bruyer, R. (1982). Role du langage et de la mémoire visuelle dans la perception des visages: effet des lésions cérébrales unilatérales. *Psychologie Française, 27,* 146–157.

Bruyer, R. (1984). Lateralized brain processing of faces and facial expressions: level of blurring and specificity. *Perceptual and Motor Skills, 59,* 545–546.

Bruyer, R., & Gadisseux, C. (1980). La reconnaissance du visage chez l'enfant normal: comparaison avec l'adulte cérébrolésé. *Enfance, 3,* 95–106.

Bruyer, R., & Velge, V. (1980). Lésions cérébrales et reconnaissance visuelle du visage humain: une étude préliminaire. *Psychologica Belgica, 20,* 125–139.

Bruyer, R., & Velge, V. (1981). Lésion cérébrale unilatérale et trouble de la perception de visages: spécificité du déficit? *Acta Neurologica Belgica, 81,* 321–332.

Bruyer, R., Laterre, C., Seron, X., Feyereisen, P., Strypstein, E., Pierrard, E., & Rectem, D. (1983). A case of prosopagnosia with some preserved covert remembrance of familiar faces. *Brain and Cognition, 2,* 257–284.

Cancellière, A. B., & Kertesz, A. (1984). Emotional expression and comprehension and the locus of lesion. *Text of a communication,* International Neuropsychological Society, Aachen, Germany.

Christen, L., & Landis, T. (1984). Prosopagnosia: A model for alternative processing of the left hemisphere. *Text of a communication,* European workshop on Cognitive Neuropsychology, Bressanone, Italy.

Cicone, M., Wapner, W., & Gardner, H. (1980). Sensitivity to emotional expressions and situations in organic patients. *Cortex, 16,* 145–158.

Clark, H. H. (1973). The language-as-fixed-effect fallacy: a critique of language statistics in psychological research. *Journal of Verbal Learning and Verbal Behavior, 12,* 335–359.

DeKosky, S.T., Heilman, K. M., Bowers, D., & Valenstein, E. (1980). Recognition and discrimination of emotional faces and pictures. *Brain and Language, 9,* 206–214.

De Renzi, E., & Spinnler, H. (1966). Facial recognition in brain-damaged patients. An experimental approach. *Neurology, 16,* 145–152.

De Renzi, E., Faglioni, P., & Spinnler, H. (1968). The performance of patients with unilateral brain damage on face recognition tasks. *Cortex, 4,* 17–34.

De Renzi, E., Scotti, G., & Spinnler, H. (1969). Perceptual and associative disorders of visual recognition. *Neurology, 19,* 634–642.

Dricker, J., Butters, N., Berman, G., Samuels, I., Carey, S. (1978). The recognition and encoding of faces by alcoholic Korsakoff and right hemisphere patients. *Neuropsychologia, 16,* 683–695.

Ellis, H. D. (1983). The role of the right hemisphere in face perception. In A. W. Young (Ed.), *Functions of the right hemisphere* (pp. 33–64). London: Academic Press.

Etcoff, N. L. (1984). Selective attention to facial identity and facial emotion. *Neuropsychologia, 22*, 281–295.

Fried, I., Mateer, C., Ojemann, G., Wohns, R., & Fedio, P. (1982). Organization of visuospatial functions in human cortex: evidence from electrical stimulation. *Brain, 105*, 349–371.

Gazzaniga, M. S., & Smylie, C. S. (1983). Facial recognition and brain asymmetries: Clues to underlying mechanisms. *Annals of Neurology, 13*, 536–540.

Grüsser, O. J., & Kirchoff, N. (1982). Face recognition and unilateral brain lesions. *Communication,* International Neuropsychological Society, Deauville, France.

Hamsher, K., Levin, H. S., & Benton, A. L. (1979). Facial recognition in patients with focal brain lesions. *Archives of Neurology, 36*, 837–839.

Hay, D. C., & Young, A. W. (1982). The human face. In A. W. Ellis (Ed.), *Normality and pathology in cognitive functions* (pp. 173–202). New York: Academic Press.

Jones, A. C. (1969). Influence of mode of stimulus presentation on performance in facial recognition tasks. *Cortex, 5*, 290–301.

Kolb, B., Milner, B., & Taylor, L. (1983). Perception of faces by patients with localized cortical excisions. *Canadian Journal of Psychology, 37*, 8–18.

Kremin, H. (1980). Recognition of faces, facial expressions, and symbolic gestures in brain damaged patients. *Text of a communication,* International Neuropsychological Society, Chianciano, Italy.

Kurucz, J., & Feldmar, G. (1979). Prosopo-affective agnosia as a symptom of cerebral organic disease. *Journal of the American Geriatrics Society, 27*, 225–230.

Kurucz, J., Soni, A., Feldmar, G., & Slade, W. R. (1980). Prosopo-affective agnosia and computerized tomography findings in patients with cerebral disorders. *Journal of the American Geriatrics Society, 28*, 475–478.

Levin, H. S., & Benton, A. L. (1977). Facial recognition in "pseudoneurological" patients. *Journal of Nervous and Mental Disease, 164*, 135–138.

Levin, H. S., Grossman, R. G., & Kelly, P. J. (1977). Impairment of facial recognition after closed-head injuries of varying severity. *Cortex, 13*, 119–130.

Levin, H. S., Hamsher, K., & Benton, A. L. (1975). A short form of the test of facial recognition for clinical use. *Journal of Psychology, 91*, 223–228.

Lewinsohn, P. M., Danaher, B. G., & Kikel, S. (1977). Visual imagery as a mnemonic aid for brain-injured persons. *Journal of Consulting and Clinical Psychology, 45*, 717–723.

Marslen-Wilson, W. D., & Teuber, H. L. (1975). Memory for remote events in anterograde amnesia: recognition of public figures from news photographs. *Neuropsychologia, 13*, 353–364.

Mayes, A., Meudell, P., & Neary, D. (1980). Do amnesics adopt inefficient encoding strategies with faces and random shapes? *Neuropsychologia, 18*, 527–540.

Meudell, P. R., Northen, B., Snowden, J. S., & Neary, D. (1980). Long-term memory for famous voices in amnesic and normal subjects. *Neuropsychologia, 18*, 133–139.

Milner, B. (1968). Visual recognition and recall after right temporal lobe excision in man. *Neuropsychologia, 6*, 191–209.

Murri, L., Arena, R., Siciliano, G., Mazzotta, R., & Muratorio, A. (1984). Dream recall in patients with focal cerebral lesions. *Archives of Neurology, 41*, 183–185.

Newcombe, F. (1974). Selective deficits after focal cerebral injury. In S. J. Dimond & J. G. Beaumont (Eds.), *Hemisphere function in the human brain* (pp. 311–334). London: Elek Science.

Newcombe, F., & Russell, W. R. (1969). Dissociated visual perceptual and spatial deficits in focal lesions on the right hemisphere. *Journal of Neurology, Neurosurgery, and Psychiatry, 32*, 73–81.

Poizner, H., Kaplan, E., Bellugi, U., & Padden, C. A. (1984). Visual-spatial processing in deaf brain-damaged signers. *Brain and Cognition, 3*, 281–306.

Pontius, A. A. (1983). Pictorial misrepresentation of spatial relations of the face by certain chronic alcoholic men: an interpretation implicating spatial aspects of memory. *Perceptual and Motor Skills, 57*, 895–910.

Sergent, J. (1984). Inferences from unilateral brain damage about normal hemispheric functions in visual pattern recognition. *Psychological Bulletin, 96,* 99–115.

Tzavaras, A., Hécaen, H., & LeBras, H. (1970). Le problème de la spécificité du déficit de la reconnaissance du visage humain lors des lésions hémisphériques unilatérales. *Neuropsychologia, 8,* 403–416.

Tzavaras, A., Hécaen, H., & LeBras, H. (1971). Troubles de la reconnaissance du visage humain et latéralisation hémisphérique lésionnelle chez les sujets gauchers. *Neuropsychologia, 9,* 475–477.

Van Lancker, D. R., & Canter, G. J. (1982). Impairment of voice and face recognition in patients with hemispheric damage. *Brain and Cognition, 1,* 185–195.

Vilkki, J., & Laitinen, L. V. (1974). Differential effects of left and right ventrolateral thalamotomy on receptive and expressive verbal performances and face-matching. *Neuropsychologia, 12,* 11–19.

Vilkki, J., & Laitinen, L. V. (1976). Effects of pulvinotomy and ventrolateral thalamotomy on some cognitive functions. *Neuropsychologia, 14,* 67–78.

Warrington, E., & James, M. (1967). An experimental investigation of facial recognition in patients with unilateral cerebral lesions. *Cortex, 3,* 317–326.

Warrington, E. K., & Taylor, A. M. (1973). Immediate memory for faces: long- or short-term memory? *Quarterly Journal of Experimental Psychology, 25,* 316–322.

Wasserstein, J., Zappulla, R., Rosen, J., & Thompson, A. L. (1983). Facial closure: interrelationships with facial discrimination, object closure and subjective contour illusion perception. *Text of a communication,* International Neuropsychological Society, Mexico City, Mexico.

Wasserstein, J., Zappulla, R., Rosen, J., & Gerstman, L. (1984). Evidence for differentiation of right hemisphere visual-perceptual functions. *Brain and Cognition, 3,* 51–56.

Wayland, S., & Taplin (1982). Nonverbal categorization in fluent and non-fluent anomic aphasics. *Brain and Language, 16,* 87–108.

Wayland, S., & Taplin, J. E. (1985a). Feature-processing deficits following brain injury I. *Brain and Cognition, 4,* 338–355.

Wayland, S., & Taplin, J. E. (1985b). Feature-processing deficits following brain injury II. *Brain and Cognition, 4,* 356–376.

Whiteley, A., & Warrington, E. K. (1979). Category-specific deficits of visual memory and visual perception. *Communication,* International Neuropsychological Society, Noordwijkerhout, The Netherlands.

Wilson, R. S., Kaszniak, A. W., Bacon, L.D., Fox, J. H., & Kelly, M. P. (1982). Facial recognition memory in dementia. *Cortex, 18,* 329–336.

Yin, R. K. (1970). Face recognition by brain-injured patients: a dissociable ability? *Neuropsychologia, 8,* 395–402.

Yin, R. K. (1978). Face perception: a review of experiments with infants, normal adults, and brain-injured persons. In R. Held, H. W. Leibowitz, & H. L. Teuber (Eds.), *Handbook of sensory physiology: Vol. VIII: Perception* (pp. 593–608). New York: Springer.

II LATERAL DIFFERENCES FOR FACE PERCEPTION IN NORMAL SUBJECTS

5 Methodological Constraints on Neuropsychological Studies of Face Perception in Normals

Justine Sergent
Montreal Neurological Institute

INTRODUCTION

By virtue of the anatomical property of the visual system whereby information presented in one lateral visual field is transmitted along neural pathways to the occipital and tectal regions of the contralateral hemisphere, the methods of experimental psychology can be, and have been, applied in a neurological context, providing a strategy to extend our understanding of the functions of the two intact cerebral hemispheres. Initially, research on cerebral lateralization of functions in normals was entirely contingent on findings from the neurological population, and early evidence of concordance between results from normal and brain-damaged subjects (e.g., Bryden, 1965; Kimura, 1966) validated the lateral tachistoscopic technique as a means of studying functional asymmetry in the intact brain. In this context, the accumulation of evidence during the 1960s of a critical role of the right hemisphere (RH) in the processing of faces (Benton & Van Allen, 1968; De Renzi & Spinnler, 1966; Hécaen & Angelergues, 1962; Milner, 1968; Newcombe, 1969; Warrington & James, 1967) prompted the investigation of this hemisphere functional specialization in normal subjects. Yet, the very first study to examine this issue failed to confirm the prediction. Rizzolatti, Umiltà, and Berlucchi (1970), using sketches of faces of famous persons presented in the right visual field (RVF) or the left visual field (LVF), found that the two hemispheres were equally efficient at processing physiognomies. The following year, however, two independent studies concurred with the neurological evidence of a RH superiority in the processing of faces. Rizzolatti, Umiltà, and Berlucchi (1971), in a go/no–go manual reaction time (RT) task with photographs of unfamiliar faces, found shorter latencies to LVF presentations, as did Geffen, Bradshaw, and Wallace (1971) in a same–different manual RT task, with Identikit faces.

This initial contradiction remained essentially unnoticed, but it has now become clear, from the results of numerous visual–laterality studies of face processing, that research with normal subjects does not yield as robust findings as research with brain-damaged patients. Despite a strong support for a critical role of the RH, there are no less than 25 articles published during the last 10 years that report data from normal subjects pointing to a specific involvement of the left hemisphere (LH) in these processes under some circumstances. Although these inconsistencies have sometimes been regarded as an indication of low reliability of tachistoscopic research in normals, they more likely reflect a bilateral mediation of face perception, along with a considerable intricacy of experimental factors involved in this type of research and a poor understanding of their interactions and of their effects on the processing organism. Indeed, the contribution of research with normals to the neuropsychological study of face perception is, in its current state, hampered by our ignorance on three crucial points. One is that we have no clear theoretical foundation of research based on the tachistoscopic mode of stimulus presentation that would allow the formulation of the problem in terms appropriate to cerebral processing. The tachistoscopic technique necessarily implies manipulation of specific variables that we tend to consider simply as methodological and technical problems whereas they pertain to substantive issues in that they determine the characteristics of the input to the brain and the particular conditions under which the brain has to operate. A second point is that we are still limited in our understanding of the spreading of neural information within and between the hemispheres, and therefore in our capacity to come up with a valid interpretation about the functions of the cerebral hemispheres from a given pattern of visual-field asymmetry. Third, the processes mediating face perception and recognition still elude us, which leaves us unable to specify the operations involved in a particular task, let alone the respective contributions of the cerebral hemispheres to these operations.

This is not to say that no progress has been made since the first study by Rizzolatti et al. (1970), but the accumulation of data has made us more aware of the complexity of the problem. The purpose of this chapter is therefore to outline some methodological constraints on neuropsychological studies of face perception in normal subjects, in an attempt to identify those factors over which control can and should be exerced, and to specify the particular influence of these factors on the processing characteristics and efficiency of the cerebral hemispheres in face perception. This chapter is not intended to be an exhaustive review of this field of research, and some factors that may contribute to variations in the patterns of results, such as age and sex, are treated elsewhere in this volume. The focus is on group studies, and individual differences are not considered, thus dealing with the underlying pattern of hemisphere specialization rather than with individual differences in drawing on hemisphere resources (see Levine, Banich, & Koch-Weser, 1984; Levy, 1983).

METHODOLOGICAL CONSIDERATIONS

The simplicity of the logic underlying visual laterality studies should not mask the complexity and the diversity of variables inherent in the experimental process. In less than a second that lasts an experimental trial, a considerable number of variables act on, and interact with, the processing organism in its dealing with the presented information. Although some of these variables are readily identifiable, for the most part they are inaccessible to observation, and only inferences from the final outcome can provide us with a gross and superficial idea of what is really going on in the brain. As noted by Ellis (1983) and by Rhodes (1984; see also Allen, 1983), several stages, or subprocessing units, compose the entire duration from input reception to response production. These subprocessors may not be equally represented in the two hemispheres and may be differentially affected by procedural variables, but no empirical study has yet been conducted within such a framework.

The invisibility of most actual factors that influence the relative efficiency of the cerebral hemispheres in processing faces imposes a very strict control over the variables that can be identified and isolated, in order to reduce to a minimum the degree of freedom within our experimental approach. It is, however, not sufficient to identify these variables, and one needs to understand the level at which they affect the processing orgasnism and the effects of their manipulation on cerebral and neural processing. This suggests that procedural variables not only bear on methodological issues but also have important theoretical implications, as is discussed in the next section. Thereafter, three main categories of variables (the human face as a stimulus, the viewing conditions, and the nature of the tasks) are examined in some detail with respect to their influence on the processing organism.

Preliminary Remarks

Methodological issues are ultimately trivial, but they are intrinsically inescapable in the experimental process, and no interpretation and conclusion has validity unless the procedural variables inherent in obtaining the data are controlled, and unless the effects of their manipulation on performance are understood. Being the means by which a stimulus and a processing organism are put in relation, these variables are an integral part of the problem of psychological investigation. The use of the tachistoscope in neuropsychological research is certainly artificial (i.e., "made with art" and unnatural), and it imposes on the brain particular conditions for the processing of information unlike those prevailing in normal circumstances. It is certainly paradoxical that, despite the extensive use of the lateral tachistoscopic technique as a means of stimulating one side of the brain, no systematic study has yet been carried out to examine how particular values of each manipulated experimental variable affect the processing efficiency of the hemispheres. The conjoint influence of experimental psychology and classical neurology on the orientation of neuropsychological research in normal subjects has probably biased researchers toward focusing on the cognitive operations and psychological functions subserved by each side of the brain, often at the expense of a consideration of the particular information to be processed. Both Garner (1970) and Gibson (1950), although quite differently, have cautioned against this type of approach and have suggested that how information is treated by an organism cannot be determined unless one specifies what this information is. More recently, Marr (1982), in still another framework, has insisted on the importance of considering how information is represented—the initial representation consisting of arrays of image-intensity values as detected by the photoreceptors in the retina—because the particular descriptions of information can greatly affect the type of operations that can be implemented. Specifying the properties of the input may then become critical to understanding how an organism processes information, especially when one attempts to study the functions of the cerebral hemispheres by stimulating them with inputs unlike those they are normally presented with. The descriptions of information in the brain is not only a function of objective variations in intensity across a stimulus, but also of the particular viewing conditions and of the retinal areas stimulated. The absence of systematic studies on the effects of variable manipulations, and therefore of objective rules governing the selection of these variables, is certainly an obstacle to progress in our understanding of functional lateralization. This is not simply a methodological problem but has considerable theoretical implications because specifying how information is represented may be necessary to understand the nature of the operations that can be implemented. In addition, evidence that visual-field advantage may shift with a change in the values of one procedural variable should caution against generalization from a single set of data and points to the relative validity of any finding.

The Human Face as a Stimulus

The human face is a complex, multidimensional, and meaningful pattern. Its richness as a stimulus and as a source of information about an individual's identity, personality, mood, and emotion makes it a unique object of research to uncover underlying visual processes and as an end in itself. However, it is probably fair to say that, thus far, the neuropsychological study of facial perception has not exploited this richness and has used rather unsophisticated means of investigation. Although the face is a three-dimensional plastic object, research has been conducted with single views of two-dimensional static faces. As noted by Bruce (1983), and by Hay and Young (1982), one fundamental property of the face is lost by this procedure, and research may simply tap *stimulus recognition* rather than *face recognition* proper. In addition, a large number of experiments have been conducted with artificially made faces, such as Photofit or Identikit, line-drawing or schematic faces.

Whether these particular experimental faces are an obstacle to accessing the processes underlying face perception is examined in this section, along with outlining some problems related to the physical properties of a face, its encoding, and the strategies that may be implemented in its processing.

The Face as a Familiar Stimulus.   As a category of visual pattern, the human face is a highly familiar class, and, every day, we perceive, discriminate, remember, and identify faces. When subjects are required to remember objects of various categories within the same experiment, they are more proficient with faces than with any other category (e.g., Freedman & Haber, 1974), and with known faces than with unknown faces (Klatsky & Forrest, 1984). Such findings have led to the suggestion that our long experience with faces enables us to access consistent dimensions that facilitate perception and memory. Goldstein and Chance (1980) have recently proposed that the repeated exposure to members of a class of objects, and particularly faces, serves to develop schemata that assist further interaction with various instances of the class, and allow fine discrimination among faces on the basis of very slight physical differences. Whether such a schema is differentially represented in the two hemispheres has not been investigated, however. Nonetheless, Hay (1981) has argued that the RH is more efficient than the LH at deciding whether a stimulus is a normal or a scrambled face, and this may be consistent with the idea of a face schema more strongly represented in the RH. However, whether this finding would hold under a variety of viewing conditions and stimulus presentation is not known.

The Experimental Face.   Neuropsychological research on face perception is conducted with a variety of types of faces, and conclusions about underlying processes in the two hemispheres usually are drawn irrespective of the particular faces that are presented. Yet, on several aspects, these different types of faces are not equivalent, and they differ in their physical characteristics, realism, and information content.

In almost all laterality studies on face perception, only one single view of each face is presented in tasks requiring discrimination or recognition of facial identity. This obviously limits the extent to which we can claim we are testing face recognition proper, and the stimuli may not be treated as faces as such but as ordinary visual pattern (Hay & Young, 1982). In fact, the capacity of human subjects to extract invariant physiognomical features from a face and to recognize it from different views has been investigated in only three studies so far. Moscovitch, Scullion, and Christie (1976) had subjects match photographs of well known singers with their caricatures and found a significant LVF advantage in latency, in contrast to an absence of hemifield difference when matching was between two caricatures or two faces. Bertelson, Van Haelen, and Morais (1979) had subjects compare two faces under two conditions: *physical identity* (same view of the same face) or *face identity* (different views of the same face). They found no difference between visual fields in the physical-identity condition but judgments of facial identity were made faster and more accurately in LVF presentations, although this effect prevailed only in "different" responses. Bertelson et al. (1979) concluded that the operations that are performed in the RH are concerned with the extraction of physiognomic invariants, but they were careful to note that the absence of field difference in "same" decisions reduces the generality of their conclusions.

St. John (1981) used three quarter views of faces and their mirror image in a same–different judgment task and found a LVF advantage for "same" and "different" decisions in three experiments, in contrast to an absence of field-difference when shoes were presented as stimuli. St. John did not discuss his finding in terms of Bertelson et al.'s (1979) distinction between physical and facial identity, but his experiments did involve facial identity, and the robust LVF superiority observed in both "same" and "different" decisions may confirm Bertelson et al.'s suggestion. The use of different views of the same face is certainly more ecologically valid in investigating the role of the hemispheres in face processing, and the RH superiority observed in such conditions may thus point to a critical contribution of this hemisphere. Although photographs of real faces, which are the only stimuli that can be used for facial identity, do not allow for objective control over variations in stimulus features across faces, they are certainly preferable over artificially made faces when the purpose of the study is to determine the capacity of the hemispheres to extract physiognomical invariants.

Another dimension that differentiates the various types of experimental faces is their composition in terms of variations in luminous intensity. Both photographs of real faces and photofit faces are black-and-white patterns, varying in shades of gray, whereas line-drawings and schematic faces are made of black lines on a white background. This creates different levels of contrast for the two categories, making the features not equally discriminable. For example, Tieger and Ganz (1979) have indicated that typical black-and-white photographs of faces have an average contrast of .50 at about 8-mL luminance, whereas line-drawing faces such as used by Sergent (1984b) have an average contrast close to .85 at the same intensity level. It is important to note that the ability to recognize faces is positively correlated with the capacity to discriminate between different patterns of shading (Benton & Gordon, 1971), and Hannay and Rogers (1979) found that LVF superiority in immediate matching of photographs of faces was positively related to brightness discrimination scores, at least in male subjects. This relation between superiority of the RH and the capacity to discriminate patterns of shading suggests that one of the factors that may determine an LVF superiority in face perception may be a greater ability of the RH to operate on low-contrast intensity variations. There is indeed evidence from normal subjects (Davidoff, 1982) as well as from brain-damaged patients (Kobayashi, Tazaki, Ishikawa, & Mukuno, 1981), that the RH plays a critical role in brightness discrimination, and has higher contrast sensitivity at low intensity. This suggests that the use of photographs and photofit faces may contribute to some extent to the finding of RH superiority in face perception, whereas line-drawing and schematic faces make less demands in terms of brightness discrimination.

This issue is further complicated, however, by the fact that the various types of faces do not convey the same amount of information. Photographs and photofit faces usually are highly detailed representations, whereas line-drawing and schematic faces only contain the essential information that characterizes a face, and may even be unrealistic representations. It is not clear how this factor affects the relative efficiency of the cerebral hemispheres. Freeman (1980, cited in Ellis, 1983) found that low-detail tracing of faces were consistently better recognized when projected in the LVF, whereas photographs of faces from which these tracings were made yielded either a RVF or no field advantage. However, there are indications that the reversed effect sometimes prevails, and that the LH may be more efficient at processing line-drawings than photographs of pictorial stimuli (Kiersch & Megibow, 1978). It is thus unclear, at present, how differences between the various types of faces, in terms of contrast and amount of information, influence the pattern of visual-field asymmetry. Both LVF and RVF superiorities already have been reported with each type of face, and it would be necessary to examine how this factor interacts with other procedural and task variables.

Although photographs of real faces clearly are desirable over other types of faces, their use reduces the possibility of evaluating performance as a function of stimulus similarity and feature differences. There is as yet no objective measure of similarity and complexity within and between stimulus sets, and using faces where alterations are made to discrete features provides the opportunity to analyze the results in a way that allows examination of the underlying operations. It has been argued (e.g., Ellis, 1981) that such artificially made faces encourage the use of a serial-processing strategy and that by using them we are only likely to produce wrong answers. Although much caution is needed when drawing inferences about underlying processes when using artificially made faces, it may not be true that they elicit a serial-processing strategy. Matthews (1978) and Sergent (1984a) have shown that even when subjects know that alterations to discrete features have been made, they do not necessarily resort to a serial-processing strategy. At the heart of this problem lies the question of whether artificial faces prevent the examination of the operations involved in real face processing, and thus whether the facial schema (cf. Goldstein & Chance, 1980) that subjects may develop is operative only with real faces.

Several arguments suggest that the use of artificially made faces does not preclude access to the processes underlying face perception. In real life situations, we are often confronted with line-drawing and schematic faces, as well as caricatures, and we have learned to deal with them and to recognize them as genuine facial representations. This suggests that a facial schema that assists our processing of faces must be flexible enough to accommodate a wide variety of facial representations. Brunswik (1956), one of the first advocates of "ecological validity" in Psychology, initiated a series of research based on schematic faces, and the use of such faces has yielded insightful information about expression and emotion (e.g., McKelvie, 1973); it is also the case that the discrimination and recognition of schematic faces is impaired following RH damage and that performance on these faces is significantly and positively correlated with that on photographs of real faces (Tzavaras, Hécaen, & LeBras, 1970). This suggests that there are common characteristics to the operations performed on photographs and schematic faces, and what is lost in ecological validity may be compensated for by the introduction of control over stimulus feature. In fact, in the same way as one cannot hear speech as noise even if one would prefer to (Fodor, 1983), one may not be able to perceive a facial representation as a simple array of intensity variations.

One last aspect that is worth considering with respect to the experimental face concerns the particular set of stimuli used in an experiment when subjects are required to make comparisons among members of a set or a decision with respect to some physical characteristics. For one thing, the size of the set may be a critical variable, and Young and Bion (1981; see also Hannay & Rogers, 1979) found a significant LVF advantage with a small set but not when twice as many faces were presented. It must be noted, however, that visual-field asymmetries have been obtained with larger sets than the large set of Young and Bion (e.g., Hilliard, 1973; Jones, 1979), and that the use of a small set does not necessarily yield field differences (e.g., Ross & Turkewitz, 1982). Moreover, the particular faces composing the stimulus set may prove crucial in determining the effect observed. For example, the finding by Yin (1969) that recognition of faces suffered more than recognition of houses from inversion was not replicated by Toyama (1975) who attributed this discrepancy to the different sets of stimuli used in the two studies. There is unfortunately no a priori way of controlling for the homogeneity, intra-similarity and internal complexity of stimulus sets. Level of performance for each face of a set, or each pair, may yield some indication about the relative ease with which it is processed in a particular task, but it provides little information for the comparison of one set with another used in a different laboratory.

There is evidence that a high level of similarity among faces of a set may result in RVF superiority, at least in "different" judgments (Fairweather, Brizzolara, Tabossi, & Umiltà, 1982; Patterson & Bradshaw, 1975; Sergent, 1982a, 1984b). In all these studies, schematic or line-drawing faces were used, but, even if this factor contributed to this outcome, it was not sufficient to account for the finding because a greater dissimilarity among these faces yielded in all cases either an absence of field advantage or an LVF superiority. There is no similar evidence with stimulus sets of photographs of real faces (but see Hellige, Corwin, & Johnson, 1984), and in fact Ellis (1983) has argued, on the basis of findings by Freeman (1980) and Young and Bion (1980), that the difficulty of discriminating among faces is not a useful basis for distinguishing the contribution of the RH and LH in processing faces. It must be noted, however, that the studies reporting RVF superiority with "different" face pairs had response latency as main dependent variable, with a relatively low percentage of errors, whereas the studies referred to by Ellis (1983) involved recognition accuracy as dependent variable, a condition that inherently imposes stimulus degradation to obtain a fair amount of errors, which in turn prevents accurate encoding of the small details that differ between highly similar faces (see following for further discussion).

Until an objective measure of facial similarity and stimulus set homogeneity with real faces is devised, researchers should be encouraged to use multiple sets of stimuli to avoid spurious findings due to a particular set, and, hopefully, to exchange such sets between them.

Encoding of Faces.   The initial encoding of faces by the visual system is based on variations of stimulus intensity over spatial intervals, followed by the recognition of the input as a face and by processing the relevant dimensions as a function of task demands. It is, however, unclear what is a relevant facial dimension and what aspects of a face serve as a basis for processing. The visual system is sensitive to variations in luminous intensity, and these variations are essentially present in the features themselves, not in smooth surfaces such as the forehead or the cheeks.

What is uncertain is whether these discrete facial features constitute the primary basis for operations performed on faces. It might as well be a cluster of features, as suggested by Shepherd, Davies, and Ellis (1981) or the facial configuration that emerges from the interrelationship among features (e.g., Sergent, 1984a). What seems to be established, however, is that the processing of facial features per se is not indispensable for face recognition. This can be illustrated in Fig. 5.1 which presents an original face (a) that has been transformed into a matrix of coarsely quantized squares (b). No single part of face (b) conveys enough information for recognition, and it is only the configuration resulting from the pattern of brightness variations that allows recognition. The configuration

a   b

FIG. 5.1 A face (a) and its spatially quantized, block-portrait, version (b). In face (b), the brightness of each square is the average of the varying brightness for that area in the original face. The low frequencies contained in the pattern of lights and darks convey the relevant information about facial configuration in such a block portrait. The high frequencies, mainly those adjacent to the image spectrum, contained in the sharp edges of the squares, prevent attending to the global pattern. The high frequencies can be filtered out by squinting, blinking, moving the picture, or looking at it from distance.

becomes the most salient property of the face when the components are blurred or, in other words, when the high frequency contents of the face have been filtered out. This does not mean, however, that the configuration is removed when the face is not blurred and, in a normal face, component and configural properties coexist (Sergent, 1984a, in press-a).

This coexistence of properties leads to an important question concerning the operations mediating face perception, and it raises difficulty in identifying the relevant parameters in an experiment in which facial features are manipulated. For example, when using artifically made faces with alterations to discrete features, these features are assumed to be the critical variables that account for variations in performance, and the results are analyzed as a function of these manipulated features (see Sergent, in press-a). Yet, changing a feature also changes the configuration of the face, and variations of performance consequent to this manipulation may not be due to processing that feature as such but to processing the new configuration that emerges from this change of feature. In the particular case of faces, this is further complicated by the fact that facial features are not equally salient and do not contribute to the same extent to face discrimination and recognition. There is a fair amount of evidence, recently reviewed by Shepherd et al. (1981) that upper features play a more critical role than lower features in assisting face recognition, and, for example, a difference in hair between two faces is detected more accurately and more quickly than a difference in mouth or in eyes. This has led Sergent and Bindra (1981; see also Fairweather et al., 1982) to assume that when two faces differ from one another on several features, subjects do not need consider all the features of a pair to make a decision but they need only consider one feature, presumably the most salient. This would imply that subjects can attend to one specific part of the face and that only the most salient feature of each face could be compared, independent of the other features.

There is evidence, however, that this assumption is false. In a recent experiment, Sergent (in preparation) found that when pairs of faces differed in the most salient feature as well as in less salient features, comparison was sigificantly faster than when faces differed only in their most salient feature. This suggests that, at least in the tachistoscopic mode of presentation, subjects do not rely on the most salient feature to make their comparison and do not parse the faces into independent component features. Instead, the faces may be encoded and processed in terms of a facial unit, and feature differences may not be treated as such but contribute to the overall configurational dissimilarity between faces. In this sense, unequal feature saliency may refer to unequal contribution of each facial feature to the face considered as a configural pattern. This suggestion is supported by the finding of Homa, Haver, and Schwartz (1976) showing that, in contrast to the "word superiority effect," it is more difficult to discriminate facial features when they are embedded within a face than when they are presented in isolation. These findings bear on the highly debated question of the nature of the operations subserved by each hemisphere. Although several authors account for findings of hemisphere asymmetry in terms of the analytic/holistic processing dichotomy, these interpretations are not based on objective criteria that would allow the specification of the underlying operations, but simply on the pattern of hemifield asymmetry. Discussion of this issue is beyond the scope of this chapter, but there is growing evidence that a feature analytic processing of faces, even in the LH, is unlikely to underly face perception (Sergent, 1984b).

Although the initial encoding processes involve the physical characteristics of the physiognomy, other encoding operations of a more abstract nature may then take place, bringing additional information about the face. Although these additional encoding operations need not be involved when subjects are required to perform simultaneous matching of two faces, they may assist memorization when face recognition is required. This probably constitutes one of the invisible variables underlying performance and over which little control can be exerced. Subjects may resort to a strategy of attributing some labels, descriptions, or names to each face so as to remember them more easily (cf. Klatsky, Martin,

& Kane, 1982). It is unclear whether such added information contributes to the pattern of results in laterality studies, and, although it may not be a primary factor and cannot substitute for the physical information, it may facilitate face recognition when task difficulty increases. It may thus be necessary to investigate whether subjects use some sort of mnemonic strategy when first presented with faces in recognition studies, and to examine whether such strategies influence the pattern of visual-field asymmetry and under which circumstances. There is a good deal of evidence that encoding faces in terms of attractiveness, likeableness, honesty (e.g., Bower & Karlin, 1974; Patterson & Baddeley, 1977; Winograd, 1976) results in better recogniton than focusing on physical features. Although there is indication that such encoding influences the pattern of hemifield asymmetry, there is no consistent pattern of hemisphere superiority across individuals (e.g., Galper & Costa, 1980; Proudfoot, 1983).

Spatial-Frequency Composition of the Human Face.   Recent evidence that the visual system filters information contained in a display into separate bands of spatial frequencies has provided a new way of describing visual patterns in terms of physical characteristics consonant with the properties of early neural processing. The visual system behaves as if it comprised multiple channels and mechanisms, each selectively sensitive to a restricted band of spatial frequency and orientation (De Valois & De Valois, 1980; Sekuler, 1974). In addition, performance in comparing or identifying visual stimuli can be accurately predicted by models of visual processing that analyzes stimuli in terms of their spatial-frequency content. For example, Gervais, Harvey, and Roberts (1984) showed that confusions in the identification of letters were best accounted for by the spatial-frequency composition of the letters, rather than feature components, suggesting that describing visual patterns in terms of their spatial-frequency contents is quite relevant to understanding higher level cognitive processing.

Results of the applications of filtering processes to the human face suggest that much of the information necessary for face recognition is conveyed by the low frequencies. This has been shown by a coarse spatial quantization of a face into a matrix of average-intensity squares (Harmon, 1973; see also Fig. 5.1), by masking with gratings of various spatial frequencies (Tieger & Ganz, 1979), and by low-pass filtering of faces (Ginsburg, 1978; see also Fig. 5.2). In all these studies, subjects had to recognize the low-frequency target in a set of unfiltered photographs of faces (i.e., a matching task). Ginsburg has further suggested that the information conveyed by the high frequencies is redundant in that it does not lead to improved recognition.

Fiorentini, Maffei, and Sandini (1983) have recently reexamined this issue and suggested that, contrary to Ginsburg's (1978) claim, information conveyed by high frequencies is not redundant and is in fact sufficient by itself to ensure face recognition. There are at least two factors that may explain this discrepancy. First, Fiorentini et al. (1983) increased the mean luminance of their high-frequency

FIG. 5.2. Gradually increasing spatial-frequency contents, by 0.5 octave steps, of the face shown in Fig. 5.1a. (I am indebted to Eugene Switkes for making this filtering possible).

faces to achieve higher visibility of the facial features than that yielded by the normal high-pass process. This is a procedure different from that used by Ginsburg (1978) who did not manipulate the inherently lower intensity level of high frequencies, and it may have increased recognition rates for high-frequency faces. Second, Fiorentini et al. (1983) did not use a recognition task but an identification task whereby subjects were first required to learn names assigned to each experimental face and later to identify each one by name. As noted by Sergent (1983b), identification may require finer information than a recognition task in which subjects only decide whether or not they have seen a given face earlier.

The results of Fiorentini et al. (1983) may then not be in contradiction with earlier suggestions and in fact complement our understanding of the role of spatial frequencies in the processing of faces. Although relatively low frequencies may be sufficient for recognition, higher frequencies help improve performance as task requirements increase. Nonetheless, as shown by Ginsburg (1978) and by Fiorentini et al. (1983), no spatial frequency bandwidth is indispensable for face processing, and either low or high frequencies are sufficient for recognition and identification. This is, in fact, consistent with the suggestion that the information conveyed by the various channels of the visual system is redundant. In addition, high spatial frequencies are more vulnerable than low frequencies to degradation, reduced contrast and luminance, motion, brief presentation, which makes the low frequencies more critical in visual pattern recognition (see Ginsburg, 1978). However, the full range of spatial frequencies usually contained in a face allows for better performance than a narrow range, as suggested by the results of a recent experiment (Sergent & Switkes, 1984) in which low-pass (0–2 c/d) and broad-pass (0–32 c/d) faces of equal mean luminance were presented in center and lateral visual fields. In all tasks (verbal identification of colleagues' faces, membership categorization, and male/female categorization, see following), response latencies were significantly longer with low- than with broad-pass faces, whereas accuracy did not significantly differ between the two types of faces. This indicates that both low and high spatial frequencies are necessary for optimal performance and that the redundancy of the input provided by the visual system is an inherent characteristic of human vision and is necessary to perform at the high efficiency typical of humans in face perception and recognition.

Conclusion.   The human face is a complex multidimensional pattern with which individuals are quite familiar and which is processed with considerable expertise. We are used to dealing with all sorts of versions of faces and, as suggested by Goldstein and Chance (1980), we may have developed some form of schema that enables us to access consistent encoding dimensions that facilitate perception and memory. Such a schema seems to be quite flexible and is adaptable to various representations of faces. There is as yet no conclusive evidence from research with normals that this schema is unilaterally represented in the brain. Nonetheless, the diverse versions of experimental faces differ with respect to their basic physical characteristics, information content, realism, depth, and only photographs of real faces allow for the investigation of hemispheric differences in extracting physiognomical invariants. Despite the evidence, reviewed earlier, of RH superiority in facial identity tasks (Bertelson et al., 1979), both hemispheres are equipped to extract physiognomical invariants. This is suggested by findings of LH superiority at identifying well known faces under particular conditions, a task that also requires the extraction of physiognomical invariants. Much research is needed to examine the extent to which these differences contribute to visual-field asymmetries, and how variables associated with the face as a stimulus interact with the viewing conditions and the task demands in determining greater contribution of one hemisphere than the other in the processing of faces.

Influence of Viewing Conditions

For a large part, neuropsychological research on face perception in normals has been carried out as if the particular mode of stimulus presentation was of no importance for the subsequent processing of information. This may be partly due to the usual description of stimuli in abstract terms and to the implicit assumption that such a description is relevant and sufficient for explaining and understanding the processes performed by the two cerebral hemispheres. It has been nonetheless mentioned, for example, that reducing stimulus presentation time makes the task more difficult (e.g., Rizzolatti & Buchtel, 1977), which it does in some circumstances, but no implication for the processing organism usually is spelled out. In fact, increasing the similarity of faces in a stimulus set also makes the task more difficult, but for different reasons.

Given the properties of the visual system, presenting information in the retinal periphery and for a brief duration has important implications for the type of information that can be extracted from the stimulus, and therefore for the description of this information in the brain. In addition, other variables that must necessarily be manipulated, such as stimulus size, luminance, and contrast, also affect the extraction process and the representaton of the stimulus. As noted earlier, how information is represented can greatly influence the type and efficiency of the operations that can be implemented. A face presented at 15 ms or 200 ms, with low luminance, is still the same face, but the visual system is sensitive to such a difference and it does not transmit to the brain the same type of information in the two conditions.

The lateral taschistoscopic mode of presentation thus induces viewing conditions different from those prevailing in normal situations. In these normal situations, we are most often processing the information at which we are looking, that is in foveal vision, and the greater acuity of central vision allows a finer and more detailed representation than peripheral viewing. This implies that the processing structures that have adapted to operating on such detailed and clear representations must operate, following lateral tachistoscopic presentation, on representations that are qualitatively different and degraded. In other words, in tachistoscopic presentations, the information extracted and transmitted by the visual system does not correspond in all its characteristics to the information that the brain is used to dealing with. These particular viewing conditions must then be taken into consideration in making inferences from tachistoscopic experiments about normal hemispheric functions.

The brain processes information in terms not akin to our usual description of scenes and objects, and describing the incoming information with metrics, or concepts, that were elaborated without understanding how the visual system analyzes and processes information may not provide a valid basis for specifying the functions of the cerebral hemispheres. There is no guarantee that the brain divides up its functions into categories that correspond to our psychological vocabulary. If specialized, the hemispheres must be specialized for physiological functions, not for psychological functions that have no one-to-one anatomical counterpart and are distributed throughout the brain. The description of the incoming information, and of its processing by the brain, in terms of spatial frequency may offer the possibility to examine hemisphere functional lateralization with a single concept that can be applied to the stimulus and the effects of procedural manipulations, while being compatible with neural processing mechanisms.

The following part of this section discusses the effects of several procedural variables inherent in lateral tachistoscopc presentations in these terms, concentrating on the essential features (see Sergent, 1983b, for a detailed discussion), along with critically assessing empirical evidence that has appeared in the last 2 years.

Procedural Variables. Among the variables that need to be manipulated, two are the sine qua non of neuropsychological investigation in normals, exposure duration and retinal eccentricity, and their particular values are constrained by the duration to trigger eye movements and the resolving power of the retinal periphery. Other variables, such as luminance, contrast, size, can be manipulated without such constraints. Each of these variables determines, in different ways, the spatial-frequency components that can be extracted from the stimulus. This implies that, when trying to specify the frequency bandwidths extracted by the visual system, no single variable is sufficient. In fact, it is the interaction among these variables that determines the level of resolution, and the effects of one variable on performance cannot be evaluated independent of the values of other variables. Consequently, manipulation of one variable in a given experiment may, or may not, affect performance depending on the extent of the manipulation and on the influence of the other variables on the extraction process.

The manipulation of these procedural variables constitutes only an indirect way of varying the spatial-frequency components available for processing, which makes Sergent's (e.g., 1982c, 1983b) interpretation of the influence of procedural variables somewhat speculative. In addition, much of the evidence bearing on the particular spatial frequencies available as a function of these variables comes from experiments examining detection of simple patterns at threshold levels, which may not always be relevant to study recognition of complex patterns. Nonetheless, experiments investigating sensory resolution at suprathreshold level usually show similar trends (Harvey & Gervais, 1978; Harwerth & Levi, 1978).

The visual system does not instantaneously extract the entire content of a stimulus, and more information becomes available as exposure duration increases, as luminance is enhanced, or as retinal eccentricity decreases (Riggs, 1971). Flavell and Draguns (1957) and Vernon (1962), discussing the microgenesis of perception, suggested that perception is a developmental process consisting of a number of distinct phases, resulting from the temporal integration of luminous energy. This integration is described by Bloch's law that states that a visual response is dependent on a reciprocal relationship of time and intensity over a critical duration. Although the time interval over which complete reciprocity holds is on the order of 100 ms for brightness discrimination, it is on the order of 300–400 ms for spatial acuity tasks (Kahneman, 1964), well above the usual exposure duration of lateral tachistoscopic presentation. Thus visual acuity develops over time and fine details become discernible later as energy is summed sufficiently to resolve the higher acuity requirements for these details (Eriksen & Schultz, 1978). In terms of spatial frequency, this implies a differential rate of extraction and integration of low and high frequencies, with lower frequencies being available earlier than higher frequencies for processing.

This microgenesis of perception is illustrated in Fig. 5.2 by showing the gradually increasing clarity achieved by a stimulus as energy, and thus resolution, increase (cf. Flavell & Draguns, 1957). The initial perception is that of a diffuse whole that then achieves figure-ground discrimination whereas the inner content remains vague. Only progressively is a greater distinctiveness of contour and inner contents realized (see Sergent, in press-b, for further discussion). Because processing does not await the full development of the percept, the low frequencies, which are extracted and integrated faster, form the initial representation of the stimulus and are thus processed first. Higher frequencies are available later and may not even be extracted if the presentation time is too brief, especially when some type of mask follows stimulus offset. The duration of this microgenesis is dependent on the luminance and the contrast of the display. For example, a 20-ms exposure may be sufficient to detect a high-frequency (16 c/d) grating, but this requires 20 times higher contrast than for a low-frequency (2 c/d) grating (Breitmeyer & Ganz, 1977). Thus, exposure duration per se does not allow the specification of the spatial-frequency content extracted by the visual system, and it cannot tell much by itself about the level of resolution of the percept.

These properties of the visual system bear on a controversy about the results of an experiment conducted with a very brief exposure duration. Ellis and Shepherd (1975), using a 15-ms exposure, found a LVF superiority in the matching of both upright and inverted faces. In contrast, Leehey, Carey, Diamond, and Cahn (1978) and Young (1984) found a LVF advantage only for upright faces and argued that, because of the 15-ms exposure, "the stimuli in Ellis and Sheperd's study were not fully encoded as faces" (Leehey et al., 1978, p. 417). Such an argument ignores the critical role of intensity in the response of the visual system. In fact, Ellis and Shepherd (1975) used a 32 ftL luminance, as well as small retinal eccentricity, and the viewing conditions in their experiment, in terms of the quality of the percept, were similar to conditions in which the stimuli would be presented for 150 ms at 3.2 ftL intensity, which are values typical of experiments with faces. In addition, the suggestion that the stimuli cannot be recognized as faces at such an exposure is relatively easy to verify. One may, for example, present well known faces to subjects and see whether they can identify them. Six students I tested in my laboratory with 20 faces of colleagues were perfectly capable of identifying each of them when the same viewing conditions as in Ellis and Shepherd's experiment were used. Obviously, the stimuli must have been perceived as faces for an identification to be achieved. This is not to say that the very short exposure used by Ellis and Shepherd did not contribute to their finding, but likely not for the reasons put forward by Leehey et al. (1978).

This controversy probably illustrates the lack of understanding and concern for basic properties of the visual system in neuropsychological research on face perception and in the use of lateral tachistoscopic presentation in general. Variations in viewing conditions across experiments imply different representations of information, and these experiments may thus not be directly comparable unless the values of the procedural variables, and their effect on the processing organism, are taken into consideration.

Empirical Findings.   Few experiments have so far examined the contribution of the manipulation of procedural variables to changes in visual-field superiorities in face perception, and no clear-cut results have yet emerged.

With respect to exposure duration, there is a general tendency for faces very briefly flashed to be better processed when presented in the LVF, and for faces presented for a relatively long duration to be better processed when appearing in the RVF (see Sergent, 1983b; Sergent & Bindra, 1981, for reviews). Experiments in which exposure duration was manipulated while all other variables were kept constant are rather inconsistent in showing an effect of presentation time on the pattern of visual-field asymmetries. Rizzolatti and Buchtel (1977) observed an increase in LVF superiority with a decrease in exposure from 100 to 20ms, but only in their male subjects. Sergent (1982c), testing only male subjects, obtained an interaction of visual field and exposure in a male/female categorization task, showing a greater improvement of RVF performance with an increase in exposure duration. However, Hellige and his colleagues (Hellige et al., 1984; Hellige & Jonnson, 1984) found no such interaction when exposure was manipulated from 10 to 100 ms or from 20 to 200 ms. Hellige and Jonnson (1984) tentatively explained this discrepancy by differences in the mode of stimulus presentation. In contrast to other studies, Hellige's experiments are conducted with a black pre- and post-exposure field, a procedure that enhances visible persistence after stimulus offset. Indeed, persistence lengthens with decrease in exposure duration (Bowling & Lovegrove, 1980), and the longer integration time of high frequencies makes the "iconic" image essentially a function of the high frequencies (Bowling, Lovegrove, & Mapperson, 1979; Di Lollo & Woods, 1981). An absence of backward mask may thus not prevent the high frequencies from being resolved even when exposure duration is very brief. Moreover, Hellige et al. (1984) used a between-subject design, whereas the reduction from 200 to 20 ms exposure in Hellige and Jonnson's (1984) within-subject study did not result in longer RT, in contrast to Sergent's results and to psychophysical findings (e.g., Kaswan & Young, 1965). This may indicate that the decrease in exposure duration in Hellige and Jonnson's (1984) experiment was not effective in reducing the level of stimulus energy, possibly because of the high luminance of the display.

Although the effect of reduction in presentation time is usually discussed in terms of stimulus degradation (e.g., Hellige, in preparation) or low-pass filtering (Sergent, 1984c), it may alternatively, or additionally, be the brief availability of sensory traces, reducing the number of processing iterations, that accounts for lower performance and differential efficiency of the cerebral hemispheres under some circumstances. There is, however, no definitive evidence for this suggestion which is supported by the finding (Sergent, 1982c, Experiment 3) that variations in exposure duration may differentially affect processing in the two hemispheres over and above variations in stimulus energy, but not by the null results of Hellige and Jonnson (1984). It seems, nonetheless, that an effect of stimulus duration on visual-field asymmetries emerges only if the manipulation of this variable is made within the critical duration over which the time-intensity reciprocity holds.

The influence of stimulus energy has also been investigated with a direct manipulation of luminance in a within-subject design (Sergent, 1982b). The results showed a relative improvement of performance in RVF presentation with enhanced intensity, suggesting that the LH benefits more than the RH from increase in stimulus energy.

Another procedural variable whose manipulation has resulted in an interaction with the visual fields is retinal eccentricity. Hellige et al. (1984; see also Wong, 1982) found that an initial LVF superiority in a visual- or memory-search task was eliminated with an increase in retinal eccentricity when the stimulus set comprised only male faces. Thus degradation resulting from projecting the faces in areas of reduced acuity was relatively more detrimental to RH than to LH processing. Hellige et al. (1984) replicated this finding when degradation was achieved by embedding a face in a matrix of dots that partially masked the face.

This pattern of results is opposite that found by Hellige (1976), Wong (1982), and Sergent (1983a) with letters as stimuli, and also opposite that of Hellige et al. (1984) when the task was a male/female categorization. Because of the critical role of task factors in Hellige et al.'s (1984) study, it is further discussed in the next section.

Conclusion.   Although few experiments have so far been designed to investigate the pattern of visual-field asymmetries in face perception as a function of the particular viewing conditions, there is sufficient evidence to suggest that the procedural variables are not without influence on the emergence and the pattern of hemisphere asymmetry. A direct implication is that one must be very careful in interpreting the results of tachistoscopic studies, and ensure that the findings would hold under different viewing conditions before attributing to one particular hemisphere some type of dominance or specialization in a given function.

In the current state of research on face perception, presentation time, retinal eccentricity, and stimulus size are always reported, while luminance seldom is, and contrast never. Yet, the last two variables are at least as important as the first three in determining the quality of the percept, and thus the representation of information in the brain, which is crucial for the explanation of results given the correlation between brightness discrimination and facial recognition (Benton & Gordon, 1971). The relatively higher proportion of RVF superiority with line-drawings than with photographs of real faces may be due, at least in part, to the higher contrast of the former than the latter. On the other hand, the finding by Hellige et al. (1984) of opposite patterns of hemifield superiority depending on whether the task is a male-face recognition with male faces as non-targets or a male/female categorization indicates that the viewing conditions are but one of the factors that influence hemispheric processing. As pointed out by Sergent and Bindra (1981), the nature of the task influences the type of information that must be processed, and performance must also be evaluated as a function of task requirements.

Role of Task Demands

The choice of specific tasks to examine the differential involvement of the cerebral hemispheres in processing faces is not without implications for the particular operations that must be carried out. Although nearly all experiments with brain-damaged patients have involved some type of matching, research with normals has been more diversified in the nature of the tasks that were required from the subjects. Yet this diversity is not always acknowledged when discussing the underlying operations, and the terminology itself is sometimes confusing (see Sergent & Bindra, 1981).

Four main types of task may be distinguished: *perceptual discrimination* (or simultaneous matching), *recognition* (or delayed matching), *categorization* (classification into a predetermined category), and *identification* (categorization of a face as that of a specific individual). These tasks differ from one another on several aspects, such as the particular mode of stimulus presentation, the nature of the response, the stimulus characteristics that need to be processed, the use of known or unknown faces, and the processing operations that must be engaged. For example, a matching task necessarily requires the presentation, either simultaneously or successively, of a target and a test face, whereas a categorization (of which an identification is the finest level) involves the presentation of a single face. Matching tasks, as well as some categorization tasks, require only one of two responses on each trial (e.g., same/different, face/non-face, male/female), whereas in identification tasks the response has to be constructed from the encoded facial features in order to access the individuality of the face, which may necessitate a finer processing of the incoming information (cf. Fiorentini et al., 1983). Identification also requires the presentation of known faces, whereas other tasks can be conducted with unknown faces as well, and there are indications that known and unknown faces may be recognized on the basis of different stimulus attributes (Ellis, Shepherd, & Davies, 1979).

In addition to these differences in task demands, a further complication arises from the type of dependent variable chosen to assess performance. Research on cognitive information processing typically is conducted with paradigms that aim at inducing some limitations on the processing organism. Response-accuracy measures are obtained under conditions of exposure that prevent the full encoding of the incoming information so as to produce an appreciable number of errors. Because the input is of less than optimal quality, the performance is state- or data-limited (Garner, 1970; Norman & Bobrow, 1975). It is in fact in the nature of any lateral tachistoscopic experiment to be state-limited, but this limitation can be considerably increased when the critical variable is response accuracy. Conversely, response-latency measures are obtained under conditions of minimal stimulus degradation and timed response. The emphasis is then put on response speed such that not enough processing capacity can be allocated to the task, making the performance resource-limited (Norman & Bobrow, 1975), in addition to the inherent state-limitation.

Although it usually is assumed that the results of these two paradigms converge on the same set of psychological processes, it is likely that this assumption is false. As suggested by Stanovitch (1979) and by Santee and Egeth (1982), performance is achieved by processing partial information in state-limited but not in resource-limited conditions. Very little investigation has been devoted to this issue in neuropsychological research, but this difference may have important implications for understanding the underlying processes. There are several examples of discrepancy between the patterns of results in latency and accuracy within the same experiment (e.g., Jonnson & Hellige, 1984; Proudfoot, 1982), and it often is the case that no hemifield difference in accuracy obtains in RT experiments (e.g., Rizzolatti et al., 1971; Moscovitch et al., 1976; Sergent, 1982a). It is therefore unlikely that hemifield asymmetries observed with these two paradigms have the same basis and tap similar stages in information processing. For instance, the two hemispheres may not be equally competent at processing degraded or partial visuospatial information, and the relative superiority of one hemisphere over the other may reflect this differential capacity rather than a specializaton in the processing of faces per se. In addition, all errors are not equivalent, and they may be due to different factors (e.g., temporary inattention, partial encoding of incoming information, decay of stored information, high similarity between the comparison stimuli) that have not yet been systematically studied.

Because of all these potential differences in terms of task demands between studies, it may not be surprising that there is as yet no conclusive evidence that one hemisphere is superior to the other in any of the main tasks, and the following presents a brief review of typical findings.

Simultaneous Matching. Simultaneous matching, or perceptual discrimination, involves the presentation of two faces that subjects must compare in terms of their sameness or difference. Few studies have used this paradigm, and they all employed RT as dependent variable. Although some authors have labelled their study an immediate matching task, their procedure implied at least .5 sec interval between the presentation of the target and test faces (e.g., Hannay & Rogers, 1979; Hilliard, 1973). Moscovitch et al. (1976) have shown that, as interstimulus interval increases beyond 100 ms, an initial absence of hemifield difference shifts to a LVF superiority.

In the four perceptual discrimination studies reported so far (Moscovitch et al., 1976; Sergent, 1982a, 1984b; St. John, 1981), all three possible outcomes (LVF, RVF, or absence of, superiority) have been found. St. John found a LVF advantage in three experiments using a 180-ms exposure with photographs of real faces presented from different angles. Sergent found a RVF advantage with pairs of line-drawing faces differing in one feature and presented for 250 ms, but not with more dissimilar pairs. Moscovitch et al. presented Identikit faces, differing in all their features, for 300 ms, and found no visual-field asymmetry. Because task demands were basically the same in these experiments, there may be no other possible explanation of these discrepancies than the differences in viewing conditions and stimuli between the studies. The RVF advantage obtained by Sergent may result from the use of a difficult task (where the difficulty is not due to degradation but to high inter-stimulus similarity), in conjunction with the presentation of highly contrasted faces for a relatively long duration, thus allowing a high level of resolution that may be necessary for the LH to operate efficiently. Moscovitch et al. also used line drawings, but of very dissimilar faces, while St. John presented black-and-white faces, thus lower contrast stimuli. The emergence of a LVF advantage in St. John's study may result from shorter exposure duration, lower luminance, and lower contrast of the faces than in the other experiments, along with the presentation of faces seen from different angles. These four studies illustrate the contribution of the various procedural variables to a given pattern of hemifield asymmetry, and the effects of these variables seem to combine in determining the relative efficiency of the cerebral hemispheres at processing faces. We are still far from understanding the level at which these variables influence processing, but the fact that those variables that affect the characteristics of the incoming information also affect the final outcome suggests that the particular representation of the faces in the brain may determine, at least in part, the processing efficiency of the cerebral hemispheres. A simultaneous matching RT task seems to be specially relevant in this respect, because the use of unfamiliar faces and timed response may impose a comparison between stimuli only in terms of their physical characteristics, which makes it essentially free of other cognitive factors that could differentially influence hemisphere processing.

Delayed Matching.   Recognition, or delayed matching, studies constitute the main body of research on face perception in normals. They require subjects to match, by a vocal or manual response, or by pointing, the memorized target with a test face presented either alone or among distractors. Usually unfamiliar faces are used, but even when known faces are presented (e.g., Leehey & Cahn, 1979; Young, 1984), subjects do not need identify the face and may recognize it without knowing whose face it is. Experiments comparing performance on recognition and identification of known faces under identical viewing conditions (e.g., Leehey & Cahn, 1979) show that subjects are able to recognize twice as many faces as they can identify.

Recognition experiments imply a delay between target and test presentation, and a different procedure is usually employed depending on whether latency or accuracy is the dependent variable. Subjects are required to memorize few targets when RT is the dependent variable, whereas accuracy studies most often involve the presentation of a larger number of targets appearing only once in each visual field (the use of very few, repeatedly presented, targets in accuracy studies may yield less robust findings, see Ross & Turkewitz, 1982, this volume).

Studies in which targets are learned prior to the experimental session have resulted in patterns of hemifield asymmetry similar to those outlined earlier for simultaneous matching task. Because few targets are used and because subjects are given ample time to study and memorize them, a fairly clear representation of the targets can then be achieved. Highly similar line-drawing faces are thus processed faster in RVF than in LVF presentations whereas more dissimilar faces, as well as black-and-white photographs result in faster match when presented in the LVF than the RVF (Fairweather et al., 1982; Moscovitch et al., 1976; Patterson & Bradshaw, 1975; Rizzolatti & Buchtel, 1977; Rizzolatti et al., 1971).

There is, however, one important exception to this general pattern, and it may be instructive to consider it in more detail. Hellige et al. (1984), using five photographs of male faces as targets and five other photographs of males as non-targets, found that degradation (induced either by increased retinal eccentricity or by masking) was more detrimental in LVF than RVF presentations. This finding departs from the frequent observation that stimulus degradation affects more LH than RH processing, and is difficult to reconcile with the view that the RH operates more efficiently than the LH on low-frequency contents of the face (Sergent, 1983b). One explanation put forward by Hellige et al. considered the degree of similarity among the faces of the stimulus set, because when targets and non-targets were more dissimilar (male/female instead of male/male), the opposite pattern of interaction prevailed, as already found by Sergent (1982c). They suggested that, if faces are fairly similar, fine details must be processed for efficient recognition, and the hemisphere the more competent at doing so will be the less affected when they are difficult to extract. That is, as long as the main differences between faces can be easily perceived, the RH may prove efficient at comparing them, but when these differences are less salient, its efficiency would decrease. Such an interpretation is consistent with the suggestion of a differential hemisphere sensitivity to spatial frequencies, and with the view that both the information available and required for processing must be considered (Sergent, 1983b). However, its validity depends on the extent of the filtering produced by an increase in retinal eccentricity. If the 9-degree displacement used by Hellige et al. filters out both intermediate and high frequencies, their finding would suggest relatively greater capacity of the LH than the RH to perform difficult visuospatial operations independent of the spatial-frequency content of the stimulus, which would disconfirm Sergent's (1983b) hypothesis. This illustrates the need for more direct manipulation of the spatial-frequency contents in order to evaluate the validity of this hypothesis.

The study by Hellige et al. (1984) raises one further important question with respect to recognition studies. As they pointed out, their results do not tell whether the effects of their manipulation was on perceptual processes or memory processes. Drawing on experiments by O'Boyle (1982) and by Wong (1982), based on Sternberg's memory-search paradigm, Hellige et al. suggested that degradation influences the encoding rather than the comparison stage. This implies that the comparison of the target and test faces was not based on visual traces of the faces in these experiments, and that subjects may have memorized the targets using some type of referent that was not influenced by the perceptual quality of the incoming information. If comparisons were based only on visual traces, the comparison time should lengthen with reduced quality of the input.

The fact that it did not raises the question of the nature of the information on which comparisons were performed. Hellige et al.'s (1984) experiments thus open the way to further investigation of two important issues: one concerns the effects of the conjunction of state- and process-limitations on hemisphere processing efficiency within the same experiment and directly bears on a spatial-frequency hypothesis of hemisphere processing asymmetry; in other words, how do the hemispheres behave when essentially low frequencies are available whereas performance on the task normally benefits from the processing of intermediate and high frequencies? The other issue concerns the respective contribution of perceptual and memory operations to patterns of hemifield asymmetry.

Recognition accuracy studies have been more consistent in their outcomes. Since the first such study by Hilliard (1973), a LVF superiority has prevailed under a variety of procedural conditions (see Davidoff, 1982; Sergent & Bindra, 1981). Typically, such experiments are conducted with poor viewing conditions and delay between target and test presentations. The net result of these manipulations is a partial encoding of the incoming information (Stanovitch, 1979) and a decay of the stored representation that seems to affect the less salient parts (Walker-Smith, 1978). Sergent and Bindra (1981) suggested that, in such conditions, what is tested may not be primarily the capacity of the hemispheres to process faces but more fundamentally their ability to deal with degraded information. Such a suggestion, however, did not take into account findings from experiments in which both upright and inverted faces are presented under the same viewing conditions in a within-subject design. Although some studies found a LVF superiority for both orientations (Bradshaw, Taylor, Patterson, & Nettleton, 1980; Ellis & Shepherd, 1975), Young (1984; see also Young & Bion, 1981) found hemifield asymmetry only for upright faces, which suggests that something related to the processing of faces per se must contribute to the LVF superiority with upright faces. Yet, the nature of such a face processor subserved by the RH remains to be specified because when commissurotomized patients are presented with faces for a long duration (e.g., Sperry, Zaidel, & Zaidel, 1979; Zaidel, 1983) or when normal subjects are presented with high quality visual information (Sergent, 1984b), the LH appears at least as competent as the RH at processing faces.

In addition, it would be necessary to determine the nature of the different processes underlying the perception of upright and inverted faces. Sergent (1984a) found that upright faces were processed on the basis of their configuration whereas inverted faces were compared essentially on the basis of their component features. Although such a finding could suggest that Young's results reflect a hemisphere difference in terms of holistic/analytic processing dichotomy, Sergent (1984b) also found that both hemispheres were capable of configural processing of faces. A possible explanation would suggest that a face schema that assists the perception of faces is bilaterally represented and allows configural processing of normally oriented faces. The processing of inverted faces may not benefit from such a schema and would require attending to local characteristics of the face that are conveyed by the higher spatial frequencies, and thus may not be as efficiently processed by the RH. More research is certainly needed to examine this issue which should prove informative for the specification of underlying processes.

Categorization Tasks.   Experiments examining hemifield asymmetry in the categorization of faces into male and female have so far consistently shown shifts in visual field advantage as a function of the quality of the input (Hellige et al., 1984; Sergent, 1982b, 1982c), making the finding by Jones (1980) of a RVF advantage for male subjects with a 200-ms exposure likely the result of the use of long exposure rather than of an assumed verbal mediation of the categorization process.

Identification of known faces involves a finer categorization than judging the sex of a face, relies on different mechanisms than recognizing unknown faces (Ellis et al., 1979), and benefits from the processing of intermediate to high spatial frequencies (Fiorentini et al., 1983). Except for one recent study by Sergent and Switkes (1984), all identification tasks have involved accuracy measures of performance.

The first study, by Marzi and Berlucchi (1977), yielded a RVF advantage, using a 400-ms exposure and faces of famous persons not seen by the subjects prior to the experiment. An opposite pattern of hemifield asymmetry was found by Leehey and Cahn (1979) and by Young and Bion (1981), with faces of colleagues or public figures, and with unilateral or bilateral presentation at 60 or 150 ms. Young and Bion found the LVF advantage only when subjects were given in advance the names of the individuals whose faces were to be presented; subjects not told in advance of the names, a procedure similar to that used by Marzi and Berlucchi (1977), displayed no hemifield asymmetry, which led Young and Bion to suggest that the necessary condition for obtaining a LVF superiority for the processing of known faces is that the subjects should know which faces to expect. Although this factor could have contributed to the different outcome of Marzi and Berlucchi's study, it is likely not a sufficient explanation (see following). An alternative explanation may come from Marzi and Berlucchi's use of long, and blocked, unilateral presentation, which may have benefited LH more than RH processing by allowing high stimulus energy.

Sergent and Switkes (1984) examined this issue further with response latency as the dependent variable so as to insure a high level of accuracy. The stimuli were 16 faces of members (professors, secretaries, graduate students, known to the subjects for at least 3 years) of the same department as the 10 subjects, presented for 100 ms at 15-mL luminance, and centered 2.7 deg from fixation. In the first experiment, high-contrast and high-resolution black-and-white faces were presented (see face a in Fig. 5.1) in three tasks run on consecutive days: a timed verbal identification (subjects calling out the name of the face), a manual membership categorization (whether the face was that of an academic or a non-academic member), and a manual male/female categorization. Because the faces were matched for age and sex, it can be asssumed that the membership categorization could be achieved only if the face was identified, as there is no physical cue indicating whether a face is that of professor or not. This task thus offered the possibility to investigate identification without naming. Exactly the same procedural conditions prevailed in the three tasks, and subjects were given 54 practice trials before each experimental session of 288 trials, and therefore knew which faces would be presented. A significant RVF superiority prevailed in the verbal identification and the membership categorization, whereas the male/female categorization yielded a non-significant LVF advantage. Error rates were less than 3% in all tasks. The results thus indicate a greater efficiency of the LH at identifying known faces, irrespective of whether the response was verbal or manual (cf. Umiltà, Brizzolara, Tabossi, & Fairweather, 1978). The main difference with previous studies is the very high accuracy, indicating that the faces were clearly encoded. The suggestion by Fiorentini et al. (1983) that identification benefits from the processing of high spatial frequencies may then support the view that the LH superiority in identifying known faces involves such a processing, provided the viewing conditions allow the extraction of these high frequencies that are inherently more vulnerable to degradation.

In a second experiment, the same tasks and procedures were again used, but two versions of each face were now presented, mixed within an experimental session: a broad-pass (0–32 c/d) face and a low-pass face (0–2 c/d, see face e in Fig. 5.2). The results are shown in Fig. 5.3 for each task as a function of visual field and type of face. Performance on broad-pass faces replicated the pattern of hemifield asymmetries obtained in the first experiment. By contrast, low-pass faces yielded longer latencies overall, and were processed significantly faster in LVF than RVF presentations in each of the tasks. These results confirm the greater capacity of the RH, compared to the LH, to operate on low-frequency contents of faces, and this differential hemispheric sensitivity to spatial frequencies may be one of the factors contributing to the usual RH superiority when the viewing conditions are such as to prevent the extraction of high spatial frequencies or when performance does not benefit from processing these spatial frequencies (see Sergent, 1985, for further discussion).

CONCLUSION

Hemifield asymmetries in processing faces are the result of a considerable number of factors, some of which pertaining to the procedural variables that must be manipulated in experimental investigations. A comprehensive account of all observed asymmetries is impossible at the moment, and the complexity of the problem never stops increasing with the accumulation of data. The now solid

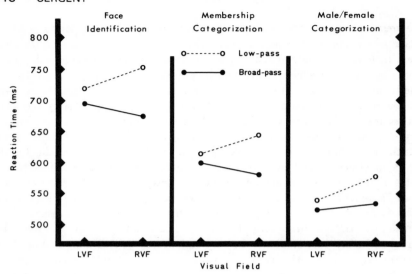

FIG. 5.3 Latencies (in ms), averaged across subjects, as a function of spatial-frequency content and visual field of presentation, to process faces in the verbal identification, the membership categorization, and the male/female categorization.

evidence that both hemispheres are competent at processing faces has shifted the attention of researchers toward specifying the nature of the contribution of the two hemispheres instead of simply trying to demonstrate hemispheric specialization in the processing of faces.

The three main categories of variables interact in complex ways to determine the final outcome. No variable as such is sufficient to account for a given pattern of results, and any finding is overdetermined by a multitude of factors whose effects on the processing organism combine to make one hemisphere more efficient than the other. Even variables that are not the object of examination in a study contribute to the outcome by creating specific conditions under which processing is taking place. Findings have been interpreted in this chapter in the context of the particular representations that can be constructed in the brain depending of procedural conditions, as a function of the requirements of the task expressed in terms of the characteristics that need to be processed. This approach offers a unitary perspective on the numerous variables that affect processing, and it frames our understanding of hemispheric asymmetries not only in terms consonant with the neural properties of cerebral operations but also with the use of a metric compatible with early visual processing and relevant in the description of higher cognitive functions (e.g., Gervais et al., 1984). Although both hemispheres are capable of processing faces, they may not be equally efficient depending on the quality of information representations and on the particular physical characteristics that carry the information relevant for the task. The RH may prove better adept than the LH when essentially low frequencies are available or are adequate for processing, while the contribution of the LH may become apparent when the processing of higher frequencies is necessary for efficient performance. However, there are limitations to this approach which cannot account for variations in visual field asymmetries when all viewing conditions are kept unchanged, unless one knows the stimulus characteristics that are relevant to achieve optimal performance in different tasks. In addition, the specification of the spatial-frequency contents that can be extracted under particular experimental conditions is quite approximative. For example, an exposure duration of 20 ms may yield a percept of higher quality than an exposure of 150 ms depending on the luminance of the display and the pre- and posttest field, as well as on the contrast of the stimuli, two factors that are most often uncontrolled in lateral tachistoscopic experiments, which makes it difficult to draw solid conclusions on the basis of indirect manipulation of spatial frequencies. Nonetheless, recent experiments that have directly manipulated the spatial-frequency contents of the stimuli (Hellige, 1984; Keegan, 1981; Kitterle, personal communication, March 3, 1985; Sergent & Switkes, 1984), irrespective of the procedural variables, have supported the suggestion of a differential hemispheric sensitivity to spatial frequencies and have encouraged the pursuit of the investigation of hemisphere functional asymmetry along these lines.

ACKNOWLEDGMENT

This chapter was supported by grants from the Fonds de la recherche en santé du Québec and the Natural Sciences and Engineering Research Council of Canada.

REFERENCES

Allen, M. (1983). Models of hemispheric specialization. *Psychological Bulletin, 93*, 73–104.

Benton, A. L., & Gordon, M. C. (1971). Correlates of facial recognition. *Transactions of the American Neurological Association, 96*, 91–96.

Benton, A. L., & Van Allen, M. W. (1968). Impairment in facial recognition in patients with cerebral disease. *Cortex, 4*, 344–358.

Bertelson, P., Van Haelen, H., & Morais, J. (1979). Left hemifield superiority and the extraction of physiognomic invariants. In I. Steele-Russell, M. Van Hof, & G. Berlucchi (Eds.), *Structure and function of the cerebral commissures*. London: Macmillan.

Bower, G. H., & Karlin, M. B. (1974). Depth of processing pictures of faces and recognition memory. *Journal of Experimental Psychology, 103*, 751–757.

Bowling, A., & Lovegrove, W. (1980). The effect of stimulus duration on the persistence of gratings. *Perception and Psychophysics, 27*, 574–578.

Bowling, A., Lovegrove, W., & Mapperson, B. (1979). The effect of spatial frequency and contrast on visual persistence. *Perception, 8*, 529–539.

Bradshaw, J. L., Taylor, M. J. Patterson, K., & Nettleton, N. C. (1980). Upright and inverted faces, and housefronts, in the two visual fields: A right and a left hemisphere contribution. *Journal of Clinical Neuropsychology, 2,* 245–257.

Breitmeyer, B., & Ganz, L. (1977). Temporal studies with flashed gratings: Inferences about human transient and sustained channels. *Vision Research, 17,* 861–865.

Bruce, V. (1983). Recognizing faces. *Philosophical Transactions of the Royal Society, London, Series, B, 302,* 423–436.

Brunswik, E. (1956). *Perception and the representation design of psychological experiments.* (2nd ed.). Berkeley: University of California Press.

Bryden, M. P. (1965). Tachistoscopic recognition, handedness, and cerebral dominance. *Neuropsychologia, 3,* 1–8.

Davidoff, J. (1982). Studies with non-verbal stimuli. In J. G. Beaumont (Ed.), *Divided visual field studies of cerebral organization.* London: Academic Press.

De Renzi, E., & Spinnler, H. (1966). Facial recognition in brain-damaged patients: An experimental approach. *Cortex, 16,* 634–642.

De Valois, R., & De Valois, K. (1980). Spatial vision. *Annual Review of Psychology, 31,* 117–153.

Di Lollo, V., & Woods, E. (1981). Duration of visible persistence in relation to range of spatial frequencies. *Journal of Experimental Psychology: Human Perception and Performance, 7,* 754–769.

Ellis, H., Shepherd, J., & Davies, G. (1979). Identification of familiar and unfamiliar faces from internal and external features: Some implications for theories of face recognition. *Perception, 9,* 431–439.

Ellis, H. D. (1981). Theories of face recognition. In G. Davies, H. Ellis, & J. Shepherd (Eds.), *Perceiving and remembering faces.* London: Academic Press.

Ellis, H. D. (1983). The role of the right hemisphere in face perception. In A. W. Young (Ed.), *Functions of the right cerebral hemisphere.* London: Academic Press.

Ellis, H. D., & Shepherd, J. (1975). Recognition of upright and inverted faces presented in the left and the right visual fields. *Cortex, 11,* 3–7.

Eriksen, C. W., & Schultz, D. W. (1978). Temporal factors in visual information processing. In J. Requin (Ed.), *Attention and performance, VII.* Hillsdale, NJ: Lawrence Erlbaum Associates.

Fairweather, H., Brizzolara, D., Tabossi, P., & Umiltà, C. (1982). Functional cerebral lateralization: Dichotomy or plurality? *Cortex, 18,* 51–66.

Fiorentini, A., Maffei, L., & Sandini, G. (1983). The role of high spatial frequencies in face perception. *Perception, 12,* 195–201.

Flavell, J., & Draguns, J. (1957). A microgenetic approach to perception and thought. *Psychological Bulletin, 54,* 197–217.

Fodor, J. (1983). *The modularity of mind: An essay on faculty psychology.* Cambridge, MA: MIT Press.

Freedman, J., & Haber, R. N. (1974). One reason why we rarely forget a face. *Bulletin of the Psychonomic Society, 3,* 107–109.

Freeman, J. (1980). *Cerebral asymmetries in the processing of faces.* Unpublished doctoral dissertation, University of Aberdeen.

Galper, R. E., & Costa, L. (1980). Hemispheric superiority for recognizing faces depends upon how they are learned. *Cortex, 16,* 21–38.

Garner, W. R. (1970). The stimulus in information processing. *American Psychologist, 25,* 350–358.

Geffen, G., Bradshaw, J., & Wallace, G. (1971). Interhemispheric effects on reaction time to verbal and nonverbal visual stimuli. *Journal of Experimental Psychology, 87,* 415–422.

Gervais, M. J., Harvey, L. O., & Roberts, J. O. (1984). Identification confusions among letters of the alphabet. *Journal of Experimental Psychology: Human Perception and Performance, 10,* 655–666.

Gibson, J. J. (1950). *The perception of the visual world.* Boston: Houghton Mifflin.

Ginsburg, A. (1978). *Visual information processing based on spatial filters constrained by biological data.* (Report No. 78–129). Wright-Patterson Air Base, OH: Aerospace Medical Research Laboratory.

Goldstein, A. G., & Chance, J. E. (1980). Memory for faces and schema theory. *Journal of Psychology, 105,* 47–59.

Hannay, H. J., & Rogers, J. P. (1979). Individual differences and asymmetry effects in memory for unfamiliar faces. *Cortex, 15,* 257–267.

Harmon, L. (1973). The recognition of faces. *Scientific American, 229,* 70–82.

Harvey, J. O., & Gervais, M. J. (1978). Visual texture perception and Fourier analysis. *Perception and Psychophysics, 24,* 534–542.

Harwerth, R. S., & Levi, D. M. (1978). Reaction time as a measure of suprathreshold grating detection. *Vision Research, 18,* 1579–1586.

Hay, D. C. (1981). Asymmetries in face processing: Evidence for a right perceptual advantage. *Quarterly Journal of Experimental Psychology, 33A,* 267–274.

Hay, D. C., & Young, A. W. (1982). The human face. In A. Ellis (Ed.), *Normality and pathology in cognitive functions.* London: Academic Press.

Hécaen, H., Angelergues, R. (1962). Agnosia for faces (prosopagnosia). *Archives of Neurology, 7,* 92–100.

Hellige, J. B. (1976). Changes in same-different laterality patterns as a function of practice and stimulus quality. *Perception and Psychophysics, 20,* 267–273.

Hellige, J. B. (1984, June). *Perceptual quality and cerebral laterality.* Paper presented at the European Conference of the International Neuropsychological Society, Aachen, Germany.

Hellige, J. B. (in preparation). Visual laterality and hemisphere specialization: Methodological and theoretical considerations. In J. B. Sidowski (Ed.), *Conditioning, cognition, and methodology: Contemporary issues in experimental psychology.* Hillsdale, NJ: Lawrence Erlbaum Associates.

Hellige, J. B., Corwin, W. H., & Johnson, J.E. (1984). Effects of perceptual quality on the processing of human faces presented in the left and the right cerebral hemispheres. *Journal of Experimental Psychology: Human Perception and Performance, 10,* 90–107.

Hellige, J. B., & Jonnson, J. E. (1984). *Effects of stimulus duration on processing lateralized faces.* Manuscript submitted for publication.

Hilliard, R. D. (1973). Hemispheric laterality effects on a facial recognition task in normal subjects. *Cortex, 9,* 246–258.

Homa, D., Haver, B., & Schwartz, T. (1976). Perceptibility of schematic face stimuli: Evidence for a perceptual Gestalt. *Memory & Cognition, 4,* 178–185.

Jones, B. (1979). Lateral asymmetry in testing long-term memory for faces. *Cortex, 15,* 183–186.

Jones, B. (1980). Sex and handedness as factors in visual-field organization for a categorization task. *Journal of Experimental Psychology: Human Perception and Performance, 6,* 494–500.

Jonnson, J. E., & Hellige, J. B. (1984). *Lateralized effects of blurring: A test of the visual spatial frequency model.* Manuscript submitted for publication.

Kahneman, D. (1964). Temporal summation in an acuity task at different energy levels - A study of the determinants of summation. *Vision Research, 4,* 557–566.

Kaswan, J., & Young, S. (1965). Effects of luminance, exposure duration and task complexity on reaction time. *Journal of Experimental Psychology, 69,* 393–400.

Keegan, J. F. (1981, June). *Hemispheric frequency analysis: Facial recognition.* Paper presented at the European Conference of the International Neuropsychological Society, Bergen.

Kiersch, M., & Megibow, M. (1978). *Hemispheric asymmetry in the recognition of tachistoscopically presented photographs and line drawings.* Paper presented at the meeting of the Western Psychological Association, San Francisco.

Kimura, D. (1966). Dual functional asymmetry of the brain in visual perception. *Neuropsychologia, 4,* 275–285.

Klatsky, R. L., & Forrest, F. H. (1984). Recognizing familiar and unfamiliar faces. *Memory and Cognition, 14,* 60–70.

Klatsky, R. L., Martin, G. L., & Kane, R. A. (1982). Semantic interpretation effects on memory for faces. *Memory and Cognition, 10,* 195–206.

Kobayashi, S., Tazaki, Y., Ishikawa, S., & Mukono, K. (1981, August). *Spatial contrast sensitivity in cerebral lesion.* Paper presented at the 12th World Congress of Neurology, Kyoto, Japan.

Leehey, S., & Cahn, A. (1979). Lateral asymmetries in the recognition of words, familiar faces and unfamiliar faces. *Neuropsychologia, 17,* 619–635.

Leehey, S. C., Carey, S., Diamond, R., & Cahn, A. (1978). Upright and inverted faces: The right hemisphere knows the difference. *Cortex, 14,* 411–419.

Levine, S., Banich, M., & Koch-Weser, M. (1984). Variations in patterns of lateral asymmetry among dextrals. *Brain and Cognition, 3,* 317–334.

Levy, J. (1983). Individual differences in cerebral hemispheric asymmetry: Theoretical and methodological considerations. In J. B. Hellige (Ed.), *Cerebral hemisphere asymmetry: Method, theory, and application.* New York: Praeger.

Marr, D. (1982). *Vision.* San Francisco: Freeman.

Marzi, C., & Berlucchi, G. (1977). Right visual field superiority for accuracy of recognition of famous faces in normals. *Neuropsychologia, 15,* 751–756.

Matthews, M. L. (1978). Discrimination of Identikit constructions of faces: Evidence for a dual processing strategy. *Perception and Psychophysics, 23,* 153–161.

McKelvie, S. J. (1973). The meaningfulness and meaning of schematic faces. *Perception and Psychophysics, 14,* 343–348.

Milner, B. (1968). Visual recognition and recall after right temporal lobe excision in man. *Neuropsychologia, 6,* 191–209.

Moscovitch, M., Scullion, D., & Christie, D. (1976). Early vs. late stages of processing and their relation to functional hemispheric asymmetries in face recognition. *Journal of Experimental Psychology: Human Perception and Performance, 2,* 401–416.

Newcombe, F. (1969). *Missile wounds of the brain: A study of psychological deficits.* Oxford: Oxford University Press.

Norman, D., & Bobrow, D. (1975). On data-limited and resource-limited processes. *Cognitive Psychology, 7,* 44–64.

O'Boyle, M. W. (1982). *Hemispheric asymmetry in memory search for four-letter names and human faces.* Unpublished doctoral dissertation, University of Southern California, Los Angeles.

Patterson, K., & Baddeley, A. (1977). When face recognition fails. *Journal of Experimental Psychology: Human Learning and Memory, 3,* 406–417.

Patterson, K., & Bradshaw, J. (1975). Differential hemispheric mediation of nonverbal visual stimuli. *Journal of Experimental Psychology: Human Perception and Performance, 1,* 246–252.

Proudfoot, R. E. (1982). Hemispheric asymmetry for face recognition: Some effects of visual masking, hemiretinal stimulation and learning task. *Neuropsychologia, 20,* 129–144.

Proudfoot, R. E. (1983). Hemispheric asymmetry for face recognition: Cognitive style and the "crossover" effect. *Cortex, 19,* 31–41.

Rhodes, G. (1984). *Lateralized processes in face recognition.* Manuscript submitted for publication.

Riggs, L. A. (1971). Visual acuity. In J. W. Kling & L. A. Riggs (Eds.), *Experimental psychology.* New York: Holt, Rinehart & Winston.

Rizzolatti, G., & Buchtel, H. (1977). Hemispheric superiority in reaction time to faces: A sex difference. *Cortex, 13,* 300–305.

Rizzolatti, G., Umiltà, C., & Berlucchi, G. (1970). Demostrazione di differenze funzionali fra gli emisferi cerebrali dell'uomo normale per mezzo della tecnica dei tempi di reazione. *Archiva Fisiologica, 68,* 96–97.

Rizzolatti, G., Umiltà, C., & Berlucchi, G. (1971). Opposite superiorities of the left and the right cerebral hemispheres in discriminative reaction time to physiognomical and alphabetical material. *Brain, 94,* 431–442.

Ross, P., & Turkewitz, G. (1982). Changes in hemispheric advantage in processing facial information with increasing stimulus familiarization. *Cortex, 18,* 489–499.

Santee, J. L., & Egeth, H. E. (1982). Do reaction time and accuracy measure the same aspects of letter recognition? *Journal of Experimental Psychology: Human Perception and Performance, 8,* 489–501.

Sekuler, R. (1974). Spatial vision. *Annual Review of Psychology, 25,* 195–232.

Sergent, J. (1982a). About face: Left-hemisphere in processing physiognomies. *Journal of Experimental Psychology: Human Perception and Performance, 8,* 1–14.

Sergent, J. (1982b). Influence of luminance on hemispheric processing. *Bulletin of the Psychonomic Society, 20,* 221–223.

Sergent, J. (1982c). Methodological and theoretical consequences of variations in exposure duration in visual laterality studies. *Perception and Psychophysics, 31,* 451–461.

Sergent, J. (1983a). The effects of sensory limitations on hemispheric processing. *Canadian Journal of Psychology, 37,* 345–366.

Sergent, J. (1983b). Role of the input in visual hemispheric asymmetries. *Psychological Bulletin, 93,* 481–512.

Sergent, J. (1984a). An investigation into component and configural processes underlying face perception. *British Journal of Psychology, 75,* 221–242.

Sergent, J. (1984b). Configural processing of faces in the left and the right cerebral hemispheres. *Journal of Experimental Psychology: Human Perception and Performance, 10,* 554–572.

Sergent, J. (1984c). Inferences from unilateral brain damage about normal hemispheric functions in visual pattern recognition. *Psychological Bulletin, 96,* 99–115.

Sergent, J. (1985). Influence of task and input factors on hemispheric involvement in face processing. *Journal of Experimental Psychology: Human Perception and Performance, 11.*

Sergent, J. (in press-a). Face perception: Underlying processes and hemispheric contribution. In G. Denes, C. Semenza, P. Bisiacchi, & E. Andreewsky (Eds.), *Perspectives in cognitive neuropsychology.* Hillsdale, NJ: Lawrence Erlbaum Associates.

Sergent, J. (in press-b). Microgenesis of face perception. In H. D. Ellis, M. A. Jeeves, F. Newcombe, & A. W. Young (Eds.), *Aspects of face processing.* Dordrecht, The Netherlands: Martinus Nijhoff.

Sergent, J. (in preparation). *Feature salience in face processing.*

Sergent, J., & Bindra, D. (1981). Differential hemispheric processing of faces: Methodological considerations and reinterpretation. *Psychological Bulletin, 89,* 541–554.

Sergent, J., & Switkes, E. (1984). Differential hemispheric sensitivity to spatial-frequency components of visual patterns. *Society for Neuroscience Abstracts, 10,* 317.

Shepherd, J., Davies, G., & Ellis, H. (1981). Studies in cue saliency. In G. Davies, H. Ellis, & J. Shepherd (Eds.), *Perceiving and remembering faces.* London: Academic Press.

St. John, R. C. (1981). Lateral asymmetry in face perception. *Canadian Journal of Psychology, 35,* 213–223.

Sperry, R., Zaidel, E., & Zaidel, D. (1979). Self-recognition and social awareness in the disconnected minor hemisphere. *Neuropsychologia, 17,* 153–166.

Stanovitch, K. E. (1979). Studies of letter identification using qualitative error analysis: Effect of speed stress, tachistoscopic presentation, and word context. *Journal of Experimental Psychology: Human Perception and Performance, 5,* 713–733.

Tieger, T., & Ganz, L. (1979). Recognition of faces in the presence of two-dimensional sinusoidal masks. *Perception and Psychophysics, 26,* 163–167.

Toyama, J. S. (1975). *The effect of orientation on the recognition of faces: A reply to Yin.* Unpublished doctoral dissertation, University of Waterloo, Canada.

Tzavaras, A., Hécaen, H., & LeBras, H. (1970). Le problème de la spécificité de la reconnaissance du visage humain lors de lésions hémisphériques unilatérales. *Neuropsychologia, 8,* 403–416.

Umiltà, C., Brizzolara, D., Tabossi, P., & Fairweather, H. (1978). Factors affecting face recognition in the cerebral hemispheres: Familiarity and naming. In J. Requin (Ed.), *Attention and performance, VII.* New York: Academic Press.

Vernon, M. D. (1962). *The psychology of perception.* Baltimore, MD: Pelican Books.

Walker-Smith, G. J. (1978). The effects of delay and exposure duration in a face recognition task. *Perception and Psychophysics, 24,* 63–70.

Warrington, E., & James, M. (1967). An experimental investigation of facial recognition in patients with unilateral cerebral lesions. *Cortex, 3,* 317–326.

Winograd, E. (1976). Recognition memory for faces following nine different judgments. *Bulletin of the Psychonomic Society, 8,* 419–421.

Wong, T. M. (1982). *Effects of retinal eccentricity and visual field of probe presentation on memory search tasks of letters and faces.* Unpublished doctoral dissertation, University of Southern California, Los Angeles.

Yin, R. K. (1969). Looking at upside-down faces. *Journal of Experimental Psychology, 81,* 141–145.

Young, A. W. (1984). Right hemisphere superiority for recognizing famous faces from internal and external features. *British Journal of Psychology, 75,* 178–184.

Young, A. W., & Bion, P. J. (1980). Absence of any developmental trend in right hemisphere superiority for face recognition. *Cortex, 16,* 213–221.

Young, A. W., & Bion, P. J. (1981). Accuracy of naming laterally presented known faces by children and adults. *Cortex, 17,* 97–106.

Zaidel, E. (1983). Advances and retreat in laterality research. *Behavioral and Brain Sciences, 6,* 523–528.

A Micro and Macrodevelopmental View of the Nature of Changes in Complex Information Processing: A Consideration of Changes in Hemispheric Advantage During Familiarization

6

Phyllis Ross-Kossak
Gerald Turkewitz
Hunter College Department of Psychology and
Departments of Pediatrics and Psychiatry
A. Einstein College of Medicine

Until recently, the processing of faces was believed to be carried out more efficiently in the right than the left hemisphere. This belief was based on evidence from numerous studies of facial recognition involving patients with unilateral cortical lesions (e.g., De Renzi, Faglioni, & Spinnler, 1968; Milner, 1968; Yin, 1970), commissurotomy patients (Levy, Trevarthen, & Sperry, 1972), and normal adults and children (e.g., Geffen, Bradshaw, & Wallace, 1971; Rizzolatti, Umiltà, & Berlucchi, 1971). However, more recent evidence indicates that processing facial information may require bilateral involvement. Thus, Hamsher, Levin, and Benton (1979) found that both right-posterior brain-damaged patients and left-hemisphere-damaged aphasic patients with an impairment in language comprehension showed defective performance on a facial recognition task. In addition, autopsy findings from patients with prosopagnosia, who show an inability to identify familiar faces, indicated the presence of bilateral lesions (Meadows, 1974). Furthermore, in studies of normal individuals it has been shown that, under certain conditions, the processing of faces may be superior in the left than the right hemisphere (Patterson & Bradshaw, 1975; Sergent, 1982a).

125

Thus, the evidence from both normal subjects and brain-damaged patients makes it clear that facial recognition may predominantly involve either the right or left hemisphere, or both hemispheres equally, depending on task constraints.

One of the proposed dichotomies regarding processing differences in the two cerebral hemispheres, which may help to explain the involvement of both hemispheres in the processing of faces, is that the right hemisphere is specialized for holistic processing and the left hemisphere for analytic processing (e.g., Bogen, 1969). With regard to faces, this view would suggest that a right-hemisphere advantage would be based primarily on attention to configurational attributes such as the contour of the face or the spatial relationships among features, whereas a left-hemisphere advantage would be based on attention to one or more distinctive features such as the eyes or nose.

The results of a study that we have done (Ross & Turkewitz, 1981) in fact shows that individuals who differ with regard to the direction of hemispheric advantage on a facial recognition task also differ with regard to the nature of the information-processing strategy used. The performance of individuals who exhibited a right-hemisphere advantage in recognizing unaltered faces was more degraded by inversion of the faces than was that of individuals with a left-hemisphere advantage, whereas that of individuals with a left-hemisphere advantage was more degraded by omission of selected facial features than was the case for individuals with a right-hemisphere advantage. These results suggest that those subjects showing a right-hemisphere advantage recognized the faces on the basis of their organizational or gestalt qualities, whereas those showing a left-hemisphere advantage based their judgments on a more analytic process involving the recognition of individual distinctive features.

One of the obvious factors that may influence the strategy utilized in recognizing a face is the extent to which the face is familiar. A face that has been seen only once will be much more difficult to identify and may require a different type of processing than the face of a colleague or friend. That this is indeed the case is indicated by the results of several studies suggesting differences in the processing of familiar and unfamiliar faces. Thus, Warrington and James (1967) found that patients with damage to the right or left sides of the brain showed no association between their ability to recognize well-known faces and their ability to recognize unfamiliar faces, suggesting that the recognition of these two types of faces requires different modes of processing. Further evidence that there is no direct relationship between processing familiar and unfamiliar faces comes from studies of patients with prosopagnosia. Although such patients have difficulty in recognizing familiar faces, they often can perform adequately on tests requiring the identification of unfamiliar faces (Benton, 1980; Malone, Morris, Kay, & Levin, 1982). In addition, in a study of normal individuals by Ellis, Shepherd, and Davies (1979), it was found that faces of well-known public figures could be recognized better by subjects when given the central portion of the face with the periphery masked than when shown the periphery of the face with the central portion masked. In contrast, when photographs of unfamiliar faces were presented with either the central portion or the periphery masked, there was no difference in subjects' ability to recognize the faces in the two conditions. This again suggests that familiar and unfamiliar faces are not processed in the same manner.

Differences in the nature of the processing of faces with different degrees and histories of familiarization clearly suggest that there would be shifts in the nature of the processing during the course of increasing familiarity with a face. To the extent that differences in hemispheric advantage reflect differences in processing, examination of such advantages and their changes with increasing familiarity could help to identify the nature of processing of familiar and unfamiliar faces. Although there have been studies that have examined the hemispheric asymmetry shown for the recognition of unfamiliar faces (e.g., Geffen et al., 1971; Hilliard, 1973; Rizzolatti et al., 1971), experimentally familiarized faces (e.g., Marzi, Brizzolara, Rizzolatti, Umiltà, & Berlucchi, 1974), famous faces (e.g., Marzi & Berlucchi, 1977), and faces of colleagues or friends (e.g., Leehey & Cahn, 1979; Young & Bion, 1981), with the exception of the work that we have done, there have been only a small handful of studies that have so much as noted shifts in hemispheric advantages within an individual and only one of these (Reynolds & Jeeves, 1978) involved responses to faces. This chapter presents a model that we have proposed concerning changes in hemispheric advantage and mode of processing during the course of increasing familiarization to a small set of faces.

Our research has stemmed from and helped to elaborate the view that there are temporal shifts in hemispheric advantage in the processing of facial information. This position is based on the view that different modes of processing complex visual information are used at different phases in the organization of such processing. The processing of perceptual information is viewed as proceeding from relatively simple to highly complex with shifts in processing mode associated with transitions in the direction of hemispheric advantage.

The proposed sequence of shifts is parallel with and in part derived from a Gibsonian, Wernerian view of perceptual learning and development. Gibson (1969) proposes two stages of perceptual learning, going from a stage in which nondifferentiated processing is utilized to a stage involving the identification of distinctive features; Werner (1957) includes a third stage that involves an integrated mode of processing. Our view of the progression of perceptual processing is that in its initial stages processing is relatively undifferentiated and performed better in the right than the left hemisphere. Following this, there is an analytic stage in which distinctive features are identified and used for making discriminations; this is posited as a left-hemisphere function. Finally, a stage is reached in which material is processed in an integrated mode that is best served by the right hemisphere. One of the principal departures of this model from previous models is that in our view processing in the right hemisphere is not a unitary function, but rather that there is a dual mode of processing in this hemisphere, a preliminary mode and a more advanced mode, and that each of these is utilized at different stages of familiarity with complex perceptual information.

Although there is as yet no empirical evidence that directly demonstrates different types of processing at different stages of familiarization with faces, Sergent (1982a, 1982b, 1983) provides evidence that at early stages in familiarization with complex figures processing is principally with regard to low-frequency information. With regard to the processing of facial information, attention to such aspects would result in a percept that consisted of an external contour with points of contrast within the face. The dominant aspect of such a percept would be the relationship of the features to each other. In phenomenological terms, we have been conceptualizing this as essentially a fuzzy face. Our conception of the percept associated with the more advanced right-hemisphere mode of processing is one in which not only are contours and the relationship of parts to each other utilized, but one in which the parts themselves have distinctive attributes. Thus, in this phase the face still consists of a contour but now includes a unique nose, mouth, etc. all integrated into an organized facial percept. According to this model, in that the final right-hemisphere mode of processing incorporates aspects of facial information that would be best attained through the use of left-hemisphere processing, it would be more advanced than the analytic left-hemisphere mode.

It should be noted that our theory is in large part overlapping with the widely held view that the right hemisphere is specialized for processing global, holistic, simultaneous information, whereas the left hemisphere is more specialized for analytic and sequential information processing (Bever, Hurtig, & Handel, 1976; Cohen, 1973; Segalowitz, Bebout, & Lederman, 1979). In addition, our theory is consistent with a more recent view of hemispheric specialization proposed by Goldberg and Costa (1981), which postulates a shift from a right- to a left-hemisphere superiority as a function of increased experience or competence with various types of perceptual as well as linguistic material. According to this view, novel tasks for which no preexisting codes or "descriptive systems" exist are performed better in the right hemisphere; however, processing that relies on the utilization of either a preexisting descriptive system, such as language or musical notations, or on one that develops in an individual during the acquisition of a novel task, is performed better in the left hemisphere. We believe that this sequence is consistent with, and characterizes to some degree, the first two stages in our model of perceptual learning.

We have reported a number of studies in which subjects have indeed shown systematic shifts in their visual field advantage (VFA) and therefore presumably in their hemispheric advantage during the course of testing. Thus when we have presented subjects with a small set of totally unfamiliar faces, we have in general found, first, that some subjects initially display a left VFA advantage (LVFA) and others a right VFA (RVFA). Second, during the course of testing both types of individuals, i.e., those who start with a left and those who start with a right VFA, show shifts in the nature of their VFA. Finally the data indicate that the nature of these shifts is different for subjects starting testing with left or right VFA's. Because preliminary data suggested that only women showed the full pattern of changes in hemispheric advantage, most of our studies were conducted using women as subjects. Unless otherwise specified the data reported therefore only refer to women.

Shifts in hemispheric advantage were examined by tachistoscopically presenting subjects with photographs of four female faces. On each trial one of the faces was presented to the left or right of a central fixation point. The subject's task was to choose the face just seen from the four faces shown on a response sheet. Testing consisted of repeated 24 trial blocks. During each block each of the faces was presented three times to the right and three times to the left of the fixation point in random order. The data were analyzed in terms of error scores during each of these blocks. Such errors were converted to an index of visual field advantage that was computed as, # errors RVF − # errors LVF/# errors RVF + # errors LVF.

Although this index which ranges from + 1.00 to − 1.00 relates reasonably well to what is generally meant by a hemispheric advantage, i.e., in general, higher indexes reflect bigger hemispheric advantages, this is not the case when only very few errors are made. Thus, for example, when only one error is made, the index is plus or minus 1.00. However, it is not at all clear that conceptually the hemispheric advantage in this case is greater than for example when 10 errors are made on one side and one on the other, resulting in an index of less than 1.00, or that the advantage is equivalent to that when 10 errors are made on one side and none on the other, which also results in an index of 1.00. This problem albeit to a lesser extent persists when two errors are made and then declines precipitously with increasing error rates. For most analyses this distortion is of relatively little moment as most of the data we report is based on error rates considerably in excess of those where the index creates any problems.

Some of the analyses we report are concerned not with the directional index described but with an absolute index, i.e., the size of advantage independent of its direction. Such an index has conceptual utility but also has mathematical properties that could complicate interpretation of results obtained when it is utilized. Thus, when the error rate is greater than 2 but less than 50%, the mean index that would be randomly generated would fluctuate between .50 and .60, which although not ideal is certainly acceptable (a random index of .50 would obviously be ideal). The problem arises when the error rate exceeds 50%. In such cases the nature of the index results in the mean randomly generated index decreasing exponentially with increases in error rate. In that the notion of a hemispheric advantage would suggest that there is in fact only a small advantage when there are many errors on both left and right visual field presentations, this mathematical constraint is probably a reasonable reflection of the limitations inherent in the concept of hemispheric advantage.

Another index that has been utilized that does not have this mathematical constraint is one in which if accuracy is greater than 50% the index is, # correct RVF − # correct LVF/# errors RVF + # errors LVF and if accuracy is less than 50%, the index is, # correct RVF − # correct LVF/# correct RVF + # correct LVF (Marshall, Caplan, & Holmes, 1975). This index has the marked disadvanatage of violating the relationship between the index and any concept of hemispheric advantage. Thus, for example, if a subject made 9 correct responses on one side and 12 on the other (out of a possible 12 on each side), the index would be 1.00, the same as it would be if 12 correct responses were made on one side and zero on the other. Clearly these identical indices do not reflect comparable hemispheric advantages. Therefore, despite its recognized imperfections, we have utilized the previously described index throughout our presentation, because we believe it superior to available alternatives, at least for our purposes.

The data from two separate studies, in which we utilized this index, indicate that during the course of testing those subjects who exhibited an LVFA on the first block of trials decreased and then increased the magnitude of this advantage, resulting in significant quadratic components on trend analyses (Ross & Turkewitz, 1982; Ross-Kossak & Turkewitz, 1984). When testing was carried out for a long enough period, i.e., more than four blocks of trials, those subjects who began with an RVFA shifted to an LVFA resulting in a significant linear trend in the magnitude of their VFA (Ross-Kossak & Turkewitz, 1984). These data indicate that there are shifts in hemispheric advantage with increasing familiarization with faces. The shifts are such as to suggest movement towards a right-hemisphere advantage and in some cases two different stages at which there is such an advantage. To the extent that the hemispheric advantage and its shifts reflect shifts in processing modes, these data are consistent with our proposed model of changes in processing with increasing familiarization.

Although the data are clear in indicating changes in hemispheric advantage during the course of testing, there are at least two different bases on which these shifts could occur. First, it is likely that during the course of testing subjects become increasingly familiar with the specific faces with which they are tested, and that changes in VFA reflect this increased familiarity with the specific faces. Thus, Young and Bion (1981) found that when subjects were tested with a small set of faces they showed a clear LVFA, whereas when tested with a large set no advantage was obtained. In that there were an equal number of trials under the two conditions, the difference in hemispheric advantage probably stems from the difference in the degree of familiarity with the specific faces obtained in the two conditions. In addition to increasing familiarity with the specific faces, it is likely that during the course of testing subjects develop a general strategy for recognizing faces under the difficult and novel conditions imposed by typical tachistoscopic tests of facial recognition. That such is indeed the case is indicated by the results of a study (Turkewitz & Ross, 1983) in which we presented one set of faces for recognition early in testing and a second set subsequently. Despite the change in faces mid-way during testing, subjects showed the same pattern of shifts in VFA as did subjects experiencing increasing familiarization with a single set of faces. Thus, subjects with an initial right-hemisphere advantage again showed a decrease and then an increase in the magnitude of their right-hemisphere advantage across trials, whereas those with an initial left-hemisphere advantage again showed a shift to a right-hemisphere advantage across trials. These shifts occurred along with a decline in errors even immediately following the shift to the new set of faces. These results suggest that subjects are able to transfer an information-processing strategy developed for processing one set of faces to a new set of faces. Thus, subjects become familiar with a process for recognizing faces in addition to becoming familiar with the unique characteristics of a particular set of faces.

The shifts in hemispheric advantage that we have thus far been considering occur over a limited time period and so can be considered a form of micro-development. The basis for our position concerning changes in processing is however based upon broader principles of perceptual development. On the basis of the proposed model of stages in the development of processing facial infor-mation, it might be the case that there are age-related differences in the type of processing and, therefore, in the associated hemispheric advantage shown in facial recognition. The literature concerning patterns of hemispheric speciali-zation for the identification of faces by children does not suggest any such age-related shifts (Broman, 1978; Marcel & Rajan, 1975; Reynolds & Jeeves, 1978; Young & Bion, 1980, 1981; Young & Ellis, 1976). However, evidence con-cerning facial identification, independent of hemispheric differences, does sug-gest that age-related shifts may indeed occur. Thus, Carey and Diamond (1977) found that children below 10 years of age showed no difference in recognizing upright and inverted faces, whereas older children did. It was suggested that these results stemmed from the older children recognizing the faces on the basis of their configurational qualities, whereas the younger children responded to individual features. Support for this interpretation is provided by another study by Diamond and Carey (1977) that, although not concerned with facial recog-nition as such, found that children below 12 years of age frequently identify photographs of different individuals as the same on the basis of a single item such as a hat, necklace, or eyeglasses. These results suggest that, on these tasks, the younger children may have relied predominantly on analytic reasoning, which presumably would be performed better in the left than in the right hemisphere, whereas the older children may have relied on a more gestalt-like processing, which presumably would be performed better in the right than in the left hemisphere.

In keeping with the proposed stages in perceptual processing, it is possible that the performance of the older children in these studies represented a mode of processing in which information concerning specific features is integrated into an organized percept, which would correspond to our advanced stage of right-hemisphere processing. The failure to find the utilization of some type of gestalt processing in the youngest children, which would correspond to our preliminary right-hemisphere strategy, may be attributable to the fact that the faces to be recognized in these studies were presented under nontachistoscopic conditions in which the faces could be clearly seen and examined for a relatively long period of time. Under these conditions, utilization of the left-hemisphere analytic mode of processing may be facilitated. In addition, Carey, Diamond, and Woods (1980), and Flin (1980) found reliably occurring reductions in facial recognition at about 11 to 12 years of age. Such reductions might well correspond to a period of reorganization consequent upon a transition to the advanced right-hemisphere mode of functioning. Such transitions are in fact frequently associated with a temporary degradation in performance (Piaget, 1970).

Further evidence of age-related changes consistent with our model of shifts in direction of hemispheric advantage is provided by the results of a study in which Reynolds and Jeeves (1978) used reaction time to examine cerebral lateralization for facial recognition in children of different ages. For the youngest group tested in this study (7–8-year-olds) no visual field superiority was found. Our reanalysis of the data for this group showed a tendency for the LVFA subjects to have slower reaction times than the RVFA subjects, $Z = 1.38, p = .08$ (Mann–Whitney U Test, $n_1 = 4, n_2 = 8$), suggesting that the subjects with a right-hemisphere advantage in this age group were utilizing a more preliminary mode of processing than that utilized by subjects with a left-hemisphere advantage. Furthermore, although there was no visual field advantage for this group when data from all days were combined, analysis indicated that, on the first day of testing, there was an LVF superiority and on the subsequent 3 days there was an RVF superiority, suggesting that these subjects were utilizing a nondifferentiated right-hemisphere mode of processing when they were relatively unfamiliar with the stimulus faces but, as they became increasingly familiar with the faces, were able to utilize the analytic left-hemisphere mode of processing. However, even with 4 days of practice, the results suggest that young children are not able to utilize the integrated right-hemisphere mode of processing.

A study that we have done (Turkewitz & Ross-Kossak, 1984) offers some further support for the view that the changes noted during microdevelopment mirror changes seen in macrodevelopment. The hemispheric advantage of children of different ages was examined on the same facial matching task that we have described. However, in part as an accommodation to the younger children's reduced attention span as well as to reduce initial task difficulty, the children were first given 3 minutes of familiarization with the four faces in full view followed by only two blocks of test trials. The reduced number of trial blocks together with the relatively high level of familiarity at the outset of testing precluded an analysis of the data in terms of sequential changes in VFA. The data were analyzed in terms of the distribution of error scores for each age group separately and for males and females separately. The shape of these distributions was then used to infer the number of different processing strategies particular types of subjects were likely to be using. At each age tested some children showed an L and others an RVFA. The error scores of 8- and 11-year-old boys and girls, both those who showed an LVFA and those who showed an RVFA, were all unimodal, suggesting that they were employing a single LVF or RVF mode of functioning. Among older (13-year-old) children and among females, those who showed an LVF advantage exhibited a bimodal distribution of error scores with some of these children being superior at matching faces and others inferior. These two modes were interpreted as reflecting use of the earlier less efficient diffuse right-hemisphere processing strategy by some of the children and the later articulated right-hemisphere strategy by others. The data as a whole were taken to indicate that at young ages some subjects utilized the primitive right-hemisphere mode of processing and others the left-hemisphere mode. Although some older individuals also utilized one or the other of these modes, at least some of them, particularly females, were also able to utilize the advanced right-hemisphere mode. Given the relatively small number of trials, i.e., two blocks, on which they were tested, it is perhaps surprising that the advanced right-hemisphere mode of processing should have been apparent in even a restricted group of subjects. However, it is likely that the pretesting familiarization under conditions of unrestricted inspection facilitated the utilization of this mode of processing.

The general outline that emerges from these studies is that there are different hemispheric advantages associated with the same formal task requirements; these advantages undergo transitions during the course of increasing familiarization; there is a phase when there is a left-hemisphere advantage and also two distinct phases in which a right-hemisphere advantage is manifested, and finally these three phases are present both on micro and macrodevelopmental scales.

These findings have implications concerning the nature of the relationships between proficiency and hemispheric advantage. Perhaps the most important of these is that no one strategy would necessarily be associated with superior performance at all stages of familiarization. For example, although a left-hemisphere analytic mode of processing might be advantageous after a certain degree of familiarity with the general characteristics of the face had been achieved, utilization of such a strategy with totally unfamiliar faces might not be successful. After a prolonged period of familiarization during which both the general characteristics of the face as well as its specific features were reasonably well known, utilization of an integrated processing strategy that takes into account both types of information might be most helpful whereas attempts at such integration early in familiarization might be premature. This way of viewing the questions suggests that a major contribution to successful matching of faces is the selection of an initially effective strategy and the changing of that strategy at an appropriate time. We in fact have data suggesting that there is a relationship between proficiency and hemispheric advantage and that this relationship is strongly influenced by the stage of familiarization and the nature of the task.

We found that subjects who showed an LVFA on the first block of trials, i.e., when the faces were still relatively unfamiliar, did better than did those showing an RVFA. Furthermore, there was a significant correlation between the direction and magnitude of subjects' VFA and their error scores (Ross-Kossak, Turkewitz, 1984). However, reexamination of the data from other studies in which there was comparable unfamiliarity with the faces on the first block of trials did not replicate this finding so that at the moment its status is questionable. However, the view that at early stages of familiarization there is some benefit to using a right-hemisphere strategy is strengthened by the finding that when subjects have little or no familiarity with the faces, it is easier or at least more typical for them to utilize a right than a left-hemisphere processing strategy. Thus in one study we found significantly more subjects showed an L than an RVFA on the first block of trials (Turkewitz & Ross-Kossak, in prep). In another study a similar finding was obtained with regard to the number of subjects showing a difference of more than one in the number of errors made on right and left visual field presentations (Ross & Turkewitz, 1982). A somewhat different analysis of the same data indicated that on the first block of trials subjects with an LVFA showed a significantly greater VFA than did those subjects who showed an RVFA. Finally, when the relationship between proficiency and magnitude of advantage was examined, it was found that initially those subjects showing a strong LVFA did better than those showing a weaker LVFA, whereas there was no comparable association between magnitude of advantage and proficiency for subjects showing an RVFA at this stage of familiarization (Ross & Turkewitz, 1982; Turkewitz & Ross-Kossak, in prep). These data suggest both a general tendency to utilize a right-hemisphere mode of processing when the faces and task are totally unfamiliar as well as a general advantage to the initial utilization of such a strategy.

The basis for the initial superiority of the right-hemisphere mode of processing can be understood in terms of the nature of the hemispheric differences in processing which we have previously noted. Thus, if initial right-hemisphere processing involves responding to general configurational aspects of the faces and left-hemisphere processing entails responding to specific features, it seems likely that effective use of specific features for matching requires more familiarity with the faces than is initially available. This suggestion is buttressed by Sergent's (1982a, 1982b, 1983) findings that at early stages of complex information processing low spatial frequency information is attended to and only later is high spatial frequency information utilized. In that specific feature identification is likely to require relatively high frequency spatial information, attempts to identify faces on this basis at early stages of familiarization would not be likely to be very successful. In addition, to the extent that a left-hemisphere advantage is in part dependent on the use of existing codes or the development of new ones (Goldberg & Costa, 1981), the attempted use of a left-hemisphere mode of processing early in familiarization would not be expected to be as effective as a right-hemisphere mode or as a left-hemisphere mode later in familiarization. Thus, we believe that the converging evidence from our own and other studies indicate that there is an advantage to utilization of the right-hemisphere mode of function at the earliest stage of familiarization.

The initial advantage that accrues to a right-hemisphere mode of processing does not appear to persist throughout the course of familiarization; rather it disappears and then reappears with greater familiarity with the task and the faces. Thus, the correlation between magnitude and direction of advantage and error scores found on the first block of trials disappeared when the first four blocks of trials were considered but reappeared when the last four were analyzed (Ross-Kossak & Turkewitz, 1984). Further evidence for the reappearance of an advantage to using a right-hemisphere mode of processing after familiarization is provided by the findings that by the end of testing better performing subjects were more likely to have an L than an RVFA. Thus, among those subjects who showed an initial LVFA, those who performed best showed a significant quadratic trend in their VFA indicating a shift towards an RVFA and back to an LVFA, whereas better performing subjects who started with an RVFA showed a significant linear trend, based on a shift to an LVFA. No such shift towards an LVFA was seen in the performance of poorer performing subjects (Ross-Kossak & Turkewitz, 1984). Furthermore, in two studies in which subjects were given a study sheet containing the faces to examine for several minutes prior to testing, subjects with an LVFA did better than those with an RVFA (Ross & Turkewitz, 1981; Turkewitz & Ross-Kossak, 1984). In addition, under these conditions older girls (13-year-olds) as well as young women (17-year-olds) showed a marked association between VFA and error scores such that those with bigger LVFAs made fewer errors than did those with RVFAs or smaller LVFAs (Turkewitz & Ross-Kossak, 1984).

The relative advantage that accrues to a right-hemisphere mode of processing at later stages of familiarization is understandable in terms of the dual nature of right-hemisphere processing that we have proposed. According to this model a right-hemisphere advantage would reflect both a relatively primitive type of holistic processing and a more advanced type in which there is integration of distinctive features into an integrated percept. The fact that at the very beginning of the task individuals with a right-hemisphere advantage performed better than those with a left-hemisphere advantage suggests as previously noted that, when a face is totally unfamiliar, the use of the early appearing right-hemisphere strategy is relatively effective. Once some familiarity with a face is achieved, and a strategy based on the identification of specific features can be effectively used, the advantage of using the initial right-hemisphere strategy disappears. The reemergence of an advantage to utilizing a right-hemisphere strategy with increasing familiarization suggests that, at this stage, such an advantage reflects a more advanced mode of processing than that used initially.

We have thus far been emphasizing the shifting nature of the relationship between a particular direction of advantage and proficiency. There is another aspect of the relationship between magnitude of advantage and proficiency that makes a rather different point and broadens our understanding of both this relationship and the role of hemisphere specialization in optimizing performance. The finding of a greater advantage to using a particular strategy at a given stage of familiarization does not preclude the possibility that an advantage accrues to the consistent short-term use of even a nonoptional strategy. That such is indeed the case was found in several studies in which the relationship between magnitude of VFA independently of its direction and error scores was examined.

In two separate studies significant negative correlations between absolute magnitude of advantage and error scores were found; this association obtained for subjects showing an RVFA as well as for those showing an LVFA (Ross & Turkewitz, 1982; Turkewitz & Ross-Kossak, in prep). These data suggest that there are advantages from consistently adopting either a short-term right-or left-hemisphere processing strategy. Other analyses suggest that the advantage of even short-term consistency is not independent of the individual's degree of familiarity with the faces. Thus, in these two studies an association between magnitude of advantage and proficiency was found on the first block of trials for subjects showing an LVFA. For subjects showing an RVFA there was no such early appearing association but one emerged during testing. This suggests that under the conditions of our test procedures, even if subjects consistently apply a feature detecting strategy, the use of such a strategy is not especially helpful until familiarity has made it possible to resolve the specific features of the face.

For both subjects showing an LVFA and an RVFA the association between magnitude of VFA and error scores did not persist throughout the course of testing. The nature of the changes in association was complex and difficult to interpret at this time. A somewhat more straightforward picture emerges from a reanalysis of the data of the 1984 Ross-Kossak and Turkewitz study. This reanalysis indicates that following the significant association between magnitude of LVFA and proficiency there was a time when there was no such association followed by the return of the association to an almost significant level at the end of testing. In terms of our model this obviously suggests advantages to the use of the primitive right-hemisphere mode of processing early in familiarization and of the advanced right-hemisphere mode following more extensive familiarization. The changes in association between proficiency and magnitude of an RVFA are somewhat more ambiguous due to the small number of subjects showing such an advantage at the end of testing.

We therefore believe that it is generally the case that at some points in familiarization there is an advantage to the consistent adoption of a particular processing strategy, and that the points when this is most useful differ depending on the strategy used. We also believe that the details concerning the timing of the optimum use of consistent strategies are a function of the particular processing requirements under investigation. Evidence for this is provided in a study in which we examined hemispheric differences in matching profiles to front face views of the same individuals (Turkewitz & Ross-Kossak, in prep). This task is a better, although by no means perfect, approximation of the everyday task of identifying individuals than is the more usual laboratory task of matching identical faces. It requires the subject to detect the invariance present in faces that differ in orientation and therefore in most stimulus attributes. Matching of such transformed faces, on any basis, is clearly more difficult than is matching identical faces. However, it seems likely that making such matches on the basis of configurational aspects is even more difficult than is making them with regard to specific features. Thus, the rotation of a face on its axis drastically alters its contour, which is one prime holistic aspect of a face. Furthermore, such rotation clearly alters the relationship between the features even when the features themselves are only perceived relatively diffusely. Although the correspondence between features in different orientations is considerably less than perfect, nonetheless, there appears sufficient invariance to make it possible to identify distinctive characteristics of a feature in a variety of orientations. For example, it seems possible to identify a thin pointed nose as such in front face as well as in profile. Nonetheless, the difficulty in abstracting the invariance specifying a specific feature in different orientations resulted in the failure to obtain any evidence for an advantage in the use of a consistent strategy at the beginning of familiarization. Thus neither subjects exhibiting a right nor those exhibiting an LVFA showed an association between magnitude of advantage and proficiency at the early stages of familiarization. However, by the second block of trials there was a significant association between magnitude of advantage and proficiency for those subjects who showed an RVFA, whereas those who showed an LVFA at this stage still showed essentially a zero order correlation. Only later in familiarization, when presumably the advanced right-hemisphere mode of processing was available, was there an association between magnitude of LVFA and proficiency. This analysis suggests that for this task the primitive right-hemisphere processing mode cannot be successfully employed and that consistent use of a left-hemisphere processing strategy can be successfully employed prior to consistent use of the advanced right-hemisphere processing mode.

Not only do the nature of the task, the degree of familiarity, and the mode of processing determine the nature of the relationship between magnitude of advantage and proficiency, but the characteristics of the subject also seem to play a determinative role in the nature of this association. Thus, on our typical task of matching identical faces, 13-year-old children (both girls and boys) showed a strong association between magnitude of advantage and proficiency; younger children, i.e., 8- and 11-year-olds, showed no such association. This was the case despite the fact that the overall error rates of the different aged children were made equivalent by adjusting the duration of presentation of the slides. This difference can be understood in relation to the finding that the young children show a significantly smaller VFA than do the older children, suggesting that within the constraints of the study they are less capable of maintaining a consistent processing strategy.

Thus far we have been considering the relationship between short-term consistency of processing strategy and proficiency in matching faces at the time when the consistency is manifest. There is, however, another aspect of the relationship that requires consideration, namely the relationship between consistency of using a particular strategy at one point in time and the level of proficiency ultimately achieved; that is, it is quite possible that use of a consistent strategy, for example, attending to specific features, may not be helpful early but the early attempt may result in better matching at a later stage in familiarization. Although cross-lagged correlations would provide some relevant information concerning this possibility, the possibility of some individuals simply being better performers than others would make interpretation of such correlations very difficult. At the moment data have not been analyzed in a manner that makes it possible to address this question.

Although the failure of most researchers to consider sequential changes in processing and hemispheric advantage in facial recognition has resulted in the presentation of data in ways that do not make it possible to address most of the issues with which we have been concerned in a detailed way, there is data that is relevant to the issue of hemispheric specialization in relation to degree of familiarity. Separate studies have examined hemispheric advantage using faces that differ in their familiarity, and comparison between the results of these studies enables some elaboration of the influence of familiarity on hemispheric advantage. The superiority of the right hemisphere in the processing of faces that are unfamiliar at the beginning of the testing has been demonstrated in studies of patients with unilateral cortical lesions (DeRenzi et al., 1968; Milner, 1968; Yin, 1970), in studies of commissurotomy patients (Levy et al., 1972), and in studies of normal adults and children (Broman, 1978; Geffen et al., 1971; Hilliard, 1973; Klein, Moscovitch, & Vigna, 1976; Marcel & Rajan, 1975; Rizzolatti et al., 1971; Young & Ellis, 1976). In contrast, in tasks involving the recognition of faces to which subjects have been familiarized prior to the experimental session, a left-hemisphere superiority is typically found (Marzi et al., 1974; Proudfoot, 1982; Umiltà, Brizzolara, Tabossi, & Fairweather, 1982). This suggests that a degree of familiarity with a face prior to testing may allow recognition judgments to be made on the basis of one or more salient features, and this type of analytic processing strategy presumably results in a left-hemisphere advantage. On the other hand, in the recognition of unfamiliar faces, subjects may have to rely on a more preliminary perception in which the individual features of the face have not been analyzed or differentiated. This type of processing presumably results in a right-hemisphere advantage.

In a recent study by Leehey and Cahn, (1979), it was found that recognition judgments for photographs of faces of colleagues with whom subjects were highly familiar were more accurate on LVF presentations. This result appears inconsistent with the RVF superiority found for the recognition of experimentally familiarized faces as they all involve the recognition of faces that are in some sense familiar. However, Leehey and Cahn suggest that differences in type of familiarity or experience that one has with faces of colleagues as opposed to faces of experimentally familiarized faces might account for the opposing directions of hemispheric advantage found for these stimuli. Faces of colleagues are encountered frequently, under a variety of transformations. This might facilitate the development of articulated integrated processing and the right-hemisphere advantage that we suggest characterizes the most advanced level of processing.

The results obtained from studies of hemispheric advantage in the recognition of famous faces are somewhat more ambiguous. In one well-known study, Marzi and Berlucchi (1977) report a left-hemisphere advantage for the recognition of famous faces; however, in two other studies a right-hemisphere advantage was found (Young & Bion, 1981; Young & Bion, 1983). There are a number of factors that might account for differences in the direction of hemispheric advantage in different studies. Thus, some studies required naming of the faces (Marzi & Berlucchi, 1977), which might induce a left-hemisphere advantage, whereas others did not. Also the nature of the famous faces used might have differed, with some of the faces being typically presented in newspapers, etc. in only one orientation and others more variably. Finally, differences in the size of the set of faces could influence the direction of hemispheric advantage.

One of the most striking findings to emerge from our studies is that when given the same task some individuals initially exhibit a right-hemisphere advantage and others a left-hemisphere advantage. It is tempting to ascribe this to differences between individuals with regard to stable characteristics. There have been studies in which associations between particular directions of hemispheric advantage on tasks involving a variety of different types of stimuli and individual characteristics have been found. This has led to the suggestion that there are right-hemisphere and left-hemisphere types of individuals. However, there are only a few such studies yielding positive results and the validity of this typology has been questioned (Beaumont, Young, & McManus, 1984). Furthermore, our finding of shifts in hemispheric advantage make any simple association between direction of advantage and individual characteristics most unlikely. It is, however, possible that a more interesting and useful typology involves the manner in which individuals shift in their strategy for processing complex information. Thus, for example, if creativity is dependent on analyzing information in a variety of ways and then integrating the results from these analyses, it is possible that the most creative individuals are those who show particular patterns of shifts in the nature of their hemispheric advantage, whereas the least creative individuals would show little or no shifting. The view that the manner of shifting processing strategies determines useful typologies has interesting implications for examining relationships between such characteristics as developmental status, including aging, and the nature of hemispheric advantage. Thus, one possibility is that at particular stages of development only one or another mode of function is available or used (indeed our data on children suggests a restriction in the number of processing modes used), so that shifts would be less likely or at least more restricted. Incomplete myellination of the corpus callosum in children might serve to isolate functions in the separate hemispheres preventing the type of integrated processing that we have suggested as underlying the advanced right-hemisphere mode of function so that a full range of switching would not be seen. Similarly, it is possible that some of the changes in cognitive functioning seen during aging result from the dissociation of the hemispheres and an ensuing reduction in flexibility of processing.

With regard to characteristics of individuals that may influence patterns of change in hemispheric advantage it should be recalled that most of the evidence that we have presented has been for female subjects. This is because in an early study we obtained evidence suggesting that only females, and older ones at that, used the advanced right-hemisphere mode of functioning. Taken together with the known superiority of women for recognizing faces (Ellis, Shepherd, & Bruce, 1973; Goldstein & Chance, 1971; Howells, 1938; Witroyl & Kaess, 1957), it seemed in fact reasonable that women were more likely to show the full range of shifts. As sex differences were not our concern at that time, and shifts in hemispheric advantage were, we restricted our studies to females. However, in view of the general finding that males tend to be more strongly lateralized than females (Springer & Deutsch, 1981), it seems likely that for certain tasks males would show an advanced mode of right-hemisphere processing whereas females would not. There is in fact some evidence suggesting that males may use the advanced right-hemisphere mode of processing in identifying male faces (Brouwers, Mononen, & Stefanatos, 1980). We also believe that males are as likely as females to utilize the advanced mode of processing on certain tasks and more likely than females to utilize this mode on still other tasks, i.e., those on which they are more proficient than females.

This raises the question of whether differences between individuals in hemispheric advantage and changes in these advantages with increasing familiarity is unique to facial recognition or whether it is a more general characteristic of complex information processing. Studies concerned with the effects of familiarity or experience on the direction of hemispheric advantage offer some support for the generality of shifts in hemispheric advantage associated with perceptual learning. Thus, with stimuli that are sequential in nature, e.g., musical notes or a series of Morse Code signals, there is evidence that familiarity causes a shift from a right- to a left-hemispheric advantage. In the processing of musical sequences, both Bever and Chiarello (1974) and Johnson (1977) found that musically naive subjects showed a left-ear, i.e., right-hemisphere advantage but musically experienced subjects showed a right-ear, i.e., left-hemisphere advantage. In addition, in the processing of Morse Code, a stronger right-ear advantage has been found in Morse Code operators than in naive subjects (Papcun, Krashen, Terbech, Remington, & Harshman, 1974). We believe that this corresponds to a shift from the first to the second stage in our model, involving a shift from nondifferentiated to analytic processing. With stimuli allowing for simultaneous as well as sequential processing, e.g., musical chords, there is evidence that familiarity causes a shift in hemispheric advantage in the opposite direction. Thus, naive subjects showed a right-ear advantage for chords, whereas musically trained subjects showed a left-ear advantage for these stimuli (Kellar & Bever, 1980). We believe that this sequence corresponds to the last two stages in our model of perceptual learning and involves a shift from analytic to integrated processing.

In addition, in a study explicitly designed to explore the generality of the facial recognition model in which the data were analyzed in terms of sequential changes in hemispheric advantage, Devenney and Turkewitz (in prep) found shifts in hemispheric advantage on a voice recognition task. This involved subjects' identification of two voices out of a set of four that were dichotically presented. Familiarization was provided only during identification testing by binaurally presenting each voice together with an identifying name, i.e., each speaker spoke the phrase "my name is" followed by her name. For dichotic presentation only the "my name is" portion of the tape was used and for identification the entire phrase including the name of all four speakers was sequentially presented. The results from this study, whereas not identical with those from the facial recognition studies, indicated substantial agreement with some of the major generalities of the facial recognition studies. Thus, some subjects showed an initial right- and others an initial left-ear advantage on this task and virtually all subjects showed systematic shifts in the direction of this advantage so that those subjects who started with a left-ear advantage shifted to a right-ear advantage and vice versa. Although there was no suggestion of the more complex right to left to right pattern of shifts in hemispheric advantage that we have found for facial recognition, differences in task difficulty and other procedural differences between the two types of tasks make the absence of perfect concordance between the two types of processing unremarkable. What is clearly evident is that systematic shifts in the hemispheric advantages associated with processing complex information is not unique to faces.

One possibility not previously addressed is that the shifts reported are not part of a tripartite pattern of information processing but rather an attenuated description of a regularly alternating pattern of shifts in processing strategy. It is possible that, were a longer series of trials used, continued shifts in hemispheric advantage would be found. Although this has not been ruled out, it is not clear what function such a pattern of shifting could serve, nor is it clear what processes later appearing hemispheric advantages could be reflecting.

We believe we have presented considerable evidence indicating that there are shifts in the hemispheric advantage associated with processing complex information and that there are associated changes in the nature of the relationship between hemispheric advantage and proficiency. In addition, we have provided some evidence that individuals who show a right-hemisphere advantage differ from those showing a left-hemisphere advantage with regard to the nature of their processing as indicated by differing effects of inversion and masking of specific features on the two types of subjects (Ross & Turkewitz, 1982). We further believe and have argued that these shifts in hemispheric advantage are likely to be based upon changes in processing strategy. Although this is perfectly reasonable, there is no data yet available that permits us to relate hemispheric shifts directly to shifts in processing strategies. In addition, although there is considerable evidence to suggest the existence of two right-hemisphere modes of information processing, the data suggesting such a dual mode is still indirect. To be convincing it will be necessary to find differences in the nature of the processing at the two proposed right-hemisphere stages. It is in this direction that future productive research must be done.

ACKNOWLEDGMENTS

This chapter is supported in part by Grant Number 13648 from the PSC-CUNY Research Award Program. We thank Drs. A. Young and E. Goldberg for their helpful comments on an earlier version of this chapter.

REFERENCES

Beaumont, J. G., Young, A. W., & McManus, I. C. (1984). Hemisphericity: A critical review. *Cognitive Neuropsychology, 1,* 191–212.

Benton, A. L. (1980). The neuropsychology of facial recognition. *American Psychologist, 35,* 176–186.

Bever, T. G., & Chiarello, R. (1974). Cerebral dominance in musicians and nonmusicians. *Science, 185,* 537–539.

Bever, T. G., Hurtig, R. R., & Handel, A. B. (1976). Analytic processing elicits right ear superiority in monaurally presented speech. *Neuropsychologia, 14,* 175–181.

Bogen, J. E. (1969). The other side of the brain II: An appositional mind. *Bulletin of the Los Angeles Neurological Society, 34,* 191–220.

Broman, M. (1978). Reaction-time differences between the left and right hemispheres for face and letter discrimination in children and adults. *Cortex, 14,* 578–591.

Brouwers, P., Mononen, L. J., & Stefanatos, G. A. (1980). Visual field differences in recognition of male and female faces. *Perceptual and Motor Skills, 51,* 627–633.

Carey, S., & Diamond, R. (1977). From piecemeal to configurational representation of faces. *Science, 195,* 312–314.

Carey, S., Diamond, R., & Woods, B. (1980). The development of face recognition—A maturational component? *Developmental Psychology, 16,* 257–269.

Cohen, G. (1973). Hemispheric differences in serial vs. parallel processing. *Journal of Experimental Psychology, 97,* 349–356.

De Renzi, E., Faglioni, P., & Spinnler, H. (1968). Performance of patients with unilateral brain damage on face recognition tasks. *Cortex, 4,* 17–34.

Devenney, D., & Turkewitz, G. (in prep). *Hemispheric advantages in voice recognition: Changes with familiarization.*

Diamond, R., & Carey, S. (1977). Developmental changes in the representation of faces. *Journal of Experimental Child Psychology, 23,* 1–22.

Ellis, H. D., Shepherd, J., & Bruce, A. (1973). The effects of age and sex upon adolescents' recognition of faces. *Journal of Genetic Psychology, 123,* 173–174.

Ellis, H. D., Shepherd, J. W., & Davies, G. M. (1979). Identification of familiar and unfamiliar faces from internal and external features: Some implications for theories of face recognition. *Perception, 8,* 431–439.

Flin, R. H. (1980). Age effects in children's memory for unfamiliar faces. *Developmental Psychology, 16,* 373–374.

Geffen, G., Bradshaw, J. L., & Wallace, G. (1971). Interhemispheric effects on reaction time to verbal and nonverbal visual stimuli. *Journal of Experimental Psychology, 87,* 415–422.

Gibson, E. J. (1969). *Principles of perceptual learning and development.* New York: Appleton–Century–Crofts.

Goldberg, E., & Costa, L. (1981). Hemisphere differences in the acquisition and use of descriptive systems. *Brain and Language, 14,* 144–173.

Goldstein, A. G., & Chance, J. (1971). Visual recognition memory for complex configurations. *Perception and Psychophysics, 9,* 237–241.

Hamsher, K. D., Levin, H. S., & Benton, A. L. (1979). Facial recognition in patients with focal brain lesions. *Archives of Neurology, 36,* 837–839.

Hilliard, R. D. (1973). Hemispheric laterality effects on a facial recognition task in normal subjects. *Cortex, 9,* 246–258.

Howells, T. H. (1938). A study of the ability to recognize faces. *Journal of Abnormal and Social Psychology, 33,* 124–127.

Johnson, P. R. (1977). Dichotically stimulated ear differences in musicians and non-musicians. *Cortex, 13,* 385–389.

Kellar, L. A., & Bever, T. G. (1980). Hemispheric asymmetries in the perception of musical intervals as a function of musical experience and family handedness background. *Brain and Language, 3,* 24–38.

Klein, D., Moscovitch, M., & Vigna, C. (1976). Perceptual asymmetries and attentional mechanisms in tachistoscopic recognition of words and faces. *Neuropsychologia, 14,* 44–66.

Leehey, S. C., & Cahn, A. (1979). Lateral asymmetries in the recognition of words, familiar faces, and unfamiliar faces. *Neuropsychologia, 17,* 619–635.

Levy, J., Trevarthen, C., & Sperry, R. (1972). Perception of bilateral chimeric figures following hemisphere deconnexion. *Brain, 95,* 61–68.

Malone, D. R., Morris, H. H., Kay, M. C., & Levin, H. S. (1982). Prosopagnosia: a double dissociation between the recognition of familiar and unfamiliar faces. *Journal of Neurology, Neurosurgery, and Psychiatry, 45,* 820–822.

Marcel, T., & Rajan, P. (1975). Lateral specialization for recognition of words and faces in good and poor readers. *Neuropsychologia, 13,* 489–497.

Marshall, J. C., Caplan, D., & Holmes, J. M. (1975). The measure of laterality. *Neuropsychologia, 13,* 315–321.

Marzi, C. A., & Berlucchi, G. (1977). Right visual field superiority for accuracy of recognition of famous faces in normals. *Neuropsychologia, 15,* 751–756.

Marzi, C. A., Brizzolara, D., Rizzolatti, G., Umiltà, C., & Berlucchi, G. (1974). Left hemisphere superiority for the recognition of well-known faces. *Brain Research, 66,* 358.

Meadows, J. C. (1974). The anatomical basis of prosopagnosia. *Journal of Neurology, Neurosurgery, and Psychiatry, 37,* 489–501.

Milner, B. (1968). Visual recognition and recall after right temporal-lobe lesions in man. *Neuropsychologia, 6,* 191–209.

Papcun, G., Krashen, S., Terbech, D., Remington, R., & Harshman, R. (1974). Is the left hemisphere specialized for speech, language, and/or something else? *Journal of the Acoustical Society of America, 55,* 319–327.

Patterson, K., & Bradshaw, J. L. (1975). Differential hemispheric mediation of nonverbal visual stimuli. *Journal of Experimental Psychology: Human Perception and Performance, 1,* 246–252.

Piaget, J. (1970). Piaget's theory. In P. H. Mussen (Ed.), *Charmichaels' manual of child psychology,* 3rd ed., Vol. 1, pp. 703–732. New York: Wiley.

Proudfoot, R. E. (1982). Hemispheric asymmetry for face recognition: some effects of visual masking, hemiretinal stimulation and learning task. *Neuropsychologia, 20,* 129–144.

Reynolds, D. M., & Jeeves, M. A. (1978). A developmental study of hemisphere specialization for recognition of faces in normal subjects. *Cortex, 14,* 511–520.

Rizzolatti, G., Umiltà, C., & Berlucchi, G. (1971). Opposite superiorities of the right and left cerebral hemispheres in discriminative reaction time to physiognomical and alphabetical material. *Brain, 94,* 431–442.

Ross, P., & Turkewitz, G. (1981). Individual differences in cerebral asymmetries for facial recognition. *Cortex, 17,* 199–214.

Ross, P., & Turkewitz, G. (1982). Changes in hemispheric advantage in processing facial information with increasing stimulus familiarization. *Cortex, 18,* 489–499.

Ross-Kossak, P., & Turkewitz, G. (1984). Relationship between changes in hemispheric advantage during familiarization to faces and proficiency in facial recognition. *Neuropsychologia, 22,* 471–477.

Segalowitz, S. J., Bebout, L. J., & Lederman, S. J. (1979). Lateralization for reading musical chords: Disentangling symbolic, analytic, and phonological aspects of reading. *Brain and Language, 8,* 315–323.

Sergent, J. (1982a). About face: Left Hemisphere Involvement in Processing Physiognomies. *Journal of Experimental Psychology: Human Perception and Performance, 8,* 1–14.

Sergent, J. (1982b). Influence of luminence in hemispheric processing. *Bulletin of the Psychonomic Society, 20,* 221–223.

Sergent, J. (1983). Role of the input in visual hemispheric asymmetries. *Psychological Bulletin, 93,* 481–512.

Springer, S. P., & Deutsch, G. (1981). *Left brain, right brain.* San Francisco: Freeman.

Turkewitz, G., & Ross, P. (1983). The development of a general strategy for the processing of facial information. *Cortex, 19,* 179–185.

Turkewitz, G., & Ross-Kossak, P. (1984). Multiple modes of right hemisphere information processing: Age and sex differences in facial recognition. *Developmental Psychology, 20,* 95–103.

Turkewitz, G., & Ross-Kossak, P. (in prep.). *Strategies for the recognition of invariant and transformed faces in relation to hemispheric differences.*

Umiltà, C., Brizzolara, D., Tabossi, P., & Fairweather, H. (1982). Factors affecting face recognition in the cerebral hemispheres: Familiarity and naming. In J. Requin (Ed.), *Attention and performance: VII* (pp. 363–374). New York: Wiley.

Warrington, E. K., & James, M. (1967). An experimental investigation of facial recognition in patients with unilateral cerebral lesions. *Cortex, 3,* 317–326.

Werner, H. (1957). *Comparative psychology of mental development.* New York: International Universities Press.

Witryol, S. L., & Kaess, W. A. (1957). Sex differences in social memory tasks. *Journal of Abnormal and Social Psychology, 54,* 343–346.

Yin, R. K. (1970). Face recognition in brain-injured patients: A dissociable ability. *Neuropsychologia, 8,* 395–402.

Young, A. W. (1984). Right cerebral hemisphere superiority for recognizing the internal and external features of famous faces. *British Journal of Psychology, 75,* 161–169.

Young, A. W., & Bion, P. J. (1980). Absence of any developmental trend in right hemisphere superiority for face recognition. *Cortex, 16,* 213–222.

Young, A. W., & Bion, P. J. (1981). Accuracy of naming laterally presented known faces by children and adults. *Cortex, 17,* 97–106.

Young, A. W., & Bion, P. J. (1983). The nature of the sex difference in right hemisphere superiority for face recognition. *Cortex, 19,* 215–226.

Young, A. W., & Ellis, H. D. (1976). An experimental investigation of developmental differences in ability to recognize faces presented to the left and right cerebral hemispheres. *Neuropsychologia, 14,* 495–498.

7 The Specificity of Face Perception: Evidence from Psychological Investigations

J. B. Davidoff
University College of Swansea

The human face is an enormously important source of information; from it we determine age, sex, race, intention, mood, and well-being. All this is done at a glance and is achieved even for unfamiliar faces. Familiar faces allow still greater possibilities. They evoke a range of associations and, as we shall see, are dealt with differently from unfamiliar faces. The importance of faces is certain, but our concern is to decide whether they are a unique form of visual input.

It could be argued that faces cannot be unique because there is some similarity between any two sources of input. At an elementary level this must be true because all light entering our eyes is in the form of electromagnetic radiation and every object is composed of variations in contrast and color. There are differences between inputs that allow categorization into objects (one class of which we know as faces), and it is possible that faces are a unique category. But, in order to decide if the class of objects called faces is unique, some criteria for uniqueness are required.

Specificity of function is intrinsic to Fodor's recent thesis (1983) on mental structure. In the absence of any other serious attempt to define specificity, we shall use the criteria he lays down. Fodor divides mind into vertical and horizontal faculties. Vertical faculties are independent input systems that he describes as domain specific computational mechanisms. These domains provide the data base for the non-specific (horizontal) thought processes. *Vertical faculties* are defined as informationally encapsulated, neurologically hard-wired, and probably innately specified. Faces are explicitly proposed by Fodor as candidates that might fulfill these requirements for a vertical faculty. The present assessment of uniqueness will therefore be governed by the extent to which faces conform to the necessary conditions laid down by Fodor for an independent input system.

INNATENESS

Taking first the innate specification component of Fodor's vertical faculties, we find little clear-cut research. A behavioral act may occasionally be determined solely by inheritance but, because stimulus, hormonal, and experiential factors are always involved, the extent of the inherited component will be difficult to assess. Ethologists tend to argue for the innateness of face processing solely on the grounds of evolutionary need. Early bonding between members of a primate species may be desirable for species survival but this cannot, as Tzavaras, Hécaen, and LeBras (1970) suggest it can, be taken as indisputable evidence for faces being the innate releasing mechanisms that accomplish imprinting.

Laboratory studies provide evidence that human infants exhibit a remarkable interest in faces from an early age. Goren, Sarty, and Wu (1975) observed that 9-minute old newborns tracked a moving schematic face in preference to similar stimuli. Less spectacularly but more reliably, Carpenter, Tecce, Stechler, and Friedman (1970) found that during the second week of life, a baby can tell its mother's face from a model of a face or an abstract model. Fantz (1961), using an attentional preference paradigm, observed that babies were more interested in a face than in a jumbled arrangement of the features that made up the face. The preference for looking at a normal face was as great at 4 days as at 5 months, suggesting an innate basis for face perception. These studies are in sharp contrast to the limited information pickup proposed by Bower (1974). He believes that young infants around 6 weeks of age are as likely to smile at two dots as at a real face. It is not until 6 months that a view of the whole face is required to elicit a smile. Bower found a similar developmental relationship of part to whole for the child's reaction to abstract shapes. He argues that faces do not constitute a particular class of objects for young infants.

Carey (1981) also argues for a development of face perception, pointing out that in studies where very early face recognition is claimed, it is not certain that it is the faceness per se of the stimuli that is being responded to. Carey suggests that within the first 2 months of life attention to faces is determined by their complexity as visual patterns. Toward the end of that time the child sees "eyes within a face," showing the beginning of a configurational analysis of the internal face features that is not properly attained for any face until around 4 months. It is concluded that the young child does not process the face in the same fashion as an adult does and that adult-like performance is achieved gradually.

Developmental studies clearly show an exceptional interest on the part of the child for the faces of others. But unless such studies consider the learning of fine discriminations possible in the first weeks of life (Bower, 1974), proof of the innateness of face preference behavior cannot be established. We require a disentangling of any unlearned responses to a face from the reinforcement benefits of face discrimination. Because we cannot deprive the newborn infant of all face experience, it is always possible to argue that face preference is due to rapid learning. With other primates, moral scruples are not always considered relevant and experience with faces can be controlled carefully. Sackett (1966) reared rhesus monkeys in isolation without the opportunity to view faces. In subsequent testing, pictures of monkeys were looked at more than were pictures of complex scenes. However, the conclusion that there is an innate species specific recognition system is open to criticism. The stimuli were not adequately controlled for complexity, and the monkeys were not deprived of views of their own bodies; it could have been nonfacial aspects of the monkey pictures that attracted attention. The monkeys behaved appropriately by withdrawing in reaction to pictures of other monkeys, but they did not show the normal response to monkeys displaying fear–a finding replicated by Miller, Caul, and Mirsky (1967). The regularity of facial expressions within a species does suggest innateness, as do the great differences between species, but research does not suggest that animals recognize as well as express emotion innately. Experience seems to be necessary for the discrimination of facial expressions.

NEUROLOGICAL CONSIDERATIONS

An innate specification for face processing could be argued from sex differences in face recognition ability. If sex differences in behavior can be determined by genetic factors, an innate causation could be proposed for any sex-related behavior. Goldstein and Chance (1971) report that females are better at recognizing photographs of faces, but there are alternative explanations apart from innate specification. It is likely that at least part of the female superiority for face recognition is a result of experience promoting an interest in faces, inasmuch as the sex of the person photographed is important (Cross, Cross, & Daly, 1971; Ellis, Shepherd, & Bruce, 1973; Witryol & Kaess, 1957). Female superiority at face recognition may also be due to personality factors. From their studies of cognitive style, Witkin, Dyk, Faterson, Goodenough, and Karp (1962) have proposed a personality dimension (field dependence–field independence) related to the extent to which reliance is placed on environmental rather than internal cues. After puberty, females are more likely to be field dependent, as measured by their performance on Witkin's Rod and Frame Test. Messick and Damarin (1964) have shown that field dependence is also positively correlated with scores on face recognition tasks; it is, therefore, no surprise that females do better at such tasks. Stronger evidence for innateness come from sex differences observed in early infancy, but here the results of research are conflicting (Fagan, 1972, 1973).

    Sex differences in face recognition occur in other areas of biologically based research. Mazzucchi and Biber (1983), reviewing neurological case reports, found that males were more liable to suffer from the severe memory disorder for familiar faces called *prosopagnosia*. The authors discount aetiology and lesion size as responsible for this sex difference and suggest instead that males and females differ in the organization of brain function. As it is a widely held belief that there is only a limited plasticity of brain function, differences in brain organization for faces can be interpreted as a preprogramming that manifests itself differently between the sexes.

Studies using brief, lateralized visual presentations with normals also have addressed the question of sex differences in the brain organization for face stimuli. The usual left visual field advantage for faces implies a right hemisphere location for processing (Davidoff, 1982; Ellis, 1981). Rizzolatti and Buchtel (1977) found no visual field advantage for female subjects and concluded that faces are represented bilaterally in the female brain. This is not the only possible interpretation of their result. Superior recognition in one visual field may be determined by processing strategy. Proudfoot (1983) found that faces judged on physical attributes were recognized better by a different hemisphere than were faces remembered by social cues. There appeared to be an arbitrary allocation of memory load between the hemispheres of the brain. The sex difference in visual field advantage for faces could therefore be due to differences in distribution of resources by females.

Preprogrammed sex differences for the brain organization of face material implies consistent sex–visual field advantage interactions, which is not the case. Some studies (Hannay & Rogers, 1979; Piazza, 1980) show no sex differences in the visual field advantage for faces, whereas McKeever and Dixon (1981) report it more likely that females show a left visual advantage for faces if affect is involved. Equally conflicting results exist for tasks requiring the discrimination of facial expression (Ladavas, Umiltà, & Ricci-Bitti, 1980; Safer, 1981). Contradictory reports are probably due more to the multidetermined visual field advantage being affected by subject, and to stimulus variables more important for the particular task used, than to any putative sex difference. For example, Pizzamiglio and Zoccolotti (1981) relate sex differences in visual field advantages found for faces to field dependence, whereas Brouwers, Mononen, and Stefanatos (1980) relate such results to whether the photographs used are of people of the same sex as the subject. Because the distribution of load between the two hemispheres appears so volatile, it is unlikely that the visual half field methodology will help us decide on the innateness issue for face processing. Furthermore, even if a sex difference in hemispheric processing does reflect differences in brain organization, it is not proven to be specific to faces. Sex differences in brain organization have been proposed for many skills (McGlone, 1980). Any difference found for faces could reflect an underlying bilaterality for all visual-spatial processing. In line with this suggestion, Davidoff (1977) found visual field advantages for dot detection that showed sex differences parallel to those reported by Rizzolatti and Buchtel (1977) for faces.

Better evidence for the hard-wiring of the visual system for faces comes from neurophysiology. Using micro-electrode implantations, Perrett, Rolls, and Caan

(1982) have recorded from cells in the superior temporal sulcus of monkeys during exposure to face and other stimuli. About one tenth of the cells gave selective responses to faces. A real human or monkey face gave responses 2 to 10 times as large as those to gratings, simple geometric stimuli or complex 3-D objects. These cells showed properties that would be essential for the recognition of a stimulus as a face rather than as a pattern. First, the cells reacted specifically to faces, i.e., they were time locked to stimulus presentation with a latency of between 80–160 msec and were unresponsive to auditory, tactile, or even other visual stimuli. Second, at least some of the cells tested gave an output that was relatively constant despite rotational transformation or alteration of color, size and distance. Third, just as for human recognition performance (Bruce, 1983), output from certain cells declined if the face was presented in profile. Face recognition, as we shall see, is possible by feature recognition or by a system that allows superior recognition from an integration of the features. Both mechanisms were found by Perrett et al. (1984) to be correlated with the output from their implanted cells. Isolating part of the face (e.g., mouth, hair) or masking out these aspects revealed that some cells responded more or less specifically to features. The organizational superiority of faces over jumbled arrangement of the features found in normals (Homa, Haver, & Schwartz, 1976) was mirrored in the output of other cells. Perrett et al. argue therefore that the neurones in the superior temporal sulcus of the monkey are part of systems specialized for faces.

The representation of faces must occur somewhere in the brain. It is important that its locus has been specifically isolated, but it has not been proven to be hard wired. Indeed, Perrett et al. (1984) have provided evidence for a learning component. They claim to have found cells that are peculiarly responsive to a particular human face often seen by the monkey. Such modification by experience would be necessary for a face recognition system, but it leaves the way open to argument that all the cell properties are a result of learning. This must be regarded as a distinct possibility, because the much simpler orientation specific cells of the visual cortex are found to be modifiable by changes in early visual experience (Blakemore & Cooper, 1970). An exact locus for the neurological correlate of face recognition is suggestive of an innate basis, but other classes of stimuli might well develop a similar locus if sufficient experience were given early in life.

THEORIES OF FACE RECOGNITION

The neurophysiological evidence for an innate component for face processsing is compelling, but it does not, as yet, constitute conclusive proof of face specificity. Looking to other areas of research, we find evidence, which might indicate specifically from our prodigious ability to deal with faces. Fodor (1983) reluctantly acknowledges the utility of this approach but is not "boundlessly enthusiastic" about it. The reluctance stems from a disinclination to assign specificity on probabilistic rather than theoretical grounds. However, without a theory, evidence can never be judged as true, it can only be given a probability of differing from chance. It therefore seems reasonable to consider studies that only point out the unusualness of faces as a class of stimuli.

RECOGNITION ABILITY

Most of us are able to discriminate thousands of faces even if we are unable to put a name to them. Bahrick, Bahrick, and Wittlinger (1975) found that the faces of old school friends could be distinguished from other faces fifteen years later. Even after a fifty year lapse, three quarters of such faces were correctly classified. A high recognition rate is also found for pictures of strangers to which we are given just one exposure (Goldstein, 1977), though evidence from cases of mistaken identity tells us that a good memory for faces is by no means mandatory (Devlin, 1976). Even if excellent performance is the rule, it does not prove the uniqueness of faces. It could well be evidence for an interest in faces rather than for a specific mechanism for face processing. An impressive memory is, in any case, also shown for the recognition of other pictorial stimuli (Nickerson, 1965; Standing, Conezio & Haber, 1970). Quite a few studies have, nevertheless, compared recognition of faces to that for other types of stimulus.

Faces were better recognized than inkblots or snow crystals, (Goldstein & Chance, 1971), houses, aeroplanes or schematic men in motion (Yin, 1969) and dogs or buildings (Scapinello & Yarmey, 1970). There is, however, little point to such comparisons unless we have adequate control over the stimuli. Studies will be worthless unless the material has been equated for familiarity and difficulty of discrimination. This conclusion applies equally to studies where faces have not been found to be better recognized than other classes of stimuli (Deregowski, Ellis, & Shepherd, 1973). Familiarity may be impossible to control, but not so difficulty level. Even if there is no suitable metric for equating discrimination levels between types of stimuli on a theoretical basis, it would be quite possible to do so in an ad hoc fashion.

Having equated performance levels, we can no longer use a simple comparison of accuracy or latency to show the unusualness of faces. However, other methodologies are available. These do not test for uniqueness but rather for independence. With the dual task methodology, independence is inferred if processing competence is unaffected by the introduction of a second task. For example, the latency for name detection from an auditory input is not increased when the subject simultaneously reads aloud (Shallice, McLeod, & Lewis, 1984). Similar experiments could be carried out with faces, though it is difficult to be optimistic about showing independence; tasks as disparate as pressure discrimination and visual counting show decrements if performed simultaneously (Woodworth & Schlosberg, 1954). Also, any conclusions drawn would have to consider the effect of practice. Neisser (1976) has shown that with extended practice, parallel processing of even complex tasks can be achieved. We must be careful to distingish independence from an increased processing capacity developing over time.

The second method for assessing independence has also activated little interest. The double dissociation method taken from neuropsychology assesses independence of function for two skills (A and B) by finding a patient group which shows impairment for A and not B and another group which shows the reverse arrangement. In this manner it has been shown, for example, that fluent speech performance is independent of visual spatial abilities (Luria, 1973). The technique has been applied to faces with a dissociation suggested between famous and unfamiliar face processing (Warrington & James, 1967). Damage to the right temporal lobe caused more impairment for tasks using known faces, and damage to the right parietal more impairment, for tasks using unfamiliar faces.

It should be possible to establish a double dissociation in normals using an interference task. A comparison might be made, say, between face and shape recognition. Having established equal performance for the two classes of stimuli without interference, we could observe the effect on shape or face recognition of filling the delay between stimulus exposure and test with a task requiring face or shape processing. The outcome of this hypothetical study showing the double dissocation is illustrated in Fig. 7.1. However, the results are unlikely to turn out this way. Cohen and Granstrom (1970) have shown that faces do interfere with the memory for geometric patterns and the reciprocal relationship would seem to be likely. It is also probable that all the interference conditions would result in poorer recognition.

If the results of this imagined study were not to come out as in Fig. 7.1, would this be taken as disproof of specific face processing? Or would we then embark on the quest for some Holy Grail to provide the class of stimuli, perhaps other shapes that did not interfere with faces and vice versa? Without a theory upon which to base the choice of comparison stimuli, there is no way of knowing whether to continue or to stop. However, it is unlikely that faces and shapes would ever interfere equally with face (or shape) recognition. Stimulus similarity of the intervening items to the to-be-remembered items is important. Although it appears that dissimilar faces produce virtually no interference with each other (Cohen & Nodine, 1978), inevitably faces will be more visually similar to other faces than to shapes. The double dissociation shown in Fig. 7.1., even if achieved, could thus result from stimulus (material) similarity rather than from any shared or separate processing mechanism. We would have shown independence, but we would not know its cause; it could be either material or mechanism specificity. Material specificity for faces may be obvious but it cannot be ignored. We shall

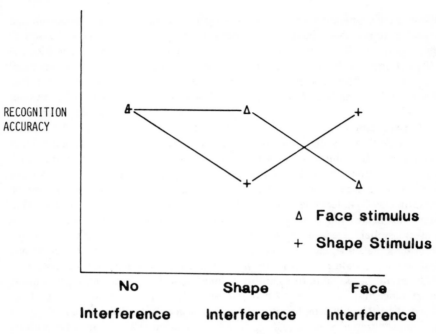

FIG. 7.1 Face and shape recognition as hypothesized under three interference conditions.

therefore consider research on the processing of face features before dealing with models of face recognition.

RECOGNITION OF FACES: FEATURES AND CONFIGURATIONS

Face features are clearly specific to faces. Certain stimuli will not do as parts of a face, though it is true we do not know the limits on shapes that will make them acceptable as face features. But even if we were able to make certain the restrictions on stimulus characteristics, this would not satisfy Fodor that faces constituted a domain. He would require evidence of specificity in processing. However, at the simplest level specificity is observed because certain parts of the face are more salient than others for recognition. The introspective report of subjects ranked the importance of face features as follows: eyes, nose, mouth, lips/chin, hair, and then ears (Laughery, Alexander, & Lane, 1971). Haig (1984) gives less importance to the nose and more to face shape, but like almost all research shows that the eyes are the most important internal face feature. Goldstein and Mackenberg (1966) found, contrary to Howells (1938), that initially showing the top half of a face was more helpful in subsequent recognition than showing the lower half. The fixation patterns used by people inspecting faces invariably starts in the upper part of the face (Walker-Smith, Gale, & Findley, 1977), and it is the eyes that receive most attention (Zusne, 1970). Infants, too, first concentrate their gaze in this region of a face and only later look at the mouth. The importance of the eyes was confirmed by Baron (1981) in his attempt to effect computer recognition of faces; it is the eyes that are first matched to the stored memory.

A preference for one face feature over the others is not really sufficient evidence for specificity. No doubt there are more and less important features used for the recognition of most classes of stimuli. It is more interesting that the precise features used to recognize a face depend on the familiarity of the face. Ellis, Shepherd, and Davies (1979) showed that well-known faces could be recognized to a fair degree of accuracy when subjects were shown only the internal features (eyes, nose, mouth) with the periphery of the face masked off. The alternative condition of masking only the internal features produced significantly worse identification. In contrast, when faces of strangers were presented, there was no difference in the ability to recognize them from either the internal or the external features.

Familarity is thus important in determining the way faces are processed; It also helps us to name faces more quickly (Bruce, 1983). Does familiarity's effect on feature recognition make faces unique? Not really, because familiarity affects other stimuli as well. Frequently used words are, for example, found to have a lower tachistoscopic threshold (Howes & Solomon, 1951). The effect of familiarity on faces, however, differs from the threshold effect with words in that the visual stimulus is itself treated qualitatively different if familiar. The examples (Fig. 7.2) taken from Palmer (1975) even show that face features can be unrecognizable out of context. Homa et al. (1976) argue that this is because faces form a meaningful configuration of features which differentially improves feature recognition. They showed that adults exposed to unfamiliar caricature faces were able to recognize the features better from a normal as opposed to a jumbled arrangement of the internal features. Recent work (Davidoff,, in prep.) has further shown that such configurational superiorities are time-locked. The advantage in retaining face features from normal faces only applies to stimulus presentations of less than 750 msecs.

A further indication that a meaningful arrangement of face features is processed in a different fashion comes from the differential improvement in recognition of the types of face features. Homa et al. (1976) showed that the eyes and mouth were much better recognized than the nose (unpublished results of the present author confirm this finding for photographs of faces). They were careful enough to match the types of feature for difficulty of discrimination so that, in isolation, there were no recognition differences. Therefore, it is important that features were not equally easy to recognize when placed together

(A) In Context   (B) Out of Context

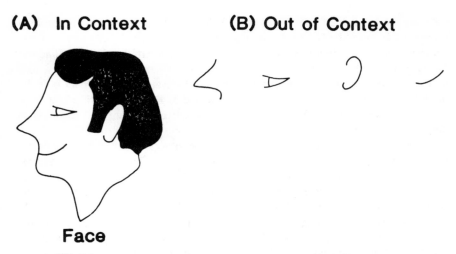

Face

FIG. 7.2. The effect of context on face feature recognition (adapted from Palmer, 1975).

as a face. Face features appear to be processed in one of two ways, depending on whether the face is regarded as separate features or as a configuration. The study of the ontogeny of face processing confirms this view.

Young children are dominated by visually striking features of a face. Even non-face features aspects of faces (e.g., glasses or hats) can determine the infant's recognition behaviour. Diamond and Carey (1977) found that 6-year-old children have difficulty in recognizing strangers if the expression is changed because, they argue, children are not remembering the whole face. Ten-year-olds do not have this problem. It is proposed that a holistic process, presumably requiring spatial integration of the features, has fully developed. Hay and Young (1982) have disputed the need for both holistic and feature based recognition mechanisms. They point out inconsistencies in the development of processing of house stimuli observed by Carey and Diamond (1977), and would rather believe that the young children could not cope with the large number of unfamiliar faces. It is certainly the case that the young children dealt with familiar faces in a similar fashion to older children. However, it is quite reasonable to suppose that young children could form mental configurations of very familiar faces but not of unfamiliar.

Faces require an integration of the features under some circumstances. This makes them unique only if configurational superiority for arrangements of visual features is restricted to face stimuli. The evidence suggests that this is not the case because there are just such effects for geometric patterns (Pomerantz, 1981; Weissstein & Harris, 1974). Does configurational processing perhaps operate in a different manner for faces? Certainly it changes the differential recognition performance of the features of the face, but even this may not be unique, because a similar change has been noted for letters in words (Davidoff, Beaton, Done, & Booth, 1982) dependent on reading skill. It was found that good readers showed better recognition for the ends of briefly presented words, whereas poor readers showed recognition in serial order from first to last letter. A similarity between words and faces with respect to configurational processing is not surprising. The experiment of Homa et al. (1976) which showed a face superiority effect was designed to parallel the word superiority effect (Reicher, 1969) in which letters embedded in words are better matched than letters presented in isolation. With extended practice Homa et al. were indeed able to demonstrate a comparable effect for their faces, explicitly arguing that faces are analogous to words.

RECOGNITION OF FACES: MECHANISMS AND MENTAL REPRESENTATIONS

The study of faces as a collection of unique features has led us to consider mechanisms of face processing. There is no evidence that any mechanism used to recognize face features is unique, but is this true for other aspects of face recognition? Goldstein and Chance (1981) argue against uniqueness, pointing out that faces behave in a similar fashion to other pictorial stimuli with respect to the effects of retention interval and exposure time on forgetting. Faces also resemble some other pictorial stimuli in not being easily coded verbally. Chance and Goldstein (1976) found that subjects were unable to recall the verbalizations they had made when first seeing faces, despite their excellent recognition of the faces at retest. Indeed, people who are capable of good verbal description of faces are not better at recognizing faces (Goldstein, Johnson, & Chance, 1979). The unimportance of verbal coding for face recognition is confirmed by studies of interference effects (Cohen & Nodine, 1978), and is similar to the limited role of verbal coding in the storage of other pictorial material. Furthermore, the logical and procedural difficulties that make uncertain the effects of intention to learn, depth of processing, and reminiscence all seem just as relevant to face memory as to memorizing other pictorial material. We must look elsewhere for evidence of the specificity of faces.

If faces are to be considered unique, they must substantiate Fodor's (1983) claim that input specificity is necessarily informationally encapsulated. By this Fodor means that the input system is a domain specified by unique processing constraints. What are the requirements of such a domain? It is certainly not intended to be the same as a modality. For the visual modality there are many domains—e.g. colour, shape, and perhaps faces. Faces are not claimed as a domain just because they are a class of visual stimuli; this would apply to other stimuli such as cows, which Fodor does not see as specific. He believes that "recognition of cows would be mediated by precisely the same mechanism that affects the perception of language, or of earthquakes or three-masted brigantines" (p. 48). Fodor argues that recognition of a cow relies on a prototype mechanism, and the identification of a particular cow on estimating the distance from the prototype by, say, angular rotation. Such a mechanism is not unique to cows; we shall see that it also proposed for faces and other classes of stimuli.

In light of the reported neurological condition (Assal, 1984; Bornstein, Sroka, & Munitz, 1969) in which farmers have complained of a specific difficulty in cow recognition, Fodor (1983) might not have chosen the best example to contrast with faces. However, the point remains that if faces are truly unlike other classes of visual stimuli, they must demand unique processing. Fodor does not tell us precisely why faces are to be regarded as a domain, but he believes that the most satisfactory reason is that, like language, there is a theory for face recognition. However, language is a much better candidate than faces for being a domain because there are known specific processing rules. Experimental research also reinforces the claim for specificity for language. For example, Liberman, Cooper, Shankweiler, and Studdert-Kennedy (1967) have shown that the same signal is heard differently depending on whether the context suggests that the sound is an utterance. There are only a few theoretically based domains besides language. Marr (1982), for example, has provided computational rules for deciding how the visual input should be divided into objects. Certain assumptions are made that, even if they eventually turn out to be wrong, nevertheless provide a theory for object recognition. Models of the mental representations of faces have not reached this stage of elaboration, but that is not to say that there are no theories of face recognition. Accounts have been recently developed (Bruce, 1979; Hay & Young, 1982), and we must consider whether these and other models incorporate any unique processing mechanisms.

Every object must be mentally represented in such a way that recognition can take place from a large, if not infinite, variety of views and illumination. For objects (including cows), Fodor considers this structural code to be a form of prototype, the input being manipulated until it matches the stored prototypical version. A similar proposal comes from the work of Cooper and Shepard (1973). They found that the time taken to match a rotated F to a vertical F depended on the extent of the rotation. The prototype would in this straightforward case be an upright F. The structural code need not be so simple. Posner and Keele (1970) conducted an experiment in which observers had to respond to dot figures that were variations on a pattern that was itself not presented. When the basic pattern was finally shown, response was rapid, indicating that the pattern acted as the structural code. Does the structural code for faces operate in the same way or in some unique fashion?

Very little research has been carried out investigating the nature of the structural code for faces. Like representations for other objects, the code would have to be able to cope with rotation. As familiarity makes faces even more resistant to rotational variation (Ellis et al., 1979), the representation must also be modifiable.

Ellis (1981) argues that the structural code is established as a summary of the different views of a face. A better structural code arises if multiple views are allowed. This is inferred from the study of Dukes and Bevan (1967), who compared learning names for faces when given multiple presentations of the identical view of a face to a condition in which different poses were shown. Subjects given the variation in pose were better able to recall the names associated with the faces when completely new poses were presented.

Not all research points to a prototype of a face being a summary of views experienced. The conclusion Ellis draws from the Dukes and Bevan experiment is only warranted if the completely new pose does not possess greater similarity to the varying poses than to the identical pose. Ellis has, in fact, conducted an experiment analogous to that of Posner and Keele, finding no evidence of a summary prototype for a class of faces. In this study, subjects appeared to retain representations of individual faces, not of the central unpresented face. There was also no evidence that we have group prototypes for categories of people. Faces could not be correctly classified as, say, a bank manager or a Scotsman, despite the belief of Light, Kayra-Stuart, and Hollander (1979) that there were such typical faces.

Perkins (1975) argues that, if we do store faces as prototypes, this could be addressed better by a nonrealistic superstimulus. The parallel is with work in ethology in which a red dot on a stick elicits gaping in herring gull chicks better than does the real beak of the parent (Tinbergen, 1957). Perkins (1975) has suggested that caricatures of faces could be just such superstimuli; but the empirical validation for this idea is nonexistent. Ellis (1981) quotes evidence that caricatures are, in fact, recognized less well than photographs, a finding that could be predicted from the work of Davies, Ellis, and Shepherd (1978), who showed that line drawings of faces were not as easy to identify as photographs. Of course, it could be argued that the caricatures used in the studies Ellis cites were not good enough to capture the essence of the person. That argument bears a distinct similarity to that used by Zuckerman and Rock (1957) to explain why certain shapes were easy to see as embedded figures, that is, the shapes chosen were not incorporated into good enough figures. This line of argument is difficult to refute but leads to circularity and is hardly satisfactory. It is more likely that caricatures act in a somewhat different fashion to photographs and are effective from an interpretation of the input rather than by direct access to the structural code.

The prototype of a face is seen by Hay and Young (1982) as a face recognition unit that acts rather like the word recognition units proposed by Morton (1969). Bruce (1983) envisages the recognition units as being activated by semantic associates to the presented face and found that search times for faces is affected by the presence of semantically related distractor items (Bruce, 1979) just as they are for letters, digits, and words. The problem of how the unit responds to variations in input is sidestepped, concentration being on the general cognitive framework instead. The threshold for evoking the unit referring to a word is lowered by priming with a related word. A similar context effect is found for faces, which is not surprising it being well known that it is harder to recognize someone encountered out of a usual setting. Watkins, Ho, and Tulving (1976) have experimentally investigated such a context effect for faces. Pairs of photographs were shown and at recognition kept either in the same pairs or repaired with other faces. The same pairs condition led to better recognition. Though the effect was small, the effect of previous context was present. Other research (Bower & Karlin, 1974; Brown, Deffenbacher, & Sturgill, 1977) has not in fact, found context effects, perhaps because the context must be relevant to the face task for it to affect retrieval (Leippe, Wells, & Ostrom, 1978).

Although the nature of the structural code for faces is unknown, such a code must perforce exist. But this necessity has long been realized (Hoffding, 1891) and is not restricted to face recognition. None of the work on the structural codes for faces requires any new mechanism. Indeed, the models of Bruce (1979) and Hay and Young (1982) owe a great deal to those already existing for word recognition. A different theory of object recognition based more on stimulus factors has been put forward by Marr (1982), but this too would apply to face recognition. In fact, part of the inspiration for Marr's ideas came from Warrington's work with brain-damaged patients, which did not distinguish between faces and objects. Warrington and Taylor (1973) found that damage to the parietal lobe of the right hemisphere causes difficulty in recognizing unusual views of objects. Such patients have equal difficulty in matching variations in views of faces.

A structural code may not be unique to faces, but it still is possible that certain transformations of the face stimulus are unique in making the code difficult to access. Yin (1969) has pointed to the disruption of face recognition if the face is inverted. The increase in errors was almost fivefold for faces but much less for houses, aeroplanes and caricatures of men in action. Similar results have been reported by Hochberg and Galper (1967), Scapinello and Yarmey (1970), and Yarmey (1971). Difficulty with inverted faces is also seen in 5- to 6-month-old infants (Fagan, 1972). However, Yin's assertion that faces must therefore be special is invalid because no control is made over the familiarity or complexity (see Goldstein & Chance, 1981) of faces compared with other types of stimuli. Our ability to deal with transformations from the prototype certainly does depend on practice. Ellis and Deregowski (1981) showed that rotational transformations from an originally presented face were less easily performed for faces of a different race from the subject's. It therefore seems appropriate to ask: If Yin had used other familiar stimuli, would the same conclusion have been reached? The answer is probably no because it is also hard to recognize familiar maps when inverted (Kanizsa, 1979, see Fig. 7.3). This conclusion is reinforced by a cartoon by Verbeek (Davidoff, 1975), which shows that clever manipulation of a figure to give a meaningful inverted display makes it particularly hard to see that there is another scene the other way up (see Fig. 7.4).

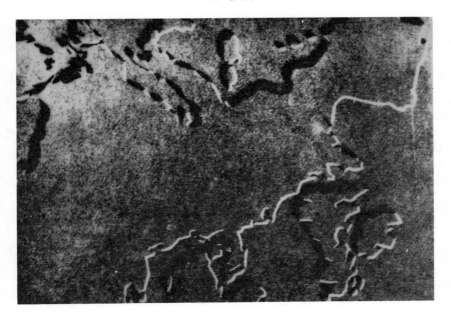

FIG. 7.3. (taken from Kanizsa, 1979).

FIG. 7.4. Cartoon by Verbeek.

Rock (1974) has pointed out that the spatial relationship between face features is disturbed by inversion. Because visual scanning movements are normally top to bottom for a face (Smith & Nielson, 1970; Walker-Smith, 1978), this over-learned viewing strategy would be hard to alter, making face recognition from inverted faces difficult. However, Bradshaw, and Wallace (1971) found that with extended practice this is not the case: subjects given sufficient experience could discriminate features in inverted faces. Other classes of stimuli disturbed by inversion would no doubt be similarly aided by practice. The finding (Yin, 1970) that, unlike normals, brain damaged patients are not disturbed by face inversion could be due to changed face scanning strategies adopted by such patients (Jones, 1969), rather than to disturbance of a face specific system.

There is a similar disruption of face recognition if there is a brightness reversal of the face as found in a photographic negative (Galper, 1970) or a lithographic negative (Phillips, 1972). Lithographic negatives are more extreme and eliminate all grey tones. However, neither of these studies compared the effects of such transformations on other stimuli. Only if such a comparison is made to equally familiar stimuli can any unique transformation be held special to faces. It must therefore be concluded that there is no good evidence that transformations of the face input provide any particular problem over that for other stimuli in accessing the structural code used for recognition.

CONCLUSION

The conclusion we must draw from the attempt to define specificity in terms of Fodor's criteria for an independent input system is clear. Faces do not have sufficient properties to be considered unique. There are material specific elements that make faces a specific class of stimuli, but there are no processing procedures that are not or could not be applied to other stimuli. No doubt the neurophysiological evidence should make us hesitate to be so adamant, but the crucial data showing that face specific cells are present in the absence of face experience are yet to be obtained. Until they are, the behavioural evidence from normal humans does not favour specificity. Still, we must not forget that the effect of experience is to produce an incredibly important class of stimuli. The face is without doubt special, even if it is not unique in terms of processing mechanisms.

REFERENCES

Assal, G. (1984). *Paper presented at the 2nd European Conference on Cognitive Neuropsychology,* Bressanone.

Bahrick, H. P., Bahrick, P. O., & Wittlinger, R. P. (1975). Fifty years of memory for names and faces: A cross-cultural approach. *Journal of Experimental Psychology: General, 104,* 54–75.

Baron, J. (1981). Mechanisms of human facial recognition. *International Journal of Man-Machine Studies, 15,* 137–178.

Blakemore, C., & Cooper, G. F. (1970). Development of the brain depends on visual environment. *Nature, 228,* 477–478.

Bornstein, B., Sroka, H., & Munitz, H. (1969). Prosopagnosia with animal faces agnosia. *Cortex, 5,* 164–169.

Bower, G. H., & Karlin, M. B. (1974). Depth of processing pictures of faces and recognition memory. *Journal of Experimental Psychology, 103,* 751–757.

Bower, T. G. R. (1974). *Development in infancy,* San Francisco: Freeman.

Bradshaw, J. L., & Wallace, G. (1971). Models for the processing and identification of faces. *Perception and Psychophysics, 9,* 443–448.

Brouwers, P., Mononen, L. J., & Stefanatos, G. A. (1980). Visual field differences in recognition of male and female faces. *Perceptual and Motor Skills, 51,* 622–633.

Brown, E., Deffenbacher, K., & Sturgill, W. (1977). Memory for faces and the circumstance of encounter. *Journal of Applied Psychology, 62,* 311–318.

Bruce, V. (1979). Searching for politicians: An information-processing approach to face recognition. *Quarterly Journal of Experimental Psychology, 31,* 373–395.

Bruce, V. (1983). Recognizing faces. *Philosophical Transactions of the Royal Society London B, 302,* 423–436.

Carey, S. (1981). The development of face perception. In G. Davies, H. D. Ellis, & J. Shepherd (Eds.), *Perceiving and remembering faces* (pp. 9–38). London: Academic Press.

Carey, S., & Diamond, R. (1977). From piecemeal to configurational representation of faces. *Science, 195,* 312–314.

Carpenter, G. C., Tecce, J. J., Stechler, G., & Friedman, S. (1970). Differential visual behavior to human and humanoid faces in early infancy. *Merrill-Palmer Quarterly, 16,* 91–108.

Chance, J., & Goldstein, A. G. (1976). Recognition of faces and verbal labels. *Bulletin of the Psychonomic Society, 7,* 384–386.

Cohen, M. E., & Nodine, C. F. (1978). Memory processes in facial recognition and recall. *Bulletin of the Psychonomic Society, 12,* 317–319.

Cohen, R. L., & Granstrom, K. (1970). Reproduction and recognition in short-term visual memory. *Quarterly Journal of Experimental Psychology, 22,* 450–457.

Cooper, L. A., & Shephard, R. N. (1973). Chronometric studies of the rotation of mental images. In W. G. Chase (Ed.), *Visual information processing* (pp. 75–176), New York: Academic Press.

Cross, J. F., Cross, J., & Daly, J. (1971). Sex, race, age and beauty as factors in recognition of faces. *Perception and Psychophysics, 19,* 393–396.

Davidoff, J. B. (1975). *Differences in visual perception.* London: Crosby Lockwood Staples.

Davidoff, J. B. (1977). Hemispheric differences in dot detection. *Cortex, 13,* 434–444.

Davidoff, J. B. (1982). Non-verbal studies. In J. G. Beaumont (Ed.), *Divided visual field studies of cerebral organization* (pp. 29–55). London: Academic Press.

Davidoff, J. B. (in prep). *Assessing the effect of faceness on the recognition of face features.*

Davidoff, J. B., Beaton, A. A., Done, J., & Booth, H. (1982). Information extraction from brief verbal displays: half-field and serial position effects for children, normal and illiterate adults. *British Journal of Psychology, 73,* 29–39.

Davies, G. M., Ellis, H. D., & Shepherd, J. W. (1978). Face recognition as a function of mode of representation. *Journal of Applied Psychology, 63,* 180–187.

Deregowski, J. B., Ellis, H. D., & Shepherd, J. (1973). A cross-cultural study of recognition of pictures of faces and cups. *International Journal of Psychology, 8,* 269–273.

Devlin, Lord Patrick. (1976). Report to the Secretary of State for the Home Department of the departmental committee on evidence of identification in criminal cases. London: Her Majesty's Stationary Office.

Diamond, R., & Carey, S. (1977). Developmental changes in the representation of faces. *Journal of Experimental Child Psychology, 23*, 1–22.

Dukes, W. F., & Bevan, W. (1967). Stimulus variation and repetition in the acquisition of naming responses. *Journal of Experimental Psychology, 74*, 178–181.

Ellis, H. D. (1981). Theoretical aspects of face recognition. In G. Davies, H. D. Ellis, & J. Shepherd (Eds.), *Perceiving and remembering faces* (pp. 171–197). London: Academic Press.

Ellis, H. D., & Deregowski, J. B. (1981). Within-race and between-race recognition of transformed and untransformed faces. *American Journal of Psychology, 94*, 23–35.

Ellis, H. D., Shepherd, J., & Bruce, A. (1973). The effects of age and sex upon adolescents' recognition of faces. *Journal of Genetic Psychology, 123*, 173–174.

Ellis, H. D., Shepherd, J., & Davies, G. M. (1979). Identification of familiar and unfamiliar faces from internal and external features: Some implications for theories of face recognition. *Perception, 8*, 431–439.

Fagan, J. F. (1972). Infants' recognition memory for faces. *Journal of Experimental Child Psychology, 14*, 453–476.

Fagan, J. F. (1973). Infants' delayed recognition memory and forgetting. *Journal of Experimental Child Psychology, 16*, 424–450.

Fantz, R. L. (1961). The origin of form perception. *Scientific American, May*.

Fodor, J. A. (1983). *The modularity of mind.* Cambridge, MA: MIT Press.

Galper, R. E. (1970). Recognition of faces in photographic negative. *Psychonomic Science, 19*, 207–208.

Goldstein, A. G. (1977). The fallibility of eyewitness. Psychological evidence. In B. D. Sales (Ed.), *Psychology in the legal process* (pp. 223–247). New York: Spectrum.

Goldstein, A. G., & Chance, J. (1971). Visual recognition memory for complex configurations. *Perception and Psychophysics, 9*, 237–241.

Goldstein, A. G., & Chance, J. (1981). Laboratory studies of face recognition. In G. Davies, H. D. Ellis, & J. Shepherd (Eds.), *Perceiving and remembering faces* (pp. 81–104). London: Academic Press.

Goldstein, A. G., Johnson, K. S., & Chance, J. (1979). Does fluency of face description imply superior face recognition? *Bulletin of the Psychonomic Society, 13*, 15–18.

Goldstein, A. G., & Mackenberg, E. G. (1966). Recognition of human faces from isolated facial features: A developmental study. *Psychonomic Science, 6*, 149–150.

Goren, C. C., Sarty, M., & Wu, P. W. K. (1975). Visual following and pattern discrimination of face-like stimuli by newborn infants. *Pediatrics, 56*, 544–554.

Haig, N. D. (1984). The effect of feature displacement on face recognition. *Perception, 13*, 505–512.

Hannay, H. J., & Rogers, J. P. (1979). Individual differences and asymmetry effects in memory for unfamiliar faces. *Cortex, 15*, 257–267.

Hay, D. C., & Young, A. W. (1982). The human face. In A. W. Ellis (Ed.), *Normality and pathology in cognitive function* (pp. 173–202). London: Academic Press.

Hochberg, J., & Galper, R. E. (1967). Recognition of faces. I. An exploratory study. *Psychonomic Science, 9*, 619–620.

Hoffding, H. (1891). *Outlines of Psychology.* London: MacMillan.

Homa, D., Haver, B., & Schwartz, T. (1976). Perceptibility of schematic face stimuli: Evidence for a perceptual Gestalt. *Memory and Cognition, 4*, 176–185.

Howells, T. H. (1938). A study of the ability to recognize faces. *Journal of Abnormal and Social Psychology, 33*, 124–127.

Howes, D., & Solomon, R. L. (1951). Visual duration thresholds as a function of word probability. *Journal of Experimental Psychology, 41*, 401–410.

Jones, A. C. (1969). Influence of mode of stimulus presentation on performance in facial recognition tasks. *Cortex, 5*, 290–301.

Kanizsa, G. (1979). *Organization in vision.* New York: Praeger.

Ladavas, E., Umiltà, C., & Ricci-Bitti, P. (1980). Evidence for sex differences in right hemisphere dominance for emotions. *Neuropsychologia, 18,* 361–366.

Laughery, K. R., Alexander, J. F., & Lane, A. B. (1971). Recognition of human faces: Effects of target exposure time, target position, pose position and type of photograph. *Journal of Applied Psychology, 55,* 477–483.

Leippe, M. R., Wells, G. L., & Ostrom, T. M. (1978). Crime seriousness as a determination of accuracy in eyewitness identification. *Journal of Applied Psychology, 63,* 345–351.

Liberman, A., Cooper, F., Shankweiler, D., & Studdert-Kennedy, M. (1967). The perception of the speech code. *Psychological Review, 74,* 431–461.

Light, L. L., Kayra-Stuart, F., & Hollander, S. (1979). Recognition memory for typical and unusual faces. *Journal of Experimental Psychology: Human Learning and Memory, 5,* 212–228.

Luria, A. R. (1973). *The working brain.* London: Penguin.

Marr, D. (1982). *Vision.* San Francisco: W. H. Freeman.

Mazzucchi, A., & Biber, C. (1983). Is prosopagnosia more frequent in males than females? *Cortex, 19,* 509–516.

McGlone, J. (1980). Sex differences in human brain asymmetry: A critical survey. *The Behavioural and Brain Sciences, 3,* 215–263.

McKeever, W. F., & Dixon, M. S. (1981). Right hemisphere superiority for discriminating memorized from non-memorized faces: Affective imagery, sex, and perceived emotionality effects. *Brain and Language, 12,* 246–250.

Messick, S., & Damarin, F. (1964). Cognitive styles and memory for faces. *Journal of Abnormal and Social Psychology, 69,* 313–318.

Miller, R. E., Caul, W. F., & Mirsky, I. A. (1967). The communication of affects between feral and socially isolated monkeys. *Journal of Personality and Social Psychology, 7,* 231–239.

Morton, J. (1969). The interaction of information in word recognition. *Psychological Review, 76,* 165–178.

Neisser, U. (1976). *Cognition and Reality,* San Francisco: W. H. Freeman.

Nickerson, R. S. (1965). Short-term memory for complex, meaningful, visual configurations: A demonstration of capacity. *Canadian Journal of Psychology, 19,* 155–160.

Palmer, S. E. (1975). The effects of contextual scenes on the identification of objects. *Memory and Cognition, 3,* 519–526.

Perkins, D. (1975). A definition of caricature and recognition. *Studies in the Anthropology of Visual Communication, 2,* 1–24.

Perrett, D., Rolls, E., & Caan, W. (1982). Visual neurones responsive to faces in the monkey temporal cortex. *Experimental Brain Research, 47,* 329–342.

Perrett, D., Smith, P. A. J., Potter, D. D., Mistlin, A. J., Head, A. S., Milner, A. D., & Jeeves, M. A. (1984). Neurones responsive to faces in the temporal cortex: Studies of functional organization, sensitivity to identity and relation to perception. *Human Neurobiology 3,* 197–208.

Phillips, R. J. (1972). Why are faces hard to recognize in photographic negative? *Perception and Psychophysics, 12,* 425–426.

Piazza, D. M. (1980). The influence of sex and handedness in the hemispheric specialization of verbal and non-verbal tasks. *Neuropsychologia, 18,* 163–176.

Pizzamiglio, L., & Zoccolotti, P. (1981). Sex and cognitive influence on visual hemifield superiority for face and letter recognition. *Cortex, 17,* 215–226.

Pomerantz, J. R. (1981). Perceptual organization in information processing. In M. Kubovy & J. R. Pomerantz (Eds.), *Perceptual organization* (pp. 141–180), Hillsdale, NJ: Lawrence Erlbaum Associates.

Posner, M. I., & Keele, S. W. (1970). Retention of abstract ideas. *Journal of Experimental Psychology, 83,* 304–308.

Proudfoot, R. E. (1983). Hemispheric asymmetry for face recognition: Cognitive style and the "crossover" effect. *Cortex, 19,* 31–41.

Reicher, G. M. (1969). Perceptual recognition as a function of meaningfulness of stimulus material. *Journal of Experimental Psychology, 81,* 275–280.

Rizzolatti, G., & Buchtel, H. A. (1977). Hemispheric superiority in reaction time to faces: A sex difference. *Cortex, 13,* 300–305.

Rock, I. (1974). The perception of distorted figures. *Scientific American, 230,* 78–85.

Sackett, G. P. (1966). Monkeys reared in isolation with pictures as visual input: Evidence for innate releasing mechanism. *Science, 150,* 1470–1473.

Safer, M. A. (1981). Sex and hemisphere differences in access to codes for processing emotional expressions and faces. *Journal of Experimental Psychology: General, 110,* 86–100.

Scapinello, K. I., & Yarmey, A. D. (1970). The role of familiarity and orientation in immediate and delayed recognition of pictorial stimuli. *Psychonomic Science, 21,* 329–330.

Shallice, T., McLeod, P., & Lewis, K. (1984). *Splitting the logogens: Are speech perception and production separate processes?* Paper presented at the meeting of the Experimental Psychology Society. London.

Smith, E. E., & Nielsen, G. D. (1970). Representations and retrieval processes in STM recognition and recall of faces. *Journal of Experimental Psychology, 85,* 397–405.

Standing, L., Conezio, J., & Haber, R. N. (1970). Perception and memory for pictures: Single-trial learning of 2500 visual stimuli. *Psychonomic Science, 19,* 73–74.

Tinbergen, N. (1957). *The Study of Instincts,* Oxford, England: Oxford University Press.

Tzavaras, A., Hécaen, H., & LeBras, H. (1970). Le problème de la spécificité du déficit de la reconnaissance du visage humain lors des lésions hémisphériques unilatérales. *Neuropsychologia, 8,* 403–416.

Walker-Smith, G. J. (1978). The effects of delay and exposure duration in a face recognition task. *Perception and Psychophysics, 24,* 63–70.

Walker-Smith, G. J., Gale, A. G., & Findlay, J. M. (1977). Eye movement strategies involved in face perception. *Perception, 6,* 313–326.

Warrington, E. K., & James, M. (1967). An experimental investigation of facial recognition in patients with unilateral cerebral lesions. *Cortex, 3,* 317–326.

Warrington, E. K., & Taylor, A. M. (1973). The contribution of the right parietal lobe to object recognition. *Cortex, 9,* 152–164.

Watkins, M. J., Ho, E., & Tulving, E. (1976). Context effect in recognition memory for faces. *Journal of Verbal Learning and Verbal Behavior, 15,* 505–517.

Weisstein, N., & Harris, C. S. (1974). Visual detection of line segments: An object superiority efect. *Science, 186,* 752–755.

Witkin, H. A., Dyk, R. B., Faterson, H. R., Goodenough, D. R., & Karp, S. A. (1962). *Psychological differentiation: Studies of development.* New York: Wiley.

Witryol, S. L., & Kaess, W. A. (1957). Sex differences in social memory tasks. *Journal of Abnormal and Social Psychology, 54,* 343–346.

Woodworth, R. S., & Schlosberg, H. (1954). *Experimental Psychology,* New York: Holt Rinehart & Winston (p. 90).

Yarmey, A. D. (1971). Recognition memory for familiar "public" faces: Effects of orientation and delay. *Psychonomic Science, 24,* 284–288.

Yin, R. K. (1969). Looking at upside-down faces. *Journal of Experimental Psychology, 81,* 141–145.

Yin, R. K. (1970). Face recognition by brain-injured patients: A dissociable ability? *Neuropsychologia, 8,* 395–402.

Zuckerman, C. B., & Rock, I. (1957). A reappraisal of the roles of past experience and innate organizing processes in visual perception. *Psychological Bulletin, 54,* 269–296.

Zusne, L. (1970). *Visual perception of form.* New York: Academic Press.

8 Subject Characteristics in Lateral Differences for Face Processing by Normals: Age

Andrew W. Young
Lancaster University

The methods used to investigate lateral differences for face processing in normal subjects can often be adapted for use with children, thus allowing the possibility of investigating the development of functional asymmetries in the normal, intact brain. This enterprise is of value in two distinct ways. Firstly, it increases our understanding of human development and the cerebral processes involved. Secondly, it increases our understanding of the mechanisms used in face processing by adults, because with increased knowledge of how these mechanisms are developed we are better able to understand their limits and their potential for further change. The importance of the topic perhaps can be most clearly seen in attempts to rehabilitate adults or children who have suffered cerebral injuries, where the kinds of technique that are thought likely to be of use will be heavily dependent on current conceptions of how the cerebral mechanisms involved in face processing are developed in the uninjured brain.

The basic simplicity of such methods as comparing the processing of stimuli presented in the left and right visual hemifields also makes them attractive research tools. There are, however, a number of problems in their application to developmental studies that need to be carefully borne in mind both when planning to undertake such studies and when evaluating their outcomes.

I have divided my discussion of the development of lateral differences for face processing into two main sections. First the studies themselves and the methods they employ are examined. This first section is divided into subsections dealing with the logic and methods used, recognition of faces of known people, recognition of faces of unknown people, the perception and production of facial expressions, and other studies involving faces. The results of these studies are then related in the second section to wider issues concerning the development of hemispheric specialization, the possibility of innate cerebral specialization for faces, and maturational changes. A brief third section providing an overview and conclusions completes the chapter.

STUDIES OF THE DEVELOPMENT OF LATERAL ASYMMETRIES FOR FACE PROCESSING

Studies of the development of lateral asymmetries for face processing are considered in subsections concerned respectively with the logic and methods used, recognition of faces of known people, recognition of faces of unknown people, perception and production of facial expressions, and other studies involving faces.

The Logic and Methods Used

The methods used in studies of lateral asymmetries in normal subjects have been reviewed by Young (1982a) and Beaumont (1983), but their application to developmental studies involves a number of problems that need to be looked at. These problems are also discussed by Witelson (1977a), Beaumont (1982), and Young (1982b, 1983). They tend to be problems that are not unique to developmental studies of lateral differences, but that are potentially present in a particularly pressing form in such studies.

Foremost among these problems is the need to control the ways in which subjects can approach experimental tasks. The use of different strategies or cognitive processes is known to influence the lateral differences obtained in a number of tasks (Bertelson, 1982; Bryden, 1978, 1982). It is thus important to try to ensure that, whenever possible, subjects of different ages are all solving the tasks in the same way. This can sometimes be achieved by instructions concerning the way in which the task is to be done or by obtaining independent evidence concerning the cognitive processes used, but it is usually more satisfactory in developmental studies to try to design the task in a way that limits the range of approaches that can be employed. Without such controls there is a real risk that findings of changes in lateral asymmetries across age will only reflect age-related changes in the strategies or cognitive processes used. Such changes are not without interest, but it is important that they are not mistaken for changes in the asymmetry of cerebral functions (see also Bertelson, 1978; De Renzi, 1982). A change in cerebral asymmetry can only be said to occur when it can be demonstrated that age differences in lateral performance asymmetries arise even though subjects of the different ages concerned are solving the tasks used in the same way.

The wide range of ages often needed in developmental studies of lateral differences can also lead to further problems linked to task difficulty. In extreme cases these will take the form of ceiling and floor effects, but there is also a problem in establishing that a task is sufficiently sensitive in both cases whenever it is found to be more difficult for one group of subjects than another (Young & Ellis, 1981). In addition, there are problems associated with the choice of an appropriate metric for comparing the sizes of lateral differences (Jones, 1983; Morris, Bakker, Satz, & Van der Vlugt, 1984).

The cause of these problems is, as Beaumont (1982) observes, to be found in the lack of a really detailed theoretical understanding of the ways in which lateral differences arise in information processing tasks. Investigators thus get caught in something of a vicious circle in which they want to gain increased understanding of lateral differences through studying their development but they need to understand lateral differences better in order to devise ways of finding out how they develop.

It's easy, however, to paint too gloomy a picture of the problems of method that beset developmental studies of lateral differences. Against this it must be pointed out that such problems are not completely intractable, and that the results of most studies of the development of lateral differences in information processing have produced consistent and convincing results (Beaumont, 1982; Witelson, 1977a; Young, 1982b, 1983). In particular, when the same lateral differences are found at different ages there are good grounds for concluding that functional asymmetry for the processes investigated has not changed across age. It is when lateral differences are found to change across age that particular caution needs to be exercised, because of the range of different potential causes that might produce such a result. It is especially difficult to mount a convincing argument that changes in laterality effects found at different ages reflect changes in cerebral asymmetry, because there are so many more prosaic alternative explanations that must be ruled out.

This point about how to interpret different kinds of result actually applies not only to developmental studies of lateral differences, but quite generally. Whenever the same findings can be made for younger and older subjects it can be inferred that young people possess the ability investigated; when differences across age are found it is always difficult to establish convincingly that young people lack some quality present in those who are older. This is because it is difficult to eliminate the possibility that the ability investigated was also present in the younger subjects but, for one of many potential reasons, they failed to display it (Bryant, 1974).

The most commonly employed method in developmental studies of lateral differences for face processing is to present stimulus faces in the left visual hemifield (LVF) or in the right visual hemifield (RVF), so that they are initially projected to the right cerebral hemisphere (LVF) or to the left cerebral hemisphere (RVF). For this method, the positions of LVF and RVF stimuli are usually specified in relation to a central point that the person acting as experimental subject is asked to fixate before each stimulus is presented. This means that some form of fixation control is desirable in developmental studies, because there are a number of reasons why children may fail to fixate centrally when instructed to do so. Failure to fixate centrally when instructed will lead to stimuli not falling in the positions in the visual field intended by the experimenter. Such fixation failures may be related in complex ways to age and task difficulty, but the most likely pattern is one in which younger subjects produce artifactual results that seem to reflect changes in lateral asymmetries across age. Fixation control is also discussed by Beaumont (1982, 1983) and Young (1982a, 1982b, 1983).

Apart from simply stressing to subjects the importance of central fixation as the best strategy to use (Marcel & Rajan, 1975; Pirozzolo & Rayner, 1979) three methods of fixation control have been employed in developmental studies of visual hemifield differences for face processing. Young and Ellis (1976) presented stimuli centrally as well as in the LVF and in the RVF, and excluded from their study children whose performance was not at least as good for central as for lateral stimuli. The reasoning behind this method is that the greater acuity of central vision should have produced better performance with central stimuli if the central spot was being fixated. This method of fixation control is simple to use, but suffers from the disadvantage that it can only eliminate subjects who did not fixate, rather than the individual trials on which central fixation did not occur. Nonetheless, the fact that 29 of the 71 children tested by Young and Ellis (1976) did not meet this simple criterion of equal or better performance with central than lateral stimuli shows the importance of some form of fixation control in studies of this type.

The second method of fixation control that has been used involves the presentation, at the fixation point on every trial, of a small digit that the subject must report. This technique, introduced by McKeever and Huling (1971), was used in Leehey's (1976) developmental studies. It is reasonably accurate, but it is unsuitable for young children and its use has always led to arguments about whether the requirement of reporting the digit interferes with the processing of the lateral stimuli (see Beaumont, 1983; Young, 1982a).

The third method of fixation control used in developmental studies is direct monitoring of the subject's eyes. This can be achieved via a video camera, which is not difficult to set up and can be arranged to be very accurate across the ranges of stimulus positions typically employed in this type of research (Reynolds & Jeeves, 1978; Young & Bion, 1980, 1981). It is surprising that it has not been more widely adopted. When a projection tachistoscope is used it may be possible to watch subjects' eyes, and this alone can attain a satisfactory accuracy (Maddess, Rosenblood, & Goldwater, 1973).

Recognition of Faces of Known People

The principal way in which we use our ability to recognize faces is to enable us to identify people we know, yet remarkably little attention has been given by psychologists to the processing of known faces (Ellis, 1981). Some recent studies have, however, begun to redress this balance (Bruce, 1983), and studies of lateral differences in the processing of known faces by adults have been reported by Leehey and Cahn (1974), Levine and Koch-Weser (1982), Marzi and Berlucchi (1977), Young (1984), and Young, Hay, McWeeny, Ellis, and Barry (1985). The typical finding has been one of LVF superiority in the identification of known faces.

Relevant developmental studies have been carried out by Leehey (1976, Experiment 3) and Young and Bion (1981, Experiment 1). In both of these studies the problem of obtaining suitable stimulus faces of known people for children to identify was solved by using their classmates.

Leehey (1976, Experiment 3) photographed a class of 8-year-old children, and used these pictures in a task in which pairs of faces were bilaterally presented (one in the LVF and one in the RVF simultaneously) for 120 ms together with a central digit, after which subjects had to report the central (fixation control) digit and pick the faces they had seen from a display of alternative choices. She used three groups of right-handed 8-year-old children as subjects; these were very familiar with the children whose faces were used as stimuli, only moderately familiar with them, or did not know them at all. The finding was one of LVF superiority for accuracy of recognition of the faces by the group who were very familiar with them; the other groups of subjects showed no difference between LVF and RVF performance.

Young and Bion (1981, Experiment 1) studied right-handed 7-year-old children, 11-year-olds, and adults, who were asked to identify by name bilaterally or unilaterally presented upright faces of classmates or colleagues presented for 150 ms. The presence of central fixation before each stimulus presentation was established by monitoring the subject's eyes with a video camera. The results of the study are shown in Fig. 8.1. The principal finding was one of LVF superiority for accuracy of naming both unilateral and bilateral upright known faces; this LVF superiority did not vary across age.

In Young and Bion's (1981, Experiment 1) study the same children and adults were also asked to identify the stimuli presented in an inverted orientation. In this condition no visual hemifield differences were found to unilateral or bilateral presentations at any age (see Fig. 8.1). The reason for using inverted faces is that inversion makes faces look rather odd, and it makes them difficult to recognize. How we do identify inverted faces is not known, but it is unlikely to depend on the normal processes involved in recognizing upright faces. The presence of visual hemifield differences only for upright faces thus shows that they can be linked to the normal processes involved in recognizing the faces, and helps to eliminate certain potential sources of artifact. The use of inverted faces is particularly useful as a means of estimating the contribution of right hemisphere perceptual superiorities to any asymmetries observed, as the next subsection of the chapter explains.

Both Leehey (1976) and Young and Bion (1981), then, have demonstrated LVF superiorities in the recognition of known faces by children. Although these

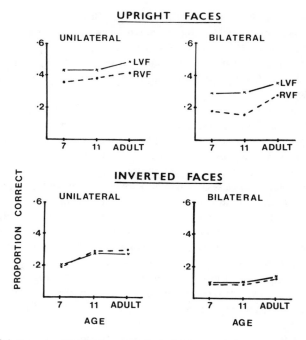

FIG. 8.1 Accuracy of children and adults in naming upright and inverted known faces from unilateral or bilateral LVF and RVF presentations. (Young & Bion, 1981, Experiment 1).

studies only sampled a few ages it seems unlikely that further studies will lead to any difference in findings, at least for this age range. This is because the recognition of familiar faces is already a very well established skill at the ages studied, and one whose nature is not held to change across this age range even by theorists who have postulated changes in the ability to encode unfamiliar faces (Carey, 1978; Carey & Diamond, 1977; Diamond & Carey, 1977).

Recognition of Faces of Unknown People

Most studies of lateral differences in face processing by children have used photographs of unknown people's faces as stimuli. Before looking at these studies in detail it is necessary to make two distinctions.

The main distinction is between knowing the face and knowing the person. In the previous subsection, studies involving known people were considered; in these studies, subjects knew both the faces used and the people they belonged to. The studies to be considered in this subsection, however, involved faces of people who were not known to the subjects (though this is not to deny that they might learn to give them simple labels). It is important to see that the fact that the people are unknown does not always mean that the faces are unfamiliar, because these can be learned during the course of the experiment. The extent to which the faces of the unknown people will become familiar will obviously vary according to the design chosen, and this factor needs to be considered when making comparisons between the results of different studies.

The second distinction is between being familiar with a face and being familiar with a particular photograph (Bruce, 1983; Hay & Young, 1982). All of the studies that have investigated lateral differences in children's recognition of the faces of unknown people have used a paradigm in which the face has to be recognized from the same photograph as that in which it was originally encountered. This method allows subjects to use strategies based on trying to identify the photograph as a visual pattern rather than trying to recognize the depicted face. A true test of face recognition would require subjects to recognize the faces they had seen in different photographs. This method of using different photographs at presentation and test has been used to investigate lateral differences in adults (Bertelson, Van Haelen, & Morais, 1979) but has not, as yet, been used with children. The methods that have been used with children have all confounded recognition of the face with recognition of the photograph. I do not mean to imply that such studies are necessarily invalid; it is quite possible that the children concerned do make use of face recognition despite this confounding. The point is simply that an alternative way of approaching the task (by trying to recognize the photograph) is available and may be used under certain circumstances (such as when recognizing the face becomes too difficult); it is thus important to try to adduce independent evidence as to which strategy was used.

The first demonstration of a visual hemifield difference for face processing in children was made by Marcel and Rajan (1975). They studied right-handed 7- to 9-year-old children who were good and poor readers, and used a threshold technique in which LVF or RVF presentation times were increased or decreased to find the lowest duration at which three correct responses were made in succession. The task involved pointing to the presented face in a display of two alternatives; the people photographed wore caps that removed hairlines from both presentation and test stimuli. Each LVF or RVF stimulus was followed by a pattern mask consisting of face fragments, and fixation was controlled by explaining that the best strategy would be to fixate centrally because the sequence of LVF and RVF presentations was unpredictable. The findings showed LVF superiority, in the form of lower thresholds, for both good and poor readers with no interaction between the size of the visual hemifield difference and the level of reading ability.

Two studies have measured the speed of children's processing of faces presented in the LVF or in the RVF (Broman, 1978; Reynolds & Jeeves, 1978). Both of these studies were modelled on the method introduced by Rizzolatti, Umiltà, and Berlucchi (1971) with adult subjects. This involves the use of a total of four faces, two of which the subject is asked to respond to, while the other two are to be ignored (go–no go task). The use of only four faces (with only one photograph of each face) means that the stimuli become well known during the course of the experiment.

There were some differences between the details of the designs adopted by Broman (1978) and Reynolds and Jeeves (1978). Broman studied entirely right-handed male subjects aged 7, 10, and 13 years. She presented stimuli for 100 ms to the 10- and 13-year-olds, but allowed this time to be increased in the case of the 7-year-olds. She did not remove the hairstyles from her stimulus faces, and paid her subjects in bubble gum trading cards. She does not mention any means of fixation control in her report, but did rely on back projection that (unlike a conventional tachistoscope) often allows the subject's eyes to be visible to the experimenter. Reynolds and Jeeves (1978), in contrast, tested entirely female subjects aged 7 to 8, 13 to 14, and 18 to 20 years; these included three left handers. A fixed presentation time of 180 ms was used at all ages, and the stimuli did not show hairlines as all four models wore a white cap (the stimuli were in fact those used by Rizzolatti et al., 1971). Central fixation was established by instructing subjects that this was the best strategy and by monitoring the subject's eyes on one block of trials; I was previously critical of the lack of direct fixation control on all blocks of trials (Young, 1982b) but am now inclined to agree with Beaumont (1982) that this is unduly harsh.

Unfortunately, the results obtained in these two reasonably carefully executed reaction time studies were discrepant. Broman (1978) found a clear LVF superiority for reaction time to faces that did not change across age; error rates also did not vary across ages or visual hemifields. Reynolds and Jeeves (1978), however, only obtained LVF superiority in their older groups of subjects, with the youngest (7- to 8-year-old) children showing no significant visual hemifield difference (the age × visual hemifield interaction was statistically significant). What makes Reynolds and Jeeves' (1978) study difficult to interpret, however, is the considerable increase in overall reaction times and the increased variance of LVF reaction times seen in this younger group, and the presence of 2 out of 12 left-handed subjects at this age. Error rates were also highest for the younger subjects (Reynolds, personal communication, 1980). It thus seems possible that the disproportionate difficulty of the task to the younger subjects may have led to a change in strategy.

Most studies of lateral differences in children's processing of unknown people's faces have used accuracy of recognition as a measure. This was first done by Young and Ellis (1976), who presented a face in the LVF or in the RVF and then asked right-handed 5-, 7-, and 11-year-old children to decide whether a second face presented a few seconds later was the same as the original. This technique was adapted from the adult study of Ellis and Shepherd (1975), and the photographs used included hairstyles. New stimuli were used for every trial, so that the faces were always unfamiliar. In order to achieve comparable overall levels of performance from the three different age groups a presentation time of

70 ms for each stimulus was used with the 5-year-olds, 50 ms with 7-year-olds, and 40 ms with 11-year-olds. Fixation was controlled by the requirement that performance with centrally presented stimuli should be equal to or better than LVF or RVF performance, and data from subjects not meeting this criterion were discounted. The finding was one of a LVF superiority that did not change across age.

Other studies involving recognition of the faces of unknown people have measured the accuracy of responses in a task involving picking out LVF and RVF faces from a display of all the possible faces that might have been presented; this has become the most commonly employed method.

Phippard (1977) presented LVF and RVF faces to groups of normal subjects aged 11–14 years and 17–23 years; although she determined the handedness of her subjects she does not state whether or not they were right-handed (presumably they were). Exposure durations were set individually to give around 50% correct performance for each subject; the average duration was 165 ms for the younger subjects and 174 ms for the older group. No fixation control is mentioned but this was again a study using a projection tachistoscope, so the subject's eyes could conceivably have been watched. LVF superiority was found only in the older subject group.

The result of no visual hemifield difference to faces for Phippard's (1977) younger subject group is inconsistent with the findings of Pirozzolo and Rayner (1979), who used a method that is in many respects similar to Phippard's. They presented faces of unknown people in the LVF or in the RVF to groups of right-handed normal and poor readers aged 10–13 years. Exposure durations were set individually to achieve around 50% correct performance, and averaged 101 ms for each subject group. Their method of fixation control was to warn subjects that the best strategy would be to fixate centrally. LVF superiorities were found in both normal and poor readers, with no relation to level of reading ability. The inconsistency between this result and Phippard's (1977) finding of no visual hemifield difference using subjects of an equivalent age and a similar procedure is hard to explain, but I suspect that it may relate to the fact that Pirozzolo and Rayner (1979) matched their face stimuli into a set that was homogeneous in background, clarity, hair color, facial expression, and orientation. This matching would make subjects more likely to adopt a strategy based on recognizing the faces, rather than looking for nonfacial cues in the photographs.

One of the largest studies in this area was carried out by Leehey (1976, Experiment 1). She tested 40 right-handed subjects at each of the ages 8, 10, 12, 14 and adult, on ability to recognize faces of people they did not know. This study employed bilateral (i.e., simultaneous LVF and RVF) presentation with a central (fixation control) digit, and a response of choosing the bilaterally presented simuli from a display. The face photographs were selected to be similar in orientation, expression and hairstyle, with the explicit intention of discouraging the use of isolated features of the pictures a a cue to aid recognition. An exposure duration of 120 ms was used at all ages. Order of reporting the bilaterally presented LVF and RVF stimuli was not controlled, and thus left open to subjects' choice (and the possibility of different directional reporting strategies at different ages). The findings of this study showed an overall LVF superiority, but this was not present at ages eight or fourteen years. The absence of LVF superiority at age 8 was replicated by Leehey (1976, Experiment 3) in a study involving 8-, 9-, 10-, and 11-year-old children. This absence of LVF superiority in 8-year-olds was interpreted by Leehey as evidence consistent with Carey and Diamond's theory that young children encode unfamiliar faces in terms of piecemeal instead of configurational features (Carey & Diamond, 1977; Diamond & Carey, 1977). Thus, her own preferred explanation of the result is that the 8-year-olds approach the task in a different way to older children, rather than that right hemisphere specialization is not present at age 8.

The studies of lateral differences in children's recognition of the faces of unknown people discussed so far do not all present consistent results. However, three points can be made. Firstly, LVF superiorities have been demonstrated in at least some studies at all of the ages that have been investigated. Secondly, there have been no reports of RVF superiority at any age. Thirdly, the developmental differences that have been found seem to be closely linked to the particular design employed, and are thus more plausibly attributed to changes in the subjects' ways of approaching the tasks than to changes in cerebral hemispheric specialization.

The weak point of these studies involving unknown faces lies in their failure to determine or to exert much control over the different approaches that subjects might be using, and more recent studies (Turkewitz & Ross-Kossak, 1984; Young & Bion, 1980) have tried to rectify this deficiency in different ways.

Young and Bion (1980) did this by comparing visual hemifield differences to upright and inverted faces. They thought that the most pressing problem of interpretation in previous studies was to distinguish LVF superiorities for face processing as such from LVF superiorities arising from the processing of presented faces as complex visual patterns. It is known that the use of complex visual stimuli other than faces can give rise to findings of LVF superiority in adults (see Davidoff, 1982; Young & Ratcliff, 1983, for reviews), and the use of tasks involving recognizing identical photographs of the faces employed often will allow subjects the option of treating the photographs presented as no more than visual patterns to be discriminated and matched to each other. However, Leehey, Carey, Diamond, and Cahn (1978) have shown that the LVF superiority for face recognition is reduced if stimulus faces are presented in an inverted orientation. Any LVF superiority arising solely from the processing of faces as visual patterns should not be affected by inversion, because a face forms an equally complex visual pattern whether it is upright or inverted. Hence, by examining the effect of inverting the stimulus faces on LVF superiorities found in children, Young and Bion (1980) reasoned that it should be possible to determine whether they arise from processing of the stimuli as faces or as complex patterns.

In their first experiment, Young and Bion (1980, Experiment 1) used small sets of only four stimulus faces; these faces thus became quite familiar during the course of the experiment. All of the faces used included hairstyles and were photographed in constant (full face) orientation with neutral expressions. One set involved faces of four unknown people that were easy to discriminate from each other, and the other set was chosen to involve four faces that were similar to each other and hence difficult to discriminate. The two sets of four faces were used as stimuli with different groups of subjects, so that any particular subject only saw a total of four different faces during the whole experiment. Pairs of faces from these sets were presented bilaterally for 150 ms to right-handed 7-, 10-, and 13-year-old children, who were asked to identify the faces seen in a display of the four faces used in the experiment. Order of report was counter-balanced by cuing the face to be reported first, and central fixation before each trial was established by monitoring the subject's eyes with a video camera. The results, illustrated in Fig. 8.2, showed a LVF superiority for upright but not for

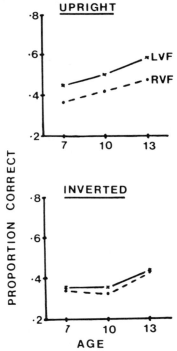

FIG. 8.2. Accuracy of children's recognition of small sets of faces of unknown people from upright or inverted bilateral presentations (Young & Bion, 1980, Experiment 1).

inverted faces at all ages. Use of the sets of faces that were easy or difficult to discriminate did not affect the size of the LVF superiority, so this factor is not shown in Fig. 8.2.

These findings were taken by Young and Bion (1980) to indicate that the task does implicate right hemisphere superiority for face processing (rather than visual pattern processing) at all ages, and that this right hemisphere superiority does not change in the age range studied. In a second experiment, Young and Bion (1980, Experiment 2) then proceeded to examine the effect of using faces that did not become so familiar to subjects. They did this by changing the set of stimuli in use at systematic intervals during the experiment, thereby increasing the size of the set of faces seen by each subject from 4 to 40. The results, shown in Fig. 8.3, again indicated LVF superiority to upright faces, but for boys only. Girls showed no visual hemifield difference at any age. No lateral differences to inverted faces were found for boys or girls at any age.

The finding of a sex difference (Young & Bion, 1980, Experiment 2) was quite unexpected. This sex difference was stable across age, and it is clear from comparison with the results of Young and Bion's first experiment that it cannot be due to any absence of functional asymmetry in females. Rather, it seems that the right hemisphere's face processing superiority is only demonstrable in female

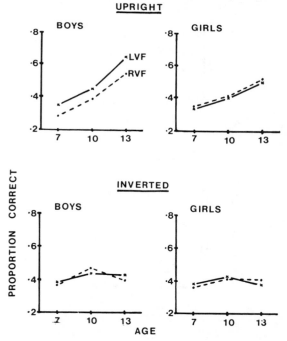

FIG. 8.3. Accuracy of children's recognition of larger sets of faces of unknown people from upright or inverted bilateral presentations (Young & Bion, Experiment 2).

subjects across a relatively restricted range of experimental conditions; a point that had previously been suggested by Rizzolatti and Buchtel (1977), and that was confirmed in a study of adults by Young and Bion (1983). Young and Bion (1983, Experiment 1) were able to show that decreasing the opportunity given to subjects to learn the faces used in the experiment eventually removed the LVF superiority for both male and female subjects, but that it affected the LVF performance of female subjects at a comparatively earlier point along the continuum of decreasing familiarity.

Young and Bion's (1980) findings thus show that LVF superiorities found in children can be taken to reflect right hemisphere superiority for face processing, but that the demonstration of LVF superiority for faces of unknown people can also depend on the use of appropriate conditions. The extent to which the faces of the unknown people become familiar during the experiment seems to be an important factor in this respect.

This approach has been extended by Turkewitz and Ross-Kossak (1984), who tried to separate different types of left and right hemisphere processing empirically, using techniques that they had developed in studies of adult subjects (Ross & Turkewitz, 1981, 1982; Ross-Kossak & Turkewitz, 1984; Turkewitz & Ross, 1983; see also Chapter 6, this volume). Turkewitz and Ross-Kossak (1984) presented faces to right-handed 8-, 11-, and 13-year-old children. They used four stimulus faces photographed in similar poses with the hairlines masked by a cap. These were presented unilaterally with the subject pointing out the face shown on each trial in a display of the four faces. Exposure durations were varied across ages (140 ms for 8-year-olds; 110 ms for 11- and 13-year-olds) to equate overall accuracy levels. No method of fixation control is mentioned but the stimuli were back projected, so that subjects' eyes could presumably be watched. The design of the study is thus similar to that of Young and Bion's (1980) first experiment, but with unilateral instead of bilateral presentation. The finding of a LVF superiority, unrelated to age, also parallels that made by Young and Bion (1980, Experiment 1) with upright faces.

Having replicated Young and Bion's (1980, Experiment 1) results in their analysis of LVF and RVF accuracies, Turkewitz and Ross-Kossak (1984) then looked more carefully at the patterns of LVF and RVF performance shown by individual subjects. From this analysis (and the results of their studies of adults) they suggested that it may be possible to identify more than one type of LVF superiority, because the error rates of subjects showing LVF superiority are often bimodally distributed. This opens up the interesting question as to how these two putative types of right hemisphere superiority are linked to differences in the age and sex of subjects and to differences in the tasks used. Further analyses of this type may help to clarify the reasons for the occasional inconsistencies already noted between the findings of earlier studies.

Most studies of the development of lateral differences in the recognition of unknown people's faces then, have been able to demonstrate LVF superiorities in children. The reasons behind cases in which LVF superiority was not found in a particular age group of subjects seem to derive from changes in the type of processing used arising from factors that are not well understood at present, but for which appropriate analytic techniques are beginning to be developed.

Perception and Production of Facial Expressions

As well as using the face as a way of establishing a person's identity, we use it to interpret people's feelings from the expressions they produce and we produce facial expressions of our own. A considerable literature of studies demonstrating the important role played by the right cerebral hemisphere in the production and perception of adult expressions has now built up (reviewed by Bryden & Ley, 1983; Campbell, 1982; and Chapters 10–12 this book). The techniques involved are at first sight readily adaptable to work with children, though few developmental studies have yet been carried out.

Asymmetries in the perception of expressions are sometimes studied in adults by means of LVF and RVF presentations of faces showing different types of expression. This technique has not, to my knowledge, been used in a developmental study; though there seems no reason why it should not be used. The study that has come closest to this approach is that of Saxby and Bryden (1984a), which did not use faces as stimuli but sentences spoken with different emotional intonations. They found left ear superiority in processing auditory emotional material in children aged 5 years and above, with no age differences in the degree of lateral asymmetry.

Studies of asymmetries in children's production and perception of facial expressions, to date, have all used methods that do not involve lateralized (LVF or RVF) stimulus presentations. Two techniques have been used; one depends on a perceptual bias toward the left that is found when right-handed people look at faces, and the other examines the asymmetry of facial expressions themselves. It is best to discuss the asymmetry of facial expressions first, as this effect needs to be controlled in the studies of perceptual bias.

In adults, the left side of a person's face often is found to be more expressive than the right side. This is thought to reflect the role of the right cerebral hemisphere in the production of expressions on the left side of the face, but the reason for the greater expressiveness of facial movements innervated by the right hemisphere is not yet properly understood (see Bryden & Ley, 1983; Campbell, 1982; Rinn, 1984, for contrasting views). In addition, the underlying pattern of innervation of facial movements is complex and it is often necessary to distinguish movements of different parts of the face and to distinguish posed from spontaneous expressions (Rinn, 1984).

The importance of distinguishing posed from spontaneous expressions is seen in the work of Ekman, Hager, and Friesen (1981), who found asymmetries in children's expressions. They studied children aged 5, 9, and 13 years, using a method involving the repeated viewing of facial actions to determine whether they were symmetrical or asymmetrical. Asymmetries favoring the left side of the face were found when the children were asked to imitate facial expression movements; no asymmetries were found in spontaneous expressions. Left and right-sided asymmetries in children's spontaneous expressions also were studied by Lynn and Lynn (1938, 1943), but their method of data presentation and analysis makes it difficult to determine whether consistent trends were found across subjects.

The simplest way of investigating asymmetries in facial expressions is to ask people to adopt certain expressions, photograph them in full-face pose, and then make composites by splitting each photograph down the vertical midline and printing the left and right side of the face together with its mirror image. The left side (+ mirror image) and right side (+ mirror image) composites can then be assessed to determine which is the most expressive. In adults, it is usually the left side composite (Bryden & Ley, 1983; Campbell, 1982; Rinn, 1984).

This technique was used by Rubin and Rubin (1980), who made composite photographs of the left and right side of the faces of left- and right-handed children aged 8–10 years adopting happy, neutral, or sad expressions. The left side and right side composites were presented to a group of 15–16-year-olds, who were asked to choose the more expressive face. Results showed a significant difference between choice of the left or right composites from the faces of the left- and right-handed children; there was a tendency for the left composites from right-handed children to be judged more expressive (though this was not statistically significant on its own) and no clear trend in the data from the left-handed children. This study thus provided evidence of asymmetry in the cerebral control of children's facial expressions in the form of a difference between right and left handers.

An extensive study is reported by Ladavas (1982). She asked right-handed children aged 4–5, 6–7, 8–9, 10–11, and 12–13 years to adopt happy, sad, and surprised expressions. The expressions of the 4- and 5-year-olds were not, however, found to reliably portray the requested emotion and were dropped from the study, leaving a group of children in the age range 6–13 years for whom left side and right side facial composites were made. These were presented side by side to eight adult judges, who were asked to choose the more expressive composite. A second group of judges then repeated this procedure but using only the upper or the lower part of the face; this was achieved by cutting each photograph along a horizontal line passing through the tip of the nose. Facial asymmetry, with the left face composites being judged more expressive, was only found in the 12–13-year-old age group; there was no significant difference between asymmetries in the upper and lower part of the face.

Two further, as yet unpublished, studies of asymmetries in facial expressions must be noted. Saxby and Bryden (1984b) used the facial composites technique with right-handed children aged 5–6, 9–10, and 13–14 years. They only found a trend toward greater expressiveness of the left composites in the oldest group, and this was itself only obtained when they adjusted the scores to take account of "baseline" asymmetries in faces with neutral expressions. The interaction of age × left or right facial composite did not, however, quite reach statistical significance ($F = 2.90$, d.f. 2,68, $0.1 > p > 0.05$). Moscovitch, Strauss, and Olds (1980) adopted a method in which judges decided which parts of the face were involved in expressions produced while children told stories. Moscovitch et al. (1980) describe these expressions as spontaneous, which in a sense they are, but it should be noted that they are not spontaneous in the sense meant by Ekman et al. (1981) because their purpose may be to heighten the effect on the other person of the story being told. A clear asymmetry toward the left side of the face was found for right-handed children aged 5–12 years, but no asymmetry was evident in 2–5-year-olds. Moscovitch et al. (1980) also made the same finding of no asymmetry in the facial expressions of 2–5-year-olds when they used the composites technique.

Taking the results of these studies of asymmetries in children's facial expressions together, it is evident that the left side of right-handed children's faces can be found to be the more expressive, but it is just as common to find no measurable asymmetry. The correct interpretation of the cases in which asymmetry was not found remains uncertain, though they cannot simply reflect a lack of hemispheric specialization for the cognitive processes involved in emotion because Saxby and Bryden (1984a) have demonstrated that such specializations are present during childhood.

There are, however, two plausible reasons for developmental changes in the asymmetry of facial expressions that have been suggested, and that need to be explored. The first (Ladavas, 1982) is that they reflect differences in the ways in which children of different ages try to produce them. This possibility is clearly seen in the fact that Ladavas was not able to get readily interpretable posed expressions from 4–5-year-olds; Ekman, Roper, and Hager (1980) have also shown that the ability to imitate facial movements improves across age. A potentially important point is that in the study of Ekman et al. (1981), which showed clear evidence of asymmetries in children, subjects were asked to imitate a facial movement, whereas in most other studies they have been asked to adopt a specified expression. The cognitive requirements of the latter task may be rather demanding for young children. The second possible reason (Saxby & Bryden, 1984b) for developmental changes in the asymmetry of facial expressions is that the relatively large deposits of subcutaneous fat in younger children's faces may tend to mask facial contours and asymmetries. This idea could readily be tested by comparing asymmetries in children with plump and lean faces.

In order to study the perceptual bias to the left that can arise when we look at a face, it is necessary to use methods that eliminate the influence of asymmetries in the production of facial expressions. It is also important to note that the use of the terms *left* and *right* for asymmetries of expression is made with respect to the face itself, whereas the use of the terms *left* and *right* in the case of perceptual bias is made with respect to the viewer's field of vision. Thus, a left sided perceptual bias will favor the right side of a seen face. The usual technique used to study this perceptual bias is to construct left or right side of the face composites and ask people which composite looks more like the original (Gilbert & Bakan, 1973; Lawson, 1978). In this case, the right side composite tends to be chosen, because it is the right side of the face that falls in the left side of the viewer's field of vision when she or he looks directly at the face. As this result is thought to reflect a fairly general perceptual bias it should not strictly be included in a discussion of facial expressions, but the only studies that have used the technique with children have looked at the perceptual bias in the context of judgments of expression, so that it is most convenient to discuss them here.

Roszkowski and Snelbecker (1982a) studied perceptual bias in children using stimuli introduced by Jaynes (1976). These stimuli consisted of a pair of schematic face composites in which the left half of one face displayed a smile and the right half a frown, and the left half of the other face displayed a frown and the right half a smile. Each subject was asked to stare at the nose of each face and then decide which face was happier. This task was given to 348 children aged 6–14 years on two occasions separated by an interval of one month. Right-handed children were found to tend to choose the face in which the smiling side fell to their left. Left-handed children showed no bias toward one face or the other. There were no age differences in the degree of perceptual bias revealed by this technique. A further study with 80 children aged 6–8 years (Roszkowski & Snelbecker, 1982b) confirmed the finding of left sided perceptual bias, and an additional study of 2,779 people aged 5–70 years (Roszkowski & Snelbecker, 1983) both confirmed the left sided perceptual bias and its relation to handedness.

The method used by Roszkowski and Snelbecker (1982a, 1982b, 1983) is appealing in its extreme simplicity and especially in that, having a forced choice and no correct answer, it avoids the problems often associated with age differences in overall accuracy. However, the actual stimuli used have been criticized by Hellige (1983) because they are not perfect mirror images of each other; Hellige's (1983) contention is that the apparent left sided perceptual bias is at least in part produced artifactually by the stimuli themselves. This is an important point, and there is thus no doubt that better stimuli could be produced for this task, but it does not explain the differences between left and right handers found by Roszkowski and Snelbecker (1982a, 1983) that do seem to argue for at least some contribution of cerebral asymmetry to the pattern of results.

Other Studies Involving Faces

Studies of cerebral asymmetries in infancy are discussed in the next section of this chapter. Two studies that do not fit neatly under the headings already used should, however, be mentioned at this point.

The first study (Moreau & Milner, 1981) showed that 5-year-old children are better able to detect stimuli touching the left side of their faces. The second study (Jones & Anuza, 1982) found a RVF accuracy superiority in boys, but no visual field differences in girls, when 3- and 4-year-olds were asked to verbally categorize (as male or female) photographs of faces presented to the LVF or RVF for 200 ms. This pattern of results is the same as that found for adults by Jones (1979, 1980), who argued that the RVF superiority derives from the involvement of a language-based decision.

HOW THE RESULTS OF STUDIES OF THE DEVELOPMENT OF LATERAL ASYMMETRIES FOR FACE PROCESSING RELATE TO WIDER ISSUES

Discussion of the relation to wider issues of the results of studies of the development of lateral asymmetries for face processing is divided into subsections concerned with the development of cerebral hemispheric specialization, the possibility of innate cerebral specialization for faces, and maturational changes.

The Development of Cerebral Hemispheric Specialization

Two major theoretical positions have dominated thinking about the development of cerebral hemispheric specialization in recent years. The first of these, deriving from a long neuropsychological tradition, was given its most influential exposition by Lenneberg (1967). Lenneberg claimed that functional asymmetry is not present in the infant brain but gradually increases in extent throughout childhood, becoming fixed at the adult level around the age of puberty. Lenneberg saw the cerebral hemispheres, in the early years of life, as equally able to acquire abilities such as language if this proved necessary (in the event of early cerebral injury, for instance).

This view that the hemispheric *lateralization* of abilities developes gradually was widely accepted at the time that it was put forward, with disputes tending to relate to points of detail such as the age at which lateralization is held to be complete (e.g., Brown & Jaffe, 1975; Krashen, 1973) and whether or not the specialized abilities of the left hemisphere lateralize concurrently with those of the right hemisphere (Corballis & Morgan, 1978).

The second major theoretical position concerning the development of cerebral hemispheric specialization has been adopted by researchers who felt that the evidence gathered in response to the interest created by Lenneberg's (1967) theory was quite inconsistent with it. For instance, neuroanatomical and functional asymmetries have been demonstrated in infant brains (Molfese, 1977; Witelson, 1983; Witelson & Pallie, 1973; Young, Lock, & Service, 1985) and detailed studies of the consequences of hemispherectomy (an operation in which an entire cerebral hemisphere is removed) have revealed that even in infancy the cerebral hemispheres do not have an equal potential for language acquisition (Dennis & Kohn, 1975; Dennis & Whitaker, 1976, 1977). In addition, performance asymmetries in children studied in a wide variety of tasks have not provided the evidence of gradual changes across age predicted by the theory of progressive lateralization of abilities (Beaumont, 1982; Bradshaw & Nettleton, 1983, Chapter 12; De Renzi, 1982, Chapter 2; Witelson, 1977a; Young, 1982b, 1983). Such findings have led to the view that functional asymmetries are typical of all ages of postnatal development, and that they reflect relatively fixed structural characteristics of the human brain (Kinsbourne, 1976; Kinsbourne & Hiscock, 1977; Young, 1982b, 1983).

The studies of lateral differences for face processing in children reviewed here are consistent with the idea that the underlying cerebral functional asymmetries do not change across age. In particular, performance asymmetries to faces have been found at almost all of the ages studied, and no findings of gradual developmental changes in lateral differences for face processing have been obtained. When developmental differences have arisen they have been in the form of a rapid shift from no lateral difference at one age to an adult-like lateral difference at the next age sampled. These rapid shifts, which are often specific to a particular type of task, are more amenable to explanation in terms of changes in the strategies or cognitive processes used to solve the task concerned than to explanation in terms of changes in cerebral asymmetry.

The failure to find evidence of developmental changes in the functional asymmetry of the cerebral mechanisms involved in face processing is consistent with evidence from studies involving the processing of other complex and largely nonverbal visual stimuli, such as pictures of human figures and collections of dots, where developmental differences in functional asymmetry also do not obtain (Witelson, 1977b; Young & Bion, 1979). This parallel should not, however, be pressed too far because of the finding made by Young and Bion (1980, 1981) that lateral differences for face processing in children can be eliminated by inverting the faces. These lateral differences are thus at least to some extent specific to the mechanisms involved in the normal processing of faces.

The Possibility of Innate Cerebral Specialization for Faces

The possibility that there might be an innate cerebral specialization for faces is suggested by a number of lines of evidence. These include the failure of studies of older children to find evidence of developmental changes in cerebral asymmetry, the evidence of neuroanatomical and functional asymmetries in the infant brain, and the fact that at least some of the skills involved in face processing are well developed even in early infancy.

The neuroanatomical evidence mostly concerns asymmetries in the areas of newborn and infant brains that will be involved in the acquisition of language skills (Chi, Dooling, & Gilles, 1977; Teszner, Tzavaras, Gruner, & Hécaen, 1972; Wada, Clarke, & Hamm, 1975; Witelson & Pallie, 1973), though asymmetries in other areas have also been reported for infant and foetal brains (Weinberger, Luchins, Morihisa, & Wyatt, 1982). The concentration of studies of infant asymmetries on the cortical language areas reflects our knowledge of neuroanatomical asymmetries in the adult brain, and should not be taken to imply that a much wider range of neuroanatomical asymmetries are not present in the brains of infants. In general, whenever an asymmetry already known to exist in adults has been looked for in the infant's brain it has been found. This makes it likely that when (or if) neuroanatomical asymmetries associated with face processing are found in the brains of adults they will be seen in infants too.

Studies demonstrating functional cerebral asymmetries in infancy have also been largely concentrated on the processing of language. However, some evidence of infant asymmetries for nonverbal stimuli does exist, including reports of greater right hemisphere involvement in the processing of simple visual stimuli (Crowell, Jones, Kapuniai, & Nakagawa, 1973; Davis & Wada, 1977) and nonverbal auditory stimuli (Gardiner & Walter, 1977; Glanville, Best, & Levenson, 1977; Molfese, Freeman, & Palermo, 1975). As was the case with the neuroanatomical asymmetries, these functional asymmetries in the infant brain show clear parallels to the functional asymmetries found in adults. Functional asymmetries to faces in infants have been reported by Barrera, Dalrymple, and Witelson (1978), Davidson and Fox (1982), and Nava and Butler (1977).

The face processing abilities of young infants, which have been investigated independently of any considerations concerning cerebral functional asymmetry, are in many respects remarkable. Infants attend readily to faces, and especially moving faces, even during the first month after birth. This phenomenon has been formally demonstrated for 2–7-week-old infants by Carpenter (1974), for 1-month-old infants by Sherrod (1979), and for 4–5-week-old infants by Hainline (1978). The results of these studies are not in complete agreement as to what it is about the face that attracts an infant's attention, though they do concur in finding faces to be more attractive to infants than other visual stimuli. There are suggestions that the source of the attention given to faces may change quite rapidly during the first couple of months. Hainline (1978), for instance, noted an increase at around 7–8 weeks in the amount of looking directed at the eyes, and Maurer and Barrera (1981) found that it was not until 2 months that infants responded to the facial configuration as a whole.

There is evidence, then, that young infants are interested in faces. As is so often the case, however, it is open to dispute whether the results considered thus far indicate an interest that is innate or one that is very rapidly learned. The findings of Goren, Sarty, and Wu (1975), however, fall powerfully on the side of the innateness claim. They were able to elicit greater interest to a moving schematic face than to moderately or highly scrambled versions of the same stimulus in infants tested immediately after birth whose median age was 9 minutes. I don't think that anyone would seriously suggest that this attentiveness had been learned in such a short time.

There is also some evidence of innateness in the infant's production and perception of expressions. This had already been suggested by Darwin (1872). The use of smiling as a social signal by infants, which usually begins during the second month after birth and can be seen as being under the control of an "innate releasing mechanism," is often cited (see Schaffer, 1971) and blind infants produce recognizable facial expressions (Fraiberg, 1977; Freeman, 1964; Thompson, 1941). In these cases the point being made is not that the phenomena are innate because they are present at birth, but that they appear in a developmental sequence whose timing is under some degree of innate control. There may, however, also be innate abilities related to the production and perception of expressions that are present at birth (Field, Woodson, Greenberg, & Cohen, 1982). Meltzoff and Moore (1977) found that infants aged 12–21 days would imitate facial gestures made by an adult (lip protrusion, tongue protrusion, and mouth opening), and Meltzoff and Moore (1983a) found evidence of the imitation of mouth opening and tongue protrusion by infants less than 3 days old. Although such findings have not always been made (Hayes & Watson, 1981; Koepke, Hamm, Legerstee, & Russell, 1983; McKenzie & Over, 1983) they have been replicated by Jacobson (1979) and Vinter (1985), and Meltzoff and Moore (1983b, 1983c) suggest a number of niceties of method that they think need to be properly observed.

The ability to discriminate different faces from each other has often been studied in infants, and a review of these studies is given by Fagan (1979). Discrimination between the faces of unfamiliar people has been shown to be possible at quite young ages (Barrera & Maurer, 1981a; Bushnell, 1982), but it is likely that the basis on which such discriminations are made becomes increasingly sophisticated during the first weeks of life. Bushnell (1982), for instance, found that 5-week-old infants relied mainly on external (hair and face shape) rather than internal facial features. Adults, of course, also rely a lot on external features in recognizing unfamiliar faces (Ellis, Shepherd, & Davies, 1978), but they can also make use of internal features when necessary. Differences between the processing of upright and inverted faces have been shown in infants aged 16 weeks (Fagan & Shepherd, 1979), 6–26 weeks (McGurk, 1970), and 5–6 months (Fagan, 1972), indicating that by these ages the mechanisms used in infant face processing have become sufficiently similar to those used by adults to show the property of orientation sensitivity.

The age at which infants become able to discriminate the faces of caretakers from those of strangers is not so well established. There is evidence of recognition of the infant's mother by age 3 months (Barrera & Maurer, 1981b; Roe, 1978; see also Schaffer, 1971), but reports of recognition at younger ages remain contentious (Melhuish, 1982).

The studies of face processing by infants provide a strong case for at least some innate component that makes the face an attractive stimulus to the baby and that allows it to begin to analyze and produce expressions. This is not, of course, to deny that learned components are then rapidly built up on this initial framework. The subtle interplay of innate and learned abilities is, for instance, readily seen in the findings of Barrera and Maurer (1981c). They showed that although 3-month-old infants could recognize and discriminate facial expressions they did so more effectively when the expressions were produced by their mothers rather than by a stranger. Thus, previous experience of a particular face seems to aid in the analysis of expression even though the basic mechanisms used in analyzing certain expressions may well be innate.

The existence of innate components in attentiveness to faces and in the ability to analyze and produce expressions would serve a most useful purpose in establishing social bonds, and in helping to provide the information on which the rapid acquisition of ability to discriminate and recognize faces depends. They may, however, be of even wider significance, because it has been found that visual monitoring of people's mouth and lip movements may play an important role in the acquisition of spoken language (Dodd, 1979; Kuhl & Meltzoff, 1982; MacKain, Studdert-Kennedy, Spieker, & Stern, 1983). It is, of course, the infant's mother whose face will usually receive the most attention, and the attention given also to her voice is well known (De Casper & Fifer, 1980; Mehler, Bertoncini, Barrière, & Jussik-Gershenfeld, 1978; Mills & Melhuish, 1974; Thoman, Korner, & Beason-Williams, 1977; Turnure, 1971). Innate interest in faces and voices, and abilities to perceive and match facial movements, may thus work together to promote the acquisition of both social and linguistic skills (see also Sullivan & Horowitz, 1983; Studdert-Kennedy, 1983; Turkewitz & Kenny, 1982).

If there is an innate component to face processing abilities this would be expected, by analogy with the other abilities already investigated in infants, to be symmetrically or asymmetrically organized in the cerebral cortex in much the same way as the corresponding part of the mechanisms used in adult face processing. The studies of cerebral asymmetries for face processing by infants that have been reported support this view, but more need to be carried out.

Maturational Changes

I have already mentioned the possibility that maturational changes may underlie certain aspects of the development of face processing abilities in early infancy. An interesting case for maturational changes has also, however, been made for much older children by Carey and her colleagues. This is now examined and related to the outcomes of developmental studies of lateral differences in face processing.

The possibility that maturational changes in face processing ability might occur in relatively old children was raised by Carey (1978), Carey and Diamond (1980), and Carey, Diamond, and Woods (1980). They noted that in tasks that required the encoding of sizeable numbers of unfamiliar faces for subsequent recognition performance improved between ages 6 and 10 years, then levelled off or even dipped slightly after age 10, with a recovery to the 10-year-old level of performance occurring by age 16 years. This pattern of development has been replicated by Flin (1980, 1985) who found that recognition of unfamiliar faces improved in the age range 6–10 years, declined at around 11–12 years, and regained its former level at about age 14 years.

It is important to note that this pattern of development is found for the recognition of unfamiliar faces; familiar faces show a quite different pattern (Carey, 1981, 1982). Carey and her colleagues (Carey, 1978; Carey & Diamond, 1980; Carey et al., 1980) suggested that the dip in ability to encode unfamiliar faces seen in the 10–16-year age range is linked to the effect on right hemisphere abilities of the maturational changes associated with puberty.

Before a maturational explanation can be seriously entertained it is necessary to rule out the idea that the dip in performance reflects nothing more than strategy changes, which might perhaps be created by the need to learn large numbers of new faces when changing to secondary schooling. Carey et al. (1980) sought to eliminate this possibility by examining the performance across age of children encoding new faces under instructions to judge the sex or the likeability of the people. They were able to show that making likeability judgments led to better performance at all ages, but that the dip at around age 12 remained. Thus the dip in performance across age is found even when subjects all use the same strategy. Comparable results have also been reported by Blaney and Winograd (1978) in a study of children and by Smith and Winograd (1978) for differences between the recognition of unfamiliar faces by younger (18–25 years) and older (50–80 years) adults. Thus there is at present no evidence to support a purely strategy-based explanation of developmental differences in ability to recognize unfamiliar faces.

Support for a connection between maturation and changes in ability to recognize unfamiliar faces was found in the study reported by Diamond, Carey, and Back (1983). They showed that girls undergoing the physical changes associated with puberty performed less well on recognition of unfamiliar faces than prepubescent or postpubescent girls of the same age.

Although some form of association between maturational changes and ability to recognize unfamiliar faces has been established by Diamond et al. (1983), its precise nature remains uncertain. Diamond et al. (1983) and Carey et al. (1980) tend to favor the view that their findings reflect maturational influences on right hemisphere abilities. They then argue that these changes should also be reflected in reduced lateral differences in the processing of unfamiliar faces at the ages concerned. This argument needs to be considered in two parts, concerning firstly whether the available evidence is consistent with it and secondly how such changes should be interpreted if they were to be found.

On the whole, the evidence does not lend itself to this view, because LVF superiorities for unfamiliar face processing have been found in the age range associated with the dip in performance. However, the studies concerned have not usually sampled more than one or two ages in the relevant range, and many employ techniques in which the faces of unknown people can become fairly familiar to the subjects. Moreover, there are hints of the predicted result in the absence of LVF superiority to unfamiliar faces shown by Phippard's (1977) 11–14-year-old and Leehey's (1976, Experiment 1) 14-year-old subject groups; this absence of LVF superiority was not, however, linked to a decline in overall performance in Leehey's results, and Phippard equated overall accuracy by varying exposure durations between subject groups. Thus, the issue cannot be regarded as settled at present.

What can be concluded, however, is that such changes do not take the form of increases or decreases in cerebral functional asymmetry. It is only on the rather restricted set of face processing skills involved in rapidly encoding considerable numbers of new faces that any difference is claimed, and it is clear that LVF superiorities *can* be demonstrated at the ages concerned. The results from Phippard's (1977) younger subject group have, for instance, already been noted as inconsistent with the finding of LVF superiority made by Pirozzolo and Rayner (1979) with a similar subject group and general procedure. It thus seems that any changes in LVF superiority found at these ages reflect changes in the way that tasks are solved that are linked both to age and to procedural variables rather than to changes in the underlying right hemisphere superiorities. This point is also accepted by Diamond et al. (1983, p. 182).

Much more needs to be known about the reasons for age differences in performance on face encoding tasks before a satisfactory explanation as to their causes can be given. The original hypothesis of shifts between piecemeal and configurational encoding offered by Carey and Diamond (1977) and Diamond and Carey (1977) was not very satisfactory (Bertelson, 1978; Flin, 1985; Young, 1983; Young & Bion, 1980). One point that has become clear, however, is that the pattern of development observed is not restricted to faces. A certain degree of face specificity was initially implied by Carey's (1978) report of no differences across age in the encoding of inverted unfamiliar faces, and by the long list of tasks that do not show a similar developmental function compiled by Carey and Diamond (1980). However, the onset of puberty has now been linked to changes in the performance of various cognitive skills (Newcombe, 1982; Newcombe & Bandura, 1983). In addition, Flin (1985) found that there *are* age differences in children's ability to encode inverted unfamiliar faces and that these seem to reflect the shape of the function found for upright faces (though the age differences are less pronounced in the case of inverted than upright faces). This finding suggests that the phenomenon reflects changes in more general skills of pattern encoding, which would be supported by Flin's (in press) results of a similar developmental function for the recognition of houses and the hint of a similar function in the recognition of pictures of flags. Figure 8.4 shows data plotted from Flin's (1980) results for upright faces and Flin's (in press) results for houses and flags. The methods used in these studies are closely similar (recognition of a set of 20 stimuli presented once only from a new set consisting of the originals and additional distractors). Although the decline in performance seems to take place about a year earlier for faces than for flags or houses this may only reflect sampling variation between the studies.

The same developmental curve has, however, also been found for the auditory encoding skills involved in recognizing unfamiliar voices (Mann, Diamond, & Carey, 1979) and there is a further hint of a similar function in the norms for the development of tonal memory reported by Spreen and Gaddes (1969).

It seems, then, that changes in level of performance at around the age of puberty can probably be shown on a number of tasks involving the encoding of novel stimuli, rather than being specific to face recognition. The list assembled here (upright unfamiliar faces, inverted unfamiliar faces, houses, flags, unfamiliar voices, tonal memory) gives the appearance that the finding holds only for stimuli that could be loosely described as nonverbal, but this may be misleading because the recognition of unfamiliar linguistic stimuli (such as pronounceable nonwords, or the names of unknown people) does not yet seem to have been studied in the same way.

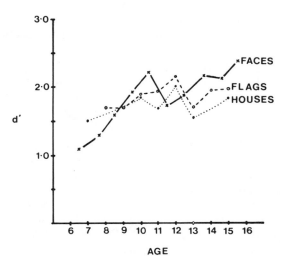

FIG. 8.4 Recognition of unfamiliar upright faces, flags, and houses by children of different ages (data from Flin, 1980; Flin, in press).

OVERVIEW AND CONCLUSIONS

Studies of age differences in lateral asymmetries for face processing mostly have been concerned with the recognition of the faces of unknown people, but other topics investigated include asymmetries in the production of facial expressions, lateral differences for identification of the faces of known people, and the perceptual bias toward the left side of the viewer's field of vision found when people look at faces.

The findings of these studies have not revealed the gradual increases in the size of lateral differences across age expected on the basis of Lenneberg's (1967) theory of the development of lateralization of abilities. Instead, two types of finding have arisen. In the first lateral asymmetries remain invariant across age; in the second there are rapid shifts from results of no lateral difference at one age to an adult-like lateral difference at the next age. This second type of finding has only arisen in some of the studies of recognition of the faces of unknown people, but it has been relatively common in the case of studies of the production of facial expressions. It has not yet arisen in the (admittedly few) studies of perceptual bias or of lateral differences for identification of the faces of known people.

I have argued that the first type of finding, in which lateral differences remain invariant across age, demonstrates the presence of cerebral asymmetries for face processing in the age range studied. Findings of the second type are best interpreted as arising from changes in the strategies or cognitive processes used, created by particular combinations of age and task requirements. This point is perhaps most easily seen in the fact that adults can also be made to shift from showing a lateral difference to showing no lateral difference simply by changing the task requirements (e.g., Young & Bion, 1983), yet no one would use this result to argue that cerebral asymmetry is not present in adulthood.

Studies of the development of lateral differences for face processing have, I believe, now reached something of a turning point at which it will become increasingly important to analyze and exert more control over these changes in strategies or cognitive processes used. There are various ways in which this might be done. One way is to seek empirical methods for distinguishing the different ways in which the task is approached; the study reported by Turkewitz and Ross-Kossak (1984) is a promising step in this direction. Another way would be to use the theoretical models of the asymmetric organization of the different functional components involved in face processing that are beginning to appear (Ellis, 1983; Rhodes, 1985) in order to derive tasks that depend primarily on a restricted set of functional components (or ideally a single functional component) for successful performance. An example of this approach in the adult literature would be the work of Hay (1981) and Young, Hay, and McWeeny (1985) who used a task in which the subject decides only whether a stimulus is a face. This eliminates many of the components involved in more complex tasks and thus limits the interpretation of any asymmetries observed; it would seem well suited to work with children.

More powerful techniques for analyzing and controlling changes in the strategies or cognitive processes used to solve experimental tasks would also benefit our understanding of the maturational changes that have been suggested, and could help to clarify any links between these changes and right hemisphere abilities. My own view is that the case for maturational changes is a good one, but that it could be as readily explained by maturational changes in the cortical areas in *both* the left and right cerebral hemispheres involved in the encoding of unfamiliar stimuli.

The most important gap in our knowledge, however, arises from the fact that there are at present so few studies of asymmetries of face processing in infants. The infant literature presents a powerful case for the innateness of certain types of response to faces, and it would be of great interest to know more about the extent to which this is reflected in an innate asymmetric cerebral organization of the processes concerned.

REFERENCES

Barrera, M. E., Dalrymple, A., & Witelson, S. F. (1978). Behavioral evidence of right hemisphere asymmetry in early infancy. *Communication* at 39th annual meeting of Canadian Psychological Association, Ottawa, Canada.

Barrera, M. E., & Maurer, D. (1981a). Discrimination of strangers by the three-month-old. *Child Development, 52,* 558–563.

Barrera, M. E., & Maurer, D. (1981b). Recognition of mother's photographed face by the three-month-old infant. *Child Development, 52,* 714–716.

Barrera, M. E., & Maurer, D. (1981c). The perception of facial expressions by the three-month-old. *Child Development, 52,* 203–206.

Beaumont, J. G. (1982). Developmental aspects. In J. G. Beaumont (Ed.), *Divided visual field studies of cerebral organization,* (pp. 113–128). London: Academic Press.

Beaumont, J. G. (1983). Methods for studying cerebral hemispheric function. In A. W. Young (Ed.), *Functions of the right cerebral hemisphere,* (pp. 113–145). London: Academic Press.

Bertelson, P. (1978). Interpreting developmental studies of human hemispheric specialization. *The Behavioral and Brain Sciences, 2,* 281–282.

Bertelson, P. (1982). Lateral differences in normal man and lateralization of brain function. *International Journal of Psychology, 17,* 173–210.

Bertelson, P., Van Haelen, H., & Morais, J. (1979). Left hemifield superiority and the extraction of physiognomic information. In I. Steele-Russell, M. W. Van Hof, & G. Berlucchi (Eds.), *Structure and function of the cerebral commissures,* (pp. 400–410). London: MacMillan.

Blaney, R. L., & Winograd, E. (1978). Developmental differences in children's recognition memory for faces. *Developmental Psychology, 14,* 441–442.

Bradshaw, J. L., & Nettleton, N. C. (1983). *Human cerebral asymmetry.* Englewood Cliffs, NJ: Prentice-Hall.

Broman, M. (1978). Reaction-time differences between the left and right hemispheres for face and letter discrimination in children and adults. *Cortex, 14,* 578–591.

Brown, J. W., & Jaffe, J. (1975). Hypothesis on cerebral dominance. *Neuropsychologia, 13,* 107–110.

Bruce, V. (1983). Recognizing faces. *Philosophical Transactions of the Royal Society, London: Series B, 302,* 423–436.

Bryant, P. E. (1974). *Perception and understanding in young children.* London: Methuen.

Bryden, M. P. (1978). Strategy effects in the assessment of hemispheric asymmetry. In G. Underwood (Ed.), *Strategies of information processing* (pp. 117–149). London: Academic Press.

Bryden, M. P. (1982). *Laterality: Functional asymmetry in the intact brain.* New York: Academic Press.

Bryden, M. P., & Ley, R. G. (1983). Right-hemispheric involvement in the perception and expression of emotion in normal humans. In K. M. Heilman & P. Satz (Eds.), *Neuropsychology of human emotion* (pp. 6–44). New York: Guilford Press.

Bushnell, I. W. R. (1982). Discrimination of faces by young infants. *Journal of Experimental Child Psychology, 33,* 298–308.

Campbell, R. (1982). The lateralisation of emotion: a critical review. *International Journal of Psychology, 17,* 211–229.

Carey, S. (1978). A case study: face recognition. In E. Walker (Ed.), *Explorations in the biology of language,* (pp. 175–201). Brattleboro, VT: Bradford Books.

Carey, S. (1981). The development of face perception. In G. Davies, H. Ellis, & J. Shepherd (Eds.), *Perceiving and remembering faces* (pp. 9–38). London: Academic Press.

Carey, S. (1982). Face perception: Anomalies of development. In S. Strauss & R. Stavy (Eds.), *U-shaped behavioral growth* (pp. 169–191). New York: Academic Press.

Carey, S., & Diamond, R. (1977). From piecemeal to configurational representation of faces. *Science, 195,* 312–314.

Carey, S., & Diamond, R. (1980). Maturational determination of the developmental course of face encoding. In D. Caplan (Ed.), *Biological studies of mental processes* (pp. 60–93). Cambridge, MA: MIT Press.

Carey, S., Diamond, R., & Woods, B. (1980). Development of face recognition—A maturational component? *Developmental Psychology, 16,* 257–269.

Carpenter, G. (1974). Visual regard of moving and stationary faces in early infancy. *Merrill-Palmer Quarterly, 20,* 181–194.

Chi, J. G., Dooling, E. C., & Gilles, F. H. (1977). Left-right asymmetries of the temporal speech areas of the human fetus. *Archives of Neurology, 34,* 346–348.

Corballis, M. C., & Morgan, M. J. (1978). On the biological basis of human laterality: I. Evidence for a maturational left-right gradient. *Behavioral and Brain Sciences, 1,* 261–269.

Crowell, D. H., Jones, R. H., Kapuniai, L. E., & Nakagawa, J. K. (1973). Unilateral cortical activity in newborn humans: An early index of cerebral dominance? *Science, 180,* 205–207.

Darwin, C. (1872). *The expression of emotions in man and animals.* London: Murray.

Davidoff, J. (1982). Studies with non-verbal stimuli. In J. G. Beaumont (Ed.), *Divided visual field studies of cerebral organization,* (pp. 29–55). London: Academic Press.

Davidson, R. J., & Fox, N. A. (1982). Asymmetrical brain activity discriminates between positive and negative affective stimuli in human infants. *Science, 218,* 1235–1237.

Davis, A. E., & Wada, J. A. (1977). Hemispheric asymmetries in human infants: Spectral analysis of flash and click evoked potentials. *Brain and Language, 4,* 23–31.

De Casper, A. J., & Fifer, W. P. (1980). Of human bonding: Newborns prefer their mothers' voices. *Science, 208,* 1174–1176.

De Renzi, E. (1982). *Disorders of space exploration and cognition.* Chichester, England: Wiley.

Dennis, M., & Kohn, B. (1975). Comprehension of syntax in infantile hemiplegics after cerebral hemidecortication: left-hemisphere superiority. *Brain and Language, 2,* 472–482.

Dennis, M., & Whitaker, H. A. (1976). Language acquisition following hemidecortication: Linguistic superiority of the left over the right hemisphere. *Brain and Language, 3,* 404–433.

Dennis, M., & Whitaker, H. A. (1977). Hemispheric equipotentiality and language acquisition. In S. J. Segalowitz & F. A. Gruber (Eds.), *Language development and neurological theory* (pp. 93–106). New York: Academic Press.

Diamond, R., & Carey, S. (1977). Developmental changes in the representation of faces. *Journal of Experimental Child Psychology, 23,* 1–22.

Diamond, R., Carey, S., & Back, K. J. (1983). Genetic influences on the development of spatial skills during early adolescence. *Cognition, 13,* 167–185.

Dodd, B. (1979). Lip reading in infants: Attention to speech presented in- and out-of-synchrony. *Cognitive Psychology, 11,* 478–484.

Ekman, P., Hager, J. C., & Friesen, W. V. (1981). The symmetry of emotional and deliberate facial actions. *Psychophysiology, 18,* 101–106.

Ekman, P., Roper, G., & Hager, J. C. (1980). Deliberate facial movement. *Child Development, 51,* 886–891.

Ellis, H. D. (1981). Theoretical aspects of face recognition. In G. M. Davies, H. D. Ellis, & J. W. Shepherd (Eds.), *Perceiving and remembering faces* (pp. 171–197). London: Academic Press.

Ellis, H. D. (1983). The role of the right hemisphere in face perception. In A. W. Young (Ed.), *Functions of the right cerebral hemisphere,* (pp. 33–64). London: Academic press.

Ellis, H. D., & Shepherd, J. W. (1975). Recognition of upright and inverted faces presented in the left and right visual fields. *Cortex, 11,* 3–7.

Ellis, H. D., Shepherd, J. W., & Davies, G. M. (1978). Identification of familiar and unfamiliar faces from internal and external features: some implications for theories of face recognition. *Perception, 8,* 431–439.

Fagan, J. F., III (1972). Infants' recognition memory for faces. *Journal of Experimental Child Psychology, 14,* 453–476.

Fagan, J. F., III (1979). The origins of facial pattern recognition. In M. H. Bornstein & W. Kessen (Eds.), *Psychological development from infancy* (pp. 83–113). Hillsdale, NJ: Lawrence Erlbaum Associates.

Fagan, J. F., III, & Shepherd, P. A. (1979). Infants' perception of face orientation. *Infant Behavior and Development, 2,* 227–234.

Field, T. M., Woodson, R., Greenberg, R., & Cohen, D. (1982). Discrimination and imitation of facial expressions by neonates. *Science, 218,* 179–181.

Flin, R. H. (1980). Age effects in children's memory for unfamiliar faces. *Developmental Psychology, 16,* 373–374.

Flin, R. H. (1985). Development of face recognition: an encoding switch? *British Journal of Psychology, 76,* 123–134.

Flin, R. H. (in press). Development of visual memory: an early adolescent regression. *Journal of Early Adolescence.*

Fraiberg, S. (1977). *Insights from the blind.* London: Souvenir.

Freeman, D. G. (1964). Smiling in blind infants and the issue of innate vs. acquired. *Journal of Child Psychology and Psychiatry, 5,* 171–184.

Gardiner, M. F., & Walter, D. O. (1977). Evidence of hemispheric specialization from infant EEG. In S. Harnad, R. W. Doty, L. Goldstein, J. Jaynes, & G. Krauthamer (Eds.), *Lateralization in the nervous system* (pp. 481–502). New York: Academic Press.

Gilbert, C., & Bakan, P. (1973). Visual asymmetry in perception of faces. *Neuropsychologia, 11,* 355–362.

Glanville, B., Best, C., & Levenson, R. (1977). A cardiac measure of cerebral asymmetries in infant auditory perception. *Developmental Psychology, 13,* 54–59.

Goren, C. G., Sarty, M., & Wu, P. Y. K. (1975). Visual following and pattern discrimination of face-like stimuli by newborn infants. *Pediatrics, 56,* 544–549.

Hainline, L. (1978). Developmental changes in visual scanning of face and nonface patterns by infants. *Journal of Experimental Child Psychology, 25,* 90–115.

Hay, D. C. (1981). Asymmetries in face processing: Evidence for a right hemisphere perceptual advantage. *Quarterly Journal of Experimental Psychology, 33A,* 267–274.

Hay, D. C., & Young, A. W. (1982). The human face. In A.W. Ellis (Ed.), *Normality and pathology in cognitive functions* (pp. 173–202). London: Academic press.

Hayes, L. A., & Watson, J. S. (1981). Neonatal imitation: Fact or artifact? *Developmental Psychology, 17,* 655–660.

Hellige, J. B. (1983). Mirror, mirror on the wall . . . Comments on the chimeric face task used by Roszkowski and Snelbecker (1982). *Brain and Cognition, 2,* 199–203.

Jacobson, S. W. (1979). Matching behavior in the young infant. *Child Development, 50,* 425–430.

Jaynes, J. (1976). *The origin of consciousness in the breakdown of the bicameral mind.* Boston: Houghton Mifflin.

Jones, B. (1979). Sex and visual field effects on accuracy and decision making when subjects classify male and female faces. *Cortex, 15,* 551–560.

Jones, B. (1980). Sex and handedness as factors in visual-field organization for a categorization task. *Journal of Experimental Psychology: Human Perception and Performance, 6,* 494–500.

Jones, B. (1983). Measuring degree of cerebral lateralization in children as a function of age. *Developmental Psychology, 19,* 237–242.

Jones, B., & Anuza, T. (1982). Sex differences in cerebral lateralization in 3- and 4-year-old children. *Neuropsychologia, 20,* 347–350.

Kinsbourne, M. (1976). The ontogeny of cerebral dominance. In R. W. Rieber (Ed.), *The neuropsychology of language* (pp. 181–191). New York: Plenum Press.

Kinsbourne, M., & Hiscock, M. (1977). Does cerebral dominance develop? In S. J. Segalowitz & F. A. Gruber (Eds.), *Language development and neurological theory* (pp. 171–191). New York: Academic press.

Koepke, J. E., Hamm, M., Legerstee, M., & Russell, M. (1983). Neonatal imitation: two failures to replicate. *Infant Behavior and Development, 6,* 97–102.

Krashen, S. (1973). Lateralization, language learning and the critical period: Some new evidence. *Language Learning, 23,* 63–74.

Kuhl, P. K., & Meltzoff, A. N. (1982). The bimodal perception of speech in infancy. *Science, 218,* 1138–1141.

Ladavas, E. (1982). The development of facedness. *Cortex, 18,* 535–545.

Lawson, N. C. (1978). Inverted writing in right- and left-handers in relation to lateralization of face recognition. *Cortex, 14,* 207–211.

Leehey, S. C. (1976). *Face recognition in children. Evidence for the development of right hemisphere specialization.* Unpublished doctoral thesis, Massachusetts Institute of Technology, Cambridge, MA.

Leehey, S. C., & Cahn, A. (1979). Lateral asymmetries in the recognition of words, familiar faces and unfamiliar faces. *Neuropsychologia, 17,* 619–628.

Leehey, S. C., Carey, S., Diamond, R., & Cahn, A. (1978). Upright and inverted faces; the right hemisphere knows the difference. *Cortex, 14,* 411–419.

Lenneberg, E. H. (1967). *Biological foundations of language.* New York: Wiley.

Levine, S. C., & Koch-Weser, M. P. (1982). Right hemisphere superiority in the recognition of famous faces. *Brain and Cognition, 1,* 10–22.

Lynn, J. G., & Lynn, D. R. (1938). Face-hand laterality in relation to personality. *Journal of Abnormal Psychology, 33,* 291–322.

Lynn, J. G., & Lynn, D. R. (1943). Smile and hand dominance in relation to basic modes of adaptation. *Journal of Abnormal and Social Psychology, 38,* 250–276.

MacKain, K., Studdert-Kennedy, M., Spieker, S., & Stern, D. (1983). Infant intermodal speech perception is a left-hemisphere function. *Science, 219,* 1347–1349.

Maddess, R. J., Rosenblood, L. K., & Goldwater, B. C. (1973). An improved technique for monitoring fixation in tachistoscopic tasks. *Quarterly Journal of Experimental Psychology, 25,* 398–403.

Mann, V. A., Diamond, R., & Carey, S. (1979). Development of voice recognition: Parallels with face recognition. *Journal of Experimental Child Psychology, 27,* 153–165.

Marcel, T., & Rajan, P. (1975). Lateral specialisation for recognition of words and faces in good and poor readers. *Neuropsychologia, 13,* 489–497.

Marzi, C., & Berlucchi, G. (1977). Right visual field superiority for accuracy of recognition of famous faces in normals. *Neuropsychologia, 15,* 751–756.

Maurer, D., & Barrera, M. (1981). Infants' perception of natural and distorted arrangements of a schematic face. *Child Development, 52,* 196–202.

McGurk, H. (1970). The role of object orientation in infant perception. *Journal of Experimental Child Psychology, 9,* 363–373.

McKeever, W. F., & Huling, M. D. (1971). Lateral dominance in tachistoscopic word recognition performances obtained with simultaneous bilateral input. *Neuropsychologia, 9,* 15–20.

McKenzie, B., & Over, R. (1983). Young infants fail to imitate facial and manual gestures. *Infant Behavior and Development, 6,* 85–95.

Mehler, J., Bertoncini, J., Barrière, M., & Jussik-Gerschenfeld, D. (1978). Infant recognition of mother's voice. *Perception, 7,* 491–497.

Melhuish, E. C. (1982). Visual attention to mother's and stranger's faces and facial contrast in 1-month-old infants. *Developmental Psychology, 18,* 229–231.

Meltzoff, A. N., & Moore, M. K. (1977). Imitation of facial and manual gestures by human neonates. *Science, 198,* 75–78.

Meltzoff, A. N., & Moore, M. K. (1983a). Newborn infants imitate adult facial gestures. *Child Development, 54,* 702–709.

Meltzoff, A. N., & Moore, M. K. (1983b). The origins of imitation in infancy: Paradigm, phenomena, and theories. In L. P. Lipsitt & C. K. Rovee-Collier (Eds.), *Advances in infancy research, Vol. 2* (pp. 265–301). Norwood, NJ: Ablex.

Meltzoff, A. N., & Moore, M. K. (1983c). Methodological issues in studies of imitation: Comments on McKenzie and Over and Koepke et al. *Infant Behavior and Development, 6,* 103–108.

Mills, M., & Melhuish, E. (1974). Recognition of mother's voice in early infancy. *Nature, 252,* 123–124.

Molfese, D. L. (1977). Infant cerebral asymmetry. In S. J. Segalowitz & F. A. Gruber (Eds.), *Language development and neurological theory* (pp. 21–35). New York: Academic Press.

Molfese, D. L., Freeman, R. B., & Palmero, D. S. (1975). The ontogeny of brain lateralization for speech and nonspeech stimuli. *Brain and Language, 2,* 356–368.

Moreau, T., & Milner, P. (1981). Lateral differences in the detection of touched body parts in young children. *Developmental Psychology, 17,* 351–356.

Morris, R., Bakker, D., Satz, P., & Van der Vlugt, H. (1984). Dichotic listening ear asymmetry: patterns of longitudinal development. *Brain and Language, 22,* 49–66.

Moscovitch, M., Strauss, E., & Olds. J. (1980). *Children's production of facial expressions.* INS conference, Chianciano (Terme), Italy.

Nava, P. L., & Butler, S. R. (1977). Development of cerebral dominance monitored by asymmetries in the alpha rhythm. *Electroencephalography and Clinical Neurophysiology, 43,* 582.

Newcombe, N. (1982). Sex-related differences in spatial ability: Problems and gaps in current approaches. In M. Potegal (Ed.), *Spatial abilities: Development and physiological foundations* (pp. 223–250). New York: Academic Press.

Newcombe, N., & Bandura, M. M. (1983). Effect of age at puberty on spatial ability in girls: a question of mechanism. *Developmental Psychology, 19,* 215–224.

Phippard, D. (1977). Hemifield differences in visual perception in deaf and hearing subjects. *Neuropsychologia, 15,* 555–561.

Pirozzolo, F. J., & Rayner, K. (1979). Cerebral organization and reading disability. *Neuropsychologia, 17,* 485–491.

Reynolds, D. McQ., & Jeeves, M. A. (1978). A developmental study of hemisphere specialization for recognition of faces in normal subjects. *Cortex, 14,* 511–520.

Rhodes, G. (1985). Lateralized processes in face recognition. *British Journal of Psychology, 76,* 249–271.

Rinn, W. E. (1984). The neuropsychology of facial expression: A review of the neurological and psychological mechanisms for producing facial expressions. *Psychological Bulletin, 95,* 52–77.

Rizzolatti, G., & Buchtel, H. A. (1977). Hemispheric superiority in reaction time to faces: A sex difference. *Cortex, 13,* 300–305.

Rizzolatti, G., Umiltà, C., & Berlucchi, G. (1971). Opposite superiorities of the right and left cerebral hemispheres in discriminative reaction time to physiognomical and alphabetical material. *Brain, 94,* 431–442.

Roe, K. V. (1978). Mother-stranger discrimination in three-month-old infants and subsequent Gesell performance. *Journal of Genetic Psychology, 133,* 111–118.

Ross, P., & Turkewitz, G. (1981). Individual differences in cerebral asymmetries for facial recognition. *Cortex, 17,* 199–213.

Ross, P., & Turkewitz, G. (1982). Changes in hemispheric advantage in processing facial information with increasing stimulus familiarization. *Cortex, 18,* 489–499.

Ross-Kossak, P., & Turkewitz, G. (1984). Relationship between changes in hemispheric advantage during familiarization to faces and proficiency in facial recognition. *Neuropsychologia, 22,* 471–477.

Roszkowski, M. J., & Snelbecker, G. E. (1982a). Validity and temporal stability of the chimeric face technique for studying hemispheric processing asymmetries: Data from 6- through 14-year-old children. *Journal of Behavioral Assessment, 4,* 209–221.

Roszkowski, M. J., & Snelbecker, G. E. (1982b). Temporal stability and predictive validity of self-assessed hand preference with first and second graders. *Brain and Cognition, 1,* 405–409.

Roszkowski, M. J., & Snelbecker, G. E. (1983). Facing up to the issues: Reply to Hellige (1983). *Brain and Cognition, 2,* 420–427.

Rubin, D. A., & Rubin, R. T. (1980). Differences in asymmetry of facial expression between left and right-handed children. *Neuropsychologia, 18,* 373–377.

Saxby, L., & Bryden, M. P. (1984a). Left-ear superiority in children for processing auditory emotional material. *Developmental Psychology, 20,* 72–80.

Saxby, L., & Bryden, M. P. (1984b). *Are children hemispherically specialized for the expression of facial emotions?* Paper presented at Canadian Psychological Association Conference, Ottawa, Canada.

Schaffer, H. R. (1971). *The growth of sociability.* New York: Penguin.

Sherrod, L. R. (1979). Social cognition in infants: Attention to the human face. *Infant Behavior and Development, 2,* 279–294.

Smith, A. D., & Winograd, E. (1978). Adult age differences in remembering faces. *Developmental Psychology, 14,* 443–444.

Spreen, O., & Gaddes, W. H. (1969). Developmental norms for 15 neuropsychological tests age 6 to 15. *Cortex, 15,* 170–191.

Studdert-Kennedy, M. (1983). On learning to speak. *Human Neurobiology, 2,* 191–195.

Sullivan, J. W., & Horowitz, F. D. (1983). Infant intermodal perception and maternal multimodal stimulation: Implications for language development. In L. P. Lipsitt & C. K. Rovee-Collier (Eds.), *Advances in infancy research, Vol. 2* (pp. 183–239). Norwood, NJ: Ablex.

Teszner, D., Tzavaras, A., Gruner, J., & Hécaen, H. (1972). L'asymétrie droite-gauche du planum temporale: a propos de l'étude anatomique de 100 cervaux. *Revue Neurologique, 126,* 444–449.

Thoman, E. B., Korner, A. F., & Beason-Williams, L. (1977). Modification of responsiveness to maternal vocalization in the neonate. *Child Development, 48,* 563–569.

Thompson, J. (1941). Development of facial expression of emotion in blind and seeing children. *Archives of Psychology, 264,* 1–47.

Turkewitz, G., & Kenny, P. A. (1982). Limitations on input as a basis for neural organization and perceptual development: a preliminary theoretical statement. *Developmental Psychobiology, 15,* 357–368.

Turkewitz, G., & Ross, P. (1983). Changes in visual field advantage for facial recognition: the development of a general processing strategy. *Cortex, 19,* 179–185.

Turkewitz, G., & Ross-Kossak, P. (1984). Multiple modes of right-hemisphere information processing: age and sex differences in facial recognition. *Developmental Psychology, 20,* 95–103.

Turnure, C. (1971). Response to voice of mother and stranger by babies in the first year. *Developmental Psychology, 4,* 182–190.

Vinter, A. (1985). La capacité d'imitation à la naissance: elle existe, mais que signifie-t-elle? *Revue Canadienne de Psychologie, 39,* 16–33.

Wada, J. A., Clarke, R., & Hamm, A. (1975). Cerebral hemispheric asymmetry in humans: cortical speech zones in 100 adult and 100 infant brains. *Archives of Neurology, 32,* 239–246.

Weinberger, D. R., Luchins, D. J., Morihisa, J., & Wyatt, R. J. (1982). Asymmetrical volumes of the right and left frontal and occipital regions of the human brain. *Neurology, 11,* 97–100.

Witelson, S. F. (1977a). Early hemisphere specialization and interhemisphere plasticity: an empirical and theoretical review. In S. J. Segalowitz & F. A. Gruber (Eds.), *Language development and neurological theory* (pp. 213–287). New York: Academic Press.

Witelson, S. F. (1977b). Neural and cognitive correlates of developmental dyslexia: age and sex differences. In C. Shagass, S. Gershon, & A. J. Friedhoff (Eds.), *Psychopathology and brain dysfunction,* (pp. 15–49). New York: Raven Press.

Witelson, S. F. (1983). Bumps on the brain: right-left anatomic asymmetry as a key to functional lateralization. In S. J. Segalowitz (Ed.), *Language functions and brain organization,* (pp. 117–144). New York: Academic Press.

Witelson, S. F., & Pallie, W. (1973). Left hemisphere specialization for language in the newborn: neuroanatomical evidence of asymmetry. *Brain, 96,* 641–646.

Young, A. W. (1982a). Methodological and theoretical bases of visual hemifield studies. In J. G. Beaumont (Ed.), *Divided visual field studies of cerebral organization* (pp. 11–27). London: Academic Press.

Young, A. W. (1982b). Asymmetry of cerebral hemispheric function during development. In J. W. T. Dickerson & H. McGurk (Eds.), *Brain and Behavioural Development* (pp. 168–202). Glasgow: Blackie.

Young, A. W. (1983). The development of right hemisphere abilities. In A. W. Young (Ed.). *Functions of the Right Cerebral Hemisphere*(pp. 147–169). London: Academic Press.

Young, A. W. (1984). Right cerebral hemisphere superiority for recognising the internal and external features of famous faces. *British Journal of Psychology, 75,* 161–169.

Young, A. W., & Bion, P. J. (1979). Hemispheric laterality effects in the enumeration of visually presented collections of dots by children. *Neuropsychologia, 17,* 99–102.

Young, A. W., & Bion, P. J. (1980). Absence of any developmental trend in right hemisphere superiority for face recognition. *Cortex, 16,* 213–221.

Young, A. W., & Bion, P. J. (1981). Accuracy of naming laterally presented known faces by children and adults. *Cortex, 17,* 97–106.

Young, A. W., & Bion, P. J. (1983). The nature of the sex difference in right hemisphere superiority for face recognition. *Cortex, 19,* 215–225.

Young, A. W., & Ellis, A. W. (1981). Asymmetry of cerebral hemispheric function in normal and poor readers. *Psychological Bulletin, 89,* 183–190.

Young, A. W., & Ellis, H. D. (1976). An experimental investigation of developmental differences in ability to recognize faces presented to the left and right cerebral hemispheres. *Neuropsychologia, 14,* 495–498.

Young, A. W., Hay, D. C., McWeeny, K. H., Ellis, A. W., & Barry, C. (1985). Familiarity decisions for faces presented to the left and right cerebral hemispheres. *Brain and Cognition, 4,* 439–450.

Young, A. W., Lock, A. J., & Service, V. (1985). Infants' hand preferences for actions and gestures. *Developmental Neuropsychology, 1,* 17–27.

Young, A. W., & Ratcliff, G. (1983). Visuospatial abilities of the right hemisphere. In A. W. Young (Ed.), *Functions of the right cerebral hemisphere* (pp. 1–32). London: Academic Press.

Young, A. W., Hay, D. C., & McWeeney, K. H. (1985). Right cerebral hemisphere superiority for constructing facial representations. *Neuropsychologia, 23,* 195–202.

9 Lateral Differences in Face Processing: Effects of Sex and Cognitive Style

Pierluigi Zoccolotti
Luigi Pizzamiglio
Dipartimento di Psicologia
Universita' di Roma - La Sapienza

INTRODUCTION

The human face represents a unique visual stimulus: It expresses a person's individuality as well as his or her moods and emotions; and the recognition of the face and its characteristics are a key medium for social interaction.

Therefore, it is not surprising that very young babies show recognition of facial stimuli, as vividly demonstrated in the well-known work by Spitz (1965). Some authors have suggested that for adults face perception also calls for specific processing characteristics, i.e., it follows a specific direct route different from that followed by recognition processes characteristic of other visual stimuli (e.g., Carey & Diamond, 1977).

From a neuropsychological standpoint, a similar claim has been made for hemispheric lateralization of face perception. Yin (1970) suggested that right hemisphere decoding of facial stimuli is independent from its superior contribution in dealing with other visuospatial material. However, evidence for this claim seems inconclusive (Ellis, 1975). More importantly, it has now been shown (Benton, 1980) that the view that face recognition occurs solely in the right cerebral hemisphere is an oversimplification. Prosopagnosia (i.e., the inability to recognize familiar faces) is usually associated with bilateral occipital-parietal damage (Meadows, 1974). As a group, patients with focal right cerebral damage show an impairment on unfamiliar face recognition when compared to patients with focal left hemispheric damage (De Renzi, Faglioni, & Spinnler, 1968; De Renzi & Spinnler, 1966; Hamsher, Levin, & Benton, 1979). However, this deficit is not an integral part of the prosopagnosic syndrome; in fact, patients who are totally unable to recognize the faces of their own relatives may have a spared ability in standard tests of the ability match unfamiliar faces (Benton, 1980). Also, within the left hemispheric subgroup of patients, those who display disturbances of aural comprehension show a selective deficit in face processing (Hamsher et al., 1979). Therefore, the contribution of each cerebral hemisphere to face processing is a research issue.

A similar conclusion is reached from studies of subjects with an intact central nervous system (CNS). In unselected samples, lateralized tachistoscopic presentation of unfamiliar faces most typically produces a left visual field (LVF) advantage, i.e., greater accuracy or faster reaction times (RT), indicating right hemisphere mediation (Geffen, Bradshaw, & Wallace, 1971; Hilliard, 1973; Rizzolatti, Umiltá, & Berlucchi, 1971). However, a right visual field (RVF) advantage has been obtained under certain conditions: after familiarization with target stimuli (Marzi, Brizzolara, Rizzolatti, Umiltá, & Berlucchi, 1974; Umiltá, Brizzolara, Tabossi, & Fairweather, 1978), when famous faces are presented (Marzi & Berlucchi, 1977; but see Levine & Koch-Weser, 1982 for divergent results), when only a few details are made crucial for recognition of schematic faces (Patterson & Bradshaw, 1975), or when the observer is required to identify the sex of the target faces (Jones, 1979, 1980; Jones & Anuza, 1982).

The interpretation of these hemifield differences is complex and goes beyond the scope of this chapter. However, it seems that factors involving task characteristics (i.e., matching vs. identification) and stimulus parameters (i.e., short vs. long exposures; schematic vs. "real" faces) interact in complex ways to moderate visual field effects for different facial stimuli (cf. Sergent & Bindra, 1981).

Along a different line of interpretation, it has been suggested that some of the variability in hemispheric laterality studies can be accounted for by individual factors. In the case of unfamiliar face recognition, Benton (1980) has observed that not all righthanded subjects show the expected LVF superiority; a consistent minority of subjects displays a RVF-left hemisphere superiority (e.g., 25% in the study of Hilliard, 1973). Similar individual differences have been reported with the use of an averaged evoked potential paradigm (Small, 1983).

Individual factors that have been considered in predicting hemispheric laterality are handedness and familial handedness (e.g., Varney & Benton, 1975), sex (for a review see McGlone, 1980), and individual cognitive style (Benton, 1980; Hannay, 1976; Oltman, 1976; Pizzamiglio & Zoccolotti, 1981b; Witkin, Goodenough, & Oltman, 1979).

The aim of this chapter is to analyze the role played by sex and cognitive style, i.e., field dependence–independence (Witkin, Dyk, Faterson, Goodenough, & Karp, 1962) in the lateralization of face perception. Although interest in these two variables stems from different theoretical sources, both have generated a sizeable body of research. The question under discussion is whether differences in strategies and level of performance related to these two variables can account for some of the variance on face lateralization over and above that due to stimuli parameters and task demands.

INDIVIDUAL DIFFERENCES IN FACE PERCEPTION: EFFECT OF SEX

Individual differences in face perception present a somewhat different picture than those found in a number of tasks involving other visuospatial material, particularly when the ability to decode socially meaningful cues from the face is investigated.

Considering gender differences, it is well known that males are more able than females in a number of visuospatial tasks after puberty (for a review see Harris, 1978). The tasks that most clearly show this superiority are those that load the factors of space visualization (e.g., the Piagetian three-mountain problem) or flexibility of closure (e.g., the recognition of embedded figures). Tasks loading on other perceptual factors (e.g., speed of closure) show less or no difference in favor of males. With regard to face perception, Maccoby and Jacklin (1975) found no reliable evidence in the literature for female superiority in the recognition, as well as in the memory, of social stimuli in general and faces in particular. However, Hall (1978), reviewing a large number of studies, demonstrated that females are slightly but consistently superior in extracting affective cues from displays depicting the face, body posture or complex visual scenes. Relevant to the present discussion, Hall (1978) identified 27 independent samples on which a separate test of the ability to recognize affect from photos of faces was made: In 18 cases the trend was toward a greater accuracy of the female subsample; the opposite effect was found in only 6 cases. Hall observed that female superiority was larger in those studies in which both visual and acoustic cues were given to the subject; this may indicate that the observed facial expression recognition superiority shown by females is part of a more general greater sensitivity to stimuli having high social interaction value. Consequently, she has attributed the difference to the characteristics of the traditional education received by girls. In contrast, it must be observed that at least some share of the male superiority in space visualization and flexibility of closure factors has been shown to depend on a genetic component linked to the X chromosome (see Harris, 1978). It is important to observe that sex differences are not present when a standard task of simultaneous matching of unfamiliar faces is given to both genders (Benton, 1980). This finding would seem to indicate that female superiority is restricted to the ability to detect facial cues, such as facial expressions, relevant to social judgment.

SEX DIFFERENCES IN LATERALITY OF
FACIAL RECOGNITION

Gender-related differences in hemispheric lateralization have been reported in a number of studies, usually indicating that females are less lateralized than males Bradshaw & Gates, 1978; Bradshaw, Gates, & Nettleton, 1977; Hannay & Malone, 1976; Kail & Siegel, 1978; Lake & Bryden, 1976; Low & Riebert, 1978; McKeever & Van Deventer, 1977; Sasanuma & Kobayashi, 1978; Segalowitz & Stewart, 1979; Tucker, 1976).

Studies dealing with laterality of facial recognition present a more complex picture depending on the nature of the task. By giving the same unfamiliar face recognition task of Rizzolatti et al. (1971) to both genders, Rizzolatti and Buchtel (1977) reported a LVF superiority for males but no lateralization for females with a 100 msec. presentation. In the attempt to investigate whether different activating conditions could be responsible for this difference, they employed a 20 msec. exposure time. Although the size of the LVF superiority increased for males, still no lateralization was present for females. This finding does not support the view that different activating conditions are required to observe laterality effects in males and females. However, Reynolds and Jeeves (1978) did find a LVF superiority for the same stimuli for adult female subjects.

Similar sex differences in laterality of face recognition have also been observed by Young and Bion both with adults (1983) and with 7- and 13-year-old children (1980), using an unfamiliar face matching test with bilaterally presented stimuli. In both studies, gender differences interacted with the level of difficulty of the face memory task: With a low ratio of stimuli to trials, both sexes showed a non-significant LVF superiority, whereas with a higher ratio, laterality effects were present for males only; an even higher ratio was used with adults only and yielded no lateralization effect for either gender and no significant decrease in overall performance (Young & Bion, 1983). The authors suggest that the nature of the observed sex differences might lie in the differential reliance of males and females on the lateral processing system for recognizing faces with increasing task difficulty. Nevertheless, other studies have failed to find sex differences in laterality for the perception of "real" faces (Leehey & Cahn, 1979; Leehey, Carey, Diamond, & Cahn, 1978) or outline face-like patterns (Bradshaw, Nettleton, & Taylor, 1981). Therefore, it is difficult to establish whether the sex differences observed by Rizzolatti and Buchtel (1977) and by Young and Bion (1980, 1983) were related to specific aspects of their methodology or whether the variability of the sex results is due to the underlying effect of other cognitive dimensions that interact with sex (Hannay, 1976).

Sex differences in laterality also have been obtained repeatedly with a task of identifying the sex of unfamiliar target faces (Jones, 1979, 1980; Jones & Anuza, 1982): Both adults and 3- and 4-year-old males showed a RVF-left hemisphere superiority for this task whereas same age females showed no hem-ifield differences. Therefore, the direction of the laterality effect depends on the nature of the task demands and the greater availability of a lateralized encoding processor in males is not restricted to right hemisphere functioning.

Less is known with respect to the recognition of familiar or famous faces. Marzi and Berlucchi (1977) obtained a RVF superiority for the recognition of famous faces by using only male subjects. In contrast, Leehey and Cahn (1979) found a LVF superiority for both familiar and unfamiliar faces; in neither case were there sex differences. Again, a LVF superiority and no sex differences were obtained by Levine and Koch-Weser (1982) using famous faces and by Young and Bion (1981) using familiar faces. It may be added that Mazzucchi and Biber (1983) reviewed all published cases of prosopagnosia and found higher incidence of this syndrome in male patients. This disproportionality exceeds the higher percentage of cerebrovascular disease in males (Mazzucchi & Biber, 1983). Although the data on normal subjects are inconclusive, the pathology seems to indicate a clear sex difference: The greater incidence of prosopagnosia in males points to a stronger functional segregation for the processes that allow the identification of highly encoded facial characteristics.

Sex differences opposite to those found for unfamiliar face recognition have been reported in some studies where the task requires the identification of the emotional content of the face, namely facial expression. Thus, Ladavas, Umiltá, and Ricci Bitti (1980), and Strauss and Moscovitch (1981) have reported larger LVF (right hemisphere) superiorities for females than for males. In a similar vein, McKeever and Dixon (1981) observed LVF superiority in a facial identity recognition task only for females when subjects were instructed to think emotionally arousing thoughts about the target faces; no laterality effects for either sex were present with the neutral instructions. However, Landis, Assal, and Perret (1979) found no sex difference in a task that required matching real-face emotional expressions to schematic expressions, and Safer (1981) found a LVF superiority for males but not for females by using the same stimulus material of Ladavas et al. (1980). In a control condition, Safer found no sex differences when the subjects were instructed to detect face identity disregarding facial expressions. It should be added that, ignoring the direction of hemispheric dif-ferences, Ladavas et al. (1980) and Safer (1981) found overall faster reaction times or better performance for females than for males, consistent with their supposedly greater accuracy in decoding emotional information from the face. No overall performance difference between genders was reported by Strauss and Moscovitch (1981), McKeever and Dixon (1981) and Landis et al. (1979).

In summary, a number of studies have reported sex differences in laterality for face perception. For tasks using unfamiliar faces, the more common finding is that of greater lateralization effects for males than females; this holds for both tasks, such as matching a target to a multiple choice array, producing a LVF superiority, and for a task of identification of the sex of the target faces that produce a RVF advantage. Studies dealing with familiar or famous faces have yielded negative results but they are too few to be conclusive. More convincing is the evidence from pathology that prosopagnosic symptoms are more frequent in males. However, a conclusion cannot be drawn until the cognitive components and the neurophysiological mechanisms underlying the prosopagnosic syndrome or the detection of face identity in general are determined.

Opposite sex differences have been reported in tasks requiring the evaluation of facial expressions. As we have seen, females show a small but reliable superiority in this type of task and these findings suggest a neuropsychological correlate of this performance difference. It must be observed that all these sex effects occur in the context of a high percentage of studies with inconsistent or negative results. It seems difficult to establish whether this inconsistency is due to differences in experimental paradigms, as suggested by Young and Bion (1983), or to underlying differences in cognitive modes of processing (Hannay, 1976). This point is examined in more depth in the final discussion.

FIELD DEPENDENCE–INDEPENDENCE AND FACE PERCEPTION

A conceptually different way of approaching individual differences in cognitive functioning is to see individual variation as an expression of a more general "cognitive style"; cognitive style indicates a grouping of consistent modes of functioning both at the perceptual and the intellectual level (Witkin, 1978). Probably, the most famous and most frequently invoked cognitive style is that of field dependence–independence (Witkin et al., 1962).

The original studies on this dimension were concerned with aspects of perceptual functioning. Here, we make reference to two perceptual situations because chronologically they were studied first, because a large amount of data has been gathered using them and, finally, because most experiments to be described are based on this type of measurement. In the first situation—the Rod and Frame Test (RFT)—the subject's task is to set a rod, surrounded by a tilted frame, to the true vertical. Field independent observers, presumably relying more on internal referents, set the rod close to the vertical, whereas field dependent observers tend to be influenced by the tilted external framework in their setting of rod position. In a second situation—the Embedded Figures Test (EFT)—field independent observers are able to restructure a complex gestalt in order to find a simple geometric figure embedded within it, whereas field dependent observers tend to be influenced by the strong gestalt organization of the larger pattern that interferes with their finding the target figure (Witkin, Oltman, Raskin, & Karp, 1971). Successful performance on these two tests is highly correlated and is taken as an indication of a more field independent approach to the perceptual field (Witkin et al., 1962).

An important aspect of these measures is their stability over time. The RFT test–retest correlations approximate .90 even in retests carried out years later in youth and adulthood, and it appears insusceptible to learning (Witkin, Goodenough, & Karp, 1967). In fact, variations occur only due to changes such as the administration of drugs, sensorial isolation, or electric shocks (Witkin et al., 1971). Performance on the EFT does vary in absolute scores as a function of learning of the situation but the scores of subjects in the retest condition maintain a very high level of correlation (Witkin et al., 1962).

An approach that is relatively field independent or relatively field dependent is not specific to any one sensory modality (e.g., visual) but is manifested in different modalities, for example, in tactile and auditory situations (Axelrod & Cohen, 1961; Pizzamiglio & Carli, 1973; White, 1954; Witkin, Birnbaum, Lomonaco, Lehr, & Herman, 1968). However, the field dependence–independence dimension does not extend to all perceptual and cognitive situations, but is manifested specifically when the task requires "breaking" an existing organization and regrouping several parts separately according to a new organization. In this regard, several factorial and correlational studies showed that performances on the RFT or the EFT are not correlated with the ability to single out an item in a distracting context or to make simple discriminations between parts of the field (Karp, 1963; Witkin et al., 1962), nor with other cognitive abilities such as verbal comprehension (Goodenough & Karp, 1961).

Relevant to the present discussion is the observation that reliable sex differences have been reported for both the performance on the RFT and the EFT; namely, males as a group tend to be more field independent than females (Witkin et al., 1962). Both cultural and genetic factors are determinants of individual position along the continuum of field dependence–independence, and they may interact in generating the gender difference. Witkin et al. (1962), examining child-rearing practices, found meaningful relationships with the cognitive style of the children. On the other hand, there also is evidence, based on linkage studies, of a genetic component associated with the X chromosome in determining the level of field dependence–independence (Goodenough, Gandini, Olkin, Pizzamiglio, Thayer, & Witkin, 1977).

The field dependence–independence dimension of cognitive style was conceived by Witkin et al. (1962) as an expression of a more general construct of psychological differentiation. In short, differentiation represents a formal, salient aspect of the organization of every psychological system. A characteristic aspect of a more differentiated system is that of demonstrating a greater level of segregation and specialization of functions of the organism. A large number of studies have demonstrated how, on the basis of the concept of differentiation, a more or less field dependent cognitive style is correlated in predictable ways with individual differences in areas such as the organization of controls, defenses, and the articulation of body schema. In this way, subjects who tend to perceive in a more independent way on the RFT and the EFT, also show a more articulated body schema (as expressed in designs of the human figure) and display more specialized control and defense mechanisms (e.g., rationalization vs. massive repression; Witkin et al., 1962).

More field independent individuals also show greater autonomy in interpersonal relationships, having internalized a series of schemas that guide them in their relations with others, but lack interest in retrieving social information; on the contrary, more field dependent individuals show less autonomy in interpersonal relationship and greater need for guidance from the other as well as enhanced attention to social information (Witkin & Goodenough, 1977).

Witkin et al. (1962) suggested that these characteristics may produce differences in the sensitivity with which field dependent and field independent observers analyze human faces. Specifically, they suggested that more field dependent individuals may be especially attentive to facial cues in order to obtain relevant interpersonal information and, as a consequence of this, they "tend to be better than field independent persons at recognizing people they have seen only briefly before" (p. 3). Evidence for this statement comes from a study from Crutchfield, Woodworth, and Albrecht (1958) in which air captains who were more field dependent on the RFT better recalled the faces of their course instructors than their more field independent colleagues.

A more systematic study was carried out by Messick and Damarin (1964) using an incidental learning paradigm. They asked their subjects to evaluate age by inspecting full-front pictures; later, they asked them to pick out these faces from a larger set of distractors. More field dependent individuals on the group EFT developed by Jackson, Messick, and Myers (1964) remembered a larger number of faces than more field independent subjects; in contrast, field dependence–independence scores did not significantly predict the ability of the subject to estimate age based on the pictures of the faces. According to Witkin and Goodenough (1977) these results indicate the greater attention that field dependent people pay to social information rather than a genuinely greater ability to interpret facial stimuli. In fact, in studies in which the subject was specifically asked to learn the target faces, no relationship emerged between memory for faces and cognitive style (e.g., Adcock & Webberley, 1971). In a recent study, Sabatelli, Dreyer, and Buck (1979) found no relationship between performance on the EFT and accuracy in interpreting facial expressions produced by a partner responding to emotional stimuli. Pellegreno and Stickle (1979) found no relationship between performance on the group EFT and accuracy in evaluating emotion category as expressed by the Pictures of Facial Affect (Ekman & Friesen, 1976). In contrast, other studies have found field dependent observers to be more proficient in the recall of socially loaded material other than faces (e.g., words) when the presentation of target stimuli was incidental to the subject's primary task (Eagle, Goldberger, & Breitman, 1969; Fitzgibbons & Goldberger, 1971; Fitzgibbons, Goldberger, & Eagle, 1965).

In summary, there is evidence for considering the relationship between field dependence–independence and the perception of human faces as a specific instance of individual differences in attending to socially relevant information. The differences between field dependent and field independent subjects do not emerge in any task dealing with recognition or memory for human faces and therefore do not derive from different perceptual abilities, but are directly connected to the degree of attentiveness to cues relevant to interpersonal relationships.

FIELD DEPENDENCE–INDEPENDENCE AND LATERALITY OF FACE PERCEPTION

Studies relating cognitive style to processes of lateralization largely have been based on the hypothesis that greater psychological differentiation as expressed by a field independent approach will be associated with a more pronounced level of segregation of function at the neurophysiological level as shown by greater hemispheric specialization (Oltman, 1976; Pizzamiglio & Zoccolotti, 1981b; Witkin et al., 1979). A number of studies using tasks mapping different sensory modalities have been consistent with this hypothesis. Relatively field independent individuals show greater left hemisphere superiority than relatively field dependent individuals in a variety of verbal tasks such as letter recognition (Manning & Ballestreros, 1982; Pizzamiglio & Zoccolotti, 1981a; Zoccolotti & Oltman, 1978), dichotic digit recall (Pizzamiglio, 1974) and recognition of stop syllables (Waber, 1976). The same relationship holds true for tasks tapping right hemisphere functioning: Field independent subjects showed greater lateralization effects in visual bilateral point localization (Ballestreros & Manning, 1981) and in unilateral tactile detection of line orientation (Zoccolotti, Passafiume, & Pizzamiglio, 1979).

The picture on the studies relating the field dependence–independence dimension to processes of lateralization of face perception is more complex. Oltman, Ehrlichman, and Cox (1977) presented faces composed of the two left or the two right hemifaces of an individual in free vision to groups of field dependent and field independent subjects. The task was to judge whether the double right or the double left face more resembled the original full-front pictures of the same subjects. Field independent subjects, but not field dependent ones, perceived the double right face as significantly more similar to the original. Following Gilbert and Bakan (1973), the authors inferred that the choice of the right hemiface, normally perceived in the LVF, can indicate a predominant involvement of the right hemisphere only in the more cognitively differentiated subjects.

Lateralized presentation of stimuli gives a different picture. In three investigations we have used the stimuli and the procedure described by Rizzolatti et al. (1971) with minor modifications (Pizzamiglio & Zoccolotti, 1981a; Pizzamiglio, Zoccolotti, Mammucari, & Cesaroni, 1983; Zoccolotti & Oltman, 1978). The subject presses a button as rapidly as possible for only two faces out of four alternatives. In all three studies, individuals who were relatively field independent in both the RFT and EFT displayed significantly faster RTs for stimuli presented to the LVF than for stimuli presented to the RVF; a trend in the opposite direction was observed for more field dependent individuals in all three studies, and was significant in the study in which the largest sample was used (Pizzamiglio & Zoccolotti, 1981a). Similar opposite hemispheric superiorities for field dependent and field independent females were also obtained by Rapaczynski and Ehrlichman (1979a) with a task involving upright faces; when stimuli were inverted, no lateralization effect occurred for either cognitive style subgroup. In this study, no difference in degree of lateralization between field dependent and field independent subjects was observed. However, it must be noted that the task (recognition of 7 faces out of a group of 14) was particularly difficult for subjects, producing RTs at around 1500 msec. It seems likely that such long reaction times are relatively unreliable and do not allow for the identification of differences in degree of lateralization. Rapaczynski and Ehrlichman (1979b) did not find hemifield differences between field dependent and field independent subjects for a monitoring task involving upright and inverted faces by the use of an EEG recording technique.

Another negative result was reported by Hannay and Rogers (1979): No sex or cognitive style difference was found for a matching task of unfamiliar faces presented for very short exposure time. Sergent and Bindra (1981) pointed out that when the stimuli are too degraded, e.g., by a very short presentation, it may become impossible to choose between alternative strategies and the subjects may be forced to respond to some elementary information such as configuration or basic properties of the stimuli. In Hannay and Rogers' (1979) paper the hemifield differences were in fact correlated with individual scores in brightness discrimination. Even if negative results can be traced to methodological differences, the nature of the opposite hemispheric superiority in field dependent and independent individuals for face lateralization is still unclear. At least two interpretations seem possible.

One is that individuals vary in their idiosyncratic level of hemispheric arousal independent of task demands (Levy, Heller, Banich, & Burton, 1983a). Individual differences in a task requiring a free vision judgment of affect from chimeric faces have been interpreted in the same way by these authors (Levy, Heller, Banich, & Burton, 1983b). If this model does account for the different lateralization among cognitive style one would expect to find that indexes of "hemisphericity," such as conjugate lateral eye movements (CLEM) to the left or the right would be related to the field dependence–independence dimension. But Shevrin, Smokler, and Wolf (1979) could not find any relationship between the performance on the portable RFT and CLEM in either direction. Schroeder, Eliot, Greenfield, and Soeken (1976) found no relationship between cognitive style and CLEM but reported a greater number of inconsistent shifters among more field dependent observers. The model proposed by Levy et al. (1983a) assumes that responses to laterally presented stimuli are influenced by two components: The idiosyncratic level of hemispheric arousal and the specialization of each hemisphere for different cognitive task. Applying this model to the data on the laterality of face recognition, the larger LVF superiority in field independent subjects would result from the additive effects of right hemisphere superiority for this stimulus material and of greater right hemisphere arousal. On the other side the smaller RVF superiority for field dependent subjects would result from left hemispheric arousal that conflicts with right hemisphere specialization for face perception. However, if this were so, one would expect an opposite pattern for the perception of verbal material. On the contrary, field dependent individuals showed smaller laterality effects in a variety of verbal tasks (Manning & Ballestreros, 1982; Pizzamiglio, 1974) even when the verbal and face recognition tasks were given to the same subjects (Pizzamiglio & Zoccolotti, 1981a; Zoccolotti & Oltman, 1978).

A second interpretation is that field dependent and field independent individuals may make a different use of cognitive strategies. In this vein, Rapaczynski and Ehrlichman (1979a) suggested that in recognizing faces field dependent individuals discriminate based on features favoring left hemisphere processing through the involvement of sequential analysis; in contrast, field independent individuals would use a gestaltic strategy favoring right hemisphere processing.

The notion that the processing of a limited set of well learned faces can follow diversified strategies has also been brought out by Ross and Turkewitz (1981) from a different perspective. In their study two subgroups of subjects among a sample unselected for cognitive style, one showing a LVF superiority and the other a RVF superiority in a face recognition task were identified. The authors investigated the question as to whether the two subgroups were systematically using different information processes, introducing two experimental manipulations: One consisted of showing inverted faces and the other of showing faces with individual features (e.g., eyes, nose) masked. The prediction was that inversion would affect only the gestalt quality of the face (Carey & Diamond, 1977)—although there is evidence against this interpretation (see Ellis, 1975)—whereas feature masking would affect the analysis of the facial cues. The LVF superior group was more affected by the first condition, whereas the RVF group by the latter manipulation of the stimuli. Ross and Turkewitz (1981) inferred that the two subgroups were using different strategies either because each of them reached a different degree of familiarization with the faces in the learning period or because they were characterized by different modes of cognitive functioning. This latter interpretation is surprisingly similar to that which can be drawn from the data on face laterality and cognitive style.

An attempt to investigate the nature of the opposite hemispheric superiorities in face perception in individuals with different cognitive style has been made recently by Proudfoot (1983) using a paradigm originally developed by Galper and Costa (1980). The experimenter attempted to induce different strategies by giving "social" and "physical" instructions to the subjects. However, the results obtained by two dependent variables (i.e., RTs and accuracy scores) lead to exactly opposite, and therefore inconclusive, results.

In summary, (a) the recognition of unilaterally presented faces shows consistent variations between different subjects, which are manifested by either left or right hemisphere superiority; (b) it seems unlikely that these differences can be accounted for by individual variations in level of hemispheric arousal, (c) instead, they can be interpreted as manifestations of diversified modes of processing information. The field dependence–independence dimension reliably predicts the direction of hemispheric lateralization in these tasks and possibly characterizes the quality of the strategy used (at least by the subjects who are extremes along this dichotomy).

In order to include these two conclusions in a larger conceptual framework, they must be seen alongside ontogenetic findings. Carey and Diamond (1977) showed a clear development moving from a feature-by-feature analysis based on facial cues and paraphernalia in young children to a more "configurational" analysis that takes into account more complex aspects of the physiognomy at older ages. Insofar as cognitive style is a manifestation of more general psychological differentiation, field dependent subjects have access only to the ontogenetically more primitive cognitive strategy whereas field independent subjects may show a more segregated set of strategies that they use alternatively when presented with different kinds of tasks (i.e., face or letter recognition).

RELATIVE CONTRIBUTION OF SEX AND FIELD DEPENDENCE IN FACE PERCEPTION

The previous discussion shows that both sex and the field dependence–independence dimension predict to some extent the perception of facial characteristics in a variety of experimental presentations. One question is whether these two variables independently affect the hemispheric processes involved in the perception of faces, or whether they can be traced to underlying variations in terms of psychological differentiation.

Pizzamiglio and Zoccolotti (1981a) investigated the relative influence of the two variables by administering a face and a letter recognition task to the same subjects. In that study, they selected two groups of equally independent subjects (one male and one female) and two groups of equally very field dependent subjects (one male and one female). There was no difference between the four cognitive groups in a test of verbal comprehension (Thurstone & Thurstone, 1947).

The results indicated that both male and female field independent subjects showed a marked RVF superiority for letter recognition and a marked LVF superiority for the recognition of faces. On the contrary, more field dependent subjects of both sexes showed smaller, although significant, LVF superiorities for both tasks. The results have been discussed previously because of their implications for the analysis of cognitive strategy. For the present discussion it is important to stress that no direct or interactive effects emerged for sex.

In a recent study of the recognition of facial expression, Pizzamiglio et al. (1983) described a complex pattern of lateralization for qualitatively different emotional expressions: As in the previous study, while field dependence–independence predicted the direction of different field effects, no sex effect was found.

These studies suggest that sex per se does not account for individual variation in two different tasks involving the processes of unknown and emotional faces, if the two genders are matched in terms of cognitive style. On the other hand, cognitive style is a reliable and independent indicator of the lateralization of perceptual processes involving faces. It must be noted that the procedure used in our studies was to select groups of subjects of the two genders exactly matched for field dependence–independence. In other investigations the groups of males and females were divided above and below the median of cognitive measures (Hannay, 1976; Hannay & Rogers, 1979); the unclear results may be due to the imprecise matching of the two subsamples.

Most studies of sex differences do not select their samples according to cognitive characteristics. Because females are significantly more field dependent than males, an unselected experimental female sample would probably be more field dependent than a similarly identified male sample.

This discussion leads to the conclusion that variations in the degree of psychological differentiation are strongly related to functional brain lateralization. Sex, which has been thought to covary with the lateralization process, does not strongly predict functional specialization. Nevertheless, among the general population it is more frequent to find a higher degree of brain lateralization in males, even if this is moderated by the cognitive characteristics. This consideration may help in interpreting data from clinical pathological studies that are bound to be restricted to the sex parameter as individual predictor.

In the introduction it was stressed that the manipulation of unfamiliar faces might be distinct from the recognition of faces that are familiar. The discussion of the relative influence of sex and field dependence–independence applies to the former task. Information regarding face identification is too limited to allow for any definite conclusions.

ACKNOWLEDGMENTS

The preparation of this paper was supported by a grant from CNR-Gruppo Scienze del Comportamento. We would like to thank M. Kinsbourne, C. Laicardi, C. Montagna, and D. Spinelli for their comments on the manuscript.

REFERENCES

Adcock, C. J., & Webberley, M. (1971). Primary mental abilities. *Journal of General Psychology, 84*, 229–243.

Axelrod, S., & Cohen, L. D. (1961). Senescence and embedded-figures in vision and touch. *Perception and Motor Skills, 12*, 283–288.

Ballestreros, R. F., & Manning, L. (1981). Dependencia-independencia de campo y differenciacion hemisferica. I asimetria derecha en una tarea de localization espacial. *Rivista di Psicologia General y Aplicada, 36*, 385–392.

Benton, A. L. (1980). The neuropsychology of facial recognition. *American Psychologist, 35*, 176–186.

Bradshaw, J. L., & Gates, E. A. (1978). Visual field differences in verbal tasks: Effect of task familiarity and sex of subjects. *Brain and Language, 5*, 166–187.

Bradshaw, J. L., Gates, E. A., & Nettleton, N. C. (1977). Bihemispheric involvement in lexical decisions: handedness and a possible sex difference. *Neuropsychologia, 15*, 277–286.

Bradshaw, J. L., Nettleton, N. C., & Taylor, M. J. (1981). Right hemisphere language and cognitive deficits in sinistrals. *Neuropsychologia, 19*, 113–132.

Carey, S., & Diamond, R. (1977). From piecemeal to configurational representation of faces. *Science, 195*, 312–314.

Crutchfield, R. S., Woodworth, D. G., & Albrecht, R. E. (1958, April). *Perceptual performance and the effective person* (WADC-TN-58-60). Lackland Air Force Base, TX: Personnel Laboratory, Wright Air Development Center, Air Research and Development Command (NTIS No. AD-151-039).

De Renzi, E., Faglioni, P., & Spinnler, H. (1968). The performance of patients with unilateral brain damage on facial recognition tasks. *Cortex, 4*, 17–34.

De Renzi, E., & Spinnler, H. (1966). Facial recognition in brain damaged patients: An experimental approach. *Neurology, 16*, 145–152.

Eagle, M., Goldberger, L., & Breitman, M. (1969). Field dependence and memory for social vs neutral and relevant vs irrelevant incidental stimuli. *Perceptual and Motor Skills, 29*, 903–910.

Ekman, P., & Friesen, W. V. (1976). *The pictures of facial affect.* Palo Alto, CA: Consulting Psychologists press.

Ellis, H. D. (1975). Recognizing faces. *British Journal of Psychology, 66*, 409–426.

Fitzgibbons, D. J., & Goldberger, L. (1971). Task and social orientation: A study of field dependence, "arousal," and memory for incidental material. *Perceptual and Motor Skills, 32*, 167–174.

Fitzgibbons, D. J., Goldberger, L., & Eagle, M. (1965). Field dependence and memory for incidental material. *Perceptual and Motor Skills, 21*, 743–749.

Galper, R. E., & Costa, L. (1980). Hemispheric superiority for recognizing faces depends upon how they are learned. *Cortex, 16*, 21–38.

Geffen, G., Bradshaw, J. L., & Wallace, G. (1971). Interhemispheric effects on reaction times to verbal and non-verbal stimuli. *Journal of Experimental Psychology, 87*, 415–422.

Gilbert, C., & Bakan, P. (1973). Visual asymmetry in perception of faces. *Neuropsychologia, 11*, 355–362.

Goodenough, D. R., Gandini, E., Olkin, I., Pizzamiglio, L., Thayer, D., & Witkin, H. A. (1977). A study of X chromosome linkage with field dependence and spatial visualization. *Behavior Genetics, 7,* 373–387.

Goodenough, D. R., & Karp, S. A. (1961). Field dependence and intellectual functioning. *Journal of Abnormal and Social Psychology, 63,* 241–246.

Hall, J. A. (1978). Gender effects in decoding non-verbal cues. *Psychological Bulletin, 85,* 845–857.

Hamsher, K. deS., Levin, H. S., & Benton, A. L. (1979). Facial recognition in patients with focal brain lesions. *Archives of Neurology, 36,* 837–839.

Hannay, H. J. (1976). Real or imagined incomplete lateralization in females? *Perception and Psychophysics, 19,* 349–352.

Hannay, H. J., & Malone, D. R. (1976). Visual field recognition memory for right handed females as a function of familial handedness. *Cortex, 12,* 41–48.

Hannay, H. J., & Rogers, J. P. (1979). Individual differences and asymmetry effects in memory for unfamiliar faces. *Cortex, 15,* 257–267.

Harris, L. J. (1978). Sex differences in spatial ability: Possible environmental, genetic and neurological factors. In M. Kinsbourne (Ed.), *Hemispheric asymmetries of function* (pp. 405–522). Cambridge, MA: Cambridge University Press.

Hilliard, R. D. (1973). Hemispheric laterality effects on a facial recognition task in normal subjects. *Cortex, 9,* 246–258.

Jackson, D. N., Messick, S., & Myers, C. T. (1964). Evaluation of group and individual forms of embedded figures measures of field independence. *Educational Psychological Measurement, 24,* 177–192.

Jones, B. (1979). Sex and visual field effects on accuracy and decision making when subjects classify male and female faces. *Cortex, 15,* 551–560.

Jones, B. (1980). Sex and handedness as factors in visual field organization for a categorization task. *Journal of Experimental Psychology: Human Perception and Performance, 6,* 494–500.

Jones, B., & Anuza, T. (1982). Sex differences in cerebral lateralization in 3- and 4-year old children. *Neuropsychologia, 20,* 347–350.

Kail, R. B., & Siegel, A. W. (1978). Sex and hemispheric differences in the recall of verbal and spatial information. *Cortex, 14,* 557–563.

Karp, S. A. (1963). Field dependence and overcoming embeddedness. *Journal of Consulting Psychology, 27,* 294–302.

Ladavas, E., Umiltá, C., & Ricci Bitti, P. E. (1980). Evidence for sex differences in right hemisphere dominance for emotions. *Neuropsychologia, 18,* 361–366.

Lake, D. A., & Bryden, M. P. (1976). Handedness and sex differences in hemispheric asymmetry. *Brain and Language, 3,* 266–282.

Landis, T., Assal, G., & Perret, E. (1979). Opposite cerebral hemispheric superiorities for visual associative processing of emotional facial expressions and objects. *Nature* (London), *178,* 739–740.

Leehey, S. C., & Cahn, A. (1979). Lateral asymmetries in the recognition of words, familiar and unfamiliar faces. *Neuropsychologia, 17,* 619–627.

Leehey, S. C., Carey, S., Diamond, R., & Cahn, A. (1978). Upright and inverted faces: The right hemisphere knows the difference. *Cortex, 14,* 411–419.

Levine, S. C., & Koch-Weser, M. P. (1982). Right hemisphere superiority in the recognition of famous faces. *Brain and Cognition, 1,* 10–22.

Levy, J., Heller, W., Banich, M. T., & Burton, L. A. (1983a). Are variations among right-handed individuals in perceptual asymmetries caused by characteristic arousal differences between hemispheres? *Journal of Experimental Psychology: Human Perception and Performance, 9,* 329–359.

Levy, J., Heller, W., Banich, M. T., & Burton, L. A. (1983b). Asymmetry of perception in free vision of chimeric faces. *Brain and Cognition, 2,* 404–419.

Low, D. W., & Riebert, C. S. (1978). Sex differences in cognitive/motor overload in reaction time tasks. *Neuropsychologia, 16,* 611–616.

Maccoby, E. E., & Jacklin, C. N. (1975). *The psychology of sex differences.* Stanford, CA: Stanford University Press.

Manning, L., & Ballestreros, R. F. (1982). Dependencia-independencia de campo y differenciacion hemisferica. II Asmetria izquierda en una tarea de reproducion de letras. *Rivista de Psicologia General y Aplicada, 37,* 637–646.

Marzi, C., & Berlucchi, G. (1977). Right visual field superiority for accuracy of recognition of famous faces in normals. *Neuropsychologia, 15,* 751–756.

Marzi, C., Brizzolara, D., Rizzolatti, G., Umiltá, C., & Berlucchi, G. (1974). Left hemisphere superiority for the recognition of well known faces. *Brain Research, 66,* 358.

Mazzucchi, A., & Biber, C. (1983). Is prosopagnosia more frequent in males than in females? *Cortex, 19,* 509–516.

McGlone, J. (1980). Sex differences in human brain asymmetry: A critical survey. *Behavioral and Brain Sciences, 3,* 215–263.

McKeever, W. F., & Dixon, M. S. (1981). Right hemisphere superiority for discriminating memorized from nonmemorized faces: Affective imagery, sex and perceived emotionality effects. *Brain and Language, 12,* 246–260.

McKeever, W. F., & Van Deventer, A. D. (1977). Visual and auditory language processing asymmetries: influences of handedness, familial sinistrality and sex. *Cortex, 13,* 225–241.

Meadows, J. C. (1974). The anatomical basis of prosopoagnosia. *Journal of Neurology, Neurosurgery, and Psychiatry, 37,* 489–501.

Messick, S., & Damarin, F. (1964). Cognitive styles and memory for faces. *Journal of Abnormal and Social Psychology, 69,* 313–318.

Oltman, P. K. (1976, September). Field independence and extent of lateralization. In B. D. Cohen (Chair), *Psychophysiological studies of field dependence-independence.* Symposium presented at the Meeting of the American Psychological Association, Washington, DC.

Oltman, P. K., Ehrlichman, H., & Cox, P. W. (1977). Field independence and laterality in the perception of faces. *Perceptual and Motor Skills, 45,* 255–260.

Patterson, K., & Bradshaw, J. L. (1975). Differential hemispheric mediation of nonverbal visual stimuli. *Journal of Experimental Psychology: Human Perception and Performance, 1,* 246–252.

Pellegreno, D., & Stickle, F. (1979). Field dependence–independence and labeling of facial affect. *Perceptual and Motor Skills, 48,* 489–490.

Pizzamiglio, L. (1974). Handeness, ear-preference and field dependence. *Perceptual and Motor Skills, 38,* 700–702.

Pizzamiglio, L., & Carli, R. (1973). Caratteristiche psicometriche di alcuni test di dipendenza indipendenza dal campo. *Archivio di Psicologia, Neurologia e Psichiatria, 34,* 276–286.

Pizzamiglio, L., & Zoccolotti, P. (1981a). Sex and cognitive influence on visual hemifield superiority for face and letter recognition. *Cortex, 17,* 215–226.

Pizzamiglio, L., & Zoccolotti, P. (1981b). Differenze individuali: Struttura cerebrale e caratteristiche cognitive. *Ricerche di Psicolgia, 20,* 205–225.

Pizzamiglio, L., Zoccolotti, P., Mammucari, A., & Cesaroni, R. (1983). The independence of face identity and facial expression recognition mechanisms: Relationship to sex and cognitive style. *Brain and Cognition, 2,* 176–188.

Proudfoot, R. E. (1983). Hemispheric asymmetry for face recognition: Cognitive style and the "crossover" effect. *Cortex, 19,* 31–41.

Rapaczynski, W., & Ehrlichman, H. (1979a). Opposite hemifield superiorities in face recognition as a function of cognitive style. *Neuropsychologia, 17,* 645–652.

Rapaczynski, W., & Ehrlichman, H. (1979b). EEG asymmetry in recognition of faces: Comparison with a tachistoscopic technique. *Biological Psychology, 9,* 163–170.

Reynolds, D. McQ., & Jeeves, M. A. (1978). A developmental study of hemisphere specialization for recognition of faces in normal subjects. *Cortex, 14,* 511–520.

Rizzolatti, G., & Buchtel, H. A. (1977). Hemispheric superiority in reaction times for faces: A sex difference. *Cortex, 13,* 300–305.

Rizzolatti, G., Umiltá, C., & Berlucchi, G. (1971). Opposite superiorities of the right and left cerebral hemispheres in discriminative reaction time to physiognomical and alphabetical material. *Brain, 94,* 431–442.

Ross, P., & Turkewitz, G. (1981). Individual differences in cerebral asymmetries for facial recognition. *Cortex, 17,* 199–214.

Sabatelli, R. M., Dreyer, A. S., & Buck, R. (1979). Cognitive style and sending and receiving of facial cues. *Perceptual and Motor Skills, 49,* 203–212.

Safer, M. A. (1981). Sex and hemisphere differences in access to codes for processing emotional expressions and faces. *Journal of Experimental Psychology: General, 110,* 86–100.

Sasanuma, S., & Kobayashi, Y. (1978). Tachistoscopic recognition of line orientation. *Neuropsychologia, 16,* 239–242.

Schroeder, N., Eliot, J., Greenfield, S., & Soeken, K. (1976). Consistency of lateral eye shift related to preschoolers' performance on an analytical perceptual task. *Perceptual and Motor Skills, 42,* 634.

Segalowitz, S. J., & Stewart, C. (1979). Left and right lateralization for letter matching; strategy and sex differences. *Neuropsychologia, 17,* 521–525.

Sergent, J., & Bindra, D. (1981). Differential hemispheric processing of faces: Methodological considerations and reinterpretation. *Psychological Bulletin, 89,* 541–554.

Shevrin, H., Smokler, I. A., & Wolf, E. (1979). Field independence, lateralization and defensive style. *Perceptual and Motor Skills, 49,* 195–202.

Small, M. (1983). Asymmetrical evoked potentials in response to face stimuli. *Cortex, 19,* 441–450.

Spitz, R. A. (1965). *The first year of life. A psychoanalytic study of normal and deviant development of object relations.* New York: International Universities Press.

Strauss, E., & Moscovitch, M. (1981). Perception of facial expressions. *Brain and Language, 13,* 308–332.

Thurstone, C. L., & Thurstone, T. G. (1947). *Primary mental abilities.* Chicago: Science Research Associates.

Tucker, D. M. (1976). Sex differences in hemispheric specialization for synthetic visuospatial functions. *Neuropsychologia, 14,* 447–454.

Umiltá, C., Brizzolara, D., Tabossi, P., & Fairweather, H. (1978). Factors affecting face recognition in the cerebral hemispheres: Familiarity and naming. In J. Raquin (Ed.), *Attention and Performance: VII* (pp. 363–374). New York: Academic Press.

Varney, N. R., & Benton, A. L. (1975). Tactile perception of direction in relation to handedness and familial handedness. *Neuropsychologia, 13,* 449–454.

Waber, D. P. (1976). Sex differences in cognition: A function of maturation rate? *Science, 192,* 572–573.

White, B. W. (1954). Visual and auditory closure. *Journal of Experimental Psychology, 48,* 234–240.

Witkin, H. A. (1978). *Cognitive styles in personal and cultural adaptation.* Boston: Clark University Press.

Witkin, H. A., Birnbaum, J., Lomonaco, S., Lehr, S., & Herman, J. L. (1968). Cognitive patterning in congenitally totally blind children. *Child Development, 39,* 767–786.

Witkin, H. A., Dyk, R. B., Faterson, H. F., Goodenough, D. R., & Karp, S. A. (1962). *Psychological differentiation.* New York: Wiley.

Witkin, H. A., & Goodenough, D. R. (1977). Field dependence and interpersonal behaviour. *Psychological Bulletin, 84,* 661–689.

Witkin, H. A., Goodenough, D. R., & Karp, S. A. (1967). Stability of cognitive style from childhood to young adulthood. *Journal of Personality and Social Psychology, 7,* 291–300.

Witkin, H. A., Goodenough, D. R., & Oltman, P. K. (1979). Psychological differentiation: current status. *Journal of Personality and Social Psychology, 37,* 1127–1145.

Witkin, H. A., Oltman, P. K., Raskin, E., & Karp, S. A. (1971). *Manual for the Embedded Figures Tests.* Palo Alto, CA: Consulting Psychologists Press.

Yin, R. K. (1970). Face recognition by brain injured patients. A dissociable ability? *Neuropsychologia, 8,* 395–402.

Young, A. W., & Bion, P. J. (1980). Absence of any developmental trend in right hemisphere superiority for face recognition. *Cortex, 16,* 213–221.

Young, A. W., & Bion, P. J. (1981). Accuracy of naming laterally presented known faces by children and adults. *Cortex, 17,* 97–106.

Young, A. W., & Bion, P. J. (1983). The nature of the sex difference in the right hemisphere superiority for face recognition. *Cortex, 19,* 215–226.

Zoccolotti, P., & Oltman, P. K. (1978). Field dependence and lateralization of verbal and configurational processing. *Cortex, 14,* 155–163.

Zoccolotti, P., Passaflume, D., & Pizzamiglio, L. (1979). Hemispheric superiorities on a unilateral tactile test: relationship to cognitive dimensions. *Perceptual and Motor Skills, 49,* 735–742.

III

NEUROPSYCHOLOGY OF FACIAL EXPRESSION

10 Production and Comprehension of Emotional Facial Expressions in Brain-Damaged Subjects

Pierre Feyereisen
Research Associate of the Belgian Fund for Scientific Research
University of Louvain
Unité de Neuropsychologie Expérimentale de l'Adulte

The neuropsychology of facial expression is based on two main assumptions: Facial movements express emotional states, and the two cerebral hemispheres are differently involved in the control and interpretation of facial expression. These assumptions may be challenged on theoretical grounds, and also on the basis of the behavior manifested by brain damaged subjects.

The hypothesis of a relationship between facial expression and emotion has been anchored in neurobiological thinking ever since Darwin (1872), according to whom the movements of the face in people and animals are related to biological functions such as protecting sense organs or to socio-sexual signaling. In such a perspective, the control the brain exerts on the facial expression in humans is thought to have evolved from neurophysiological mechanisms underlying primate facial behavior. The problem with this view is that it is not known precisely how emotion and facial movement are related: Darwin used a much broader definition of emotion (including, for example, maternal behavior) than is common today, and some of his explanations have to be reformulated in more contemporary terms. Furthermore, animal studies suggest that different mechanisms have to be conceived for the control of simple reflexive behavior (e.g., startle, pain expressions), of built-in social reactions (e.g., threat, submissive responses), and of affective evaluation (e.g., avoidance, pleasure). We thus have to define what is meant by "expression of emotion". The emotional behavior of brain-damaged human subjects may allow us to choose among rival conceptions.

The last decade of neuropsychological research on facial expression has been dominated by attempts to demonstrate lateral differences in facial motility and in the perception of facial cues. It is hypothesized that the right hemisphere is

221

dominant in the processing of facial expressions. If such an hypothesis is confirmed, the question arises of the specificity of the process: Is this competence particular, or is it related to other cognitive operations in visuo-spatial processing or in emotional behavior? Again, analysis of the impairments following brain lesions may answer some of these questions.

THE EXPRESSION OF EMOTION BY
FACIAL MOVEMENTS

The first problem concerns the relation between emotion and facial motility: How does emotion control the face and how does the face code for emotion?

How Does the Face Express Emotions?

Emotion is a much debated issue in psychology, and the profusion of theories in the field has been viewed as a sign of immaturity (see open peer commentaries on Panksepp, 1982, and Scherer, 1984; see also the papers collected by Plutchik & Kellerman, 1980). In the absence of a formal definition of emotion, mild agreement exists on the tenet that emotion is a constellation of different behavioral phenomena: physiological arousal (heart rate, perspiration, etc.), specific motor responses (facial expressions, aggressive movements, etc.), subjective feelings, and the alteration of instrumental activity (speech, problem solving, etc.). The problem is to specify how these different aspects are related, and, for our present purposes, how facial movements express emotion. Several solutions have been proposed, each of which has different implications as far as neural control is concerned. Three sets of conceptions may be distinguished: peripheral theories, cognitive theories and comprehensive theories.

Peripheral Theories: Facial Movements Come First.   The peripheral theories consider that affects result from the perception of bodily changes. It has recently been suggested by Tomkins (1962, 1980) that affects are primarily facial behavior: The muscular responses located in the face generate sensory feedback that is evaluated to produce emotional feelings. "These organized sets of responses are triggered at subcortical centers where specific programs for each distinct affect are stored." (Tomkins, 1980, p. 142)

In this perspective, there is a limited number of fundamental emotions (or facial affect programs): joy, sadness, anger, fear, interest, disgust, and a few others. More complex feelings arise from the simultaneous activation of different programs. For example, anxiety is a blend of fear with another emotion, depression a set with sadness as a key element, and hostility a compound of anger and disgust (Izard, 1977). From this point of view, the question of how facial movements express emotion is meaningless because facial movements precede emotional evaluation.

There is ample experimental evidence to suggest that voluntary modification of facial expression interferes with feelings, and it has recently been shown that posing for a facial expression also influences autonomic activity (Ekman, Levenson, & Friesen, 1983; see review in Feyereisen & de Lannoy, 1985, chap. 7).

The facial feedback hypothesis remains highly controversial, however. One problem concerns individual differences in facial expressivity (Buck, 1980; Zuckerman, Klorman, Larrance, & Spiegel, 1981). There is little evidence to indicate that the most expressive individuals experience the most intense emotions; on the contrary, a significant negative correlation between facial behavior and electrodermal response is observed. This suggests two individual strategies in coping with emotional situations: externalizing and internalizing. Another problem is with the temporal course of the association between facial movement and other emotional cues: How are the rapid muscular responses related to slower vegetative activity? In the vicarious conditioning of facial movements (Dimberg, 1982; Vaughan & Lanzetta, 1980) facial behavior and galvanic skin response appear to be unrelated or negatively correlated.

As far as the behavior of brain-damaged subjects is concerned, the facial feedback hypothesis suggests that facial activity and emotional response would be dissociable in only one way: Emotional indifference could happen in spite of intact facial behavior if the feedback is no longer interpreted, but reduced facial motility would always affect the ability to experience emotion. Moreover, strong assumptions are made about the existence of "facial programs", i.e., built-in mechanisms liable to disruption by subcortical brain lesions.

Cognitive Theories: Feelings Come First.   The main concern of cognitive theories is to account for subjective feelings as resulting from the evaluation of the physiological arousal and of the situation (for reviews see Cotton, 1981; Leventhal, 1980; Reisenzein, 1983; Schachter, 1975). Thus, not much attention is paid to facial behavior, but there is a tendency to consider facial expressions, like other emotional expressions, as secondary reactions.

Mandler (1980) says: The facial expressions are the result of cognitive evaluations of the world and of internal states. The simple fact that human beings can display facial expressions in the absence of emotional states suggests the parallel to language in general. I can make a face to signal disgust without being disgusted just as I can say "That is terrible!" without referring to anything at all (p. 239). Correlatively, the face may express the diversity of the cognitive states— irony, perplexity, boredom, etc.—which are not necessarily conceived as combinations of elementary affects.

The key function of cognitive evaluation suggests the dependence of facial expression on intellectual functioning: parallel development in ontogenesis and simultaneous disruption in non-specific disorders (mental retardation, dementia, etc.). Thus, disorders of facial expression are expected in people impaired in affective judgments. Moreover, partial dissociations could be predicted as a result of focal brain damage; facial inexpressivity would not imply reduced emotionality. However, hypo–arousal or the inability to infer emotional meanings could result in a lowering of facial activity; such an association is also assumed by the facial feedback hypothesis on the basis of a causal relationship of inverse directionality.

Comprehensive Theories: Parallel Processing of Facial Movements and Feelings.   In fact, peripheral and cognitive theories are not truly incompatible. For example, primary facial reactions and more controlled voluntary facial movements might correspond to distinct aspects of the emotional expression. Ekman (1971) argues for such a distinction in his two–stage *neuro-cultural theory of emotion,* where "neuro refers to the facial affect program—the relationships between particular emotions and the firing of a particular pattern of facial muscles" (p. 222). In a second step, the facial program is submitted to *display rules* learned during childhood and shaped by culture. These rules lead subjects to exaggerate, suppress, or modify their facial appearance according to the demands of the social environment. Alternative to this sequential model is parallel processing model suggested by Leventhal (1980): "Emotional experience emerges from an interaction of volitional and spontaneous motor scripts . . . We feel emotion when the spontaneous motor system overrides the control of the voluntary system . . . When the volitional system overrides the spontaneous one, in contrast, we experience controlled action" (p. 169).

From these perspectives one may expect dissociations of spontaneous and voluntary facial behavior in brain-damaged subjects: some disorders could specifically impair either the automatic path or the ability to modify facial appearance on demand.

However, these synthetic approaches remain unclear about the relationships between facial expressions and emotional feelings in the automatic stage of the process. We understand that, according to the cognitive and the comprehensive theories, voluntary control of facial motor system would be related to mental representations of the situation and of internal states. But the triggering of spontaneous facial movements is not well described. Are facial programs to be conceived as mechanisms by which perceived key physical events release pre-wired combinations of facial movements? The psychological literature does not provide data favoring such a view, but the facial feedback hypothesis rests implicitly on it. Or is another kind of mental representations to be advocated for the activation of facial movements? These representations would be distinct from rules of civility or from the "concepts of self" implied by voluntary control but specific to the automatic path: fast affective categorization, detection of discrepancies between expectations and perceived stimuli, etc. In other words, we are left with either a reformulation of the cognitive theories (feelings come first) or a modified version of the facial feedback hypothesis (the inability to repress automatic facial reactions is the input to the mental affective representations).

Different predictions of theories of facial expression on the consequences of cerebral lesions make the analysis of pathological data useful. Indeed, there is ample evidence that emotional behavior is affected by brain damage. Along with experimental studies on animals, human pathology indicates the critical role of anatomical structures, cortical and subcortical, belonging to the limbic system (for reviews, see Damasio & Van Hoesen, 1983; Dimond, 1980, Chapter 5; Poeck, 1969). Moreover, facial movement is also disturbed by brain lesions. Are dissociations between automatic and voluntary facial behavior evidenced? Are facial–movement disorders and emotional disturbances always associated?

Emotion and Brain Damages

Human emotional behavior seems to be related to the activity of the temporal and frontal lobes. Bilateral lesions of the temporal lobe result in the *Klüver-Bucy syndrome,* which was first described in monkeys then observed in human pathology. In nonhuman primates extended bilateral ablations of the anterior temporal lobe impair the use of affiliative signals. Frequency of vocalizations, facial expressions, and grooming is considerably reduced (see Kling & Steklis, 1976; Steklis & Raleigh, 1979 for reviews). In a semi-natural environment such animals remain isolated from the group (Myers & Swett, 1970). In the laboratory, changes in sexual and maternal behavior are also observed (Franzen & Myers, 1973). Homologous bilateral lesions in man cause dramatic alteration of socio-emotional behavior: placidity, absence of anger and fear, hypersexuality, and bulimia. Since Poeck's (1969) review several such çases have been described (Friedman & Allen, 1969; Gascon & Gilles, 1973; Marlowe, Mancall, & Thomas, 1975). Recently, 12 cases of Klüver-Bucy syndrome of various etiologies—encephalitis, trauma, Pick's and Alzeimer's diseases—resulting generally in extended lesions have been reported (Lilly, Cummings, Benson, & Frankel, 1983). In addition to emotional disorders, the patients showed amnesia, aphasia, visual agnosia, or dementia. Such a general disruption of emotional and cognitive processes renders the experimental investigation of these cases of little use for the dissociation of specific mechanisms involved in facial expression.

In contrast to the emotional indifference observed in the Klüver-Bucy syndrome is the behavior of subjects with temporal lobe epilepsy, who are described as being prone to attribute emotional meaning to perceived stimuli. This emotionality has been interpreted as resulting from hyperactivation of the connections between the temporal lobes and the related structures (Bear, 1979). Interictal personality changes could follow, but the specificity of the pattern remains controversial (Bear & Fedio, 1977; Mungas, 1982; Rodin & Schmaltz, 1984). On the other hand, unilateral temporal lobectomy influences the rating of affective materials: Subjects with left temporal excisions judge scenes and words as more neutral and less pleasant than do normal subjects (Fedio & Martin, 1983). But, on the other hand, epileptic patients do not report more fearfulness than normal subjects (Strauss, Risser, & Jones, 1982). They feel more afraid of social events, like speaking in public, and they have sexual anxieties (becoming homosexual, etc.) that could result from problems in psycho-social adjustment rather than from the activation of an hypothetical emotional center.

Lesions of the prefrontal cortex (dorsolateral or orbitofrontal) in monkeys produce changes in social behavior similar or even more dramatic than those observed after temporal lesions (Kling & Steklis, 1976; Raleigh & Steklis, 1981). Animals keep a "poker face", but when attacked they produce screams and grimaces (Franzen & Myers, 1973). This suggests that the motor mechanisms for facial expression might remain spared. In man, indifference, reduction of anxiety, and akinetic mutism are observed after bilateral damage of the cingulate gyrus, an associative structure connecting the hippocampus to the frontal lobes (Damasio & Van Hoesen, 1983; Poeck, 1969). Frontal lobe lesions have also been shown to alter social behavior and to result in euphoria or irritability (Angelergues, Hécaen, & Ajuriaguerra, 1955; Hécaen & Albert, 1975), but in no way is the pathology so severe as in the Klüver-Bucy syndrome. Indeed, we know of no detailed case study or any experimental investigation of emotional disorders after frontal lobe damage. One exploratory attempt to analyze management of social interactions after frontal lobe damage is the study of Deutsch, Kling, and Steklis (1979) where verbal and nonverbal behavior was recorded in a semi-natural situation: subject alone in a waiting room, introduction of a silent confederate, conversation. However, the small size of the samples of frontal and non-frontal lesions and the lack of a non–neurological control group make the interpretation of the observed nonsignificant statistical differences difficult.

A general problem in the assessment of emotional behavior after temporal and frontal lesions is the association of cognitive and affective disorders. Bilateral lesions of the temporal lobe impair memory; frontal lobe lesions disturb attentional mechanisms and problem solving, and disturbances of perceptual or linguistic processes regularly interfere with the study of emotional behavior. Is emotional indifference an inability to extract specific emotional meaning from the situation or does the flattening of affect result from the absence of anticipatory behavior making the subject undisturbed by unexpected events? Or does this indifference result from reduced attention or from impaired perceptual analysis? Does it mean that emotion and cognition are intrinsically connected, or that extended lesions are likely to impair several independent functions? The same problem arises in the analysis of emotional processing in senile and presenile demented patients.

A related issue is the question of whether emotional disorders after brain lesions are the direct result of the destruction of specific control centers or the secondary consequences of motor, perceptual, mnesic, or linguistic deficits (Seron

& Vanderlinden, 1979). The "catastrophic reaction" or depression in aphasic patients (Gainotti, 1969, 1972; Robinson & Benson, 1981; Robinson, Kubos, Starr, Rao, & Price, 1984) could more plausibly be due to the psycho-social adjustment to the language impairment than to the desinhibition of a hypothetical "sadness" center located in the left hemisphere. Similarly, in the emotional changes following head trauma more distress is experienced six months after the accident than earlier, whereas cognitive functioning does not deteriorate (Fordyce, Roueche, & Prigatano, 1983).

In spite of these difficulties in assessing the nature of the emotional changes after brain damage, it remains that pathological cases evidence objective modifications of the emotional reactivity, and thus provide an opportunity to analyze the relationships between facial expressions and other aspects of emotional behavior. Unfortunately, we have found no systematic descriptions of facial behavior in subjects with emotional disturbances (see, however, the analysis of nonverbal communication in depressed and schizophrenic subjects, which is beyond the scope of the present chapter, and is reviewed in Feyereisen & de Lannoy, 1985, chap. 9). We do not know the effects of bilateral focal lesions of the temporal lobes, which are probably involved, as suggested by ablation studies in nonhuman primates, in the control of facial expression. Moreover, facial behavior in cases of hyper–reactivity to emotional stimuli remains unassessed. Nevertheless, the relationships between emotional behavior and facial expression might be examined in another interesting pathological population. Numerous clinical studies bear on the disorders of the facial movements in brain–damaged subjects. Are these movement disorders associated with changes in emotional behavior?

How Does the Brain Control Facial Expressions?

A common assumption in several theories of emotion is that emotional behavior, including facial expressions, is part of adaptative patterns inherited through phylogeny. Thus, they belong to the repertoire of the species, and the notion of a "facial program" expresses the idea of a relatively automatic triggering of facial movements by the situation itself or by some representation of this situation. Unfortunately, the neurophysiological mechanisms involved in such an automatic control have yet to be adequately described, and we do not know exactly what the notion of facial program refers to. The motor control of facial movements operates at different levels, and pathological facial behavior may be observed with lesions of different structures (see Borod & Koff, 1983; Rinn, 1984, for reviews).

The facial musculature is directly dependent on the facial nerve nucleus via the seventh cranial nerve (Graham & House, 1982). This nucleus is located in the caudal part of the pons and comprises different cellular groups, which show a somatotopic organization (Brodal, 1969; Dubner, Sessle, & Storey, 1978). The lateral and the ventrolateral groups control the muscles of the mouth region, whereas the dorsolateral group (pars intermedia) is involved in the control of frontalis, orbicularis oculi, and corrugator supercilii muscles. The facial nerve nucleus receives inputs from different parts of the brain: other nuclei of the stem (olive, etc.), central nuclei (red nucleus, globus pallidus, etc.), and cortex. The corticobulbar tract cross completely for fibers concerning the lower part of the face, whereas there is only a partial crossing for the tract involved in the musculature surrounding the eyes. A lesion of the peripheral facial nerve causes Bell's palsy, usually unilateral, which abolishes all the movements of a hemiface. A more central lesion spares the movements of the upper part of the face (blinking, frowning, etc.) while disrupting movements of the lower part (chewing, mouth opening, etc.).

Some positive manifestations of the pathology of peripheral motor control have also been described. Irritation of the facial nerve causes involuntary contractions of the face (hemifacial spasm). These spasmodic movements are often precipitated by voluntary movements (e.g., chewing) or by emotional arousal. Sometimes, however, they can be suppressed by voluntary control (Nudleman & Starr, 1983).

The role of the central nuclei in the control of facial expression is not well documented. The hypothalamus and the dorsal thalamus, in association with related structures, probably intervene (Kahn, 1966). Patients suffering from a pathology of the caudate nucleus in Parkinson's disease are characterized by a reduction of the spontaneous facial activity or amimia (Buck & Duffy, 1980). The eye blink rate is lowered and sensitive to pharmacological control (Karson, 1983; Karson, Burns, Lewitt, Foster, & Newman, 1984). Positive manifestations of subcortical disorders have been described under the heading of *Meige's disease* or *Brueghel's syndrome* (Altrocchi & Forno, 1983; Mardsen, 1976; Meige, 1910; Tolosa, 1981; Tolosa & Klawans, 1979). In Mardsen's series, *thirteen* patients presented spasmodic contractions of the orbicularis oculi causing eye closure (blepharospasm); *nine* patients had spasmodic contraction of the mouth (oromandibular dystonia), and *seventeen* patients manifested a combination of the two symptoms. Again, distinct mechanisms for the control of upper and lower part of the face are evidenced. The pathological mechanism of Meige's disease is unknown, but it has been attributed to a disorder of the basal ganglia.

Another pathology of spontaneous facial movements is the involuntary release of laughter and crying by nonspecific and various stimuli (for reviews, see Black, 1982; Poeck, 1969). This disorder may arise as a consequence of very diverse lesions including cortical lesions as assumed in so-called gelastic epilepsy (see Myslobodsky, 1983, for a review) or subcortical lesions in the pseudo-bulbar palsy (caudate nucleus, thalamus, substantia nigra, etc.). Outbursts of laughter or crying are usually reported without associated change of emotional experience. Other changes in facial expression giving the appearance of sadness, fear, surprise, etc. have also been described at the onset of focal seizures, but modifications of emotional feelings have not been studied in this context (Strauss, Wada, & Kosaka, 1983).

Evidence of cortical control of facial expression is given by subjects suffering from frontal lesions (Laplane, Orgogozo, Meininger, & Degas, 1976; Laplane, Talairach, Meininger, Bancaud, & Orgogozo, 1977). Facial paresis on the contralateral side is observed after damage to the supplementary motor area (medial part of the frontal lobe). More facial asymmetry is shown in spontaneous emotional movement than in voluntary movement, whereas a lesion of the motor cortex (facial hemiparesis) causes the inverse: impaired voluntary movements but intact spontaneous smiling (Monrad-Krohn, 1924). Kolb and Milner (1981) systematically observed spontaneous facial expressions produced during neuropsychological testing: brow raising, smiling, lips tightening, sticking tongue out, etc. The subjects with left or right frontal lesions produced fewer movements than patients with temporal or parietal lesions. Thus, a critical role of the frontal lobe is again suggested, but the nature of this contribution—motor, emotional, or cognitive—remains to be determined.

Conclusions

Disorders of facial activity in brain-damaged subjects are often studied on their own without reference to the emotional meaning of the movement. Thus, the present body of pathological data does not support or refute any given theory of facial expression because critical observations are still lacking. Moreover, attention has been concentrated on the form of the movement, rather than on the eliciting conditions. Thus, the notion of a facial program remains conjectural. The only element in its favor could be the automatic release of crying or laughter; outbursts of anger have also been observed after brain lesions (Poeck, 1969; Reeves & Plum, 1969), but there is little evidence for the storage of other facial configurations. In addition, some elements argue for a distinction between automatic and voluntary processes, thus favoring the comprehensive theories of emotional expression. The facial feedback hypothesis has gained little support, even if subjective feelings and facial movements have never been recorded simultaneously in a systematic way: pathological laughter is not followed by changes in emotionality, and there is some evidence for a dissociation of motivational and motor mechanisms of facial expression. Thus, reduced facial activity could be due either to an inability to control facial musculature or to emotional indifference. Such a dissociation would better fit the cognitive theories of emotional expression as would the coincidence of cognitive and emotional disturbances in frontal and temporal lobes lesions.

However, these cognitive theories are also the readiest to question the assumption that facial movements express emotions. Some strong emotional experiences are better characterized by bodily changes and vocalization than by typical facial expressions. Inversely, several spontaneous facial expressions are not unanimously interpreted as emotional, and the face can express more various mental processes than just emotional ones. Similarly, if the interpretation of facial expressions in others does not imply the recall of subjective emotional experience or proprioception of the automatically copied model, facial movements could conceivably be understood without any reference to an implicit theory of emotion. Nevertheless, despite the imprecision of what could be called emotional processing, there is a tradition of considering right hemisphere as dominant in producing facial movements in response to emotional stimuli as well as dominant in understanding facial expressions of emotions.

THE LATERALITY ISSUE: RIGHT AND LEFT HEMISPHERE LESIONS COMPARED

The hypothesis of right-hemisphere dominance in the processing of emotional facial, vocal, and verbal expressions is suggested by data gathered from normal and brain damaged subjects (see Campbell, 1982; Seron & Vanderlinden, 1979; Tucker, 1981, for reviews). Right-hemisphere contribution is also hypothesized in the recognition of neutral faces. Right- and left-hemisphere lesions are thus expected to have different effects on the processing of emotional facial expressions. However, the question remains open as to whether this right-hemisphere contribution is related to the emotional nature of the process or to the particularity of the face as a stimulus or as muscles system (Gainotti, 1984). The dissociation of performance in brain-damaged subjects would constitute a major argument for the specificity of the processes at both the expressive and the receptive levels.

The Production of Facial Expressions

Hypotheses raised by the asymmetry of the face in normal subjects posing for an emotion (see reviews in Borod & Koff, 1981; Campbell, this volume; Sackeim & Gur, 1982) may be examined as far as unilateral brain lesions affect facial expression. Is the contribution of the right hemisphere in motor control related to performances in face recognition (mobilization of the face template)? Do laterality effects result from the competence of the intact hemisphere or from the suppression of the inhibitory influences of the other damaged hemisphere? Are lateral differences influenced by the spontaneous or the voluntary nature of the produced movement?

   Clinical observations suggest intact spontaneous facial gesturing in *left-hemisphere-damaged (LHD)* aphasic subjects and lack of expression in *right-hemisphere-damaged (RHD)* patients. Golper and Gordon (1984) made silent films of patients during conversations and reported that RHD subjects were more often recognized by naive judges as neurological patients than were aphasics. These RHD patients were said to be lacking in facial expression, to show more facial asymmetry, and to look "slow" or "blank". In the two cases reported by Ross and Mesulam (1979), the RHD patients are described as inexpressive: Their facial expressions lacked variety. They lost the ability to cry and laugh, although they experienced emotions and had no difficulty in judging emotions in other people. Associated deficits are the loss of affective intonation of speech and weakness of the left hemiface. Extended lesions were observed in the right posterior frontal and anterior parietal lobes. The basal ganglia were spared in one case, but not in the other.

Aphasics do not suffer from comparable deficits (Katz, Lapointe, & Markel, 1982). Indeed, no statistical differences appear when rates, durations, and mean durations of six co-verbal behaviors, among them eye-brow raising and smiling, are compared in aphasic and normal subjects. Correlations with linguistic performance as assessed by the Porch Index of Communicative Ability indicate an inverse relationship between verbal score, on the one hand, and smile rate and duration of eye contact, on the other. These nonverbal signals could serve as compensatory devices to maintain the social bond in conversation when speech is impaired. This *communicative competence* of aphasic patients is in accordance with the pragmatic adjustment shown by these patients in experimental tasks (see review in Foldi, Cicone, & Gardner, 1983).

A systematic investigation of facial expressivity in brain-damaged subjects was conducted with the slide-viewing paradigm, where the inadvertent facial behavior of the subject is filmed during slide presentations (Buck & Duffy, 1980; Duffy & Buck, 1979). The film is then presented to judges who are asked to rate expressiveness and to guess the kind of slide viewed. The slides belong to one of four categories: familiar people, pleasant landscapes, unpleasant scenes, and strange photographic effects. The number of correct responses and expressiveness measure are the dependent variables. In the first report (Duffy & Buck, 1979), a group of RHD subjects was nonsignificantly less accurate than aphasics in facial sending; aphasics did not differ from normal subjects and their performance did not correlate with their scores in the Porch Index of Communicative Ability or with their scores in a pantomime expression test. In the second analysis of the data (Buck & Duffy, 1980), severe aphasics were excluded and an additional control group of subjects with Parkinson's disease was tested. This time, the RHD subjects were found to be less accurate than normal and aphasic subjects, and just above the chance level of 25%. The subjects with Parkinson's disease scored at chance level and were judged as less "expressive" than RHD subjects who did not differ from normal subjects in this respect. All groups showed similar performances across the slide categories; decreasing accuracy from familiar, scenic, unusual, to unpleasant slides. An exception to this pattern was the performance of aphasics, which was above 40% accuracy in the four categories.

Reduced emotional expression in RHD subjects has also been shown by Borod, Koff, Perlman, and Nicholas (1985). In this study, subjects were presented pleasant and unpleasant scenes and were instructed to "describe their feelings and reactions". Records of the session were shown to judges who rated the utilization of three channels: facial expression, intonation, and speech. The analysis of variance of the rating scores showed a group-by-channel interaction: The LHD subjects were judged to use the facial and the vocal channels the most and the speech channel the least. Inversely, the RHD subjects were rated as more expressive in the speech channel than in the facial and vocal channels. The subjects with right frontal lesions received the lowest score in the facial channel. In RHD and LHD subject groups, facial expressiveness correlated with the use of emotional intonation, but neither measures correlated with speech expressiveness.

The hypothesis of a right hemisphere dominance in the control of spontaneous emotional movements must be qualified by the possible influence of the emotional valence. Some observations suggest different lateralization for positive and negative emotions, i.e., joy and surprise versus sadness, anger, fear, and disgust (see Bruyer, 1980 and Tucker, 1981, for reviews). For example, electrical stimulation of the brain more often produces feelings of well being on the left side and irritability and anxiety on the right (Sem-Jacobsen & Styri, 1975). Sackeim et al. (1982) presented a retrospective analysis supporting the hypothesis of a left-hemisphere dominance in the expression of happiness. Destructive unilateral lesions were assumed to desinhibit the other, intact hemisphere, whereas irritative lesions in epilepsy would activate the mechanisms located in the damaged hemisphere. In 109 cases of pathological laughing and crying, laughter occurred more frequently in RHD subjects and crying in LHD subjects. However, this pattern differed according to the sex of the subjects. An analysis of the three-way contingency tables provided by the authors (sex by lesion lateralization by emotional valence) indicates that the association of laughter and crying with right and left lesions, respectively, strongly depends on the sex variable. The other observation favoring the hypothesis of differential lateralization is the left localization of the majority of epileptic foci causing irrepressible laughing (Myslobodsky, 1983; Sackeim et al., 1982). However, the opposite pattern, i.e., epileptic outbursts of crying (dacrystic epilepsy) is very infrequent and we do not know the proportion of left foci in the consulting epileptic population. Thus, the statistical significance of the data cannot be determined. Systematic observations do not confirm different emotional reactions according to the lateralization of the epileptic focus. The self-reporting of fear does not differ between groups, but the mean fear score tends to be superior for left temporal epilepsy (Strauss et al., 1982). Analysis of the spontaneous facial expressions occurring at the onset of seizures does not reveal differences in emotional valence according to the side of the focus (Strauss et al., 1983). Thus, the hypothesis of a right hemisphere dominance restricted to the negative emotions still lacks empirical support as far as the expressive behavior of the brain-damaged people is considered.

The normal spontaneous facial activity of aphasic subjects contrasts with their impairments demonstrated by oral apraxia tests. Mateer and Kimura (1977) devised two nonverbal tasks: imitation of single oral movements (tongue protrusion, blowing, etc.) and imitation of multiple movements (sequence of three single movements). The performance of nonfluent aphasics was defective in both tasks, whereas fluent aphasics scored below control groups (RHD, LHD subjects without aphasia) in the second task only. A particular intervention of the left hemisphere in motor control is also evidenced by an experiment of Bruyer and Guérit (1983), where the subjects were requested to maintain a posture for thirty seconds. Some items involved facial movements, like closed eyes, but others did not. The mean inhibition time was lower for the LHD than for the RHD subjects, which suggests a superiority of the left hemisphere in the inhibition of movement.

Different effects of left-hemisphere lesions on the production of spontaneous and voluntary facial movements led Buck (1982) to hypothesize opposite cerebral lateralization according to the nature of the movement. The hypothesis of left-hemisphere dominance in the control of voluntary movements can economically account for several data: (a) Overall greater emotional expressivity of aphasic subjects would result from a desinhibition of spontaneous movements, and reduced expression in RHD patients would be due to a shift of the balance toward inhibition by the intact left hemisphere, (b) Facial asymmetry favoring the left side of the face in posing for emotions would be due to the stronger inhibitory influence of the left hemisphere on the right hemiface, and (c) A stronger inhibition would be exerted on negative than on positive expressions; thus, the more controlled sad expressions would appear more asymmetrical than the happy ones.

Unfortunately, this explanation is too simplistic in the light of several contradictory findings. As far as spontaneous facial expression is concerned, Kolb and Milner (1981) observed similar activity after right and left excisions in the temporal and parietal lobes. Administration of sodium asmytal reduces facial expression regardless the side of the injection. On the other hand, when the asymmetry of the mouth opening is measured in aphasic subjects, lateral differences appear to vary with the nature of the task; smiles are left-sided, whereas greater right opening is observed during word list generation and other verbal tasks (Landis & Graves, 1983). These data suggest bilateral control of the spontaneous facial expression. Voluntary movements are also influenced by left- and right-hemisphere lesions. If asymmetry in posed facial expression is, as according to Buck's hypothesis, mainly dependent on the inhibition of the right hemiface by the left hemisphere, then a left-hemisphere lesion would make the face more symmetrical, and a right-hemisphere lesion would not change, or would increase, facial asymmetry. Bruyer (1981a) analyzed facial asymmetry in brain-damaged subjects with normal judges choosing left or right composites as the most expressive. For sad and neutral poses, composites contralateral to the lesion were judged less expressive, which could be due to mild motor weakness of the hemiface controlled by the damaged hemisphere. No asymmetry appeared in posing for smiles in any of the groups. In a preliminary study, Borod and Koff (1982) also reported an inversion of the normal facial asymmetry in RHD subjects. Similarly, epileptic subjects posing with a smile or smiling spontaneously showed a contralateral weakness to the side of the focus, regardless the right or left localization (Remillard, Andermann, Rhi-Sausi, & Robbins, 1977). These observations suggest a specific role of the right hemisphere in the control of facial expression and not just a greater inhibition by the left hemisphere. This role could be related to other right hemisphere advantages in motor control such as in copying static hand configurations (Kimura & Vanderwolf, 1970).

In summary, clear evidence for lateral differences in brain control on facial expressions does not make the interpretation of the observations obvious. More precisely, it is not clear whether right hemisphere superiority relies on the emotional nature of the movement or on the peculiarities of the face as a motor system. Facial inexpressivity of RHD subjects could be due either to a disturbance of the control mechanisms of facial movements or to an inability to experience emotions in experimental or everyday situations. Thus it is interesting to compare performances on the expressive and receptive levels, i.e., to analyze facial processing when no motor performance is required.

The Comprehension of Facial Expressions

The hypothesis of right-hemisphere dominance in emotional processing has inspired several studies on the interpretation of facial expression in brain-damaged subjects. The first systematic observations were published in 1980 by Cicone, Wapner, and Gardner, and by DeKosky, Heilman, Bowers, and Valenstein. Cicone et al. (1980) compared four groups; 18 LHD, 21 RHD, 13 lobectomized schizophrenics, and 10 normal subjects. The processing of facial expression was examined in a task where subjects chose the stimulus corresponding to the target face from four photographs. The target represented an emotional expression belonging to one of the six categories: positive emotions (joy, surprise) and negative emotions (sadness, disgust, fear, anger). The multiple choice gave the correct response, an expression of the same polarity, an expression of the opposite polarity, and a neutral expression. A significant group effect on the number of errors was observed, each group differing from each other, except the RHD and the schizophrenic groups, which showed similar impairment. There was also a group-by-emotion interaction; the happy face was often correctly interpreted by the normal and LHD subjects but rarely so by the RHD subjects. The groups also differed by the nature of their errors. Most subjects chose the face of the same polarity more often than the face of the opposite polarity, but the RHD subjects showed the reverse pattern. It was thus suggested that the impairments evidenced by the LHD and the RHD subjects were of distinct natures.

In DeKosky et al.'s (1980) study, three groups of subjects (nine RHD subjects with hemineglect, nine conduction aphasics, and nine neurological controls) processed facial expressions in four conditions: (1) making same/different judgments of facial identity on two photographs bearing a neutral expression, (2) naming the emotional facial expression shown on a photograph, (3) pointing to the face expressing the named emotion, and (4) making same/different judgments of emotional expressions. Significant differences between the groups appeared in each condition: The RHD subjects were impaired relative to the control subjects for all the conditions. The aphasic subjects performed normally in the two judgment tasks but not in the verbal tasks. This result was expected as far as naming is concerned, but the impaired pointing in subjects with spared comprehension of isolated words was more surprising. Moreover, when the groups were equalized by taking into account their scores in the facial identity judgment, the two brain-damaged groups showed similar impairments in the three emotional tasks. These results again suggest disturbances of different natures in RHD and in LHD subjects.

In order to distinguish different kinds of impairments in the processing of emotional expression, several hypotheses have been examined: deficits in RHD subjects would be related to other visuo-spatial or emotional disorders, whereas deficits in LHD subjects would be related to language disturbances.

Relations to Other Visuo-Spatial Impairments.   Difficulties of RHD subjects in interpreting facial expression have been associated with the presence of unilateral spatial agnosia (DeKosky et al., 1980; Goldblum, 1980; Kremin, 1980). Bruyer (1981b) also found poorer performances in subjects with left hemianopia. The possible role of a general disturbance of the visuo-spatial processes may be further examined in relating impairment with facial expressions to the disturbances of the facial recognition (prosopagnosia).

This hypothesis, however, has gained little support in current research. The possible influence of prosopagnosia is suggested by covariance analysis in the study of DeKosky et al. (1980) and by the positive correlation between scores of facial recognition and emotional expressions matching in Kremin's (1980) sample, but the correlations are much lower in other studies (Cicone et al., 1980; De Kosky et al., 1980). Independence is also suggested by a re-analysis of previous results by Bruyer (1984) where RHD subjects' impairment was unchanged when the score in facial recognition was introduced as a covariate. The case of prosopagnosia described by Bruyer et al. (1983) showed no disturbance in tests involving emotional facial expressions. Unfortunately, these tests have rarely been applied to the other cases of prosopagnosia described in the literature. Other arguments for the separability of the processes underlying facial recognition and interpretation of facial expressions come from the null correlation between the two experimental scores in senile dementia (Kurucz & Feldmar, 1979) and from the fact that in electrical stimulation of the right hemisphere of epileptic patients disruption of either facial recognition or interpretation of facial expression is observed, whereas no site has been found to be associated with the disturbance of both these functions (Fried, Mateer, Ojemann, Wohns, & Fedio, 1982).

An experimental analysis of the relationship between facial recognition and interpretation of facial expression was conducted by Etcoff (1984). Two actresses posed, expressing joy or sadness, and the subjects classified the stimuli according to the model or to the emotion in three conditions: (1) correlation of facial expression and facial identity, (2) constant association of one woman with one emotion and variable association for the other, and (3) orthogonal variations in the two dimensions, expression and identity. A parallel task involved geometric figures differing by shape and/or color. The assumption of the paradigm was that integrated processing of the two dimensions will make the three conditions more difficult from the first to the third whereas no differences between the conditions would appear if the two dimensions of the stimulus are processed separately. The results showed a significant group-by-condition-by-dimension interaction. The conditions did not differ in the parallel task with geometric figures. In processing faces the LHD did not differ from the normal subjects, but the RHD subjects made more errors and performed more slowly in the orthogonal condition. Thus, facial expression and facial identity appear to be separately processed by subjects with an intact right hemisphere while right-hemisphere lesions disrupt both the processes. However, the two impairments could be independent as some RHD subjects showed disparity in their scores in tests on facial identity or facial expression.

Relationships to Other Emotional Judgments. If the interpretation of facial expression is independent as regards the processing of facial identity is it then determined by the emotional nature of the stimulus? Similar performances of RHD subjects were observed in matching pictures of emotional scenes and in processing facial expressions of emotions (Cicone et al., 1980; De Kosky et al., 1980). On the other hand, Goldblum (1980) noted that RHD subjects are more impaired in interpreting emotional faces than in processing conventional gestures, whereas the two conditions did not yield different results with aphasic and normal subjects. Kremin (1980) obtained the same pattern of results, although in her sample, the two performances in aphasic and in RHD subjects correlated. The emotional nature of the stimulus could thus be a critical factor.

Other data, however, do not support this hypothesis. Subjects with senile dementia made more errors in a verbal task of pointing to a face expressing the named emotion than in a nonverbal task showing the face that expressed a different emotion in an array of three (Brosgole, Kurucz, Plahovinsak, & Gumiela, 1981). These demented subjects have also been shown to be able to interpret postural expressions of emotions better than facial expressions (Brosgole, Kurucz, Plahovinsak, Sprotte, & Haveliwala, 1983). These results suggest a relatively specific disorder restricted to some tasks involving particular stimuli. The deficit of the RHD subjects could also be limited to some experimental conditions. Cicone et al. (1980) found a significant group-by-condition interaction due to a superior performance of RHD subjects in the verbal description of an emotional scene. In this condition, these subjects were thus able to infer emotional meanings. Accordingly, the authors suggested that the difficulty with facial expressions could rather be located in the inability to "relate this emotional inferential process to the stimulus at hand". This cognitive impairment might be related to other disturbances in RHD subjects, especially in appreciating humor (Brownell, Michel, Powelson, & Gardner, 1983; Gardner, Ling, Flamm, & Silverman, 1975; for a review, see Gardner, Brownell, Wapner, & Michelow, 1983). Similarly, Kolb and Taylor (1981) found the perception of emotion to be dissociated in facial and verbal stimuli. Subjects with excision of different parts of the right hemisphere were found to be impaired in matching emotional faces, but they scored near normal level and higher than patients with excision in the left hemisphere in describing verbally persons experiencing emotional events. Similar to the data of Cicone et al. (1980), this result suggests that RHD patients could be helped in processing emotional materials by the verbal nature of the task.

An alternative hypothesis could be that interpreting facial expression is a specific process. The interpretation of emotional cues in several channels, as tested in the Profile of Nonverbal Sensitivity (PONS), was most impaired by right hemisphere damages when subjects had to process facial expressions, whereas little impairment was evidenced in the processing of vocal or postural cues (Benowitz et al., 1983). On the other hand, modifications of the emotional behavior after right hemisphere lesions could be unrelated to the disturbances in facial processing. Zoccolotti, Scabini, and Violani (1982) replicated the results of Morrow, Vrtunski, Kim, and Boller (1981) who demonstrated reduced electrodermal activity in RHD subjects viewing emotional slides relative to the galvanic skin responses of normal and LHD subjects. Taking the scores in a test of facial expression interpretation as a covariate did not reduce this difference, which suggests the independence of the two performances.

Relation to Language Disturbances.   The hypothesis of a specific processing of facial expressions seems to be relatively well supported as far as the behavior of RHD subjects is concerned. However, it does not account for the impairment of aphasic subjects, which was first reported by Cicone et al. (1980) and De Kosky et al. (1980), and then confirmed by Goldblum (1980), and Blunk (1982). In Katz' (1980) study the aphasics did not differ as a group from normal subjects, but a deficit was observed in the five most severe cases. Highly divergent explanations for the deficit shown by aphasic subjects have been proposed.

Because De Kosky et al. (1980) observed more severe disturbances in the verbal tasks, in spite of the intact auditory comprehension of their aphasic subjects, they suggested a disconnection between the verbal function and the "emotional areas" of the right hemisphere. But such an explanation would not account for the deficit observed in other studies using nonverbal tasks. Some authors suggest a covert linguistic mediation in matching facial expressions, but LHD patients without aphasia do not score significantly better than aphasic subjects in these tasks (Goldblum, 1980; Kremin, 1980). In these cases perceptual processes might be disturbed by posterior lesions, but a visual field defect does not seem to be a critical factor in LHD subjects (Bruyer, 1981b; Goldblum, 1980). On the basis of significant correlation between verbal and nonverbal matching of facial expressions and of gestures Kremin (1980) argues for a general disturbance of comprehension, which would not be material specific. Similarly, an inability to match facial expressions could be related to other well-documented nonverbal impairments in matching tasks involving sounds, colors, pictures, or pantomime (see e.g., Feyereisen & Seron, 1982). This impairment of analytic competence has been interpreted as resulting from an inability to extract relevant information in order to associate conceptually related elements. For example, in the study of Feyereisen, Seron, and de Macar (1981), aphasic subjects manifested more difficulty in matching physiological gestures (expression of fear, of pain, stretching, crying, etc.) with pictures of eliciting situations than was the case for pantomimed use of objects (cigarette, guitar, comb, toothbrush, etc.). The same difference was observed when verbal labels were substituted for gestures. It was thus suggested that the impairment was not related to the perceptual analysis of the signal but to the cognitive operations of matching the signal and the eliciting situation.

This raises the question of the conditions in which processing of emotional faces is studied in brain damaged subjects. Impairments in matching tasks do not imply an inability to use facial cues in social interpretation. Moreover, several experimental paradigms for the study of facial processing by normal children and adults, like vicarious conditioning or combinations of facial and contextual cues, have, to our knowledge, never been applied to neurological populations. Even when several experimental conditions are designed, such as those by De Kosky et al. (1980), the group-by-condition interaction has not been thoroughly analyzed or possible dissociations examined in the study of individual cases. Does not the simple fact that both RHD and LHD patients exhibit difficulties in interpreting facial expressions indicate that the two hemispheres intervene in the experimental tasks dealing with facial expressions? This will have to be kept in mind in future research aimed at specifying the nature of the impairment resulting from unilateral brain damages.

Cooperation of the Two Hemispheres?   Apart from studies evidencing more severe disturbances in RHD than in LHD subjects in interpreting facial expressions, other data do not show statistical differences between these two groups. We have in mind the studies by Kremin (1980), Kurucz, Soni, Feldmar, and Slade (1980), and Prigatano and Pribram (1982). The results of the two last studies are difficult to interpret because of the verbal nature of the experimental task, which could have disturbed aphasic subjects, and because of the small size of the sample, which could have favored the type II error in the statistical inference (non significant results do not necessarily mean absence of true differences). More interesting in these studies is the fact that the most impaired population turned out to be that of bilateral brain-damaged subjects, among whom, in the group of Prigatano and Pribram (1982), four out of five had frontal lesions. This result could be related to a disturbed interpretation of facial expression in the schizophrenic subjects who had undergone a bilateral frontal lobectomy (Cicone et al., 1980; Stuss & Benson, 1983).

Diffuse lesions like those observed in senile dementia are also shown to impair comprehension of facial expressions in naming and verbal pointing tasks (Brosgole et al., 1983; Kurucz & Feldmar, 1979; Kurucz, Feldmar, & Werner, 1979). These observations could be related to deficits in interpreting facial expressions evidenced in mentally handicapped children (Gray, Fraser, & Lendar, 1983; Lambert & Defays, 1978) and in schizophrenic subjects (Cutting, 1981; Dougherty, Bartlett & Izard, 1974; Muzekari & Bates, 1977; Walker, Marwit, & Emory, 1980; Walker, McGuire, & Bettes, 1984), some of whom are suffering from diffuse brain damage (Seidman, 1983). Along with the very poor performance of split-brain subjects in interpreting facial expression (Benowitz et al., 1983), these observations suggest that both hemispheres have to cooperate to understand emotion in facial movements. The conditions for such cooperation cannot be identified until the nature of the contribution of each hemisphere is specified.

CONCLUSIONS

In fact, laterality effects in facial processing will guard their mystery as long as there is no established theory on emotional expression or on comprehension of emotion. Because the lack of basic data and the tentative nature of the existing theories render inconclusive the first issue raised (How does the face express emotions?), it is impossible to relate observed differences between RHD and LHD subjects to other lateral differences in cognitive processing. However, it remains that empirical data are as respectable as Lord Mayors and that any attempt to design a general theory of hemispheric specialization has to take account of the effects of brain damage on facial processing as artefacts or as predictable effects, whether the laterality effects are due to the nature of the stimulus (verbal versus nonverbal), to the kind of processing (global versus analytic), or to the physical properties of the processed material.

Regarding the problematic issue of specificity of facial processing, two avenues may be explored. One is to view the concept of emotion as a remnant of prescientific thought. Experimental analysis will thus dissolve this pseudoobject by finding specific explanations for the various behavioral phenomena collapsed under the emotional heading or for the different kinds of subjective experience—fear, pleasure, contempt, perplexity, etc.—that receive an emotional label. The other way is to consider that the true emotions we experience constitute a special cognitive domain. To some extent, emotional evaluation has properties of a module as an input system in Fodor's (1983) sense. On the one hand, they are rapid, mandatory, and give only limited access to consciousness. Zajonc (1980,

1984) argues for very rapid affective categorization and that preferences need no inferences. On the other hand, however, affects are not domain-specific, because the class of inputs arousing emotional evaluation appears to be unlimited. They are poorly encapsulated, too, because past experience and knowledge modify emotion. It could be, then, that they are not comparable with other perceptual operations. Nevertheless, the exploration of emotion as a particular mode of information processing is not really incompatible with the first approach we mentioned, which dismisses the concept of emotion. Indeed, it seems necessary for any theory of emotion to specify the extent to which facial expression is related to emotional evaluation, and whether facial expression and the interpretation of facial cues imply some common subprocesses. It is unfortunate that the behavior of brain damaged people has not yet been analyzed from such a perspective.

REFERENCES

Altrocchi, P. H., & Forno, L. S. (1983). Spontaneous oral-facial dyskinesia: neuropathology of a case. *Neurology, 33,* 802–805.

Angelergues, R., Hécaen, H., & Ajuriaguerra, J. (1955). Les troubles mentaux au cours des tumeurs du lobe frontal. A propos de 80 observations dont 54 avec troubles mentaux. *Annales médico-psychologiques, 113-II,* 577–642.

Bear, D. M. (1979). Temporal lobe epilepsy: a syndrome of sensory limbic hyperconnection. *Cortex, 15,* 357–384.

Bear, D. M., & Fedio, P. (1977). Quantitative analysis of interictal behavior in temporal lobe epilepsy. *Archives of Neurology, 34,* 454–467.

Benowitz, L. L., Bear, D. M., Rosenthal, R., Mesulam, M. M., Zaidel, E., & Sperry, R. W. (1983). Hemispheric specialization in nonverbal communication. *Cortex, 19,* 5–11.

Black, D. W. (1982). Pathological laughter, a review of the literature. *The Journal of Mental and Nervous Disease, 170,* 67–71.

Blunk, R. (1982). Recognition of emotion and physiognomy in right- and left-hemisphere damaged patients and normals. Deauville: *Communication* at the INS Meeting.

Borod, J. C., & Koff, E. (1982). Facial asymmetry and lateral dominance in normal and brain-damaged adults. Pittsburgh: *Communication* at the INS Meeting.

Borod, J. C., & Koff, E. (1983). Asymmetries in affective facial expression: behavior and anatomy. In N. Fox & R. Davidson (Eds.), *The psychobiology of affective development* (pp. 293–323). Hillsdale, NJ: Lawrence Erlbaum Associates.

Borod, J. C., Koff, E., Perlman, M., & Nicholas, M. (1985). Channels of emotional expression in patients with unilateral brain damage. *Archives of Neurology, 42,* 345–348.

Brodal, A. (1969). *Neurological anatomy in relation to clinical medicine* (2nd ed.). New York, London, & Toronto: Oxford University Press.

Brosgole, L., Kurucz, J., Plahovinsak, T. J., & Gumiela, E. (1981). On the mechanism underlying facial-affective agnosia in senile demented patients. *International Journal of Neurosciences, 15,* 207–215.

Brosgole, L., Kurucz, J., Plahovinsak, T., Boettcher, P., Sprotte, C., & Haveliwala, Y. A. (1983). Facial affect recognition in normal preschool children and in senile elderly persons. *International Journal of Neurosciences, 20,* 91–102.

Brosgole, L., Kurucz, J., Plahovinsak, T. J., Sprotte, C., & Haveliwala, Y. A. (1983). Facial- and postural-affect recognition in senile elderly persons. *International Journal of Neurosciences, 22,* 37–46.

Brownell, H. H., Michel, D., Powelson, J., & Gardner, H. (1983). Surprise but not coherence: sensitivity to verbal humor in right-hemisphere patients. *Brain and Language, 18,* 20–27.

Bruyer, R. (1980). Implication différentielle des hémisphères cérébraux dans les conduites émotionnnelles. *Acta psychiatrica Belgica, 80,* 266–284.

Bruyer, R. (1981a). Asymmetry of facial expression in brain damaged subjects. *Neuropsychologia, 19,* 615–624.

Bruyer, R. (1981b). Perception d'expressions faciales émotionnelles et lésion cérébrale: influence de la netteté du stimulus. *International Journal of Psychology, 16,* 87–94.

Bruyer, R. (1984). Lateralized brain processing of faces and facial expressions: levels of blurring and specificity. *Perceptual and Motor Skills, 59,* 545–546.

Bruyer, R., & Guérit, J. M. (1983). Hemispheric differences in the voluntary inhibition of movement. *Brain and Cognition, 2,* 251–256.

Bruyer, R., Laterre, C., Seron, X., Feyereisen, P., Strypstein, E., Pierrard, E., & Rectem, D. (1983). A case of prosopagnosia with some preserved covert remembrance of familiar faces. *Brain and Cognition, 2,* 257–284.

Buck, R. (1980). Nonverbal behavior and the theory of emotion: the facial feedback hypothesis. *Journal of Personality and Social Psychology, 38,* 811–824.

Buck, R. (1982). A theory of spontaneous and symbolic expression: implications for facial lateralization. Pittsburg: *Communication* at the INS Meeting.

Buck, R., & Duffy, R. J. (1980). Nonverbal communication of affect in brain damaged patients. *Cortex, 16,* 351–362.

Campbell, R. (1982). The lateralization of emotion: a critical review. *International Journal of Psychology, 17,* 211–229.

Cicone, M., Wapner, W., & Gardner, H. (1980). Sensitivity to emotional expressions and situations in organic patients. *Cortex, 16,* 145–158.

Cotton, J. L. (1981). A review of research on Schachter's theory of emotion and the misattribution of arousal. *European Journal of Social Psychology, 11,* 365–397.

Cutting, J. (1981). Judgment of emotional expression in schizophrenics. *British Journal of Psychiatry, 139,* 1–6.

Damasio, A. R., & Van Hoesen, G. W. (1983). Emotional disturbances associated with focal lesions of the limbic frontal lobe. In K. M. Heilman & P. Satz (Eds.). *Neuropsychology of human emotion* (pp. 85–110). New York & London: Guilford Press.

Darwin, C. (1965). *The expression of the emotions in man and animals.* Chicago & London: The University of Chicago Press. (Original work published 1872).

De Kosky, S. T., Heilman, K. M., Bowers, D., & Valenstein, E. (1980). Recognition and discrimination of emotional faces and pictures. *Brain and Language, 9,* 206–214.

Deutsch, R. D., Kling, A., & Steklis, H. D. (1979). Influence of frontal lobe lesions on behavioral interactions in man. *Research Communications in Psychology, Psychiatry and Behavior, 4,* 415–431.

Dimberg, U. (1982). Facial reactions to facial expressions. *Psychophysiology, 19,* 643–647.

Dimond, S. J. (1980). *Neuropsychology: A textbook of systems and psychological functions of the human brain.* London: Butterworth.

Dougherty, F. E., Bartlett, E. S., & Izard, C. E. (1974). Responses of schizophrenics to expressions of the fundamental emotions. *Journal of Clinical Psychology, 30,* 243–246.

Dubner, R., Sessle, B. J., & Storey, A. T. (1978). *The neural basis of oral and facial function.* New York & London: Plenum Press.

Duffy, R. J., & Buck, R. W. (1979). A study of the relationship between propositional (pantomime) and subpropositional (facial expression) extraverbal behaviors in aphasics. *Folia Phoniatrica, 31,* 129–136.

Ekman, P. (1971). Universals and cultural differences in the facial expressions of emotion. In J. K. Cole (Ed.), *Nebraska Symposium on Motivation, vol. 19* (pp. 207–283). Lincoln: University of Nebraska Press.

Ekman, P., Levenson, R. W., & Friesen, W. V. (1983). Autonomous Nervous System activity distinguishes among emotions. *Science, 221*, 1208–1210.

Etcoff, N. L. (1984). Selective attention to facial identity and facial emotion. *Neuropsychologia, 22*, 281–295.

Fedio, P., & Martin, A. (1983). Ideative-emotive behavioral characteristics of patients following left or right temporal lobectomy. *Epilepsia, 24* (Suppl. 2), S117–S130.

Feyereisen, P., & de Lannoy, J. D. (1985). *Psychologie du Geste.* Bruxelles & Liège: P. Mardaga.

Feyereisen, P., & Seron, X. (1982). Nonverbal communication and aphasia, a review: I. Comprehension. *Brain and Language, 16*, 191–212.

Feyereisen, P., Seron, X., & de Macar, M. A. (1981). L'interprétation de différentes catégories de gestes chez des sujets aphasiques. *Neuropsychologia, 19*, 515–521.

Fodor, J. A. (1983). *The modularity of mind.* Cambridge, MA: The MIT Press.

Foldi, N. S., Cicone, M., & Gardner, H. (1983). Pragmatic aspects of communication in brain-damaged patients. In S. J. Segalowitz (Ed.), *Language function and brain organization* (pp. 51–86). New York & London: Academic Press.

Fordyce, D. J., Roueche, J. R., & Prigatano, G. P. (1983). Enhanced emotional reactions in chronic head trauma patients. *Journal of Neurology, Neurosurgery and Psychiatry, 46*, 620–624.

Franzen, E. A., & Myers, R. E. (1973). Neural control of social behavior: prefrontal and anterior temporal cortex. *Neuropsychologia, 11*, 141–157.

Fried, I., Mateer, C., Ojemann, G., Wohns, R., & Fedio, P. (1982). Organization of visuospatial functions in human cortex: evidence from electrical stimulation. *Brain, 105*, 349–371.

Friedman, H. M., & Allen, N. (1969). Chronic effects of complete limbic lobe destruction in Man. *Neurology, 19*, 679–690.

Gainotti, G. (1969). Réactions "catastrophiques" et manifestations d'indifférence au cours des atteintes cérébrales. *Neuropsychologia, 7*, 195–204.

Gainotti, G. (1972). Emotional behavior and hemispheric side of the lesion. *Cortex, 8*, 41–55.

Gainotti, G. (1984). Some methodological problems in the study of the relationships between emotion and cerebral dominance. *Journal of Clinical Neuropsychology, 6*, 111–121.

Gardner, H., Brownell, H. H., Wapner, W., & Michelow, D. (1983). Missing the point: the role of the right hemisphere in the processing of complex linguistic material. In E. Perecman (Ed.), *Cognitive processing in the right hemisphere* (pp. 169–191). New York & London: Academic Press.

Gardner, H., Ling, P. K., Flamm, L., & Silverman, J. (1975). Comprehension and appreciation of humorous material following brain damage. *Brain, 98*, 399–412.

Gascon, G. G., & Gilles, F. (1973). Limbic dementia. *Journal of Neurology, Neurosurgery and Psychiatry, 36*, 421–430.

Goldblum, M. C. (1980). La reconnaissance des expressions faciales émotionnelles et conventionnelles au cours de lésions corticales. *Revue neurologique, 136*, 711–719.

Golper, L. A. C., & Gordon, M. E. (1984). Coverbal behavior and perceptions of organicity. Aachen: *Communication* at the INS Meeting.

Graham, M. D., & House, W. F. (Eds.). (1982). *Disorders of the facial nerve.* New York: Raven Press.

Gray, J. H., Fraser, W. L., & Lendar, I. (1983). Recognition of emotion from facial expression in mental handicap. *British Journal of Psychiatry, 142*, 566–571.

Hécaen, H., & Albert, M. C. (1975). Disorders of mental functioning related to frontal lobe pathology: In D. F. Benson & D. Blumer (Eds.), *Psychiatric aspects of neurologic disease* (pp. 137–150). New York, San Francisco, & London: Grune & Stratton.

Izard, C. E. (1977). *Human emotions*. New York & London: Plenum Press.

Kahn, E. A. (1966). On facial expression. *Clinical Neurosurgery, 12,* 9–22.

Karson, C. N. (1983). Spontaneous eye blink rates and dopaminergic systems. *Brain, 106,* 643–653.

Karson, C. N., Burns, S., Lewitt, P. A., Foster, N. L., & Newman, R. P. (1984). Blink rates and disorders of movement. *Neurology, 34,* 677–678.

Katz, R. C. (1980). Perception of facial affect in aphasia: In R. H. Brookshire (Ed.), *Clinical aphasiology. Proceedings of the conference* (pp. 78–88). Minneapolis: BRK Publishers.

Katz, R. C., LaPointe, L. L., & Markel, N. N. (1978). Coverbal behavior and aphasic speakers. In R. H. Brookshire (Ed.), *Clinical aphasiology. Proceedings of the conference* (pp. 164–173). Minneapolis: BRK Publishers.

Kimura, D., & Vanderwolf, C. H. (1970). The relation between hand preference and the performance of individual finger movements by left and right hands. *Brain, 93,* 769–774.

Kling, A., & Steklis, H. D. (1976). A neural substrate for affiliative behavior in nonhuman Primates. *Brain, Behavior and Evolution, 13,* 216–238.

Kolb, B., & Milner, B. (1981). Observations of spontaneous facial expression after cerebral excisions and after intracarotid injection of sodium amytal. *Neuropsychologia, 19,* 505–514.

Kolb, B., & Taylor, L. (1981). Affective behavior in patients with localized cortical excisions: role of lesion site and side. *Science, 214,* 89–91.

Kremin, H. (1980). Recognition of faces, facial expressions and gestures in brain damaged patients. Chianciano: *Communication* at the INS Meeting.

Kurucz, J., & Feldmar, G. (1979). Prosopo-affective agnosia as a symptom of cerebral organic disease. *Journal of the American Geriatrics Society, 27,* 225–230.

Kurucz, J., Feldmar, G., & Werner, W. (1979). Prosopo-affective agnosia associated with chronic organic brain syndrome. *Journal of the American Geriatrics Society, 27,* 91–95.

Kurucz, J., Soni, A., Feldmar, G., & Slade, W. R. (1980). Prosopo-affective agnosia and CT findings in patients with cerebral disorders. *Journal of the American Geriatrics Society, 28,* 475–478.

Lambert, J. L., & Defays, D. (1978). La compréhension d'expressions faciales chez des arriérés mentaux et normaux. *Psychologie, 37,* 216–224.

Landis, T., & Graves, R. (1983). Mouth asymmetry variation with task in aphasia. Lisbon: *Communication* at the INS Meeting.

Laplane, D., Orgogozo, J. M., Meininger, V., & Degas, J. D. (1976). Paralysie faciale avec dissociation automatico-volontaire inverse par lésion frontale. Son origine corticale. Ses relations avec l'AMS. *Revue neurologique, 132,* 725–734.

Laplane, D., Talairach, J., Meininger, V., Bancaud, J., & Orgogozo, J. M. (1977). Clinical consequences of corticectomies involving the supplementary motor area in Man. *Journal of the Neurological Sciences, 34,* 301–314.

Leventhal, H. (1980). Toward a comprehensive theory of emotion. In L. Berkowitz (Ed.), *Advances in experimental social psychology, Vol. 13* (pp. 139–207). New York & London: Academic Press.

Lilly, R., Cummings, J. L., Benson, D. F., & Frankel, M. (1983). The human Klüver-Bucy syndrome. *Neurology, 33,* 1141–1145.

Mandler, G. (1980). The generation of emotion: a psychological theory. In R. Plutchik & H. Kellerman (Eds.), *Emotion, theory, research, experience. Vol. 1: Theories of emotion* (pp. 219–243). New York & London: Academic Press.

Mardsen, C. D. (1976). Blepharospasm-oromandibular dystonia syndrome (Brueghel's syndrome). A variant of adult-onset torsion dystonia? *Journal of Neurology, Neurosurgery and Psychiatry, 39,* 1204–1209.

Marlowe, W. B., Mancall, E. L., & Thomas, J. J. (1975). Complete Klüver-Bucy syndrome in Man. *Cortex, 11,* 53–59.

Mateer, C., & Kimura, D. (1977). Impairment of nonverbal oral movements in aphasia. *Brain and Language, 4,* 262–276.

Meige, H. (1910). Les convulsions de la face, une forme clinique de convulsion faciale bilatérale et médiane. *Revue neurologique, 21,* 437–443.

Monrad-Krohn, G. H. (1924). On the dissociation of voluntary and emotional innervation in facial paresis of central origin. *Brain, 47,* 22–35.

Morrow, L., Vrtunski, B., Kim, Y., & Boller, F. (1981). Arousal responses to emotional stimuli and laterality of lesion. *Neuropsychologia, 19,* 65–71.

Mungas, D. (1982). Interictal behavior abnormality in temporal lobe epilepsy. *Archives of General Psychiatry, 39,* 108–111.

Muzekari, L. H., & Bates, M. (1977). Judgment of emotions among chronic schizophrenic. *Journal of Clinical Psychology, 33,* 662–666.

Myers, R. E., & Swett, C. Jr. (1970). Social behavior deficits in free-ranging monkeys after anterior temporal cortex removal: a preliminary report. *Brain Research, 18,* 551–556.

Myslobodsky, M. S. (1983). Epileptic laughter. In M. S. Myslobodsky (Ed.), *Hemisyndromes: Psychobiology, neurology, psychiatry* (pp. 239–263). New York & London: Academic Press.

Nudleman, K. L., & Starr, A. (1983). Focal facial spasm. *Neurology, 33,* 1092–1095.

Panksepp, J. (1982). Toward a general psychobiological theory of emotions. *The Behavioural and Brain Sciences, 5,* 407–467.

Plutchik, R., & Kellerman, H. (Eds.). (1980). *Emotion, theory, research, experience. Vol. 1: Theories of emotion.* New York & London: Academic Press.

Poeck, K. (1969). Pathophysiology of emotional disorders associated with brain damage. In P. J. Vincken & G. N. Bruyn (Eds.), *Handbook of clinical neurology: Vol. 3. Disorders of higher nervous activity* (pp. 343–367). Amsterdam & New York: North-Holland & Wiley.

Prigatano, G. P., & Pribram, K. H. (1981). Perception and memory of facial affect following brain injury. *Perceptual and Motor Skills, 54,* 859–869.

Raleigh, M. J., & Steklis, H. D. (1981). Effects of orbitofrontal and temporal neocortical lesions on the affiliative behavior of vervet monkeys (Cercopithecus aethiops Sabaeus). *Experimental Neurology, 73,* 378–389.

Reeves, A. G., & Plum, F. (1969). Hyperphagia, rage and dementia accompanying a ventromedial hypothalamic neoplasm. *Archives of Neurology, 20,* 616–624.

Reisenzein, R. (1983). The Schachter theory of emotion: Two decades later. *Psychological Bulletin, 94,* 239–264.

Remillard, G. M., Andermann, F., Rhi-Sausi, A., & Robbins, N. M. (1977). Facial asymmetry in patients with temporal lobe epilepsy. A clinical sign useful in the lateralization of temporal epileptogenic foci. *Neurology, 27,* 109–114.

Rinn, W. E. (1984). The neuropsychology of facial expression: a review of the neurological and psychological mechanisms for producing facial expressions. *Psychological Bulletin, 95,* 52–77.

Robinson, R. G., & Benson, D. F. (1981). Depression in aphasic patients: frequency, severity and clinical-pathological correlations. *Brain and Language, 14,* 282–291.

Robinson, R. G., Kubos, K. L., Starr, L. B., Rao, K., & Price, T. R. (1984). Mood disorders in stroke patients. *Brain, 107,* 81–93.

Rodin, E., & Schmaltz, S. (1984). The Bear-Fedio personality inventory and temporal lobe epilepsy. *Neurology, 34,* 591–596.

Ross, E. D., & Mesulam, M. M. (1979). Dominant language functions in the right hemisphere? *Archives of Neurology, 36,* 144–148.

Sackeim, H. A., & Gur, R. C. (1982). Facial asymmetry and the communication of emotion. In J. T. Cacioppo & R. E. Petty (Eds.). *Social psychophysiology.* New York: Guilford Press.

Sackeim, H. A., Greenberg, M. S., Weiman, A. L., Gur, R. C., Hungerbuhler, J. P., & Geschwind, N. (1982). Hemispheric asymmetry in the expression of positive and negative emotions. *Archives of Neurology, 39,* 210–218.

Schachter, S. (1975). Cognition and peripheralist-centralist controversies in motivation and emotion. In M. S. Gazzaniga & C. Blakemore (Eds.), *Handbook of psychobiology* (pp. 529–564). New York & London: Academic Press.

Scherer, K. R. (1984). Les émotions: fonctions et composantes. *Cahiers de Psychologie cognitive, 4,* 9–39.

Seidman, L. J. (1983). Schizophrenia and brain dysfunction: an integration of recent neurodiagnostic findings. *Psychological Bulletin, 94,* 195–238.

Sem-Jacobsen, C. N., & Styri, O. B. (1975). Manipulation of emotion: Electrophysiological and surgical methods. In L. Levi (Ed.), *Emotions: Their parameters and measurement* (pp. 645–676). New York: Plenum Press.

Seron, X., & Vanderlinden, M. (1979). Vers une neuropsychologie humaine des conduites émotionnelles? *L'Année psychologique, 79,* 229–252.

Steklis, H. D., & Raleigh, M. J. (1979). Behavioral and neurobiological aspects of primate vocalization and facial expression. In H. D. Steklis & M. J. Raleigh (Eds.), *Neurobiology of social communication in primates* (pp. 257–282). New York & London: Academic Press.

Strauss, E., Risser, A., & Jones, M. W. (1982). Fear responses in patients with epilepsy. *Archives of Neurology, 39,* 626–630.

Strauss, E., Wada, J., & Kosaka, B. (1983). Spontaneous facial expressions occurring at the onset of focal seizure activity. *Archives of Neurology, 40,* 545–547.

Stuss, D. T., & Benson, D. F. (1983). Emotional concomitants of psychosurgery. In K. M. Heilman & P. Satz (Eds.), *Neuropsychology of human emotion* (pp. 111–140). New York & London: Guilford Press.

Tolosa, E. S. (1981). Clinical features of Meige's disease (idiopathic orofacial dystonia). A report of 17 cases. *Archives of Neurology, 38,* 147–151.

Tolosa, E. S., & Klawans, H. L. (1979). Meige's disease: a clinical form of facial convulsion bilateral and medial. *Archives of Neurology, 36,* 635–637.

Tomkins, S. S. (1962). *Affect, imagery and consciousness: Vol. 1. The positive affects: Vol. 2. The negative affects.* New York & London: Tavistock-Springer.

Tomkins, S. S. (1980). Affect as amplification: some modifications in theory. In R. Plutchik & H. Kellerman (Eds.), *Emotion, theory, research, experience: Vol. 1. Theories of emotion* (pp. 141–164). New York & London: Academic Press.

Tucker, D. M. (1981). Lateral brain function, emotion and conceptualization. *Psychological Bulletin, 89,* 19–46.

Vaughan, K. B., & Lanzetta, J. T. (1980). Vicarious instigation and conditioning of facial expressive and autonomic responses to a model's expressive display of pain. *Journal of Personality and Social Psychology, 38,* 909–923.

Walker, E., Marwit, S. J., & Emory, E. (1980). A cross-sectional study of emotion recognition in schizophrenics. *Journal of Abnormal Psychology, 89,* 428–436.

Walker, E., McGuire, M., & Bettes, B. (1984). Recognition and identification of facial stimuli by schizophrenics and patients with affective disorders. *British Journal of Clinical Psychology, 23,* 37–44.

Zajonc, R. B. (1980). Feeling and thinking: preferences need no inferences. *American Psychologist, 35,* 151–175.

Zajonc, R. B. (1984). On the primacy of affect. *American Psychologist, 39,* 117–123.

Zoccolotti, P., Scabini, D., & Violani, C. (1982). Electrodermal responses in patients with unilateral brain damage. *Journal of Clinical Neuropsychology, 4,* 143–150.

Zuckerman, M., Klorman, R., Larrance, D. T., & Spiegel, N. H. (1981). Facial autonomic and subjective components of emotion: The facial feedback hypothesis versus the externalizer-internalizer distinction. *Journal of Personality and Social Psychology, 41,* 929–944.

11 Asymmetries of Facial Action: Some Facts and Fancies of Normal Face Movement

Ruth Campbell
Department of Experimental Psychology,
University of Oxford, U.K.

We are not generally aware that the smiles, the frowns, the expressions of greeting or disdain that constitute the "rapid signs" (Ekman, Friesen, & Ellsworth, 1972) of face language are notably asymmetric. In contrast, we can, and do, observe unimanual behavior to be consistently asymmetric and design tools to accommodate the right handed user. Therefore, the first question to be asked must be: Are face action asymmetries real? In particular, is one side of the face consistently used in nonverbal expression, and is this side generally one and the same for the population as a whole? That is, are face actions asymmetric in a directionally consistent way, as are manual asymmetries? If this can be established, a host of questions follow. What psychological significance would such actions carry? On what are they based? Why are they not more noticeable?

ARE FACE ACTION ASYMMETRIES REAL?

The first question is whether face action asymmetries are a natural feature of communication: Do they occur in the field, rather than only in the laboratory? Just one report gives us an indication of an answer, and this was more of a pilot for later laboratory studies than a systematic ethological investigation. Moscovitch and Olds (1982) made two natural observational studies. In one, they watched "friends, acquaintances, and T.V. and film personalities—in short, anyone who caught our eye," for short periods of time. In the other, they kept close watch on 45 cafe clients, observing their gestures over a 3-minute period and noting

247

whether each gesture was bilateral or asymmetric to the left or right. In both cases, where face actions were observed to be asymmetric, more left than right actions emerged. However, asymmetric actions were less likely to be seen than bilaterally symmetrical ones. In the cafe study of a total of 510 recorded expressions, "138 were left sided, 63 right sided, and 310 bilateral" (p. 75).

Before dismissing the significant advantage of left over right recorded asymmetries as negligible in contrast to the bilateral actions, it should be noted that this apparent lack of asymmetry could reflect a conservative scoring method. Only *very* asymmetric actions are likely to be noted when observations are made, as these were, in real time. Consistent judgments of face action can be obtained by offering judges a forced choice (e.g. Campbell, 1982a). Although the Moscovitch and Olds' study provides a useful lead, the study of spontaneous asymmetries of face actions in a natural setting is a fruit ripe for research picking.

Elicitation studies tend to confirm left-facedness. These are reviewed briefly to indicate the general pattern of the findings and their range, before considering the neuroanatomical basis and psychological import of such asymmetries as do occur. Borod and Koff (1984) provide a useful review of the major methodological issues in the study of face action asymmetries, as well as a thorough tabulation of the studies to date. The present chapter, of necessity, covers some of this ground but concentrates more on the possible psychological bases for the effects that occur. Clinical aspects of face asymmetries are not covered here (see Feyereisen, this volume).

PULLING FACES ON COMMAND

According to Borod, Koff, and Caron (1983), Charles Darwin appears to have been the first systematic investigator of asymmetries in normal facial actions. "Following reports that Australian natives, when angry, drew the upper lip to one side or the other, Darwin instructed four subjects to uncover the canine tooth on one side of the face in sneering. Two could expose the canine on the left side, one only on the right side, and the fourth on neither side" (p. 94).

Fortunately, more recent studies with larger numbers of subjects have demonstrated directional consistency in facial asymmetries for some, if not for all, face movements. Chaurasia and Goswami (1975), in the largest scale study to date, asked 330 Indian college students, bank employees, and their families to perform five different unilateral face actions to command, on each side of the face in turn. These included winking, lateral eye movement, and eyebrow raising. Under these conditions, bilateral movements were rarely observed (3% of all actions), and most subjects were better able to perform these actions on the left than on the right side of the face. Handedness played a significant role: 59% of right handers were left-faced for all actions, although only 29% of left-handers were left faced. The relationship between hand preference and facedness re-emerges as a problematic aspect of facedness in this chapter.

The generally greater judged motility of the left than of the right side of face has received independent, if sometimes partial, corroboration in a number of other studies. Koff, Borod, and White (1981) and Borod and Koff (1983) have shown that there is left-facedness for unilateral face actions, such as winking and pulling ones mouth up or down and to one side. Their posers were American college students and staff members. Because Chaurasia and Goswami (1975) had demonstrated the same phenomenon for Indians, it appears that across the two cultures tested left-facedness is not susceptible to cultural pressures. Alford (1983) also reports left-facedness for such actions on demand, but significantly so only for men, not for women. In this study, men were also generally more facile at face actions than were women. In both Alford's and Koff et al.'s study left-facedness was more pronounced for lower face (mouth) than for upper face (eye and eyebrow) actions. The implications of this are discussed later.

Left-facedness may also extend to *bilateral* actions performed on command. In one study (Campbell, 1982a) I asked 16 people to "pull their face up and down as quickly and as strongly as possible." While they were doing this, I videotaped them for 10 seconds at a time. Face movement was significantly more likely to be judged greater on the left than on the right side of face.

Asking people to make unilateral or bilateral face movements of this sort is a task somewhat removed from normal face actions. Face actions are usually expressive or emotive signs—functional, not in terms of the muscles recruited, but in terms of a particular behavioral state. Smiles, sneers, grief, and greetings are all recognisable, categorical face signs. Although some of these may be signs of internal states (the emotions) and are therefore communicative in a secondary way, others have primary communicative intent. That is, some are concerned with the management and production of information in a social interaction, rather than the expression of an internal emotional state. Such signs are called expressive gestures by Ekman, Hager, and Friesen (1981). Despite the theoretical importance of this distinction, it is not always clear to what extent a particular face action may be one or the other. Interpretation depends on the setting as well as on the possible differentiable characteristics of the various face states. Does left-facedness occur when we ask people to pose emotions or to make other functional, communicative face signs? Does it occur when more clearly emotional (spontaneous) expressions are elicited in the laboratory?

A number of studies have addressed themselves to the first question, which may generally be answered in the affirmative. Borod, Koff, and White (1983) report the left of face is judged to move more than the right when posing some emotions on request. The requested expressions included happiness, sexual arousal, confusion, sadness, and disgust. In an earlier study, Borod and Caron (1980) investigated asymmetries for other posed facial expressions, including, clowning, toughness ("look like a gangster"), greeting, and flirtatiousness. In these studies, left-facedness was more pronounced and more general for negative expressions than for positive ones (flirtation, happiness, clowning). Tone of emotion interacted with sex of poser; men tended to be more left-faced than women in expressing positive emotions. (Borod, Koff, and White, 1983; Borod, Caron, & Koff, 1981).

Borod et al.'s (1983) studies used videotapes of posed expressions; however, similar results occur when still photographs are used. One technique is to construct face composites comparing symmetrical face photographs derived from the left- face and its mirror half with the corresponding symmetrical right-face composites. Sackeim and Gur (1978) found that left-left composite pictures of particular emotions were generally judged to be expressing emotion more intensely than right-right composites. The photographs that they used were of individuals trained to mimic natural emotions by discrete muscle training techniques (Ekman & Friesen, 1975). They were not photographs of naive projectors of emotion. The emotions judged included sadness, fear, anger, disgust, happiness, and surprise. Once again, a positive emotion (surprise) was not notably left-faced although all the other emotions were. In the Sackeim and Gur study only 12 individual posers were seen. In Borod's studies it is usual for 30–40 posers to be examined for each face action. In one study (Campbell, 1978) using photocomposites, I found that smiles seem to be left-faced. However, a fuller investigation of a set of 20 posers revealed a more complex situation (Campbell 1979a, Experiment 4). When the pairs, left-left and right-right, of symmetrical face composites were shown side by side for the judgment, "which looks happier?" the face derived from the poser's left-face was reliably judged to be happier. However, when all the faces were presented in random order for scalar rating of happiness, there was no consistent pattern for one side of a person's face to be reliably rated happier than the other side, despite significant interjudge reliability on how expressive these symmetrical composites were. But when the corresponding symmetrical composites of the relaxed facial expression of these same posers were presented for the judgment "which looks sadder?" significant left-facedness occurred, and did not disappear when tested by rating technique rather than forced choice. I conclude that photographs of smiles may be slightly left-faced, whereas photographs of relaxed faces look much sadder on the left than on the right of face. In other experiments (Campbell 1978, Exp. 1; Heller & Levy, 1981) subjects were asked to judge *asymmetric* face composites, left-face smiling and right-face relaxed and vice-versa, for happiness. The fact that these judgments were significantly left-faced could therefore be due to an additive effect of a small asymmetric smile and a large sad-looking relaxed face asymmetry.

What of spontaneous facial expressions? It should be clear from the discussion so far that studies have relied on expressions elicited in the laboratory, usually to visual stimuli, such as horrific pictures or funny movies. Whether or not spontaneous emotional arousal in real life is adequately simulated by such studies is an open question. However, the general finding, from the extremely limited number of studies performed to date, is that such emotional expressions, if they are asymmetric at all, tend to be left-faced. Once again, the smile provides a notable exception.

Lynn and Lynn (1938, 1943) observed that youngsters could, and often did, smile asymmetrically and that this was consistently so for each individual. However, analysis of over 400 spontaneous smiles revealed no left-facedness, but rather a more or less even distribution of those who smiled leftwards and those who smiled to the right. It is possible that failure to find left-facedness in these adolescents reflects a slowly maturing tendency for smiles, as well as other expressions, to become left-faced. Inspection of videotapes of *adults* who had been told a joke or watched a pleasant film (Ekman et al., 1981) led these investigators to the same conclusion: Spontaneous smiles, the only emotion recorded with sufficient frequency for reliable analysis, were roughly equally divided between those that were expressed more strongly to the left than to the right and vice versa. Two points may be made about these recent, essentially negative results: First, the number of observations was not large in this study, because the inspection was posthoc. Second, the judgment of asymmetry was made on the basis of the "final state" of the smile, that is its spatial extent at the moment when it was judged to be greatest. There may be some asymmetry in the *dynamics* of the smile.

The most well-structured experimental investigation to date, that of Borod, Koff, and White (1983), did not find general left-facedness for judged movement of smiles expressed in response to pleasant pictures. Rather, with their 18 male and 18 female (all right-handed) subjects there was, as with posed expressions, an interaction. Men expressed smiles leftwards, women did not. Chaurasia and Goswami (1975) noted that the majority of spontaneous smiles they observed while testing for unilateral asymmetries were left-sided. It would be interesting to know if these, too, were sex-dependent. Borod et al. (1983) found that responses of disgust or sadness to pictures of unpleasant or distressing stimuli were consistently left-faced in this group of subjects, with no interaction of sex and facedness. Thus, overall, there was an interaction between tone of emotion, facedness, and sex of poser. Although spontaneous negative emotions were consistently left-faced, positive ones were only so for men.

Borod et al. (1983) study's primary concern was to see whether posed facial gestures, "look happy, look sad", and spontaneously elicited ones in response to arousing pictures would show differential asymmetries. They did not; posed and spontaneous expressions were indistinguishably left-faced. It would be interesting to know whether posed expression asymmetry predicted spontaneous asymmetry across individuals. Borod and her collaborators have used such correlative techniques to show the absence of a relationship between hemiface size and facility (Koff et al., 1981).

More recently, Dopson, Beckwith, Tucker, and Bullard-Bates (1984) report an interaction between the degree of judged asymmetry of a posed and a spontaneous emotion. In their study, undergraduate subjects were given mood induction training to generate happy and sad moods, respectively. In this state, and unknown to them, photographs of their facial expressions were taken from a one-way mirror. Then, while still in the induced mood, they were asked to pose a sad and a happy expression for the camera. The left side of face composite photographs were rated (by 34 judges) to be more expressive than the right side photographs, but only for the spontaneous, covertly photographed, expressions and not for the posed ones. Interestingly, no further interaction was reported between type of expression, sidedness, and spontaneity. Smiling a posed smile when one is feeling happy does not make it appear more left-faced than trying to pose a sad face.

The importance of these studies, for unilateral actions, for bilateral actions, and for posed and spontaneous expressions, is that a general pattern of left-facedness, tempered by potentially interesting psychological variables, such as hand preference, sex, and type of mood, emerges. This pattern is not very pronounced, but it is consistent across a number of different investigations using different techniques. Moreover, certain variables do *not* affect it. Hemiface size, although consistently asymmetric, does not affect judgments of left-facedness in face actions, nor does it appear to affect judgments of emotional intensity (Koff et al., 1981).

With one exception, there are no reports of right-facedness for nonspeech facial actions. When Borod and Koff (1983) asked their righthanded subjects to move *either* side of their face in a unilateral action, the right, rather than the left face, was preferentially moved. Therefore, left-facedness would seem to be real, in a somewhat constrained and circumscribed way. These constraints, however, do have psychological significance and we must next ask what this general pattern of weak left-facedness means? The answer depends on some knowledge of the neuroanatomical control process involved. An outline sketch of these processes follows.

THE NEUROANATOMICAL BASIS FOR ASYMMETRIC FACIAL ACTIONS

Neuroanatomists concur that the cortico-bulbar tracts of the facial nerve, those that mediate voluntary facial movements, are crossed. Thus, the frontal lobe of the right hemisphere can be considered to control those parts of the facial nerve that supply the left half of the face from the bulbar nuclei, whereas the left hemisphere has corresponding control over the right-face half. However, there is little agreement on the site(s) of the crossover (Brodal, 1965; Kuypers, 1958; Miehlke, 1973). Moreover, according to most neuroanatomists, crossed distribution of these tracts is observed only in the lower face musculature. The forehead and eye region, served by the corrugator and orbis orbiculari muscles, are generally thought to be bilaterally innervated from each bulbar nucleus to both sides.

Thus, clinically, hemiparesis of the lower face, accompanied by intact voluntary movement of the upper part of the face, denotes a central, unilateral lesion. If there is complete paralysis of the half-face a more peripheral lesion is implicated. It should be noted, however, that this is the orthodox opinion. There are less orthodox ideas about the distribution of the voluntary efferents of the facial nerve. In particular, Monrad–Krohn (1924) suggested that the whole distribution of the facial nerve can be considered functionally crossed. More details on this controversy can be seen in Borod and Koff (1984), Thompson (1982), and van Gelder (1981).

For present purposes, however, the proposal that the lower face musculature reflects crossed control, while the upper face parts are bilaterally innervated, may help to substantiate the finding that for unilateral and bilateral face actions on command, lower face asymmetries (mouth stretching up or down or to one side, moving the jaw area) may be more consistently expressed asymmetrically than movements of the upper face (eye-closure and forehead wrinkling) (Alford, 1983; Borod & Caron, 1980). However, it does not explain why these actions should be left-faced, nor why there appear to be strong individual consistencies in the ability to move parts of the upper face on command, even when there is no overall directional consistency across subjects. If the forehead and eye region are equally well innervated from either or both sides, why is it not the case that individuals find it equally easy to close either eye, or lift either eyebrow? There is little doubt, anecdotally or experimentally, (Alford & Alford, 1981) that they do not.

Remember, too, that while asymmetries of the lower face for nonfunctional face actions are left-sided, it is not reliably or generally so for the expression of a smile, the most widely investigated spontaneous facial expression. This is usually (Borod & Koff, 1984; Ekman et al., 1981) taken to mean that voluntary and involuntary tracts of the facial nerve are subject to different degrees of asymmetric distribution. This point is discussed later.

A further point on which several neuroanatomists agree, but which has received scant attention from psychologists, is that right hemisphere control over the left-face half may be greater than left hemisphere control over the right half. The possibility, of dominance of right hemisphere control for (hemiface) actions, arises from studies of hemispherectomised patients (Crockett & Estridge, 1951; Peele, 1961; Zollinger, 1935). van Gelder (1981) writes: "According to Kuypers, the right motor cortex dominates the left, giving off more fibres to the facial nucleus, especially the left facial nucleus" (p. 2).

A similar pattern, but in the opposite direction, was noted by Teuber (1962) for hand movements. He suggested that there was unequal crossed cortical control of voluntary hand movements, with the left hemisphere dominating such actions. Additionally, he suggested rather more ipsilateral innervation for the left hemisphere to the hand, so that the left hemisphere exerted control not only over the right hand but also, to some extent, over the left hand. This was not as marked for the right hemisphere acting on the left hand. If this is the case, the contrasting pattern of crossed cortical dominance of hand and face movements might indicate a neat complementary cortical distribution of function. During a single behavioral event, the left hemisphere may be controlling hand and speech movement and the right hemisphere the facial accompaniments to these actions. Distributed cortical control of this sort would allow for such synchronous, simultaneous behavior to occur with more efficiency than if the hemispheres had to share the task, in particular, its bilateral aspects in real time. This point, completely speculative, is elaborated further in the following discussion on the possible explanations for left-facedness.

EXTRAPYRAMIDAL TRACTS AND INVOLUNTARY FACIAL ACTIONS

Although there is reasonable consensus on the distribution of the pyramidal tracts of the facial nerve that descend from the cortex, the same is not true for those parts of the facial nerve that have subcortical connections (extrapyramidal fibers). There sometimes appear to be as many posited pathways for these tracts as there are neuroanatomists to describe them. van Gelder (1981) writes: "Whether these pathways are crossed and/or uncrossed and how they distribute to the upper and lower parts of the face remains questionable" (p. 4).

Another longstanding problematic question concerns the differentiation of function implied by the dissociation of cortical and subcortical tracts. Classically, the distinction is between voluntary and involuntary actions. In terms of face actions, this distinction may not always be easy to make. It is fairly clear that in response to demands, such as, "close one eye," "move your mouth to one side," or "smile please!" there is very large voluntary component. Some posed facial expressions may also be largely under voluntary control. However, as Ekman et al. (1981) point out, it all depends on how the pose is elicited and how the poser goes about following instructions; for example, "look sad." Is a Stanislavskian state of identification undertaken? Are certain muscle actions made that are known by the poser to mimic sadness? Does the poser simply have a vague idea of what sadness looks like which he tries to project? To what extent do these different mechanisms for posing an expression recruit voluntary and involuntary aspects of emotion? The problem is that for normal face action there is no independent criterion of voluntary and involuntary facial actions available. More precisely, no such independent criterion has been sought in studies of either posed or of spontaneous emotion.

For Ekman et al. (1981) the distinction between expressive gestures and spontaneous emotions is used as an independent discriminator between voluntary (gestural) and involuntary (emotional) face actions. They, further, take the view that involuntary face actions will be expressed symmetrically, a view which can be neither supported nor refuted on the basis of the contradictory neuro-anatomical evidence. Thus, these investigators concluded that the Moscovitch and Olds' (1982) finding that left-facedness occurred when people recounted emotional episodes reflected *gestural*, hence voluntary, control. In their own post-hoc investigations of videotapes of people responding to jokes or pleasant events, they found little evidence of asymmetry. This was because these were, in a sense, less voluntary responses. Alternative explanations appear likely in the face of Borod, Koff, & White's (1983) finding that there is no distinguishable difference between posed and spontaneous emotions in terms of their expressed asymmetry. Both are left faced; both show an interaction between type of mood and sex of poser. Of course, Ekman et al. (1981) could apply the same rationale to these results as to those of Moscovitch and Olds (1982). Any attempt to summarize facedness effects in spontaneous expression on the basis of current knowledge would be premature. Our knowledge of the precise paths of sub-cortically elicited face actions presents a confused picture and the functional expression of such emotional actions is not independently defined. This must remain an area of conjecture until more data accumulates from clinical as well as (or even rather than) from normal sources.

The Neuroanatomical Basis of Skilled, Fine Movements

A different distinction can be drawn in contrasting voluntary and involuntary fiber tracts. Fine, skilled motor control is associated with activation of the pyramidal tracts; whereas, by contrast, gross, habitual, uncoordinated movements can be effected by the extrapyramidal fibers. Thus, for arm and hand movement, it is noted that gross actions may be intact following focal cortical lesions; although, fine sequencing, for example, sequences of finger movements, may be damaged. According to Grossman (1967): "The most prominent feature of the deficit *(unilateral transection of cortical efferents)* is the nearly complete loss of the precise movements which are essential for any type of skilled or learned pattern of motor co-ordination" (pp. 248–249).

The issues of learning, sequencing, and precision in normal face actions, at the present, are almost completely unexplored. One study may be considered to provide some indirect evidence. Ekman and Friesen (1975) trained a number of people to project facial emotions by explicitly instructing them in the use of particular face muscle groups and by extensive and intensive feedback on their abilities to project a range of facial expressions. Photo composites of these faces are judged to express emotions more intensely when they are composed of left-left rather than of right-right halves (Ekman, 1980; Sackeim & Gur, 1978). It is then possible that left-face facility in facial action may reflect greater trainability of the right hemisphere for expressive face actions; however, this must be an extremely speculative proposal.

Hemispheric Specialization and Hemiface Action

The main purpose of this neuroanatomical excursion along the facial nerve is to provide a basis for discussing the possible ways in which face action asymmetries may reflect what is known of the somewhat, independent and specialized functions of each cerebral hemisphere. A number of possibilities exist, all speculative. It is here that the dearth of detailed observations and relevant data is most apparent and flights of theoretical fancy correspondingly unconstrained. It is important to clarify the possible relationship(s) between hand preference and facedness before these speculations start.

1. Hand Preference: A Simple Relationship?   Borod and Caron, 1980, at first entertained the idea that handedness predicts facedness in such a way that a right-handed person is likely to be left-faced and vice versa. This is not the case. Left and right handers alike are strongly left-faced for posed smiles (Campbell 1978, 1979b; Heller & Levy, 1981). Borod, Caron, & Coff (1981) find no direct relationship between hand preference and facedness for the display of a range of posed facial expressions. Koff et al. (1981) found no significant effect of hand-preference on unilateral face action asymmetry (mouth and eye movements on command to one or other side). Borod et al. (1981) however, did find that one unilateral face action, the ability to draw one's mouth to one side in a "Cagney face," in response to the instruction "look tough," was significantly correlated with hand preference. Left-handers tend to move the right half-face; right handers the left half-face. Their subjects were 19 left-handed and 29 right-handed adults.

2. Hand Preference: A Complex Relationship?   The failure to find that hand preference predicts facial asymmetries is not too surprising. Hand preference is a poor predictor of cerebral laterality for language. Although most right-handers have left hemisphere language representation, the site (or sites) of language representation for a given left-hander is hardly predictable (Hécaen & Ajuri-aguerra, 1964). For language lateralization, handedness predicts the shape of the distribution curve; that is, it is useful in terms of population, if not individual, prediction. For left-handers the distribution of language lateralization is bimodal; a proportion show right hemisphere dominance, a majority left hemisphere dominance, and a small (variable) number show neither. It is perhaps to differences in the *range* of facedness asymmetries that we should look in comparing left and right handers. As yet, the samples investigated have been too small (typically 20–30 left-handers) to compare with right-handers. By analogy with language lateralization we should be prepared to find that left-handers *as a group* are more variable in their facedness asymmetries than are right-handers.

Taking this view, in one of my own studies, (Campbell 1979a, Experiment 7), I found that one aspect of 24 left-handers' performance, sensitivity to expressor asymmetry in face pictures, although not significantly different from that of right-handers in terms of central tendency, differed significantly in terms of variation. The range of right-handers' scores was significantly smaller than that of left-handers. Furthermore, a population–based viewpoint may help to explain why effects of hand preference on facial asymmetry have been reported in some studies; for example, the large scale study of Chaurasia and Goswami (1975) and Moscovitch and Olds' (1982) study. If the distribution of facedness is more variable for left-handers than right-handers we would expect sample differences sometimes to be apparent across studies. Indeed, the discovery of any *direct* association between facedness and handedness would seem to imply more peripheral factors. Thus, the association of handedness with displayed toughness in Borod et al.'s experiment (1981), and my own finding (Campbell 1979a, Exp. 8) that, when relaxed, left-handers are judged to be sadder looking on the right side of the face than on the left, (in significant contrast to right handers) suggests that hand preference and facedness may both be direct, linked, manifestations of the same process; however, this process is not necessarily one of cerebral lateralization. It could perhaps be due to differences in myotonic tone on the side of the body ipsilateral to the preferred hand; a point that finds some support in Borod et al.'s (1981) report that strength of hand actions, rather than speed, related best to posed toughness asymmetries. A similar point may be made in relation to eye preference, which is generally more closely associated with facedness than is hand preference. It may also be noted that Rubin and Rubin (1980) found facedness for posed smiles correlated negatively with hand preference in seven year old children. Since Ladavas (1982) found no consistent facedness in children of this age, Rubin and Rubin's study may have been tapping such a myotonic variable.

Borod et al. (1981), however, go further than this. Because they do not find a significant difference between handedness groups in the projection of posed emotions, other than toughness, neither in terms of central tendency nor (apparently) in terms of distribution, they suggest that emotional expression is a right hemisphere function that is independent of hand preference. They may well be right; however, this is just one of several possible explanations of facedness in terms of right hemispheric actions. The time has come to list these explanations.

1. The Right Hemisphere Is Specialized in the Interpretation and Expression of All Emotion.   There is a good deal of evidence that emotional stimuli are more effectively processed by the right than by the left hemisphere. In this volume, Ley and Strauss (chapter 2) indicate how this may apply to the interpretation of facial expressions. The major part of this advantage is not necessarily due to the emotional salience of the stimuli (for right hemisphere superiorities obtain for a range of other nonverbal tasks,) and the *structural* qualities of the emotional stimulus may not always be clearly distinguished from the effects of emotion, per se. Moreover, the relationship between lateralized effects in the interpretation and in the expression of emotion must be carefully drawn. Interactions can be observed between expressed mood and the interpretation of emotion (see Campbell, 1982b).

However, there are more important reasons to query the "right hemisphere emotion" hypothesis. In any simple form it must predict emotional expression is right hemisphere directed. If it is, spontaneous emotion will involve the right hemisphere preferentially more than will posed emotion. Therefore, some distinction is needed, in terms of facedness, between posed and spontaneous emotions. The only get-out from this point of view is that we do not really know how the right hemisphere may influence the expression of spontaneous emotion, because it is not clear whether or not the extrapyramidal tracts of the facial nerve are crossed (previously discussed). Yet the data here are equivocal. Dopson et al. (1984) find that spontaneous expressions are more left-faced than posed ones. But Borod and White's (1983) demonstration that posed and spontaneous elicited expressions are equally left-faced could occur if the extrapyramidal and the pyramidal tracts both were crossed. Allowing for this, however, the failure to find a clearly replicable distinction between posed and spontaneous expression in terms of facedness must weaken the hypothesis. Perhaps more importantly, the finding that left-facedness occurs for face actions that are neither spontaneous expressions of emotion, emotional gestures, nor posed emotions, but rather simple motoric actions (raise your eyebrow; pull out your mouth to one side, move your face up and down) suggests that there is more to left-facedness than an emotion hypothesis would imply. Failure to find a direct relationship between facedness for such actions and facedness for emotional gestures (Borod & Koff, 1983) does not necessarily imply that there is no relationship at all. In this study, which apparently used the same subjects as reported in Borod, Koff, and White (1983), the investigators found left-facedness for both types of action, but no significant relationship across subjects for judged asymmetry of these actions. It should be noted that this is an extremely stringent test of such a relationship. As Graves, Goodglass, and Landis (1982) point out in another context, the failure to find marked correlations between measures does not necessarily mean that these measures are not all of the same process; they may, for instance, be differently contaminated by unrelated processes. It depends on ones theoretical standpoint just how one interprets the nature of the semihidden intervening variables.

2. The Right Hemisphere is Specialized for the Expression of Negative Emotions; the Left Hemisphere is Specialized for the Expression of Positive Emotions or Positive Emotions are not Lateralized.   This hypothesis was first entertained to deal with the apparent inconsistencies in reports of facedness for smiles. It is based on the possibility that in the *interpretation* of emotion there may be some distinction between the hemispheres as a function of mood state (see Ley & Strauss, this volume). Borod, Koff, and White's (1983) study indicates that negative expressions of mood, whether posed or spontaneous, are more reliably left-faced than are positive expressions. They are obtained more consistently for both men and women whereas, left-facedness for smiles is seen in men but not in women. Although it is possible to ascribe this difference directly to sex differences in lateralization, such differences have been reported for language and for visuospatial lateralization (McGlone, 1980); this may not be the only, or the most likely reason for men and women to differ in facedness for smiles. Alford (1983) suggests another possibility, whereas, Fairweather (1982) offers some convincing reasons for doubting that men and women differ markedly in cerebral lateralization.

If the lateralization of the smile were, in a sense, weaker than that of negative expressions, we might expect hand preference, which bears a known, if indirect relationship to lateralization, to interact with the type of mood expressed, just as sex difference is said to interact. Smiles *may* be less strongly left-faced than other expressions, however possibilities other than reduced right-hemisphere involvement, have not been explored to account for this difference. Do smiles, perhaps, use bilaterally innervated muscle groups more than negative expressions? Is the projection of negative expressions more dependent on the lower face musculature? Unilateral actions are more likely to be observed in the lower part of the face, at least when these are voluntary actions. The hypothesis of differential right hemisphere activation for negative emotional expression still does not predict left-facedness for nonemotive actions. If smiles are less lateralized because they implicate the negative right hemisphere less, then what of face actions with no emotive component? They should be less left-faced even than smiles.

To summarize, although both variants of the right hemisphere emotion hypothesis offer plausible explanation for left-facedness, the explanation is weak on two counts: First, it is by no means clear in what ways the right hemisphere is specialized for emotional expression, rather than interpretation. Second, the hypothesis fails to predict left-facedness for nonemotional face acts, except as a secondary consequence of right hemisphere emotional facility.

3. The Right Hemisphere is Specialized in Directing Nonspeech Associated Movements by Default.   The production of speech is accompanied by more right than left side of mouth opening (Graves, 1983; Graves, Goodglass, & Landis, 1982); the production of speech is further accompanied by more right than left handed gestures (Kimura, 1973a, 1973b). Despite some critical interpretations

(Hager & van Gelder, 1985), it seems likely that left hemisphere activation leads to these right-directed actions; the picture is confirmed by studies of unilateral lesioned patients (Graves & Landis, in press; Kimura & Archibald, 1974).

If activation and recruitment of left hemisphere processes leads to such right-sided actions, then, because the production of a nonverbal commentary should synchronize with speech output, an efficient mechanism would be one that distributed the control of such processes to a linked, but relatively independent, cerebral site. That is, the production of expressive signs to accompany speech will be delegated to the right hemisphere by *default*; the distribution of the two modes of communication requiring, for efficiency, two cerebrally distinct loci. A number of possibilities follow from such a conceptualization. One possibility is that left-hemisphere speech localization should predict facedness in a fairly circumscribed way; however, this has not yet been conclusively tested. It may be worth noting that Ladavas (1982), in a study of the development of facedness, finds left-facedness for posed expressions to emerge at around the age of 11 years; an age that follows complete speech lateralization. Another possibility is that patients with unilateral brain lesions and cerebral commissurotomy patients will not be able to control voice and face in the same, coordinated fashion as normal individuals, but may make do with other mechanisms of metacontrol. The relationship between speech and nonverbal communication, in terms of the integration and output of a set of smooth, well regulated communicative signs, is underresearched both in normal and clinical populations. The present conjecture is likely to remain just that for some time.

Two findings may be relevant: firstly, Moscovitch and Olds (1982), in the laboratory study in which their subjects recounted emotional experiences, found that it was possible to classify hand gestures that occurred during speech into those that accompanied a facial expression and those that did not. There was a right hand advantage only in the latter condition. Secondly, Dimond and Harries (1984) report that adult humans, unlike other primates, touch their chin with their hand a great deal. They claim that left-hand chin touching occurs significantly more than right-hand chin touching and it usually accompanies speech.

It is possible, then, that gestures, including hand movements, that accompany speech may not be specifically tied to speech output. Rather, they may reflect the expression of a somewhat autonomous system of communication that is under right hemisphere control and, therefore, tends to be left-sided. An urgent question for future research is to investigate correlations between facedness for speech and for nonspeech actions.

4. Face Actions, Excluding Those Pertaining to Speech Output, are Structurally Suited to Right Hemisphere Specialized Processes. The right and left hemispheres may differ in their control of face actions because, at the most central level, the motor schemata for facial expressive signs are more suitably realized by the right than by the left hemisphere. Although the right hemisphere may have perceptual advantages over the left, for example, in identifying facial expressions, (see Ley & Strauss, this volume; Sergent, this volume), they do not necessarily account directly for expressive asymmetries. However, such perceptual specializations may help to establish motor schemata efficiently.

That the expression of facial signs must be mediated by such high level perceptuo-motor schemata is an assumption that cannot be fully justified here. However, it is difficult to understand how one could effectively obey the command "smile" or "look grouchy" without such central, abstract representations. Indeed, because Ladavas (1982) reports that children under six years old were unable to pose expressions that could be reliably rated by adult judges, such schemata are likely to be achieved through intensive cognitive work. Moreover, emotional concealment would be very hard to envisage in a framework that lacked this highest representational level. The most useful starting point for this speculation is its end. The goal of a proposed facial expression is a single, roughly discrete act in which a set of face muscles move synchronously to express a particular communicative intent. By contrast, the goal of a proposed speech act is a correctly ordered temporal arrangement of articulated speech sounds to achieve a particular communicative intent. We know, from the evidence of speech errors and timing, that this output sequence is hierarchically organized with linguistic variables (syntax, morphology, semantics, phonology, articulation) manifest at different levels of organization (Butterworth, 1981). Moreover, at each level, segmentation of items represented in the speech plan is implied. The correct sequential order of segments is critical to correct categorical speech. Thus, sequential order in speech generates distinctive categorical events; "dog" and "god" are not the same thing at all, despite their common constituent phonemes. Only the order in which they are produced distinguishes them and this order *must* be represented in the speech plan. By contrast, in facial expression, although one can distinguish a sequence, such as a frown followed by an eyebrow raise from the opposite sequence of events, these two differently ordered acts do not signal single, categorically distinct objects of representation. Moreover, it is not even demonstrably the case that there is functional segmentation of face acts in the spatial, rather than the temporal dimension. Face expression blends— a smile on the mouth occurring synchronously with anxious eyes—are exceptional and unreal—at this highest functional level facial communication does not comprise hierarchically organized, segmentable units of expression.

The modulation of communicative intent also shows interesting similarities and differences when facial expression and speech are compared. If I wish to make an expressive point more strongly by means of facial action, I move the relevant muscles more, longer, or harder. If I wish to perform or modulate a speech act I can do it two ways: I can vary the prosodic aspects, including duration and intensity of parts of the message; or I can, laterally, rephrase the message. One cannot rephrase a nonverbal communication within the same domain. Thus, modulation of communicative intent is essentially analogue in nature for facial actions, but does not have to be so for speech acts.

We may characterize the functional differences between speech acts and face acts at the highest level as follows: Face acts are rigidly and globally organized; they do not demand segmentation nor hierarchical levels of organization. Modulation of face acts is, essentially, gradeable and analogue in nature. Moreover, it is quite likely that these features are not structurally independent. By contrast, speech act schemata, although necessarily organized as wholes, must be fully decomposable into segments that are functionally independent at different levels of structural representation; in order to allow for a far wider range of means to effect the communicative act. Although analogue modulation is possible, it is not the only, or even the preferred, means of modifying a message. It should not be inferred, from this caricature of the necessary types of structure for face and speech acts, that functional synergistic characteristics are implied in faces but not speech. The discovery of high level invariance in a range of motor acts (Viviani & Terzuolo, 1983) is the strongest possible evidence for high level, abstract motor schemata that control such acts. However, the invariance of face acts is at an even higher level, one at which the communicative intent is first specified.

Although this distinction, essentially between global and analyzable representations, does seem to characterize right and left hemisphere functions, respectively, the distinction is not usually applied to motoric representational levels. However, the possibility that the hemispheres are so organized is strongly suggested by studies where the more usual distinction between visual and verbal skills does not hold. For example, the right hemisphere is better able than the left to detect prosodic modulation in speech (Safer & Leventhal, 1977). Moreover, characteristic hemisphere differences may be found *within* modalities (Lake & Bryden, 1974), which can be explained only in terms of cognitive structure or style differences between the hemispheres.

The contention, then, is that the right hemisphere is structurally better suited to the representation of face act schemata than is the left hemisphere; left-facedness follows because of the crossed distribution of the facial nerve. This hypothesis has a number of testable predictions. If such lateralization of cognitive structure is important, then, because the right of the mouth tends to move more during the expression of verbal speech (Graves, 1983), varying the prosodic envelope of the speech act may reduce or eliminate such right-facedness and would implicate analogue processes known to utilize right hemisphere mechanisms. On the other hand, where a series of face acts are to be performed, it is possible that left-facedness may be reduced or eliminated because the sequential ordering constraints may call upon left hemisphere processing capacities.

These four explanations of a right hemisphere basis to left-facedness are not mutually exclusive. For instance, the right hemisphere movement ideas can subsume the emotion hypothesis, because emotional expression may be *structurally* suited to the right hemisphere; and the movement idea may be subsumed within an emotion hypothesis (Borod & Koff, 1984). Because different proposals suggest different experiments and observations, further data will clarify the best fitting hypothesis. A final possibility, however, remains to be considered.

5. Left-facedness as a Learned Ability: Interactions Between Expressor and Interpreter Asymmetries of Facial Expression.   One proposal for left-facedness (Campbell, 1978) was that it might reflect a learned response consequent to cerebral asymmetries in the interpretation of facial expression. It has been noted (Bruyer, 1981) that the side of the face that expresses most strongly is not the side that most people notice more. In looking at faces, it is the left-as-you-see-it-side, normally, the right side of the poser's face, that is more salient, for both identification (Gilbert & Bakan, 1973) and for judgments of expression (Campbell, 1978). Nor is such interpretor asymmetry confined to centrally viewed, tachistoscopic presentations, where the stimuli project directly to one or the other hemisphere. It also holds true for free viewing conditions (Levy, Heller, Banich, & Burton, 1983; Zoccolotti & Oltman, 1978).

One way in which such interpretor asymmetries could determine left-facedness is: A good expression could be assumed to be one that appears symmetrical. Because the left side, from where the viewer sees it, is more salient, a truly symmetrical expression will appear unbalanced and asymmetrical; it will seem to be too expressive on the viewer's left. Levy (1976) has shown that aesthetic balance in pictures is better when the pictorial weight is on the right rather than on the left side. A left-faced expression will seem more balanced to a viewer than will a truly symmetrical one; therefore, it is likely to elicit a more suitable response from the viewer and will be shaped in the expressor, accordingly. Furthermore, if it is the case that the right hemisphere is implicated more in negative than positive interpretation (Campbell, 1982b; Ley & Strauss, this volume; Tucker, 1981) then interpretor asymmetry could interact with the shaping of facedness, giving rise to more left-directed negative than positive facial expressions.

However, proven relations between interpretor and expressor asymmetry are sparse; those that are available suggest that the link is not a close one. In two quite independent studies with face composite photographs, it has been shown that despite left and right handers being indistinguishable in terms of expressor asymmetries (both smile leftwards), right and left handers differ significantly in terms of their asymmetric sensitivity to the lopsided smile. Thus, right-handers are more sensitive to smiles appearing on the left-as-they-see-it side of the face, usually the expressor's right, while left-handers show the opposite preference pattern; they are more sensitive to smiles that occur on the right-as-they-see-it side.

In one of these studies (Heller & Levy, 1981) 12 left-handers viewed five right-handed posers and four left-handed posers. In the other (Campbell 1979a,

Experiment 8), 33 left-handers viewed 20 faces of right-handers. Despite the difference in the numbers and the nationalities of the subjects, the findings in each experiment are completely congruent. Therefore, it is likely that this complex effect is rather strong. Moreover, within each study there is no sign of a significant correlation between interpretor and expressor asymmetries. These effects are noninteractive; they are additive across subjects. In terms of the "shaping" hypothesis, this should mean that the burden of the shaping of the left-facedness of left-handers' smiles is due to the fact that left-handers live in a right-handed world, rather than to viewing oneself in the mirror and adjusting one's expressions accordingly. Some preliminary complexities in asymmetries of preference for self-image are discussed in the study by Strauss & Kaplan (1980).

Although interpretor asymmetries do not seem to affect the metrical judgment of asymmetries in sizes of body parts by trained judges (Koff, Borod, Nicholas, & White, 1983), there is no reason to doubt that they may operate in observations of face action. To the extent that people generally take more account of the side that is less expressive, left-faced asymmetries tend to be hidden in everyday viewing. One answer to the question posed at the beginning of the chapter is: Left-facedness occurs, but may be essentially invisible because of compensatory interpretor asymmetries. This hypothesis is in need of stringent testing.

One way to examine, and therefore control, interpretor bias in judgments of facial asymmetries, is to inspect mirror-reversed as well as normally oriented pictures. Interpretor asymmetries will emerge as a consistent asymmetric choice that is independent of orientation; whereas expressor bias will change with orientation of the stimulus. This technique may pick up different sorts of asymmetry. This is made clear from a study of moving faces, where judges viewed videotapes of 16 people pulling faces and speaking the alphabet (Campbell, 1982a). Left-facedness was reliably indicated for pulling faces, however, there was a strong and independent left bias in the viewers of this task; there was a more pronounced left than right choice when the faces were seen in the mirror-reversed than in the normal orientation. In viewing faces that were speaking, however, there was neither an expressor bias nor an interpretor bias. Thus, any cerebral asymmetries that lead to left bias, in looking at the movement of silent faces, seem to disappear when looking at speaking faces. Perhaps hearing speech shifts biasing strategy away from the right hemisphere and towards the left hemisphere. The failure to demonstrate expressor asymmetries need not weaken Graves' (1983) finding that there is more pronounced right than left mouth opening in speech. In Graves' examinations a strictly metrical technique is used to assess asymmetry. Under the rather different conditions of judging "which side moves more?" movement, not size of change, is udged and judgments are made in real time. These factors could easily hide a real asymmetry in speech actions. Just as with nonverbal face actions, there do not seem to be strong correlations between expressor asymmetries for speech and measures of language interpretation lateralization (Graves, 1983; Graves, Goodglass, & Landis, 1982). What still remains to be investigated in detail is the interplay between expressor and interpretor asymmetries of speech in an experimental setting. Investigations are currently underway on the lateralization of lipread speech in normally hearing individuals (Campbell, 1986).

The chapter opened with the question Are there consistent asymmetries of facial action? Left-facedness is a feature of nonverbal facial actions and right-mouthedness appears to be a feature of seen speech. The implication of this is: The cerebral hemispheres are differentially involved in face and speech acts. Exactly what characterizes this differential involvement is still problematic. The discussion offered here will have proved useful if it tweaks a corner of the veil that masks the moving face.

ACKNOWLEDGMENTS

I would like to thank Joan Borod, Thedi Landis, Jerre Levy, and Ronald vanGelder who commented wisely and generously on this chapter. Their critical support is most warmly acknowledged, although not all of their points are accommodated here. This chapter was written while the author was supported by the Medical Research Council of Great Britain at University College London.

REFERENCES

Alford, R. D. (1983). Sex differences in lateral facial facility; the effects of habitual functional concealment. *Neuropsychologia, 21,* 567–570.

Alford, R. D., & Alford, K. F. (1981). Sex differences in the expression of emotion. *Neuropsychologia, 19,* 605–608.

Borod, J., & Caron, H. S. (1980). Facedness and emotion in relation to lateral dominance, sex, and expression type. *Neuropsychologia, 18,* 237–242.

Borod, J., Caron, H. S., & Koff, E. (1981). Asymmetry in positive and negative facial expressions: sex differences. *Neuropsychologia, 19,* 819–824.

Borod, J., & Koff, E. (1983). Hemiface mobility and facial expression asymmetry. *Cortex, 19,* 327–332.

Borod, J., Koff, E., & Caron, H. S. (1983). Right hemisphere specialisation for the expression and appreciation of emotion: a focus on the face. In E. Perecman (Ed.), *Cognitive processing in the right hemisphere* (pp. 83–109). New York: Academic Press.

Borod, J., Koff, E., & White, B. (1983). Facial asymmetry in posed and spontaneous expressions of emotion. *Brain and Cognition, 2,* 165–175.

Brodal, A. (1965). *The cranial nerves.* Oxford: Blackwell.

Bruyer, R. (1981). L'asymétrie du visage humain: état de la question. *Psychologica Belgica, 21,* 7–15.

Butterworth, B. (Ed.). (1981). *Language production I,* London: Academic Press.

Campbell, R. (1978). Asymmetries in interpreting and expressing a posed facial expression. *Cortex,* *16,* 473–481.

Campbell, R. (1979a). *Cerebral asymmetries in looking at faces and in facial movements.* Unpublished doctoral dissertation.

Campbell, R. (1979b). Left-handers' smiles. *Cortex, 15,* 571–579.

Campbell, R. (1982a). Asymmetries in moving faces. *British Journal of psychology, 73,* 95–103.

Campbell, R. (1982b). The lateralisation of emotion: a critical review. *International Journal of Psychology, 17,* 211–219.

Campbell, R. (1986). The lateralisation of lipreading: A first look. *Brain and Cognition, 5,* 1–22.

Chaurasia, B. D., & Goswami, H. K. (1975). Functional asymmetry in the face. *Acta Anatomica, 91,* 154–160.

Crockett, H. G., & Estridge, N. M. (1951). Cerebral hemispherectomy; a clinical, surgical and pathological study of four cases. *Bulletin of the Los Angeles Neurological Society, 18,* 71–87.

Dimond, S., & Harries, R. (1984). Face touching in primates and man. *Neuropsychologia, 22,* 227–234.

Dopson, W. G., Beckwith, B. E., Tucker, D. M., & Bullard-Bates, P. C. (1984). Asymmetry of facial expression in spontaneous emotion. *Cortex, 20,* 243–251.

Ekman, P. (1980). Asymmetry in facial expression. *Science, 209,* 833–834.

Ekman, P., & Friesen, W. V. (1975). *Unmasking the face.* Englewood Cliffs, NJ: Prentice–Hall.

Ekman, P., Friesen, W. V., & Ellsworth, T. (1972). *Emotion in the human face; guidelines for research and an integration of findings.* New York: Pergamon Press.

Ekman, P., Hager, J., & Friesen, W. V. (1981). The symmetry of emotional and deliberate facial actions. *Psychophysiology, 18,* 101–106.

Fairweather, H. (1982). Sex differences: little reason for females to play midfield: In J. G. Beaumont (Ed.), *Divided visual field studies of cerebral organization* (pp. 147–190). London: Academic Press.

Gilbert, C., & Bakan, P. (1973). Visual asymmetry in the perception of faces. *Neuropsychologia, 11,* 355–362.

Graves, R. (1983). Mouth asymmetry, dichotic ear advantage and tachistoscopic visual field advantage as measures of language lateralization. *Neuropsychologia, 21,* 641–649.

Graves, R., Goodglass, H., & Landis, T. (1982). Mouth asymmetry during spontaneous speech. *Neuropsychologia, 20,* 371–381.

Graves, R., & Landis, T. (in press). Hemispheric control of speech expression in aphasia: A mouth asymmetry study. *Archives of Neurology.*

Grossman, S. (1967). *Textbook of physiological psychology.* New York: Wiley.

Hager, J., & Van Gelder, R. (1985). Note: Asymmetry of speech actions. *Neuropsychologia, 23,* 119–120.

Hécaen, H., & Ajuriaguerra, J. (1964). *Left-handedness, manual superiority and cerebral dominance.* New York: Grune & Stratton.

Heller, W., & Levy, J. (1981). Perception and expression of emotion by right-handers and left-handers. *Neuropsychologia, 19,* 262–272.

Kimura, D. (1973a). Manual Activity during speaking I, right-handers. *Neuropsychologia, 11,* 45–50.

Kimura, D. (1973b). Manual Activity during speaking II, left-handers. *Neuropsychologia, 11,* 51–55.

Kimura, D., & Archibald, Y. (1974). Motor functions of the left hemisphere. *Brain, 97,* 337–350.

Koff, E., Borod, J., Nicholas, M., & White, B. (1983). Is there a bias in size measurements taken from mirror reversed photographs of body parts? *Perceptual & Motor Skills, 57,* 211–214.

Koff, E., Borod, J., & White, B. (1981). Asymmetries for hemiface size and mobility. *Neuropsychologia, 19,* 825–830.

Kuypers, H. G. J. M. (1958). Corticobulbar connections to the pons and lower brainstem in man. *Brain, 81*, 364–388.

Ladavas, E. (1982). The development of facedness. *Cortex, 18*, 535–545.

Lake, D. A., & Bryden, M. P. (1976). Handedness and sex differences in cerebral asymmetries. *Brain and Language, 3*, 266–282.

Levy, J. (1976). Lateral dominance and aesthetic preference. *Neuropsychologia, 14*, 431–445.

Levy, J., Heller, W., Banich, M. T., & Burton, L. A. (1983). Asymmetry of perception in free viewing of chimeric faces. *Brain and Cognition, 2*, 404–419.

Lynn, J. G., & Lynn, D. R. (1938). Face-hand laterality in relation to personality. *Journal of Abnormal and Social Psychology, 33*, 291–322.

Lynn, J. G., & Lynn, D. R. (1943). Smile and hand dominance in relation to basic modes of adaptation. *Journal of Abnormal and Social Psychology, 38*, 250–276.

McGlone, J. (1980). Sex differences in human brain asymmetry: a critical survey. *Behavioral and brain science, 3*, 215–263.

Miehlke, A. (1973). *Surgery of the facial nerve*. Philadelphia: Saunders.

Monrad-Krohn, G. H. (1924). On the dissociation of voluntary and emotional innervation in facial persis of central origin. *Brain, 47*, 22–35.

Moscovitch, M., & Olds, J. (1982). Asymmetries in spontaneous facial expressions and their possible relation to hemispheric specialisation. *Neuropsychologia, 20*, 71–81.

Peele, T. W. (1961). *The neuroanatomic basis for clinical neurology*. New York: McGraw-Hill.

Rubin, D. A., & Rubin, R. T. (1980). Differences in facial asymmetry between left and right-handed children. *Neuropsychologia, 16*, 473–481.

Sackeim, H. A., & Gur, R. C. (1978). Lateral asymmetry in intensity of emotional expression. *Neuropsychologia, 16*, 473–481.

Safer, M., & Leventhal, H. (1977). Ear differences in the evaluation of emotional tone of voice. *Journal of Experimental Psychology: Human Perception and Performance, 3*, 75–82.

Strauss, E., & Kaplan, E. (1980). Lateralised asymmetries in self perception. *Cortex, 16*, 283–293.

Teuber, H. (1962). Effects of brain wounds; implications of right or left hemisphere in man. In V. Mountastle (Ed.), *Interhemispheric relations and cerebral dominance* (pp. 131–157). Baltimore: Johns Hopkins Press.

Thompson, J. K. (1982). Neuroanatomy, hemisphericity and facial asymmetry. *Neuropsychologia, 20*, 699–701.

Tucker, D. M. (1981). Lateral brain function in emotion and conceptualization. *Psychological Bulletin, 89*, 19–46.

van Gelder, R. (1981). *Neuroanatomy and facial asymmetry*. Internal publication of the I.L.O. Dept. Psychology Free University of Amsterdam.

Viviani, P., & Terzuolo, C. A. (1983). The organization of movement in handwriting and typing. In B. Butterworth (Ed.), *Language production II* (pp. 103–146). London: Academic Press.

Zoccolotti, P., & Oltman, P. K. (1978). Field dependence and the lateralisation of processing. *Cortex, 14*, 155–163.

Zollinger, R. (1935). Removal of the left cerebral hemisphere. *Archives of Neurology and Psychiatry (Chicago), 34*, 1055–1064.

12

Hemispheric Asymmetries in the Perception of Facial Expressions by Normals

Robert G. Ley
Simon Fraser University

Esther Strauss
University of Victoria

> *As a rule a man's face says more of interest than does his tongue . . . it is the monogram of all his thoughts and aspirations.*
> Schopenhauer "On Physiognomy" (1851).

Interpersonally, the human face serves two primary purposes: communication and identification. For example, in most social situations, it is important to know whether the person standing before you is happy, angry, or sad, and additionally (perhaps principally), whether that person is your spouse, department chairman, or physician. As indicated elsewhere in this book, much of the research on face recognition (especially that conducted before the late 1970s) ignored or confused these purposes and treated the face somewhat monolithically. In other words, when regarding the face (experimentally), emotional expression has at times been considered as simply another facial feature, like a nose or an eye. This philosophical or methodological shortcoming is perhaps analogous to viewing the *Mona Lisa* without attending to her smile.

At present, the relatively naive 1970s approach to the study of face and expression recognition has been superceded by a 1980s sophistication. On the basis of recent research (e.g., Sergent & Bindra, 1981), if one embarks on a study of facial identity and emotional expressions, it is imperative that the erstwhile researcher consider a host of stimulus, task and subject variables that have been shown to moderate the perceptual effects. Thus, in researching face and facial emotion perception, one may want to control for famous or unfamiliar faces (Levine & Koch-Weser, 1982), cartoons or photographs (Ley & Bryden, 1979; Strauss & Moscovitch, 1981), labeling strategies (Safer, 1981), as well as subjects' sex, handedness, and cognitive style (Heller & Levy, 1981; Ladavas, Umiltá, & Ricci-Bitti, 1980; Pizzamiglio, Zoccolotti, Mammucari, & Cesaroni, 1983), to name but a few.

Granted, in the normal course of human interaction and perception (i.e., that which is not scientifically controlled in the lab), it is exceedingly difficult to separate the stimulus impact of a face from its emotional expression. This consideration leads to wondering whether a facial expression must also necessarily convey an emotional expression (i.e., even a "blank" face perhaps conveys boredom or indifference). At any rate, there is some putative evidence to suggest that one can experimentally (and statistically) dissociate the process of face recognition from emotional expression recognition (Ley & Bryden, 1979; Safer, 1981; Strauss & Moscovitch, 1981). From a neuropsychological standpoint, this dissociation is important, inasmuch as different cerebral hemispheric mechanisms may underlie each of these perceptual processes.

In the following, we review studies of hemispheric asymmetries for face and facial expression perception and consider whether these asymmetries are related to the emotional valence of the expression (e.g., positive vs. negative affect). All of the studies we examine have been undertaken with normal as opposed to brain-damaged subjects. We also consider whether face and expression recognition involves different information processing mechanisms.

HEMISPHERIC ASYMMETRIES AND EMOTIONAL VALENCE

People can distinguish emotional from non-emotional faces. They can consistently classify facial expressions into six basic categories (e.g., happiness, sadness, surprise, anger, fear, and disgust). They also can distinguish a variety of instances within each of these six sets and rate these instances with regard to emotional intensity. The cerebral mechanisms supporting these operations must be "finely tuned" to facilitate the large number of discriminations that can be made and to account for the constancies in emotional expression perception. The first section of this chapter reviews evidence on the contributions of each cerebral hemisphere to the processing of facial expressions. Moreover, because facial expressions are good indicators of underlying emotional states (Ekman & Oster, 1979), studying them also may provide a window on the more general problem concerning the cerebral representation of emotion.

There are two important and contrasting views on the nature of the representation of emotion in the cerebral hemispheres. One proposal is that the right hemisphere is dominant for all emotions (e.g., Bryden & Ley, 1983; Gardner, 1975).

Alternatively, it is posited that the right hemisphere processes negative affect, whereas the left hemisphere processes positive (e.g., Tucker, 1981). In light of this debate, this section examines not only whether hemispheric asymmetries exist in the processing of facial expressions, but also whether these asymmetries are related to emotional valence.

Because variations in task requirements may have implications for interpretation, our discussion of the literature is organized around the three major methodological approaches that have been employed in emotional expression recognition studies: (a) same–different recognition, (b) detection of emotional as opposed to non-emotional faces, and (c) judgment of degree and direction of emotionality. Although Sergent (this volume) has thoroughly reviewed the methodological factors inherent in lateral asymmetries for face perception (see chapter 3), we use methodology as an organizing framework for our review and for the most part avoid specific commentary about methodological considerations. The studies we review have all relied on the divided visual half-field technique. Before turning to the relevant literature, some brief comments about this approach are in order.

In the divided visual field technique, a stimulus is presented briefly (via tachistoscope or "back-projection") to the right and/or left visual field. The rationale underlying this procedure derives from the fact that the visual cortex receives input from only the contralateral visual half-field. A stimulus projected to the left visual field (LVF) will be received first by the right hemisphere (RH), whereas a stimulus presented to the right visual field (RVF) will be received first by the left hemisphere (LH). Laterality effects exist in divided visual field studies because one hemisphere is more proficient than the other in processing certain types of material or at carrying out certain operations. For example, it is generally accepted that LH superiorities exist for perceptual tasks that involve verbal/linguistic stimuli (Springer, 1979), whereas the RH has an advantage for perceptual tasks that can be broadly construed as visual-spatial in nature (Ornstein, Johnstone, Herron, & Swencionis, 1980).

It is important to note that visual laterality measures do seem to be related to hemispheric asymmetry. Strauss, Wada, and Kosaka (in press) examined epileptic patients whose speech dominance had been ascertained using the carotid amytal technique. On a verbal visual half-field task, normal right-handed people and patients with speech located in the left hemisphere were more likely to show a RVF superiority, whereas patients with right or bilateral speech representation tended to show a bias in favor of the LVF. Additional support for the utility of the divided visual half-field technique comes from the comparison of normal right- and left-handed people. Because the incidence of atypical speech lateralization is higher in left- than in right-handers (e.g., Branch, Milner, & Rasmussen, 1964; Goodglass & Quadfasel, 1954; Penfield & Roberts, 1959; Rasmussen & Milner, 1977; Strauss & Wada, 1983), laterality effects on visual half-field tasks should be reversed or attenuated in left-handers. This does indeed seem to be the case (see Bryden, 1982, for a review).

Same–Different Recognition

Most studies that elucidate the contributions of each hemisphere to the processing of facial expressions have used a memory paradigm. In such protocols, subjects indicate whether test faces presented to either the right or left visual field display the same affect as a target face retained in memory over a prolonged time interval (see Table 12.1). Overall, these studies have reported a LVF/RH superiority for processing both positive and negative facial expressions. One of the first studies to raise the question of the lateralization of perceiving facial expressions was conducted by Suberi and McKeever (1977). Photographs of four actors, projecting happy, sad, angry, and neutral facial expressions, were presented briefly in either the right or left visual field. Three groups, each consisting of 24 women, were exposed to systematically varied stimulus conditions. Group "neutral" subjects were exposed exclusively to neutral faces. Two of the stimulus faces served as targets and the other two served as non-targets. Group "emotional" subjects were exposed only to emotional target and non-target faces. This group included three subgroups of subjects, each subgroup exposed only to happy, or sad, or angry faces. Group "mixed" was exposed to both neutral and emotional faces. In all groups, subjects studied and committed to memory only the two target stimuli prior to the discrimination task. Subjects indicated, by pressing keys, whether test faces were the same as, or different from, the memorized target faces. Analysis of the response latencies revealed a LVF superiority that was most pronounced for those subjects who had memorized emotional as opposed to neutral target faces. Moreover, the LVF effect appeared to hold for all three emotional expressions (sad—36.5 msec; happy = 26.5 msec; angry = 15.8 msec). It is worth noting that this study does not show a LVF superiority for the recognition of particular expressions. It suggests only that the right hemisphere is called upon in discriminating emotional from non-emotional faces.

However, Ley and Bryden (1979) did investigate the recognition of specific facial expressions. Cartoon line drawings of five adult men, each depicting five emotional expressions ranging from extremely positive to extremely negative, were exposed briefly in the right or left visual field. The unilaterally presented target face was immediately followed by a centrally presented test face. Right-handed men ($n = 3$) and women ($n = 17$) were asked to state whether the emotional expressions of the two faces were the same or different. Analysis of the errors revealed that subjects were more accurate in judging emotional expressions presented to the left, rather than to the right visual field. Moreover, the visual field differences were greatest for the extreme emotional expressions. The LVF superiority was highly significant for the extremely positive and extremely negative emotional expressions but not statistically significant for the mildly

"Memory-Paradigm" Investigations of Facial Expression Recognition in Normal Subjects

Author	Task Demand	Response	Measure	Ss	Results
Buchtel et al., 1978	Match to previously presented affective category	Key press	RT	16m RH	LVF effect for happy & sad, RVF for neutral
Campbell, 1978	Delayed matching of chimeric faces. Which face looked happier?	Vocal	Preference	12m 12f RH	Preference for smile in LVF
Hansch & Pirozzolo, 1980	Match to previously presented target word.	Key press	RT	21m 15f RH	RVF effect for verbal conditions, LVF effect for nonverbal conditions.
Heller & Levy, 1981	Delayed matching of chimeric faces. Which face looked happier?	Vocal	Preference	12m RH 12m LH	Preference for smile in LVF but only for RH
Ladavas et al., 1980	Match to previously designated affective category	Key press	RT	12m 12f RH	LVF effect but only for females
Landis et al., 1979	Simultaneous match central cartoon to lateral photo	Key press	RT	12m 12f RH	Overall LVF effect
Levy et al., 1983	Compare pairs of chimeric faces. Which face looks happier?	Vocal	Preference	70 m 41f RH 62m 49f LH	LVF effect for RH & LH but the left bias larger for RH
Ley & Bryden, 1979	Match to subsequently presented target	Vocal	Accuracy	3m 17f RH	LVF effect most pronounced for extreme emotions
Natale et al., 1983	Exp't 2: Rate pos-neg of chimeric faces	Lever	Rating	22m 16f RH 38m 26f LH	LVF presentations judged more accurately
	Exp't 3: Judge whether composites expressed a pos or neg mood	Vocal	Rating	15m 15f RH	Composites judged pos when in RVF
Pizzamiglio et al., 1983	Match to previously presented affective category	Key press	RT	16m 16f RH	Field indep Ss showed LVF effect for disgust & fear. RVF effect for anger

Study	Task	Response	Measure	Subjects	Results
Reuter-Lorenz & Davidson, 1981	Two laterally presented faces, one emot, one neut. Indicate side of emotional face	Key press	RT	28 RH	RVF superiority for accuracy. For RT, RVF effect for happy, LVF effect for sad
Reuter-Lorenz et al., 1983	Two laterally presented faces, one emot, one neut. Indicate side of emotional face	Key press	RT	10m 10f RH / 5m 5f LH inv / 5m 5f LH noninv	RH: RVF effect for happy, LVF effect for sad. LH inv showed sim trend while LH non-inv showed opp trend
Safer, 1981	Match to previously presented target. Ss encouraged to adopt empathy or labeling strategy when viewing target	Vocal	Accuracy	36m 53f RH	LVF effect for men
Strauss & Moscovitch, 1981	Exp't 1: Simultaneous match 2 lateral photos for 1 of 3 exp.	Key press	RT	16m 16f RH	For same responders, LVF effect. For diff responders, men esp fast for RVF/RH responses.
	Exp't 3: Match to memorized target for either of 2 presented faces	Key press	RT	12m 12f RH	For same responders, LVF effect for women. Men showed LVF bias only when both faces had same exp. For diff responders, men esp fast for LVF/RH responses.
Suberi & McKeever, 1977	Match to memorized target	Key press	RT	72f RH	Overall LVF effect

positive, neutral, and mildly negative emotional expressions. Thus, this study shows an overall LVF/RH superiority for recognizing strong emotional expressions, but does not show laterality differences between positive and negative emotional expressions.

Other researchers (Buchtel, Campari, DeRisio, & Rota, 1978; Hansch & Pirozzolo, 1980; Strauss & Moscovitch, 1981) have replicated the finding of a LVF/RH superiority for the recognition of facial expressions. In the study by Hansch and Pirozzolo (1980), the stimuli consisted of photographs developed by Ekman and Friesen (1975) of models posing happy, angry, and surprised expressions. In contrast to Ley and Bryden (1979), who required subjects to compare pairs of facial expressions, Hansch and Pirozzolo (1980) had their subjects (21 men : 15 women) match a laterally presented facial expression to an oral cue word that was given just prior to the facial stimulus. In addition, subjects had to determine whether non-emotional faces, emotional and non-emotional words matched previously presented cue words. Analysis of the reaction-time data revealed a significant LVF advantage for the nonverbal recognition tasks (face and facial expression) and a RVF superiority for the verbal recognition tasks (emotional and non-emotional word), suggesting that it is the verbal–nonverbal nature of the task and not the emotionality of the stimulus that determines laterality effects (see also Berent, 1977; Kolb & Taylor, 1981; Strauss, 1983, for the same view). No examination of the relation between laterality and type of affect was reported.

Buchtel, Campari, DeRisio, and Rota (1978) presented photographs of students, each showing a happy, neutral, and sad expression, in either the right or left visual field. Half of the male subjects were told to press a key following the presentation of a happy face and the other half had to make the same response to the appearance of a sad face. When the other kind of face appeared, subjects were to refrain from responding. The subjects were not aware that neutral targets also were introduced. Responses to sad and happy expressions were significantly faster for LVF presentations, whereas responses to the neutral faces were faster for RVF presentations. Moreover, there was no tendency for the neutral face to be judged more often as happy or sad depending on the receiving hemisphere. Thus, these findings also provide no support for the proposal that the left and right hemispheres differentially mediate positive and negative affect, respectively.

Strauss and Moscovitch (Experiment 3, 1981) presented pairs of Ekman faces, displaying happy, sad, or surprised expressions, to either the right or the left visual field. For one third of the right-handed subjects, the target affect was happy. For one third, the target was sad, and for the remainder, the target was surprised. The subjects were required to determine, by pressing a key, whether either of the two faces of a pair displayed the designated expression. Analysis of the reaction-time data indicated that when the response was "same-as-target," women showed an overall LVF advantage. Men showed a LVF bias only when both members of a laterally presented pair of faces showed the same expression.

When the response was "different-than-target," perceptual asymmetries did not emerge for women. Men were particularly fast for right-hand responses made to LVF presentations. Thus, although there were some sex-related differences in performance, overall both men and women tended to show a LVF advantage. Additional analyses revealed that the LVF effect held for all three expressions (happy = 18 msec; sad = 16 msec; surprised = 15 msec).

Other researchers have replicated the finding of a LVF superiority for expression recognition, but only in specific subgroups of the population. A study by Safer (1981) reported that sex of the subject was related to the laterality effect. The stimuli consisted of the Ekman faces displaying six different emotions: happiness, sadness, surprise, anger, fear, and disgust. Right-handed men (n = 36) and women (n = 53) stated whether pairs of facial expressions represented the same or different emotion. The first expression in each pair was presented centrally to both hemispheres, whereas the second expression was exposed briefly to either the right or left visual field. Subjects were encouraged to adopt either an empathy or labeling strategy when viewing the target expressions. A significant LVF superiority in accuracy occurred, but only for the male subjects. Women showed no visual field bias. The effect of type of expression on the lateralization process was not examined.

In contrast to the findings by Safer (1981), Ladavas, Umilta, and Ricci-Bitti (1980) reported that only women, not men, showed a LVF superiority for expression recognition. Their stimuli also consisted of the Ekman faces, displaying six different emotions. Right-handed men (n = 12) and women (n = 12) had to determine, by pressing a key, whether the unilaterally presented facial expressions matched a previously designated affective category. Analysis of the response latencies revealed a clear-cut LVF superiority, but only for women. Ten of the 12 women but only 6 of the 12 men showed a LVF advantage. Finally, there was no indication in their data of a visual field by emotion interaction, again providing no evidence of an emotional polarity between the hemispheres.

Pizzamiglio et al. (1983) have suggested that the presence of conflicting evidence regarding sex-related differences in expression recognition may be due to underlying differences in individual cognitive style. Their task was similar to the one used by Ladavas et al. (1980). The stimuli consisted of the Ekman photographs, faces displaying happiness, sadness, surprise, anger, fear, and disgust. Right-handed men (n = 16) and women (n = 16) classified as being field-dependent or field-independent, had to indicate, by pressing a key, whether the unilaterally presented facial expressions matched a previously designated affective category. Analysis of the response latencies revealed no significant gender-related effects. However, the dimension of individual cognitive style proved to be a determinant of perceptual asymmetries. Field-independent people showed a significant LVF superiority for disgust and fear and a RVF superiority for anger. Field-dependent subjects did not show any significant visual field differences. It is worth noting that the data from this experiment also do not support the proposal that the left and right hemispheres subserve positive and negative affect, respectively, because a RVF superiority emerged only for anger.

The findings of McKeever and Dixon (1981) also highlight the importance of cognitive style for explicating sex differences in discriminating memorized from nonmemorized faces. In a rather unique study, which might be construed as a hybrid of the Suberi and McKeever (1977), Buchtel et al. (1978) and Safer (1981) procedures, McKeever and Dixon (1981) unilaterally presented face photographs depicting objectively neutral emotional expressions. Subjects were to differentiate previously memorized target from nontarget faces via a manual response. However, in an interesting twist, McKeever and Dixon required one half of the subjects to imagine that something "terribly sad" had happened to the stimulus persons and that they were "very saddened, frantically unhappy, and deeply depressed" despite displaying neutral affective expressions. Subjects were also encouraged to think of personal experiences in which they (i.e., the subjects participating in the experiment) had the same kind of sad feelings as the target individuals. Reaction time latencies showed that a LVF superiority in target detection existed for females who were given the emotional-imagery instructions. In contrast, visual field asymmetries did not exist for female subjects in a "neutral-imagery" condition, which was designed to avoid emotional arousal or identification with the target individuals. Quite surprisingly, male subjects failed to show a LVF advantage in either condition. However, for both males and females, LVF superiorities were strongly associated with the perceived emotionality of the faces. In short, McKeever and Dixon showed that RH effects for affectively neutral faces could be shown for females, if emotional-imagery augmented memory storage, as well as for both sexes if emotionality was attributed to the faces.

The investigations just reviewed have relied on memory paradigms. Both Landis, Assal, and Perret (1979) and Strauss and Moscovitch (1981) have examined the contribution of each hemisphere to the perception of facial expressions by employing memory-free recognition tasks. In the study by Landis et al. (1979), right-handed men ($n = 12$) and women ($n = 12$) had to compare a centrally presented cartoon face to a laterally displayed photograph of a familiar person. The two pictures were shown simultaneously for a brief time and the subjects were required to determine, by pressing a key, whether the pair members displayed the same expression (happy, angry, astonished). If the pair members did not match, no response was to be given. Analysis of the response latencies revealed faster times for LVF than RVF presentations. Landis et al. did not report analyses on the relation between laterality and specific types of expressions.

In the study by Strauss and Moscovitch (Experiment 1, 1981), the stimuli consisted of the Ekman photographs displaying happy, sad, and surprised expressions. These stimuli were paired with one another and this pairing resulted in four different stimulus combinations. In one set, there were pairs in which both the face and the expression were the same (SFSE). Another combination consisted of pairs of different people displaying the same expression (DFSE). In a third combination, the pair members were of the same people displaying different expressions (SFDE). For the remaining combination, pairs consisted of different people displaying different expressions (DFDE). Right-handed men ($n = 16$) and women ($n = 16$) were shown a pair of faces simultaneously in one visual half-field and they were required to judge whether the pair members displayed the same expressions. Analysis of the response latencies revealed that perceptual asymmetries emerged only when judging that pair members displayed the same emotional expression (SFSE, DFSE). Such judgments were made faster by both men and women when the stimulus pairs were presented to the LVF, as compared to the RVF. Additional analyses revealed no clear laterality differences between positive and negative emotional expressions. For women, a LVF advantage was found for all expressions. For men, there was a LVF superiority for surprised expressions, whereas visual field differences were not observed for sad and happy expressions.

Without exception, the visual half-field studies just reviewed report that normal right-handed people manifest a LVF superiority for recognizing both positive and negative facial expressions. It may be useful to focus on the consistency of the finding. The LVF advantage emerges on same–different recognition tasks with or without a memory component. It is found with reaction-time or recognition accuracy as the dependent measure. It occurs when photographs of real people or caricatures are used and it even exists for cross-modal or cross-contextual comparisons such as when cartoons are compared to photogaphs, as well as when facial expressions are matched to words. There are some reports of sex-related differences, but the results are contradictory and open to other interpretations. Thus, given the conventional position that the visual field effect is at least partially due to hemispheric asymmetry, it would seem that for most right-handed people, the right hemisphere plays the critical role in recognizing both positive and negative emotional facial expressions.

EXPRESSION DETECTION

Up to this point, we have reviewed 11 studies that found evidence of right hemisphere dominance in the processing of both positive and negative facial expressions. All of these investigations used a same-different recognition paradigm. Reuter-Lorenz and her colleagues (Reuter-Lorenz & Davidson, 1981; Reuter-Lorenz, Givis, & Moscovitch, 1983) took a different approach and reached a different conclusion. They report that the right hemisphere advantage applies only to negative emotional expressions. In the initial study by Reuter-Lorenz and Davidson (1981), the stimuli consisted of the Ekman faces displaying happy, sad, angry, and neutral expressions. Emotional and neutral facial expressions of the same individual were presented simultaneously, one to each visual field.

Right-handed subjects ($n = 28$) were asked to identify the side that contained the emotional face by pressing the right or left key on a response box. Only the data analyses for the happy and sad expressions were reported. Overall, subjects were more accurate for RVF than LVF presentations. On the other hand, analysis of the response latencies revealed that happy faces were associated with the faster reaction times in the RVF, whereas sad faces were responded to more quickly in the LVF.

A subsequent study by Reuter-Lorenz, Givis, and Moscovitch (1983) replicated and extended the initial findings. In addition to examining right-handers (10 men : 10 women), asymmetries in affect perception also were evaluated in inverted (5 men : 5 women) and non-inverted (5 men : 5 women) left-handers. The rationale underlying the inclusion of inverted and non-inverted left-handers derives from the notion (Levy & Reid, 1976, 1978) that hemispheric organization differs in these two groups. According to Levy and Reid, inverted left-handers, like normal right-handers, presumably have language represented in the left hemisphere, whereas non-inverted left-handers are considered to have language located in the right hemisphere (but see Ajersch & Milner, 1984; Strauss, Wada, & Kosaka, 1984; Weber & Bradshaw, 1981). As in the initial study, an emotional face (happy or sad) was presented to one visual field and a neutral face to the other. The subject's task was to indicate the side on which the emotional face was presented. For right-handers and inverted left-handers, responses to happy faces were faster for RVF presentations, whereas responses to sad faces were faster for LVF presentations. A reversal of this pattern of results was found for the non-inverted left-handers, suggesting that the task is indeed sensitive to functional hemispheric asymmetry.

The explanation for these findings is not certain although Reuter-Lorenz and her colleagues (Reuter-Lorenz, Givis, & Moscovitch, 1983) have suggested two possibilities. One explanation is that the left and right hemispheres are indeed differentially specialized for positive and negative affect, respectively. By asking subjects simply to detect emotion, rather than to match the expression with some exemplar, they may have obtained a measure of emotion perception that was less confounded by cognitive factors. That is, differential lateralization for different emotional valences may be evident when subjects rely on more immediate emotional reactions rather than on their cognitive appraisal of the stimulus. The alternative explanation is that the discrimination of happy and sad faces may be accomplished by using different cognitive strategies. Happy faces may be recognized by detecting or scrutinizing a specific facial feature, such as the mouth, an analytic task for which the left hemisphere is presumably specialized (Bradshaw & Nettleton, 1981). Identifying sad faces may require that information from various parts of the face be related to each other, a holistic process that presumably requires the right hemisphere. Methodological differences also might account for findings of left and right hemispheric advantages for stimuli of positive and negative emotional valence. For example, Reuter-Lorenz and

Davidson (1981) used exposure durations around 300–350 msec, which are much longer than those used in studies showing exclusively right hemispheric effects. Sergent and Bindra (1981) state that exposure duration is a critical variable in face recognition studies. Additional studies are needed to decide the issue.

JUDGMENT OF DEGREE AND DIRECTION OF EMOTIONALITY

The few studies that have examined the judgment of emotionality report conflicting findings (Campbell, 1978; Heller & Levy, 1981; Levy, Heller, Banich, & Burton,1983; Natale, Gur, & Gur, 1983). Campbell (1978) presented tachistoscopically photographs (10 men : 19 women) of facial composites, half the face smiling and the other half neutral. On each trial, a pair of stimuli was shown with a brief delay separating the presentation of each pair member. In one member of each pair, the smiling half-face was in the LVF and in the other pair member, the smiling half-face was in the RVF. Both right-handed men ($n=$ 12) and women ($n = $ 12) judged faces as happier when the smiling half-face was in the LVF and a neutral expression in the RVF.

Heller and Levy (1981) replicated and extended the findings of Campbell (1978). Photographs of facial composites (9 men), half the face smiling and the other half not smiling, were presented tachistoscopically. Right-handed ($n = $ 12), but not left-handed ($n = $ 12) men rated the faces as happier when the smiling half-face was in the LVF. Heller and Levy point out that the failure to observe a significant visual field bias for left-handers is consistent with neurological evidence that left-handers are heterogeneous in their patterns of lateralization, and provides support for the suggestion that the visual field advantage found in right-handers derives from cerebral asymmetry of function.

Recently, Levy and her colleagues (Levy, Heller, Banich, & Burton, 1983) have shown that it is not necessary to restrict initial input to a single hemisphere to elicit a perceptual bias. They devised a task in which left- ($n = $ 111) and right-handers ($n = $ 111) were asked to judge which of two chimeric faces (one with the smile on the left-side, the other its mirror image) looked happier. Subjects had unlimited time to view the stimuli. Both right- and left-handers showed significant leftward biases, but the bias for right-handers was larger than that for left-handers, suggesting that the free-vision task is sensitive to functional hemispheric asymmetry as well.

The findings of Campbell (1978) as well as Levy and her colleagues (Heller & Levy, 1981; Levy et al., 1983) suggest that right-handed people perceive faces as happier when the smile is presented to the LVF/RH. Contrary results are reported by Natale, Gur, and Gur (1983). In one of their studies (Experiment 2), right- ($n = $ 38) and left-handed ($n = $ 64) men and women were presented with happy, sad and mixed (half happy, half sad) chimeric faces, projected to either the left or right visual field, for exposure durations allowing only the detection of the existence of a face. The subjects were required to rate each face on a 7-point scale ranging from very sad to very happy. The rating was done by moving a lever up or down to marked positions. The authors report that although LVF presentations were judged more accurately, there was no visual field asymmetry in response bias. There also were no handedness effects.

In the study just described, subjects had to discriminate between positive and negative expressions. In a subsequent study (Experiment 3), subjects did not have to make this differentiation because each stimulus contained both types of emotion. Chimeric faces (half the face happy, half sad) were presented to either the right or left visual field, for exposure durations that allowed the subjects to perceive the existence of two expressions on the face. Right-handed men ($n = 15$) and women ($n = 15$) were asked to judge categorically whether the face appeared to express a more positive or a more negative mood. Chimeric faces presented to the RVF received more positive judgments, whereas stimuli presented to the LVF did not produce biases. The investigators concluded that the right hemisphere is more accurate in recognizing emotional valence, whereas the left hemisphere has a bias to perceive emotional expressions as positive.

The results of studies on the judgment of emotionality in chimeric faces do not lend themselves to easy interpretation. Of four studies, three (Campbell, 1978; Heller & Levy, 1981; Levy et al. (1983) found evidence in favor of the view that facial expressions are perceived more positively when presented to the LVF/RH and one (Natale, Gur, & Gur, 1983) found the opposite, a RVF/LH positive bias. Methodological differences may have contributed to the inconsistency in the findings. By way of explanation, Campbell (1978) and Levy and her colleagues (Heller & Levy, 1981; Levy et al., 1983) asked subjects to contrast pairs of composite photographs (one half smiling, the other half neutral) and then judge which pair member looked happier. On the other hand, Natale et al. (1983) asked subjects to judge whether the mood expressed in a laterally presented photograph (one half smiling, the other half sad) was predominantly positive or negative. It is possible that the task developed by Natale et al. (1983) is more dependent on emotional, as opposed to cognitive processes, than are those tasks that involve the comparison of composite faces. Alternatively, the finding of a left hemisphere positive bias may reflect a chance result and thus the neuro-psychological implications of the Natale et al. finding are not immediately clear.

ARE THE PROCESSORS FOR
FACIAL EXPRESSIONS UNIQUE?

To recapitulate the gist of the foregoing review: Over the past decade, much research has repeatedly shown a LVF superiority for the recognition of all kinds of human faces (cartoons, photographs, familiar, unfamiliar, etc.). It is assumed that this visual field asymmetry reflects a right hemispheric advantage for face perception. The present review also has marshalled considerable evidence indicating a LVF (and presumed RH) bias for recognizing both positive and negative emotional facial expressions. Some question exists as to whether the two effects (e.g., face perception and emotional expression perception) are independent and manifestations of different, perhaps neuroanatomically distinct, right hemispheric mechanisms. Early formulations for these data posited that face recognition tasks drew upon the well-known right hemispheric superiority for processing and encoding complex visual-spatial stimuli (e.g., Ornstein et al., 1980), whereas facial expression recognition requisitions the right hemispheric advantage for processing emotional stimuli (e.g., Bryden & Ley, 1983). In addition to the question of the dissociability of facial identity and facial expression recognition, controversy exists as to whether face recognition itself is a specific ability or merely an extension of the right hemisphere advantage for visuospatial functions. The latter question is beyond the purview of the present chapter, but suffice it to say that the aggregate of evidence drawn from normal (McKeever & Dixon, 1981) and neurological populations (Yin, 1970) suggests that face recognition is not mediated by the same neural substrate that underpins recognition of other visual–spatial patterns.

Let us turn to an examination of the evidence favoring the proposition that the processors for facial identity and expression are unique and specific to each task.

As a first step, it is important to note that some clinical reports describe patients who are unable to identify emotional expressions (in photographs), but remain able to recognize faces. More specifically, Kolb, Milner, and Taylor (1983) found that although right hemispheric frontal damage impaired expression recognition, facial identity recognition was preserved. Likewise, Cicone, Wapner, and Gardner (1980) discovered no relationship between patients' performance on an emotional perception and face perception task. Although an obvious explanation for these clinical neuropsychological data is that face and expression perception involve different processing mechanisms, it is always dangerous to make assertions about normal brain functions based on observations of brain-damaged populations. Additionally, at least one methodologically sound study reports findings contrary to the aforementioned. Dekosky, Heilman, Bowers, and Valenstein (1980) showed that an impairment in face recognition also disturbed emotional expression recognition (for both faces and emotionally laden scenes) implying that the same defect was disrupting both face and emotional expression perception. Furthermore, most prosopagnosics (a neurological syndrome indexed by the inability to recognize familiar faces) are able to recognize emotional expressions (Hecaen & Albert, 1978).

As indicated previously, studies of normal subjects yield rather conclusive evidence that the RH is superior to the LH in both recognizing faces and emotional expression. Logically, it would seem to follow that if different patterns of lateralization accompany each of these perceptual tasks, then it can be reasonably concluded that different processors are functioning in each task (or at least that the same neuroanatomic mechanism is functioning in quite different ways for each task). Consistent with this supposition, divergent lateralization patterns have been found for the recogniton of facial emotions and identity.

The most compelling evidence favoring distinct processors for faces and emotional expressions is derived from the experimental and statistical dissociation of these effects. A few researchers have provisionally demonstrated such independence. For example, Ley and Bryden (1979) had subjects judge on each trial, the sameness or difference of both the emotional expression and the identity of pairs of faces. Although Ley and Bryden found LVF superiorities for both facial identity and emotion recognition, analyses of covariance indicated that face recognition did not affect emotional expression recognition, whereas the converse was true. Additionally, laterality coefficients for each subject for face and emotion recognition accuracy were not correlated. In short, Ley and Bryden's findings suggest the extricability of face and expression perception. Likewise, Pizzamiglio et al. (1983) found that a LVF advantage for identifying emotional expressions was preserved when the subjects' performance on a face recognition task was partialled out. Pizzamiglio et al. conclude that "the recognition of emotion in the human face requires a separate and independent process (than face identity recognition) preferentially lateralized in the right hemisphere" (p. 185).

Although most researchers in this domain find LVF superiorities in processing emotional expressions and facial identity, one can compare the configuration of lateral asymmetries for each task. Such a comparison should further elucidate whether face and expression perception rely on distinct processors. In fact, such comparative opportunities exist, and some investigators have found that the lateral asymmetries for facial expression and identity perception often vary in "size" or degree. For example, there is a tendency for LVF superiorities to be greater for judgments that involve emotional expression rather than facial identity. Along these lines, Suberi and McKeever (1977) found a greater LVF advantage in face discrimination when subjects had memorized emotional, as opposed to neutral targets (for which a smaller LVF superiority existed). Although this study does not show a LVF superiority for the identification of emotional expression per se, it does indicate that face recognition is augmented by emotional expression in the memory set. Such augmentation, plus the finding that interhemispheric differences in discrimination time were due to increased LH latencies for emotional stimuli, refutes the possibility that the processing of emotional faces is subserved by the same mechanisms that operate for neutral faces.

Ley and Bryden (1979) found different patterns of lateralized performance both within the emotional expression task as well as between facial expression and facial identity recognition tasks. In the first case, more extreme or intense emotional expressions (especially negative) were more accurately recognized and matched than were less intense, neutral emotional expressions. These differences emerged while face identity was held constant. McKeever and Dixon's (1981) findings have a similar implication. In their facial discrimination task, the degree of the RH bias was correlated with the degree of emotion ascribed to the target faces. In short, the LVF superiority appeared "tied" to the degree of expressed emotion.

In the second case, Ley and Bryden (1979) and others (McKeever & Dixon, 1981; Suberi & McKeever, 1977) have shown that LVF/RH superiorities for emotional expression recognition are greater than those for face recognition, even when subjects are required to make both judgments about the same stimulus. On the other hand, Safer (1981) found the right hemisphere superiority for face recognition to be significantly greater than that which existed for expression recognition.

Despite these differences in direction, one can provisionally conclude that the well-established LVF superiority for face recognition cannot account for all of the expression recognition effect. This conclusion is founded on the observation that different patterns of lateralization are obtained as a function of emotional expression (whether this "resides" in the stimuli or the subject), when the subject is judging facial identity and expression.

Further evidence differentiating face and expression perception tasks (despite overall LVF superiorities for each task) is provided by Strauss and Moscovitch (1981). They found that an expression recognition task had longer response times than a face recognition task that employed the same stimuli and procedure. Although these tasks were similarly lateralized, the difference in reaction time latencies again suggests that different processing mechanisms are invoked for face and emotional expression perception.

Another approach to evaluating the relative independence of processes subserving facial expression and facial identity recognition is to evaluate the influence of stimulus features, such as spatial complexity or individual difference variables, such as sex, handedness, or cognitive style on the perceptual effects. The influence and nature of the latter individual difference variables is comprehensively reviewed elsewhere in this book and is given little consideration here. Suffice it to say that findings of sex differences in recognizing emotional expressions, when sex differences in recognizing faces are not found (e.g., Safer, 1981), further suggest that the gender differences in emotion recognition is not due to differing visual–spatial abilities between the sexes. This conclusion implies that the hemispheric mechanisms for recognizing emotional expressions are different than those for recognizing faces. However, it is important to note that evidence pertaining to the relationship between sex and emotional expression recognition is very complex and contrary (Ladavas et al., 1980; Strauss & Moscovitch, 1981). Sex differences also seemingly interact with cognitive style

(Pizzamiglio et al., 1983) and further experimentation is necessary to clarify these conflictual findings, such that the implications for the independence of facial identity and emotional expressiveness can be known.

But what of facial stimulus features? As mentioned in our introductory commentary, by definition (and by observation) a "face" intrinsically combines (and for experimental purposes, confounds) visual–spatial complexity and emotionality. Although some researchers (Ley & Bryden, 1979) claim to have dissociated these effects, McKeever and Dixon (1981) cogently argue that one cannot rule out the possibility that spatial complexity is enhanced by emotional expressivity. Consequently, in the Ley and Bryden study, it could be posited that the weaker face recognition effect disappeared due to the loss of visual–spatial variance. However, McKeever and Dixon were able to hold constant the spatial complexity of their facial stimuli. By deploying neutral faces as stimuli, McKeever and Dixon are able to exclusively attribute the observed LVF advantage to emotional factors (rather than visual-spatial features), albeit the effect inheres in the subjects, not the stimuli. Thus, McKeever and Dixon refute the possibility that the right hemispheric superiority (or mechanism) for processing visual–spatial patterns also subserves face recognition. Furthermore, their results suggest that LVF effects due to "perceived emotionality" in faces also are not attributable to RH visual–spatial dominance.

The work of Pizzamiglio et al. (1983) provides additional evidence favoring the independent lateralization of facial emotion features from visual–spatial factors. Like Ley and Bryden, these researchers found that a LVF effect for emotional expressions was preserved when performance on face identity recognition was statistically removed. However, Pizzamiglio et al. also noted slightly different patterns of lateralization for different emotional expressions, although substantive differences between positive and negative emotions were not in evidence. Quite ingeniously, Pizzamiglio et al. were able to analyze the number of facial units represented in their stimulus faces, which also varied in expressivity. Although they found a positive correlation between facial complexity and reaction time, this relationship was independent of the degree and direction of the visual field advantage for different emotional expressions. In short, although few researchers have meticulously controlled the confounding effect of spatial complexity on the emotionality of stimulus faces, provisional evidence suggests that separate mechanisms subserve facial identity and emotional expression recognition.

Few researchers of face and emotional recognition have considered the extent to which facial or emotional stimuli have imageable components or the ways in which subjects use imagery-based cognitive strategies for meeting task requirements. Given emerging clinical and experimental evidence attesting to the right hemispheric mediation of cognitive and perceptual processes involving imagery (Ley, 1983), it seems prudent for future researchers to evaluate whether facial stimuli engender imaging. For instance, it is relatively easy to imagine (so to speak) that the presentation of familiar faces might prompt image-laden associative networks. Some investigators have required subjects to use emotional-imagery for encoding target faces (e.g., McKeever & Dixon, 1981) and their results suggest that right hemispheric advantages for face or emotional expression recognition are facilitated by imagery-based mnemonic or labeling strategies. One wonders whether separate processors also uniquely mediate the recognition of imageable stimuli as they seemingly do for face and emotional expression recognition. Although definitive evidence is not yet available, a series of experiments hint at the independent influence of affect and imagery on emotion recognition in both visual and auditory sensory domains (Ley & Bryden, 1983).

On the basis of the foregoing evidence, the question "Are the processors for facial expression unique?" should be answered in the affirmative. Although much of the evidence is circumstantial (and influenced by stimulus and subject variables), it does converge to substantiate the proposition that independent right hemispheric mechanisms underlie recognition of facial identity and emotional expression. Furthermore, these processes seem separate from those that underpin a more general, right-hemispheric visual–spatial dominance. A countervailing position is principally anchored by the findings of Hansch and Pirozzolo (1980). They obtained LVF advantages for both emotional and neutral faces that mitigates against the separation of emotional processing from facial recognition. Hansch and Pirozzolo also simultaneously found RVF effects for both neutral and emotional words indicating that the nature of the task (verbal vs. nonverbal) had a larger effect than the emotionality of the stimulus. However, the use of verbal cues and stimuli, as well as very brief exposure durations (50 msec) may have contributed to a type of information processing that differentially attenuated right hemispheric dominance for affective stimuli.

SUMMARY

In summary, a few general statements can be made. First, in right-handed people, the right hemisphere plays the critical role in recognizing both positive and negative expressions. When subjects are required to match expressions with some target, both types of emotional stimuli show a LVF bias. Second, although the evidence is slim, differential lateralization of positive and negative expressions occasionally has been shown and is perhaps more likely to occur for tasks that require minimal cognitive processing. When subjects are asked to detect or rate emotionality, rather than match the expression with some exemplar, then there is some evidence of a LVF/RH bias for negative expressions and a RVF/LH bias for positive expressions. However, these results are open to other interpretations. Third, there are a few reports of sex-related differences, but the findings are contradictory. For the most part, studies have found that men and women perform in a similar manner. A final area of convergence in the literature, and one that deserves emphasis, is that right-handed people are more likely than some left-handed individuals to show the LVF effect, suggesting that it is cerebral asymmetry that induces the perceptual asymmetry.

Clinical reports of brain-damaged individuals and studies of normals show that different patterns of lateralization accompany face and emotional expression perception. Additionally, these effects have been experimentally and statistically dissociated. The size and degree of LVF superiorities for faces and emotions also vary. These results strongly suggest that the processors for facial identity and expression are independent and unique to each task. Future research endeavors should control for the influence of stimulus variables, such as visual spatial complexity and imageable features; subject variables, such as sex, handedness, and cognitive style; as well as varying task requirements, such as same-different or verbal vs. nonverbal judgments.

REFERENCES

Ajersch, M. K., & Milner, B. (1984). Handwriting posture as related to cerebral speech lateralization, sex and writing hand. *Human Neurobiology, 2,* 143–146.

Berent, S. (1977). Functional asymmetry of the human brain in the recognition of faces. *Neuropsychologia, 15,* 829–831.

Bradshaw, J., & Nettleton, N. (1981). *Human cerebral asymmetry.* Englewood Cliffs, NJ: Prentice-Hall.

Branch, C., Milner, B., & Rasmussen, T. (1964). Intracarotid sodium amytal for the lateralization of cerebral speech dominance. *Journal of Neurosurgery, 21,* 399–405.

Bryden, M. P. (1982). *Laterality: Functional asymmetry in the intact brain.* New York: Academic Press.

Bryden, M. P. & Ley, R. G. (1983). Right hemisphere involvement in the perception and expression of emotion in normal humans. In K. Heilman & P. Satz (Eds.), *The neuropsychology of emotion* (pp. 6–44). New York: Academic Press.

Buchtel, H., Campari, F., DeRisio, C., & Rota, R. (1978). Hemispheric difference in the discrimination reaction time to facial expressions. *Italian Journal of Psychology, 5,* 159–169.

Campbell, R. (1978). Asymmetries in interpreting and expressing a posed facial expression. *Cortex, 14,* 327–342.

Cicone, M., Wapner, W., & Gardner, H. (1980). Sensitivity to emotional expressions and situations in organic patients. *Cortex, 16,* 145–158.

Dekosky, S. T., Heilman, K. M., Bowers, D., & Valenstein, E. (1980). Recognition and discrimination of emotional faces and pictures. *Brain and Language, 9,* 206–214.

Ekman, P., & Friesen, W. V. (1975). Measuring facial movement. *Journal of Environmental Psychology and Nonverbal Behavior, 1,* 56–75.

Ekman, P., & Oster, H. (1979). Facial expressions of emotion. *Annual Review of Psychology, 30,* 527–554.

Gardner, H. (1975). *The shattered mind.* New York: Knopf.

Goodglass, H., & Quadfasel, F. H. (1954). Language laterality in left-handed asphasics. *Brain, 77,* 521–548.

Hansch, E. C., & Pirozzolo, F. J. (1980). Task relevant effects on the assessment of cerebral specialization for facial emotion. *Brain and Language, 10,* 51–59.

Hecaen, H., & Albert, M. L. (1978). *Human neuropsychology*. New York: Wiley-Interscience.

Heller, W., & Levy, J. (1981). Perception and expression of emotion in right-handers and left-handers. *Neuropsychologia, 19*, 263–272.

Kolb, B., Milner, B., & Taylor, L. (1983). Perception of faces, facial expressions and emotion by patients with localized cortical excisions. *Canadian Journal of Psychology, 37*, 8–18.

Kolb, B., & Taylor, L. (1981). Affective behavior in patients with localized cortical excisions. Role of lesion site and side. *Science, 214*, 89–91.

Ladavas, E., Umilta, C., Ricci-Bitti, P. E. (1980). Evidence for sex differences in right hemisphere dominance for emotions. *Neuropsychologia, 18*, 361–366.

Landis, T., Assal, G., & Perret, E. (1979). Opposite hemisphere superiorities for visual associative processing of emotional facial expressions and objects. *Nature, 278*, 739–740.

Levine, S. C., & Koch-Weser, M. P. (1982). Right hemisphere superiority in the recognition of famous faces. *Brain and Cognition, 1*, 10–22.

Levy, J., Heller, W., Banich, M. T., & Burton, L. A. (1983). Asymmetry of perception in free viewing of chimeric faces. *Brain and Cognition, 2*, 404–419.

Levy, J., & Reid, M. (1976). Variations in writing posture and cerebral organization. *Science, 194*, 337–339.

Levy, J., & Reid, M. (1978). Variations in cerebral organization as a function of handedness, hand posture in writing and sex. *Journal of Experimental Psychology: General, 107*, 117–144.

Ley, R. G. (1983). Cerebral laterality and imagery. In A. A. Sheikh (Ed.), *Imagery: Current theory, research and application* (pp. 252–287). New York: Wiley & Sons.

Ley, R. G., & Bryden, M. P. (1979). Hemispheric differences in recognizing faces and emotions. *Brain and Language, 7*, 127–138.

Ley, R. G., & Bryden, M. P. (1983). Right hemispheric involvement in imagery and affect. In E. Perecman (Ed.), *Cognitive processing in the right hemisphere* (pp. 111–123). New York: Academic Press.

McKeever, W. F., & Dixon, M. S. (1981). Right hemisphere superiority for discriminating memorized from nonmemorized faces: affective imagery, sex and perceived emotionality effects. *Brain and Language, 12*, 246–260.

Natale, M., Gur, R. E., & Gur, R. C. (1983). Hemispheric asymmetries in processing facial expressions. *Neuropsychologia, 21*, 555–566.

Ornstein, R., Johnstone, J., Herron, J., & Swencionis, C. (1980). Differential right hemisphere engagement in visuospatial tasks. *Neuropsychologia, 18*, 49–64.

Penfield, W., & Roberts, L. (1959). *Speech and brain mechanisms*. Princeton, NJ: Princeton University Press.

Pizzamiglio, L., Zoccolotti, P., Mammucari, A., & Cesaroni, R. (1983). The independence of face identity and facial expression recognition mechanisms: Relationship to sex and cognitive style. *Brain and Cognition, 2*, 176–188.

Rasmussen, T., & Milner, B. (1977). The role of early left-brain injury in determining lateralization of cerebral speech functions. *Annals of the New York Academy of Sciences, 299*, 355–369.

Reuter-Lorenz, P., & Davidson, R. J. (1981). Differential contributions of the two cerebral hemispheres to the perception of happy and sad faces. *Neuropsychologia, 15*, 609–614.

Reuter-Lorenz, P. A., Givis, R. P., & Moscovitch, M. (1983). Hemisphere specialization and the perception of emotion: evidence from right-handers and from inverted and non-inverted left-handers. *Neuropsychologia, 21*, 687–692.

Safer, M. A. (1981). Sex and hemisphere differences in access to codes for processing emotional expressions and faces. *Journal of Experimental Psychology: General, 110*, 86–100.

Sergent, J., & Bindra, D. (1981). Differential hemispheric processing of faces: Methodological considerations and reinterpretation. *Psychological Bulletin, 89*, 541–554.

Springer, S. (1979). Speech perception and the biology of language. In M. Gazzaniga (Ed.), *Handbook of behavioral neurobiology* (pp. 153–173). New York: Plenum.

Strauss, E. (1983). Perception of emotional words. *Neuropsychologia, 21*, 99–104.

Strauss, E., & Moscovitch, M. (1981). Perception of facial expressions. *Brain and Language, 13,* 308–332.

Strauss, E., & Wada, J. (1983). Lateral preferences and cerebral speech dominance. *Cortex, 19,* 165–177.

Strauss, E., Wada, J., & Kosaka, B. (1984). Writing hand posture and cerebral speech dominance. *Cortex, 20,* 143–147.

Strauss, E., Wada, J., & Kosaka, B. (in press). Visual laterality effects and cerebral speech dominance determined by the carotid amytal test. *Neuropsychologia.*

Suberi, M., & McKeever, W. F. (1977). Differential right hemispheric memory storage of emotional and nonemotional faces. *Neuropsychologia, 5,* 757–768.

Tucker, D. M. (1981). Lateral brain function, emotion and conceptualization. *Psychological Bulletin, 89,* 19–46.

Weber, A. M., & Bradshaw, J. L. (1981). Levy and Reid's neurological model in relation to writing hand/posture: An evaluation. *Psychological Bulletin, 90,* 74–88.

Yin, R. K. (1970). Face recognition by brain injured patients: A dissociable ability? *Neuropsychologia, 8,* 395–402.

Author Index

Subject Index